C# Programmer's Reference

Grant Palmer

Wrox Press Ltd. ®

C# Programmer's Reference

© 2002 Wrox Press

First Printed in April 2002

Published by Wrox Press Ltd,
Arden House, 1102 Warwick Road, Acocks Green,
Birmingham, B27 6BH, UK
Printed in the United States
ISBN 1-861006-30-6

Trademark Acknowledgments

Wrox has endeavored to provide trademark information about all the companies and products mentioned in this book by the appropriate use of capitals. However, Wrox cannot guarantee the accuracy of this information.

Credits

Author
Grant Palmer

Commissioning Editor
Julian Skinner

Technical Editors
Chris Goode
Jon Hill

Index
Michael Brinkman

Author Agent
Charlotte Smith

Project Manager
Christianne Bailey

Technical Reviewers
Andreas Christiansen
Mitch Denny
Brian Hickey
Shefali Kulkarni
Johan Normén
Gavin Smyth

Proof Reader
Lisa Stephenson

Production Coordinator
Natalie O'Donnell

Cover
Chris Morris

Managing Editor
Louay Fatoohi

About the Author

Grant Palmer is the IT tool development lead for the Eloret Corporation under a contract with the NASA Ames Research Center. Grant develops standalone and web-based programs for scientific applications.

He has been programming since the days of the punch card and has a wide experience with Java, C, C++, FORTRAN, and most recently with the exciting new language C#. Grant lives in Chandler, Arizona with his beautiful wife, Lisa, and his two sons, Jackson and Zachary.

Acknowledgments

I would like to dedicate this book to my mother and father.

I would like to acknowledge Julian Skinner, Chris Goode, and Chris Matterface, the production team at Wrox who guided me in the writing of this book. They are largely responsible for taking my original concept of a C# programmer's reference and refining it down to the book you have in your hands. I would also like to thank Gavin Smyth, Brian Hickey, Mitch Denny, and all the other technical reviewers. Their insightful (and sometimes biting) comments greatly increased the quality of this book, and I learned a lot about C# from them in the process. I also must thank my wife Lisa for putting up with me and for taking care of our two wild boys during the writing of this book.

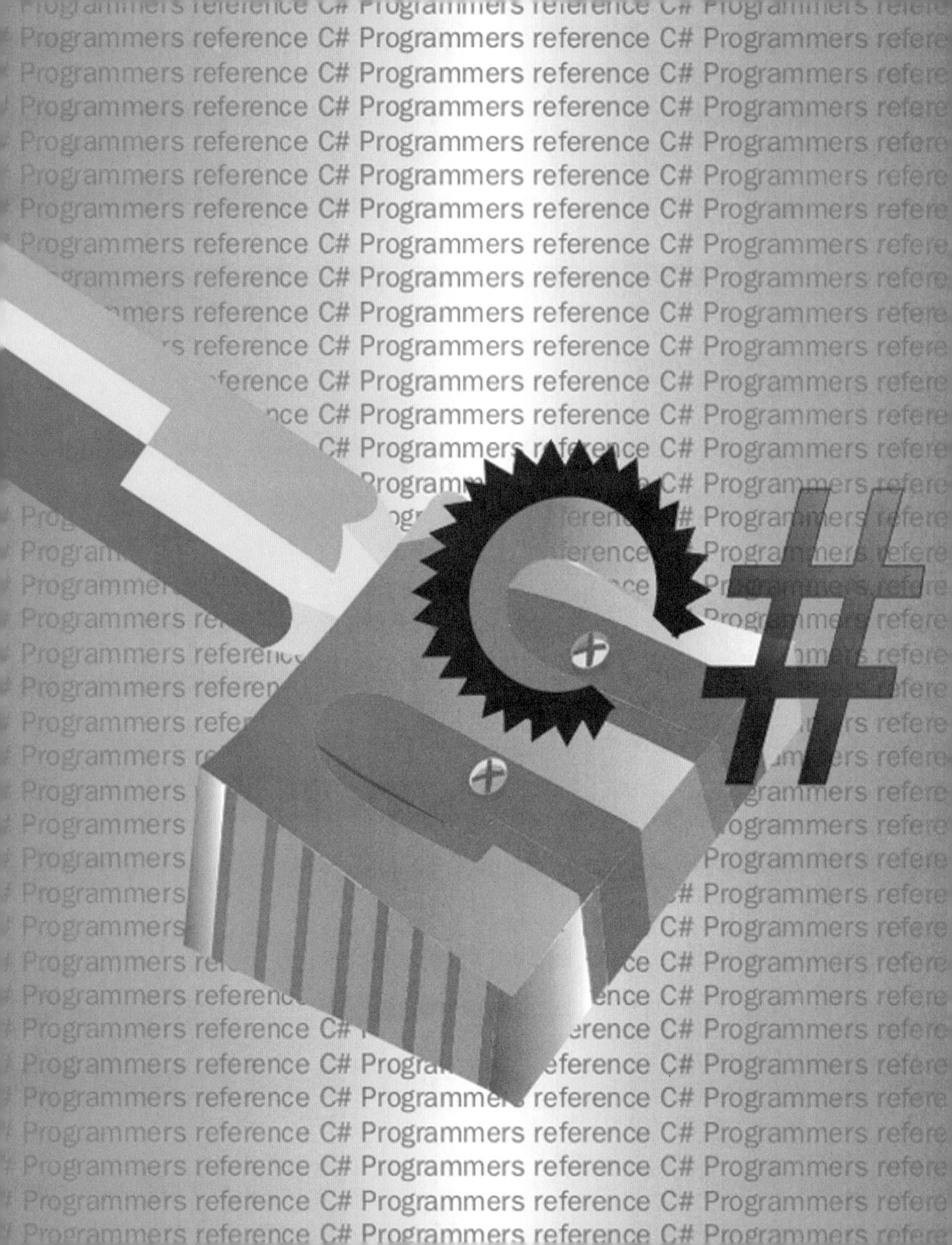
Programmers reference C#

Table of Contents

Table of Contents

Table of Contents

Table of Contents

vi

Table of Contents

Table of Contents

Table of Contents

C# Programmers reference

Introduction

The .NET Framework – of which the C# compiler is a part – is Microsoft's revolutionary new platform for developing applications and managing their run-time execution. Besides development tools – such as the brand new C# language and new versions of old favorites (including Visual Basic, C++, and JScript) – the .NET Framework has two main components: a run-time environment (similar in many ways to the Java Virtual Machine) called the **Common Language Runtime** (CLR), and a vast library of classes providing almost all the common functionality we need to develop applications on the Windows platform. It's important to stress that the .NET Framework isn't itself an operating system, but sits on top of the OS. At the moment, the only implementation of .NET is for Windows, but other implementations (in particular for Linux) are already in progress. These implementations will all include a C# compiler.

The .NET Framework comes in a variety of flavors. In order to run .NET applications, the host computer must have .NET installed. For clients, such as Windows applications, we will need to include a cut-down redistributable version of the Framework with our code in order to ensure that the client can run the program. While this version of .NET can be installed on Windows 9x/ME machines, and can be used (together with any text editor) to write and compile C# programs, serious development requires the full version of the **.NET Software Development Kit** (SDK). This can be freely downloaded from Microsoft's MSDN web site, and includes a raft of tools and documentation, as well as .NET itself. This version can be run on Windows NT4, 2000, or XP.

Finally, for serious development, we need an Integrated Development Environment (IDE) with features for debugging code, IntelliSense, auto-completion, and so on. The standard IDE for C# development is **Visual Studio .NET** (VS.NET), which is specially designed for writing .NET applications, and generates a lot of the standard boilerplate code for projects such as Windows applications and Windows services. VS.NET itself comes in several varieties, from the Visual C# .NET Standard Edition (which only supports the C# language), to Visual Studio .NET Enterprise Architect, which allows development of applications in C#, Visual Basic .NET, and C++, and comes with a raft of important utilities such as Visio (an OO design tool). All versions of VS.NET ship with the .NET SDK.

The Common Language Runtime

The Common Language Runtime is the real core of the .NET Framework. The CLR manages the execution of our code at runtime. The C# compiler (and other language compilers that target the CLR) compile not into native code, but into a low-level language called **Intermediate Language** (IL). At runtime, this IL code is Just-In-Time (JIT) compiled into native code. This JIT compilation allows optimizations to be made for the operating system and hardware in use, thus offsetting to a large degree the performance cost of the compilation (as opposed to prior compilation to native code).

The Virtual Execution System

The component of the CLR that manages the run-time execution of .NET code is known as the **Virtual Execution System** (VES). One of the chief benefits of managed code is **garbage collection**. In earlier languages, where the developer is responsible for releasing all resources used by the program, subtle and hard-to-detect bugs were often introduced when developers didn't free a resource once it had been used. Because the system had no way of reclaiming the memory used by these resources, the performance of the application progressively deteriorated over time. While developers are still responsible for releasing unmanaged resources, and still need to release expensive resources as soon as possible, the .NET garbage collector will destroy any managed objects that can no longer be accessed from any thread in the process, and will free up their memory.

The Common Type System

We mentioned earlier that all .NET code is compiled to a low-level language known as Intermediate Language prior to installation of the application. Because of this, a very high degree of interoperability between languages is possible – .NET standardizes the way methods are called, the type system used by all languages, and so on. True, COM did much of this as well, but .NET goes much further – we can even derive classes in one .NET language from a base class written in another. The way .NET achieves this is through the **Common Type System** (CTS). The CTS defines the primitive data types available in all languages, and the format and behavior of complex types. While not every compiler will support every feature of the CTS, there is a subset called the **Common Language Specification** (CLS), which every compiler *must* support. This means that there is a common set of types that every .NET language is guaranteed to recognize, and so long as only these types are used, our code will be accessible from any other .NET language. We will look at the CTS and the C# type system in more detail in Chapter 2.

Assemblies

.NET code is deployed as a logical unit known as an **assembly**. An assembly can be a class library (DLL), a console or Windows application, a Windows service, or even an ASP.NET page (ASP.NET is the .NET equivalent of ASP, but, like everything else in .NET, is much more than merely a new incarnation of the existing technology). Assemblies can consist of one or many physical files, or even (if it is a dynamic assembly, stored entirely in memory) no files at all.

As well as the actual code, assemblies contain **metadata** – data about the assembly. Every assembly has two distinct types of metadata – **assembly metadata** and **type metadata**. The assembly metadata is data about the assembly itself (for example, the version and build numbers of the assembly). This is also known as the assembly's **manifest**. The type metadata contains information about the types defined in the assembly, and their public members.

Because all this metadata is contained within the assembly itself, assemblies don't need a special installation process – we can just copy the file(s) to the target machine. There is no central registry, where information about all .NET components must be stored. Because assemblies don't need to be registered and assigned a unique ProgID, multiple versions of a component can be installed on the same machine (side-by-side versioning). This ensures that we no longer have the situation known as "DLL Hell", where one application would overwrite an existing version of a shared component, and break the application that originally installed it – every application can install its own version of the component, without affecting existing versions.

By default, assemblies are private, and can only be accessed from code running in the same directory. However, it's also possible to share assemblies by storing them in the **Global Assembly Cache** (GAC). Such assemblies can be accessed by code from other applications, even if it doesn't know the exact location where the assembly file is stored. Shared assemblies must be signed with a certificate to ensure they can't be corrupted by other programs.

COM interoperability

While all this makes life considerably easier for the developer, there's one potential problem – because .NET is entirely new in almost every respect, you can't easily mix managed .NET code with legacy COM code. Microsoft solved this by supplying tools that can generate COM type libraries for .NET assemblies, and that can read COM type libraries and use them to generate .NET wrappers. This system provides a fairly seamless interoperability between .NET and COM in usual circumstances, but problems can obviously occur when marshaling more complex data types.

The Framework class libraries

One of the best things about .NET is the huge number of class libraries supplied. These replicate the functionality of the vast majority of Windows API functions, as well as a whole host of higher-level operations such as data access, XML serialization, and string and collection handling. It's impossible to write any meaningful program in C# without using these libraries – even simple console IO is dependent on the .NET classes! We'll look at a few of the most important of these libraries in the second half of this book, but we'll briefly mention here a couple of the larger libraries which we couldn't cover without expanding the book to many thousands of pages. The classes (like all .NET types) are organized into hierarchical namespaces, very similar to Java packages.

Windows forms

One of the most important of these class libraries is the `System.Windows.Forms` namespace. This provides functionality for creating form-based Windows applications, similar to Visual Basic forms or MFC applications. Because everything is handled through the .NET classes, we don't need to handle Windows messages directly, so creating Windows applications in C# is much easier than in MFC!

Web forms

Web forms are the ASP.NET equivalent to Windows forms. ASP.NET introduces the new concept of server controls, which reside on the server (and can therefore maintain state to a limited degree), but generate HTML and JavaScript code to send to the client, and react to client input. This model allows server controls to be programmed in a similar way to Windows controls – the application can handle client-side events on the server, because JavaScript code is generated which causes a postback when an event such as a button click occurs.

ADO.NET

ADO.NET is the data access API for .NET. Like its precursor, ActiveX Data Objects, ADO.NET is a simple object model that provides classes for connecting to a data source, executing commands, and retrieving and manipulating data. Also like ADO, it uses different data providers to access different types of data source (these include OLE DB and ODBC data providers, as well as a provider for SQL Server, so almost any data source accessible to ADO is also available to ADO.NET). The most important difference lies in ADO.NET's support for XML. Although later versions of ADO had limited supported for saving and loading files using a specific XML schema, ADO.NET can read any XML-formatted data, and uses XML as its method for storing and transporting data.

Remoting

Remoting is roughly the .NET equivalent of DCOM. It is a (very large) class library which uses a proxy/stub system to make and process calls between process boundaries. Messages are passed between the client and server through a series of sinks; each of these sinks can process the message in some way (such as serializing it into a binary or SOAP format). Remoting allows cross-process calls to be made in any format, and over any transport.

What does this book cover?

This book provides a comprehensive reference to the C# language and the core .NET class libraries which you will need to use in every C# program. The chapters in this book can be divided into three main sections:

❑ The first half of the book looks in detail at every aspect of the C# language itself, in a sequence of short, very fast-paced chapters designed especially for easy reference.

❑ The second half looks at the types defined in the most commonly used class libraries and their methods and properties, with examples of their use.

❑ The third section consists of a couple of appendices that cover the keywords that have special meaning in C#, and the recommended naming conventions that should be adhered to when programming in C#.

Who is this book for?

This book is ideal for anyone who already knows the basics of C#, but needs a concise reference to the language and to the class libraries which they use constantly. While it's not intended as a tutorial, it will also be great for anyone who:

❑ Already knows the syntax of a related C-style language

❑ Likes to pick up languages through short code examples

❑ Has some experience of C# but who feels happiest having a hard-copy reference to hand while coding

What do you need to use this book?

The main prerequisite for this book is to have a machine with the .NET Framework installed. .NET currently comes in two "flavors":

- ❑ The .NET Framework Redistributable – the full framework on its own. Includes everything you need to run any .NET application. Approximate size: 20 Mb.

- ❑ The .NET Framework SDK (Software Development Kit) – the full framework plus samples and tutorials that you can refer to in order to learn more about .NET. Approximate size: 130 Mb.

Both of these are available for free download from http://msdn.microsoft.com/.

A copy of Microsoft Visual C# .NET or Microsoft Visual Studio .NET Professional or higher is optional. Visual Studio .NET is available to MSDN subscribers as part of the MSDN Professional or higher subscriptions, or it is available to purchase online.

This book is editor-neutral, so anyone who does not own a copy of Visual Studio .NET should still find that the content in this book is useful.

Conventions

We've used a number of different styles of text and layout in this book to help differentiate between the different kinds of information. Here are examples of the styles we used and an explanation of what they mean.

Code has several fonts. If it's a word that we're talking about in the text – for example, when discussing the `FileStream` object – it's in this font. If it's a block of code that can be typed as a program and run, then it's also in a gray box:

```csharp
using System;

public class HelloWorld
{
  public static void Main()
  {
    Console.WriteLine("Hello");
  }
}
```

Sometimes we'll see code in a mixture of styles, like this:

```csharp
public static void Main()
{
  Console.WriteLine("Hello");
  Console.WriteLine("World");
}
```

In cases like this, the code with a white background is code we are already familiar with; the line highlighted in gray is a new addition to the code since we last looked at it.

Advice, hints, and background information come in this type of font.

> **Important pieces of information come in boxes like this.**

Bullets appear indented, with each new bullet marked as follows:

- ❏ **Important Words** are in a bold type font.

- ❏ Words that appear on the screen, or in menus like Open or Close, are in a similar font to the one you would see on a Windows desktop.

- ❏ Keys that you press on the keyboard, like *Ctrl* and *Enter*, are in italics.

Customer support

We always value hearing from our readers, and we want to know what you think about this book: what you liked, what you didn't like, and what you think we can do better next time. You can send us your comments, either by returning the reply card in the back of the book, or by e-mail to feedback@wrox.com. Please be sure to mention the book title in your message.

How to download the sample code for the book

When you visit the Wrox site, http://www.wrox.com/, simply locate the title through our Search facility or by using one of the title lists. Click on Download in the Code column, or on Download Code on the book's detail page.

When you click to download the code for this book, you are presented with a page with three options:

- ❏ If you are already a member of the Wrox Developer Community (if you have already registered on ASPToday, C#Today, or Wroxbase), you can log in with your usual username and password combination to receive your code.

- ❏ If you are not already a member, you are asked if you would like to register for free code downloads. In addition, you will be able to download several free articles from Wrox Press. Registering will allow us to keep you informed about updates and new editions of this book.

- ❏ The third option is to bypass registration completely and simply download the code.

Registration for code download is not mandatory for this book, but should you wish to register for your code download, your details will not be passed to any third party. For more details, you may wish to view our terms and conditions, which are linked from this page.

Once you reach the code download section, you will find that the files that are available for download from our site have been archived using WinZip. When you have saved the files to a folder on your hard drive, you will need to extract the files using a decompression program such as WinZip or PKUnzip. When you extract the files, the code is usually extracted into chapter folders. When you start the extraction process, ensure your software (WinZip, PKUnzip, etc.) is set to use folder names.

Errata

We've made every effort to make sure that there are no errors in the text or in the code. However, no one is perfect and mistakes do occur. If you find an error in one of our books, like a spelling mistake or a faulty piece of code, we would be very grateful for feedback. By sending in errata you may save another reader hours of frustration, and, of course, you will be helping us provide even higher quality information. Simply e-mail the information to support@wrox.com, your information will be checked and, if correct, posted to the errata page for that title, or used in subsequent editions of the book.

To find errata on the web site, go to http://www.wrox.com/, and simply locate the title through our Advanced Search or title list. Click on the Book Errata link, which is below the cover graphic on the book's detail page.

E-mail support

If you wish to directly query a problem in the book with an expert who knows the book in detail then e-mail support@wrox.com A typical e-mail should include the following things:

❑   The **title of the book, last four digits of the ISBN**, and **page number** of the problem in the Subject field.

❑   Your **name**, **contact information**, and the **problem** in the body of the message.

We won't send you junk mail. We need the details to save your time and ours. When you send an e-mail message, it will go through the following chain of support:

❑   Customer Support – Your message is delivered to our customer support staff, who are the first people to read it. They have files on most frequently asked questions and will answer anything general about the book or the web site immediately.

❑   Editorial – Deeper queries are forwarded to the technical editor responsible for that book. They have experience with the programming language or particular product, and are able to answer detailed technical questions on the subject.

❑   The Authors – Finally, in the unlikely event that the editor cannot answer your problem, he or she will forward the request to the author. We do try to protect the author from any distractions to their writing; however, we are quite happy to forward specific requests to them. All Wrox authors help with the support on their books. They will e-mail the customer and the editor with their response, and again all readers should benefit.

The Wrox Support process can only offer support to issues that are directly pertinent to the content of our published title. Support for questions that fall outside the scope of normal book support is provided via the community lists of our http://p2p.wrox.com/ forum.

p2p.wrox.com

For author and peer discussion join the P2P mailing lists. Our unique system provides **programmer to programmer**™ contact on mailing lists, forums, and newsgroups, all in addition to our one-to-one e-mail support system. If you post a query to P2P, you can be confident that it is being examined by the many Wrox authors and other industry experts who are present on our mailing lists. At p2p.wrox.com you will find a number of different lists that will help you, not only while you read this book, but also as you develop your own applications. Particularly appropriate to this book are the pro_windows_forms and the vs_dotnet lists.

To subscribe to a mailing list just follow these steps:

1.   Go to http://p2p.wrox.com/.

2.   Choose the appropriate category from the left menu bar.

3.   Click on the mailing list you wish to join.

4.   Follow the instructions to subscribe and fill in your e-mail address and password.

5.   Reply to the confirmation e-mail you receive.

6.   Use the subscription manager to join more lists and set your e-mail preferences.

Why this system offers the best support

You can choose to join the mailing lists or you can receive them as a weekly digest. If you don't have the time, or facility, to receive the mailing list, then you can search our online archives. Junk and spam mails are deleted, and your own e-mail address is protected by the unique Lyris system. Queries about joining or leaving lists, and any other general queries about lists, should be sent to listsupport@p2p.wrox.com.

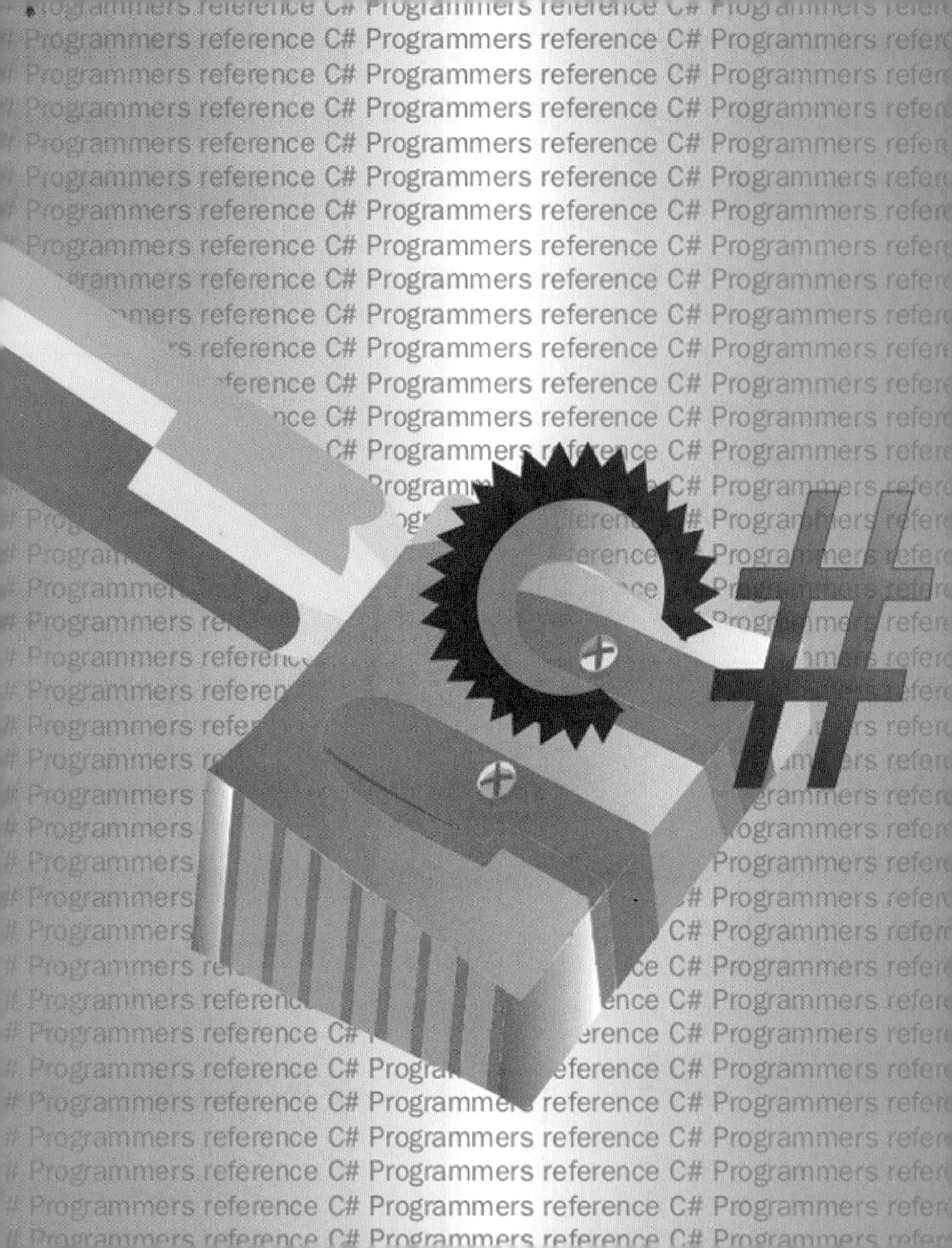
C# Programmers reference
C#

1

Compilation and program structure

This chapter reviews some basic elements of C# programming that you'll need to be familiar with when looking at any of the other chapters in this book. The C# language traces its lineage back to C and C++, so if you have any experience with those languages (or, for that matter, with Java), a lot of what is described in this chapter will look familiar.

In this chapter we will:

❑   Review basic C# syntax – what the various punctuation marks represent, and how to use them

❑   Introduce the `Main()` method – the entry point for a C# program

❑   Talk about how to compile a C# program – including descriptions of the compiler options

❑   Present a discussion of namespaces – what they are, how to create them, and how to access them

Basic C# syntax

When you look at a C# program listing, you'll see punctuation marks including colons, semicolons, and parentheses throughout the code. These characters are used to define and delimit the elements of a C# program. A list of the characters and a description of what each does is provided below.

Colons ':'

❑   indicate inheritance

❑   indicate that a class is implementing an interface

❑   precede the `base` and `this` keywords in constructor initializers

❑   terminate labels in `switch` statements

❑   appear in the ternary operator

Semicolons ';'

❑   indicate the end of a code statement

Braces '{ }'

- ❏ delineate code blocks such as namespace, class, and function bodies
- ❏ are used as scope delimiters
- ❏ are part of an array initialization statement

Brackets '[ ]'

- ❏ are part of an array declaration statement
- ❏ are used to access an element of an array or a collection
- ❏ are used to apply attributes to code elements

Parentheses '( )'

- ❏ enclose arguments passed to methods and constructors
- ❏ are part of function declaration statements
- ❏ are part of a casting, boxing, or unboxing statement
- ❏ can be used to isolate a code element
- ❏ define the evaluation order of an expression

Comments

There are two standard ways of writing a comment in C#. A **single-line comment** is denoted by two forward slashes. A **delimited comment** begins with the characters / * and ends with * /.

```
// This is a single line comment

/* This is a
   delimited
   comment */
```

You can place the single-line comment marker, //, anywhere inside a single-line or delimited comment. The following two lines are both acceptable:

```
/* This is a comment // forward slashes won't matter */
// This is // okay too
```

You can't, however, nest delimited comments. This will not compile:

```
/* This is /* not going */ to work */
```

The first comment is open until the * / syntax is reached, so the / * between is and not is simply passed over. The * / between going and to closes the first comment, leaving the end of the line – to work * / – to stand alone. This is not legal C# code.

*The Microsoft C# compiler makes available a third type of comment: an **XML documentation** **comment**. This is a single-line comment that's denoted by* three *forward slashes, ///. This type of comment can be processed by the compiler and placed in an XML file. Documentation comments are covered in detail in Chapter 20.*

Example: Syntax and comments

This example demonstrates how all of the characters described above can be used in a C# program. Don't worry if you don't understand the code completely – everything in this program is described somewhere in this book!

```csharp
using System;

/* The Test class creates an array of floats, a
   Quad object, and a Triangle object. It then
   writes out the areas of the Quad and Triangle. */
class Test
{
  public static void Main()
  {
    float[] vals = {(float)2.0, (float)3.0};

    Quad q = new Quad(vals[0], vals[1]);
    Triangle t = new Triangle(vals[0], vals[1]);
    Console.WriteLine("quad area is {0}", q.GetArea());
    Console.WriteLine("triangle area is {0}", t.GetArea());
  }
}

public abstract class Shape
{
  protected float width;
  protected float height;

  public Shape(float w, float h)
  {
    width = w;
    height = h;
  }

  public abstract float GetArea();
}

// The Quad class encapsulates a quadrilateral
public class Quad : Shape
{
  public Quad(float w, float h) : base(w, h)
  {}

  public override float GetArea()
  {
    return width * height;
  }
}
```

```
// The Triangle class also derives from the Shape class
public class Triangle : Quad
{
  public Triangle(float w, float h) : base(w, h)
  {}

  public override float GetArea()
  {
    return 0.5F * width * height;
  }
}
```

Output:

```
quad area is 6
triangle area is 3
```

At the top of the code, a delimited comment describes the Test class. Braces are used to enclose the blocks of code that form the class and method bodies. An array of float values is defined using brackets, and the array's elements are initialized by two values enclosed in braces. The values are converted from doubles to floats using a cast expression that features parentheses.

A single-line comment describes the Quad class, and both Quad and Triangle are written as derived classes of the Shape class – the inheritance is indicated with a colon. The Quad and Triangle class constructors invoke the Shape class constructor by using the base keyword after a colon. Throughout the entire program, semicolons are placed at the end of every statement, and parentheses are placed around the argument list of every method.

The Main() method

Every program needs an entry point, the place where execution begins. In C#, the entry point is the Main() method. Other C-based languages (C, C++, Java) use the main() method (small "m") as their entry point, but the concept is the same.

Every C# application must define at least one Main() method. It's possible to define more than one Main() method, but then you must use the /main compiler option to specify which one will serve as the entry point.

Because the Main() method is called before any class or structure instances are created, it must be declared static. There are several acceptable signatures for the Main() method:

```
public static void Main()
public static int Main()
public static void Main(string[] args)
public static int Main(string[] args)
```

The last two versions are used to pass command-line arguments to the `Main()` method – any arguments are passed as an array of `string`s. (You could of course use the proper class name `String` rather than the alias `string`.) The return type of the method must be either `void` or `int`; the latter mirrors the C convention of using the return value to indicate the manner in which the program terminated. A value of zero means the program exited normally; a non-zero return value means that an error occurred.

For an example of a `Main()` method, look at the example in the *Basic C# syntax* section above.

Compiling a C# program

How would you compile the example program from the *Basic C# syntax* section? If the `Test`, `Shape`, `Quad`, and `Triangle` class definitions were contained in a single file named `Test.cs`, you could simply type the following at the command line:

```
csc Test.cs
```

This would invoke the C# compiler and generate an executable file named `Test.exe`; this file would be placed in the directory from which the compiler was invoked. Unlike languages such as C and C++, the C# compiler does not produce machine code. Instead, C# programs are compiled into an intermediate language called **Microsoft Intermediate Language** (**MSIL**). MSIL is machine-independent code that contains instructions for a 'virtual' processor, similar in concept to Java's byte code. When the program is executed, the .NET runtime converts the MSIL code into machine code.

Actually, the compiler command listed above is shorthand for this command:

```
csc /t:exe Test.cs
```

The `/t` (or `/target`) syntax specifies what kind of output file will be created – the `:exe` here indicates that the target is a console application – usually, an EXE file. However, `/t:exe` is the default option, and does not have to be specified.

Another possible configuration would arise if the `Shape`, `Quad`, and `Triangle` class code listings existed in a separate file named `Shape.cs`. In this situation, you can cause the two source files to be compiled together by specifying them both on the command line:

```
csc Test.cs Shape.cs
```

> *As you'd expect, this syntax can be extended to compile any number of files together, and you can even use wildcards – csc *.cs, for example, compiles all the CS files in the current directory.*

If you anticipate that the definitions contained in the `Shape.cs` file will be used in a number of executable projects, another possibility is to compile it into a non-executable file that will be loaded by the .NET CLR at runtime. This is how you specify a **library** as the compilation target:

```
csc /t:library Shape.cs
```

This will generate a dynamic-link library file named Shape.dll, rather than an executable. Then, in order to compile the Test.cs file, we must reference the library that contains the Shape, Quad, and Triangle classes. This is done using the /r (or /reference) option:

```
csc Test.cs /r:Shape.dll
```

The third possible 'target' option is a reminder of the fact that you don't *have* to create a .NET assembly when you compile C# code. The Shape.cs file could have been compiled into a **module** (an executable file without a manifest) using this command:

```
csc /t:module Shape.cs
```

As a result of this command being issued, a file called Shape.netmodule will be created in the current directory. In order to use this in the creation of an EXE, another new compiler option is required:

```
csc Test.cs /addmodule:Shape.netmodule
```

The fourth and final 'target' option is useful when you want to compile a Windows application (one that, by default, does not have a console window). It is the /t:winexe option:

```
csc /t:winexe Test.cs Shape.cs
```

The /t and /r compiler options are the ones you'll use most often, but there are many others that allow you to customize the compilation process in different ways. The following list contains some of the other compiler options you might need, along with a short description of each.

Compiler Option	Description
@<filename>	Specifies a **response file** that contains a list of compiler commands. These commands will be executed as if they were typed in at the command line.
/addmodule:<module>	The specified module (or list of modules) will be included in the assembly.
/checked<+->	The /checked or /checked+ syntax specifies that integer overflows will raise a run-time error. The /checked- option disables overflow checking.
/codepage:<id>	Specifies the code page used for all source code in the compilation.
/debug<+->	Enables or disables debugging information. Debugging is disabled by default.
/define:<name> /d:<name>	Defines the specified preprocessor symbol.
/doc:<filename>	Processes XML documentation comments and outputs to the specified file.
/help /?	Lists all compiler options to standard output.
/incremental<+-> /incr<+->	If enabled (/incremental or /incremental+), only methods that have been altered since the previous compilation will be compiled.

Compiler Option	Description
`/main:<class>`	Specifies which `Main()` method will serve as the entry point of the program.
`/optimize<+->` `/o<+->`	Enables (+) or disables (–) compiler optimizations. The optimizations are enabled by default.
`/out:<filename>`	Specifies an output file name.
`/recurse:<dir\file>`	Searches subdirectories for source code to compile.
`/reference:<assembly>` `/r:<assembly>`	Imports the contents of one or more assemblies.
`/resource:<filename>` `/res:<filename>`	Embeds the specified .NET resource into the output file.
`/target:<option>` `/t:<option>`	Specifies the format of the output file. Valid options are `exe`, `library`, `module`, and `winexe`.
`/unsafe`	Allows compilation of code marked by the `unsafe` keyword. See Chapter 17 for more on unsafe code.

This list and the previous descriptions cover some but not all of the compiler options available to you. For a complete list of the available compiler options, consult the Microsoft documentation.

Namespaces

A **namespace** is a logical grouping of C# classes, interfaces, delegates, enumerations, and other types. For instance, when you need to use a regular expression, you can look inside the `System.Text.RegularExpressions` namespace for types relating to that topic. Namespaces are also used to prevent naming conflicts between types. If you were to use a library in your application, and a type defined in that library had the same name as a type that you've defined, there could be a problem. If, however, the types in the library were contained inside a separate namespace, no such problem could arise.

The .NET Framework class library is itself organized as a series of namespaces. When you develop your own C# code, you can place it inside a namespace that you define – if you don't specify otherwise, it will automatically be placed into the nameless, global namespace. To create a namespace, simply use the `namespace` keyword to define a block of code, as in the following example.

Namespaces can be nested, and, unlike classes, namespaces don't have to be contiguous blocks of code. Elements in a namespace can be placed in different source files, and one source file can contain several namespaces.

Example: Namespaces

```
namespace Animals
{
  namespace Birds
  {
    public class Sparrow
    {
      // Code listing for Sparrow class
    }
  }
}
```

In the above example, the `Sparrow` class is being placed in the `Animals.Birds` namespace. The full name of the `Sparrow` class becomes `Animals.Birds.Sparrow`. As they are developed, additional types can be placed in the `Animals.Birds` namespace in a similar fashion. For instance, if you write the `Finch` class and want to put it in the `Animals.Birds` namespace, you might type:

```
namespace Animals.Birds
{
  public class Finch
  {
    // Finch class code
  }
}
```

There are, of course, some rules when constructing namespaces. Every type definition within a namespace must be unique, so you couldn't define (say) two `Sparrow` classes in the `Animals.Birds` namespace. Also, you're free to name your namespaces as you choose, but for consistency's sake Microsoft has provided some guidelines:

- The first letter of each word in a namespace name should be capitalized

- The first part of a namespace name is generally a company or an organization name

- The second part of a namespace name should be the name of the associated technology, followed by optional feature and design names

If you worked for the Acme Engines Corporation, for example, you might define a namespace called `AcmeEngines.FuelInjector.Diesel`.

One way to access a type contained in a namespace is to write the full name of the type, *including the namespace in which it resides*. For example, the following program uses classes from the `System` and `System.Text.RegularExpressions` namespaces:

```
public class UsingDemo
{
  public static void Main()
  {
    System.String str = "Zachary is three";
    System.Text.RegularExpressions.Regex regex =
                    new System.Text.RegularExpressions.Regex("three");
    System.Console.WriteLine(regex.Replace(str, "four"));
  }
}
```

Output:

```
Zachary is four
```

As you can see, using the full type name can be quite cumbersome. Fortunately, C# provides the `using` keyword, which works rather like the `import` statement in Java, or the `#import` statement in Microsoft Visual C++ – it's placed at the top of a program and references a given namespace. You then have access to all of the types in that namespace without having to specify their 'full' names. The example shown above can be simplified significantly by employing the `using` keyword:

```
using System;
using System.Text.RegularExpressions;

public class UsingDemo2
{
  public static void Main()
  {
    String str = "Zachary is three";
    Regex regex = new Regex("three");
    Console.WriteLine(regex.Replace(str, "four"));
  }
}
```

Output:

```
Zachary is four
```

Summary

In this chapter, we've looked at three things that will be important in every C# application you ever write: C# syntax, the C# compiler, and C#'s use of namespaces.

With regard to the first of these, we looked at the different possible meanings of punctuation marks when they appear in code listings, at how to form comments correctly, and at the `Main()` method. For the compiler, we looked at the creation of four different types of file, and at the compiler options necessary in order to build applications from these files. Lastly, under the topic of namespaces, we looked at their use in organizing and simplifying code, and saw how they can make writing type libraries an altogether safer proposition.

In the next chapter, we'll move on to look at C#'s built-in type system, and how you can manipulate it to get the flexibility you need in your applications.

Programmers reference C# Programmers reference C# Programmers reference

2

The C# type system

The type is the basic building block of any C# program. Every piece of data in a C# program has a strongly-defined type (there is no variant type or direct equivalent). This is true not just of the primitive types such as bytes and integers, but also of objects, structs, and enumerations. A variable's type identifies its nature, both to the developer, and to the compiler and runtime. The C# language and .NET Framework define an efficient system for categorizing, accessing, and manipulating different types.

In this chapter we will:

❑ Discuss the Common Type System that provides the basic framework for inter-language operability

❑ Present the .NET Framework type hierarchy

❑ Outline the differences between value and reference types

❑ Overview the basic categories present in the type hierarchy, as well as the predefined value and reference types

❑ Talk about how one type can be converted, or cast, into another type

The Common Type System

The Common Type System (CTS) is the specification that defines a set of predefined types, as well as the behavior of all types in C# and in the .NET Framework. It defines a standardized framework by which types are declared, used, and managed, and thus facilitates the integration of types written in different programming languages. It defines basic rules that types written in different languages must follow to ensure type safety and optimized performance.

> *The CTS specification can be found in* `Partition I Architecture.doc` *in the* `Tool Developers Guide\docs` *subfolder of the* `FrameworkSDK` *folder. If you have installed the .NET Framework, this folder resides within the* `Microsoft.NET` *folder in your* `Program Files` *folder. With Visual Studio .NET, the folder is within the* `Microsoft Visual Studio .NET` *folder, which can also be found in the* `Program Files` *folder.*

The Common Language Specification

Not all .NET languages support all types defined in the CTS , so any classes with members of an unsupported type may be unusable from some languages. To facilitate interoperability between languages, the **Common Language Specification** defines a subset of the CTS, which *must* be supported by all .NET languages. Types which aren't supported by the CLS can still be used internally by classes that are exposed to other languages, but shouldn't be exposed as public fields or as parameters or return values to public methods.

The type hierarchy

One of the things the CTS defines is a type hierarchy, shown in the figure below. Beyond describing the different predefined types available, the type hierarchy also points out where user-defined types reside in the hierarchy. Each of these types will be described in more detail in this and subsequent chapters.

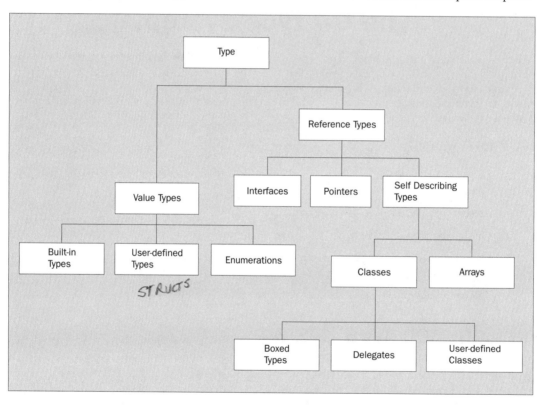

The stack and the managed heap

The CTS distinguishes between two basic categories of types – **value types** and **reference types**. The fundamental difference between these two categories lies in how they are stored in memory. .NET uses two different physical blocks of memory to store data – the **stack** and the **managed heap**. The stack stores data on a First In, Last Out (FILO) basis. Value types always take up a predefined number of bytes of memory (for example. an `int` will always take up four bytes, whereas the number of bytes taken up by a `string` will vary depending on the length of the string), and when a value-type variable is declared, the appropriate amount of memory is allocated on the stack (except for value-type members of reference types, such as an `int` field of a class), and this space in memory is used to store the value held by the variable. .NET maintains a stack pointer which contains the address of the next available memory location on the stack; when a variable goes out of scope, the stack pointer is moved back by the number of bytes occupied by the freed variable, so that it still points to the next available address. (Because the stack is FILO-based, the top variable on the stack will always go out of scope before those below it; this has important implications for variable scope in C#, covered in more detail in Chapter 5.)

Reference variables also make use of the stack, but in this case the stack only contains a reference to another memory location, rather than an actual value. This location is an address on the managed heap. As with the stack, a pointer is maintained which contains the address of the next free location on the heap. However, the heap is not FILO-based – because references to objects can be passed around within our program (for example, as arguments to method calls), objects on the heap do not go out of scope at a predetermined point in the program. In order to free up memory allocated on the heap once it is no longer required, .NET periodically performs a **garbage collection**. The garbage collector recursively examines all the object references in the application; the memory used by any object to which there are no active references is inaccessible to the program, and can be reclaimed. To do this, the garbage collector shifts all the objects (unless fixed in memory with the `fixed` keyword) in subsequent memory locations down to occupy the unused space (this is possible because of .NET's type safety – the type of all objects on the heap is set when the object is declared – and because .NET doesn't by default allow direct access to memory locations).

Be aware that compiler optimizations may result in an actual process that varies somewhat from the above discussion – this is more a conceptual guide to how the stack and heap work than an absolute description of what happens in every case.

Value types

Value types represent primitive values such as integers or floating-point values. There are three general categories of value types: enumerations, which are described in detail in Chapter 10; built-in value types; and user-defined value types, or structs. As we have seen, value types store their data directly on the stack. Since parameters are by default passed by value in C#, when a value-type parameter is passed into a method, a new copy of the value is created; any changes made to the parameter won't result in changes to the variable passed into the method. Method parameters are discussed in detail in Chapter 12.

Built-in value types

The .NET Framework provides a number of predefined value types. These represent various integer, floating point, character, and Boolean values. In other programming languages these are often referred to as primitive data types. The built-in data types of the .NET Framework are defined as structures and can be found in the `System` namespace. A list of the built-in value types available in C# is given below:

Struct Name	C# Alias	IL Alias	CLS-Compliant	Description	Range
Boolean	bool	bool	Yes	Boolean value	true or false
Byte	byte	unsigned int8	Yes	8-bit unsigned integer	0 to 255
Char	char	char	Yes	16-bit Unicode character	
Decimal	decimal	(Not an IL primitive type)	Yes	128-bit high precision	±1.0E-28 to ±7.9E+28 (and 0.0) decimal notation
Double	double	float64	Yes	64-bit double precision floating point	±5.0E-324 to ±1.7E+308 (and 0.0) floating point number
Int16	short	int16	Yes	16-bit signed integer	-32768 to 32767
Int32	int	int32	Yes	32-bit signed integer	-2,147,483,648 to 2,147,483,647 (-2.15E+9 to 2.15E+9)
Int64	long	int64	Yes	64-bit signed integer	-9,223,372,036,854,775,808 to 9,223,372,036,854,775,807 (-9.22E+18 to 9.22E+18)
SByte	sbyte	int8	No	8-bit signed integer	-128 to 127
Single	float	float32	Yes	32-bit single precision floating point	±1.5E-45 to ±3.4E+38 (and 0.0) floating point number
UInt16	ushort	unsigned int16	No	16-bit unsigned integer	0 to 65535
UInt32	uint	unsigned int32	No	32-bit unsigned integer	0 to 42,949,667,295 (0 to 4.29E+9)
UInt64	ulong	unsigned int64	No	64-bit unsigned integer	0 to 18,446,744,073,709,551,615 (0 to 1.84E+19)
IntPtr	–	native int	Yes	Signed integer of a platform-specific size (for example 32-bit on a 32-bit system)	(Platform-specific)
UIntPtr	–	native unsigned int	No	Unsigned integer of a platform-specific size	(Platform-specific)
Typed Reference	–	typedref	No	Pointer to a memory location where data is stored, together with a representation of the type stored at that location	

Notice that decimal is treated here as a primitive, since it has a C# alias, although it is actually a composite type when compiled to IL. The last three types (IntPtr, UIntPtr, and TypedReference) are primitive types in IL, but don't have C# aliases, and can't be instantiated using a normal assignment; instead we need to use the types' constructors or other keywords.

Platform-specific integers

The two platform-specific integral types, IntPtr and UIntPtr, are used for native resources such as window handles. The size of such resources will vary according to the hardware and operating system in use, but will always be big enough to hold a pointer on the system (hence the name). For example, to retrieve the handle for a Windows Form we can use:

```
IntPtr hWnd = this.Handle;
```

Note that IntPtr is CLS-compliant, but the unsigned equivalent, UIntPtr, is not.

Typed references

The last type – TypedReference – is by far the least common, and its use is poorly documented, so we'll take a moment to look at it. It represents data by containing both a reference to the location in memory where the data is stored, and a run time representation of the type of this data. Only local variables and parameters may be of the TypedReference type – fields cannot be typed references. The TypedReference type is not CLS-compliant.

There are a number of undocumented C# keywords (completely absent from the C# language specification) which we can use to create and manipulate variables of this type. We can create a typed reference from a variable using the __makeref keyword:

```
int i = 32;
TypedReference tr = __makeref(x);
```

The original type of the variable represented by the typed reference can be found using the __reftype keyword:

```
Type t = __typeref(tr);
```

Finally, the value can be extracted from the TypedReference using the __refvalue keyword:

```
int j = __refvalue(tr, int);
```

Typed references can be used to represent method arguments in variable argument lists (varargs). Such argument lists can be passed into methods and accessed with the (similarly undocumented) __arglist keyword:

```
// Method with a variable argument list
// We use the __arglist keyword to represent this
public static void PrintToConsole(__arglist)
{
    // Create a System.ArgIterator object to loop through the args
    ArgIterator ai = new ArgIterator(__arglist);
```

```
   // Each item in the ArgIterator is a TypedReference,
   // and we can convert them to objects using the
   // TypedReference.ToObject() static method

   while (ai.GetRemainingCount() > 0)
   {
     TypedReference tr = ai.GetNextArg();
     Console.WriteLine(TypedReference.ToObject(tr));
   }
}

// Main method from which we call our varargs method
public static void Main()
{
   // Define some parameters with different types
   int x = 23;
   string y = "a string";
   double z = 19.25;

   // Call our variable argument method, passing
   // the arguments in, again using the __arglist keyword
   PrintToConsole(__arglist(x, y, z));
}
```

Note that, because this code uses undocumented keywords (which aren't guaranteed to work in future versions of C#), it isn't generally advisable to take this approach – for a cleaner way of doing this, see the section on the `params` *keyword in Chapter 12.*

Declaring a built-in value-type variable

The C# language is strongly typed – the type of every variable must be specified when the variable is declared. There are two ways to declare a built-in value-type variable. You can use the full struct name or use the alias. For instance, the following are identical:

```
// Using the full struct name
System.Int32 width;

// Using the C# alias
int width;
```

Both of these statements declare 32-bit integer variables. Using the alias produces more compact, readable code and is the preferred method, although the compiled IL code is identical. We can initialize a value type when it is declared by including a value in the variable declaration statement:

```
int height = 4;
```

Literal values

The right-hand side of the above statement is called a numeric literal. You have to be a little careful if there is a type conflict. Integer literals default to the smallest type possible into which the value will fit – `int`, `uint`, `long`, `ulong`, in that sequence – and floating-point literals default to `double`. If we wish to mark a literal as having a different data type from the default, we can add a suffix to the literal to make its type explicit (these suffixes are not case-sensitive):

Type	Suffix
uint	u
long	l
ulong	ul
float	f
decimal	m

For instance, the following statement won't compile:

```
float amount =  23.7;
```

This won't compile because the literal 23.7 is assumed to be of type double. In this case you would have to use the following syntax:

```
float amount = 23.7F;
```

All integral types can take values in either hex or decimal notation. In the former case, the literal is prefixed with 0x; for example:

```
int height = 0xFFFF;
```

Note that C# does not support octal literals.

Literals of type char are enclosed in single quotes:

```
char firstInitial = 'G';
```

As well as character literals, we can use Unicode values (four-digit hex codes prefixed by \u) and (variable-length) hex values prefixed by \x to represent char values. We can also cast integer values to char. The following statements are all identical:

```
char c = 'X';          // Character literal
char c = '\u0058';     // Unicode value
char c = '\x58';       // Hex value
char c = (char)88;
```

Finally, a char can also contain one of the following escape sequences:

Sequence	Description	Hex Code
\'	Single quote	0027
\"	Double quote	0022
\\	Backslash	005C
\0	Null	0000
\a	Alert	0007

Table continued on following page

Sequence	Description	Hex Code
\b	Backspace	0008
\f	Form feed	000C
\n	Newline	000A
\r	Carriage return	000D
\t	Tab character	0009
\v	Vertical tab	000B

The unescaped literal characters ', \, and newline are not permitted in chars.

User-defined value types

The C# language allows the creation of user-defined value types. A user-defined value type will be defined as a struct that derives from the System.ValueType class. Structs are covered in detail in Chapter 8. A user-defined value type can contain fields, properties, methods, and events. If the user-defined type is boxed, it will have access to the virtual methods defined in the System.ValueType and System.Object classes. Boxing is described later in this chapter. Value types are by their nature sealed – no other type can derive from them (this is implicit – the sealed modifier can't be explicitly added to structs).

Reference types

The second major branch of the type hierarchy tree corresponds to reference types. Reference types contain a pointer to a location on the heap where the object itself is stored. Because they only contain a reference, not the actual values, reference-type variables passed into method calls will be affected by any changes made to the parameter within the body of the method, and are therefore similar in some ways to reference parameters.

Let's look at what happens when a string variable is declared and passed as a parameter into a method:

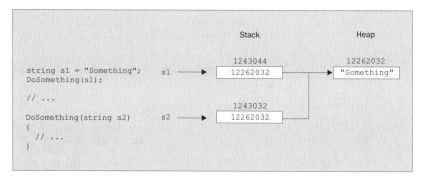

When the string variable s1 is declared, a value is pushed onto the stack which points to a location on the heap; in the figure above the reference is stored at address 1243044, and the actual string is stored at address 12262032 on the heap. When the string is passed into a method, a new variable is declared on the stack (this time at location 1243032) corresponding to the input parameter, and the value held in our reference variable – the memory location on the heap – is passed into this new variable.

Reference types include pointer, interface, and self-describing types. Pointer types are used to store the address of another object, and are only permitted in unsafe code in C# (see Chapter 17). An interface defines the contract which implementing classes or structs must adhere to (the methods, properties, fields, etc. they must expose), but doesn't provide any implementation for those members. Interfaces are described in more detail in Chapter 9.

Self-describing reference types include class types and arrays. An array represents a set of elements, which can be value or reference types. An array is a reference type even if its elements are value types. Details on how to create and manipulate arrays are provided in Chapter 6.

Classes are user-defined reference types (very similar in functionality to structs). They can contain data members (fields, constants) and function members (methods, properties, events, operators, constructors, and destructors). According to object-oriented programming principles, a class will define all of the functionality needed to manipulate its data members. Classes are described in more detail in Chapter 7.

A delegate is a reference type that refers to a method, similar to a function pointer in C++ (the chief difference is that delegates include the object on which the method is invoked). Delegates provide a type-safe and secure way to reference a method defined in another object, and can refer to a static, virtual, or instance method. Delegates are extensively used in event handling, and are discussed in more detail in Chapter 15.

Predefined reference types

There are two reference types that are given special treatment in the C# language, and which have C# aliases like those for the predefined value types. The first is the Object class (the C# alias is object, with a lower-case o). This is the ultimate base class of all value and reference types. Because all .NET types derive from Object, inheritance from Object is assumed and does not have to be declared. The Object class defines methods to compare two objects to return the hash code, a Type object, and a String representation of the object. A complete description of the Object type can be found in Chapter 22. Because all types derive from Object, it is possible to cast any type to an Object, even value types. This process of casting value types to Object is known as boxing, and we will look at it in more depth shortly. Boxing is also the magic which lies behind the apparent paradox that all value types derive from a reference type.

The other class given special treatment by the C# language is the String class. A string represents an immutable sequence of Unicode characters. This immutability means that once a string has been allocated on the heap, its value will never change. If the value is altered, .NET creates an entirely new String object, and assigns that to the variable. This means that in many ways strings behave like value rather than reference types – if we pass a string into a method, and alter the parameter's value within the method body, that won't affect the original string (unless of course the parameter is passed by reference). C# provides the alias string (with a lower-case s) to represent the System.String class. If you're using String in your code, the using System; line must be at the top of your code. Using the built-in alias string means this line is no longer necessary.

Strings can be created using the usual constructor syntax or by using what is called a string literal. The following three expressions are all valid ways to create a String object:

```
String strA = new String('A', 5); // Sets strA to "AAAAA"
string strB = "Zachary";
String strC = @"This line can wrap,
and can contain backslashes (\), etc.";
```

The first version uses one of the String class constructors (other overloads can take a char array, or a pointer to a char array). The second and third statements simply assign a string literal to the variable. If the @ character is placed before the literal text, it indicates that the string will be read "verbatim" – this allows the literal to span multiple lines and to contain escape characters.

The String class defines methods that can be used to concatenate two strings. We can also use the + operator for this purpose:

```
String str = "Hello";
String str2 = str + " There";
```

We can extract a character at a given position in the String by using an indexer syntax:

```
String str = "Bye Bye";
char firstChar = str[0];
```

Chapter 22 contains a complete description of the properties, methods, and operators defined in the String class. Indexers are covered in Chapter 14.

Mutable strings

Because strings are immutable, it requires three separate strings every time we perform a concatenation. For example, take the C# code:

```
string s1 = "Hello";
string s2 = s1 + " There";
string s3 = s2 + " John";
```

This code requires five separate strings to be loaded, as can be seen from the IL code it compiles to:

```
.locals init (string V_0, string V_1, string V_2)
IL_0000:  ldstr      "Hello"    // Load the string "Hello"
IL_0005:  stloc.0               // Pop the value into variable V_0
IL_0006:  ldloc.0               // Push V_0 onto the stack
IL_0007:  ldstr      " There"   // Load the string " There"
// Call the String::Concat() method
IL_000c:  call       string [mscorlib]System.String::Concat(string,
                                                            string)
IL_0011:  stloc.1               // Pop the return value into V_1
IL_0012:  ldloc.1               // Push V_1 onto the stack
IL_0013:  ldstr      " John"    // Load the string " John"
// Call String::Concat() again
IL_0018:  call       string [mscorlib]System.String::Concat(string,
                                                            string)
```

As well as the three hard-coded strings, two strings are created by the calls to String::Concat() – each change to the string results in a new String object being allocated on the heap.

It's possible to get round the immutability of strings by using a StringBuilder object (this resides in the System.Text namespace, and is covered in detail in Chapter 26). The StringBuilder represesents a mutable sequence of characters, and it can therefore be more efficient than strings if we're performing a lot of concatenation. The equivalent C# code using a StringBuilder would be:

```
StringBuilder sb = new StringBuilder("Hello");
sb.Append(" There");
sb.Append(" John");
```

This compiles to the IL code:

```
.locals init (class [mscorlib]System.Text.StringBuilder V_0)
IL_0000:  ldstr       "Hello"
IL_0005:  newobj      instance void
                      [mscorlib]System.Text.StringBuilder::.ctor(string)
IL_000a:  stloc.0
IL_000b:  ldloc.0
IL_000c:  ldstr       " There"
IL_0011:  callvirt    instance class [mscorlib]System.Text.StringBuilder
                      [mscorlib]System.Text.StringBuilder::Append(string)
IL_0016:  pop
IL_0017:  ldloc.0
IL_0018:  ldstr       " John"
IL_001d:  callvirt    instance class [mscorlib]System.Text.StringBuilder .
                      [mscorlib]System.Text.StringBuilder::Append(string)
```

In this case, we only have the three hard-coded strings, plus our single instance of the StringBuilder class – the calls to StringBuilder::Append() don't result in new instances of the StringBuilder. While there's no perceptible performance gain in this instance, the difference is startling when concatenation is repeated many times – in a test, 50,000 iterations of a simple concatenation took on average 18 milliseconds with the StringBuilder, but 423 milliseconds with standard strings!

User-defined reference types

The C# language lets us create our own user-defined classes, as well as arrays, delegates, and interfaces. Indeed, most programming work will probably involve defining new reference types. User-defined reference types can be written to do almost anything, and can make use of any combination of built-in types.

Determining a type

There are two ways to determine the type of a variable. We can use the GetType() method defined in the Object class. This method returns a Type object representing the type of a variable. Alternatively, we can use the typeof operator that does the same thing. The typeof operator takes as its argument either the fully qualified name of a type or a type alias.

Example: Determining a type

In this simple example, the TypeDemo class defines a method named DoStuff(). This method takes an object argument. Inside the DoStuff() method, the GetType() method is called to return a Type object corresponding to the input argument, and the typeof operator is used to return a Type object corresponding to the String class. The two Type objects are compared.

The DoStuff() method is called twice. The first time the method is passed a double as an argument. The second time the method is called it is passed a string:

```
using System;

public class TypeDemo
{
  public static void Main()
  {
    DoStuff(32.45);
    DoStuff("Hello");
  }

  public static void DoStuff(object obj)
  {
    if (obj.GetType() == typeof(string))
      Console.WriteLine("Argument was a string");
    else
      Console.WriteLine("Argument was not a string");
  }
}
```

Output:

```
Argument was not a string
Argument was a string
```

In this example, we used the alias for the String class. We could also have used the syntax typeof(System.String). Determining an object's type is an important element of reflection. See Chapter 25 for more details on reflection, and for other examples of using GetType() and typeof.

Casting

When assembling the classes and methods provided by the .NET Framework into your own application, it may be necessary to convert one data type to another. For instance, consider the following code that uses a FileStream object to read data from a file. The Read() method reads a specified number of bytes from the input stream and places them into a byte[] array. The Length property of the FileStream is used to designate how many bytes to read:

```
FileStream fs = File.Create("data.inp");
byte[] buf2 = new byte[fs.Length];
int k = fs.Read(buf2, 0, fs.Length);
```

This code will not compile. The problem is that the Read() method takes an int as its third argument, but the Length property returns a long. The system attempts to perform an implicit conversion from long to int, but this is not allowed because it is a narrowing conversion (64-bit to 32-bit). If we were trying to convert from an int to a long, this would be a widening conversion, and could be done implicitly.

The solution is to cast the `long` explicitly to an `int`. This is done by placing the desired cast type inside parentheses before the value or object to be cast. In our previous example, it would look like this:

```
if (fs.Length <= int.MaxValue)
    int k = fs.Read(buf2, 0, (int)fs.Length);
```

Because narrowing conversions can result in loss of data, we check that the actual value will fit in an `int` before making the conversion. An alternative approach would be to use the `checked` operator, which will cause an error to be thrown if the conversion would result in loss of data. The `checked` operator is covered in Chapter 3.

Casting can be performed on both value and reference types. As was previously noted, some casts will be performed implicitly by the compiler. These are widening conversions, going from a smaller data type to a larger one. The implicit conversions supported by C# are:

From	To
byte	decimal, double, float, int, long, short, uint, ulong, ushort
char	decimal, double, float, int, long, uint, ulong, ushort
float	double
int	decimal, double, float, long
long	decimal, double, float
sbyte	decimal, double, float, int, long, short
short	decimal, double, float, int, long
uint	decimal, double, float, long, ulong
ulong	decimal, double, float
ushort	decimal, double, float, int, long, uint, ulong

Any conversion not listed in the above table must be performed explicitly using a cast. Note that we cannot implicitly or explicitly cast a `bool` into another type. We must also be careful when performing a narrowing conversion. For example, if we try to cast a `long` to an `int` and the value of the `long` is greater than the maximum value of an `int`, the statement will compile, but the cast will not be properly performed. Using the `checked` operator can help detect conversion overflows. We will look in more detail at casting between reference types in Chapter 7, including defining custom casts for class types.

Boxing and unboxing

Both value types and reference types are derived from the `Object` class. This means that any method that takes an object argument, for instance, can be passed a value type. Similarly, a value type can call an `Object` class method:

```
int j = 4;
string str = j.ToString();
```

What is happening here is another example of type casting. If you recall, a value-type variable contains data stored on the stack. You might wonder how such a variable could call a reference-type method. The answer is that the value-type variable is implicitly cast into a reference type in a process called **boxing**. Conceptually, this is achieved by creating a temporary reference-type "box" corresponding to the value type (although the exact process may vary due to compiler optimizations). This is what happens in IL:

```
IL_0000:  ldc.i4.4          // Load the int 4 onto the stack
IL_0001:  stloc.0           // Pop the value off the stack and into V_0
IL_0002:  ldloca.s   V_0    // Push the address of variable V_0
                            // onto the stack

// Call Int32::ToString()
IL_0004:  call         instance string [mscorlib]System.Int32::ToString()
```

The key instruction here is `ldloca.s V_0`, which loads a managed pointer to the V_0 variable – it is this managed pointer, not the value itself, against which the `ToString()` method is called.

We can also explicitly box a value following the normal casting syntax:

```
int j = 4;
object obj = (object)j;
```

We can convert a previously boxed variable back into a value type using the same casting syntax:

```
int k = (int)obj;
```

There are several limitations on unboxing. You can only unbox a variable that has previously been explicitly boxed. The normal casting limitations also apply. For instance, if we box a `long` into an object, we can't unbox the object into an `int`, although we can of course explicitly cast the `long` to an `int` once we've unboxed it:

```
long l = 1000;
object o = (object)l;
int i = (int)((long)o);
```

Summary

We've taken a look into some of the core features of C# in this chapter. The format and behavior of types in .NET is defined by the Common Type System (CTS). Not all types defined by the CTS are available to all .NET languages, so the Common Language Infrastructure defines a subset of the CTS, called the Common Language Specification, which specifies the types that *all* .NET languages *must* support. The types available when working with C# can be either value or reference types, and this distinction points to the memory allocation system under the hood.

In this chapter we've looked at:

❑   The Common Type System

❑   The .NET Framework type hierarchy

❑   The differences between value and reference types

❑   The basic categories present in the type hierarchy, as well as the predefined value and reference types

❑   How one type can be converted, or cast, into another type

❑   How value types can be "boxed" into reference types

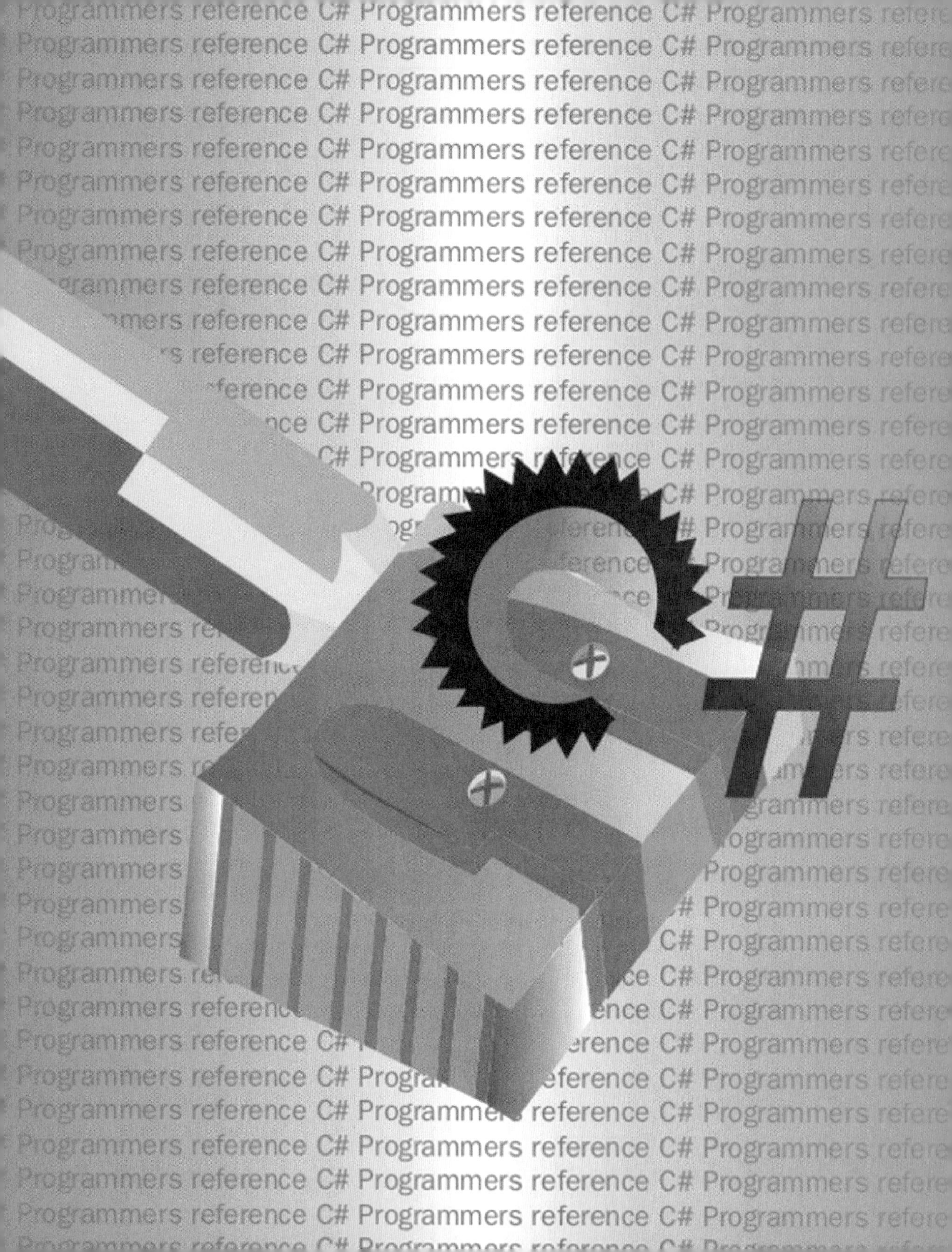
Programmers reference C#

3

Operators

Like any good programming language, C# defines a number of operators to facilitate various mathematical, logical, and other functions. Most of them are C-based and will look familiar to anyone with a C, C++, or Java background. You can also develop your own versions of some of the operators in a process known as operator overloading.

In this chapter, we'll look at:

❑ Mathematical operators

❑ Assignment operators

❑ Relational operators

❑ Logical operators

❑ Object operators

❑ Indirection and address operators

❑ Some miscellaneous operators

❑ Operator overloading

Mathematical operators

The mathematical operators cover the basic arithmetic functions as well as incrementing and decrementing a value.

Operator	Description
+	Addition or positive value
−	Subtraction or negative value
*	Multiplication
/	Division

Operator	Description
~	Bitwise complement operator
%	Modulus
++	Pre- or post increment
--	Pre- or post decrement

The +, -, !, ~, *, ++, --, and cast operators are called **unary** operators. The increment and decrement operators can be expressed in both a prefix and a postfix manner. When the operator is placed before a variable, the increment/decrement operation is performed before any assignments are made. If the operator is placed after the variable, the increment/decrement is performed after any assignments are made. For example:

```
int a = 10;
int b = ++a;
```

In this code, the value of b will be 11 because the increment takes place first. If the code was written like this:

```
int a = 10;
int b = a++;
```

then the value of b will be 10 because a will be assigned to b before a is incremented. In both cases the variable a will have the value 11 after the second statement is executed.

Operator precedence

When an expression contains multiple operators, the order in which these operators are applied can affect the outcome, so the operators are allocated a precedence that defines the exact order in which operators must be applied to an expression. For this reason, a-b/c is evaluated as a-(b/c). The following table shows the list of operator precedence, in order of precedence from highest to lowest.

Category	Operators
Primary	x.y, f(x), a[x], x++, x--, new, typeof, checked, unchecked
Unary	+, -, !, ~, ++x, --x, (T)x
Multiplicative	*, /, %
Additive	+, -
Shift	<<, >>
Relational and type testing	<, >, <=, >=, is, as
Equality	==, !=

Category	Operators
Logical AND	&
Logical XOR	^
Logical OR	|
Conditional AND	&&
Conditional OR	||
Conditional	?:
Assignment	=, *=, /=, %=, +=, -=, <<=, >>=, &=, ^=, |=

Assignment operators

The assignment operators are used to assign the value of one variable to another. There are also assignment operators that combine an assignment with a mathematical or logical operation. The last five operators in the assignment operator table are infrequently used. While they are perfectly valid syntax, they can make a code listing a bit harder to follow.

Operator	Description
=	Assignment operator
+=	a+=b is equivalent to a = a + b
-=	a-=b is equivalent to a = a - b
*=	a*=b is equivalent to a = a * b
/=	a/=b is equivalent to a = a / b
%=	a%=b is equivalent to a = a % b
<<=	a<<=b is equivalent to a = a << b
>>=	a>>=b is equivalent to a = a >> b
&=	a&=b is equivalent to a = a & b
^=	a^=b is equivalent to a = a ^ b
|=	a|=b is equivalent to a = a | b

Example: Assignment operators

In this simple example, the += operator is used to compute the sum of a group of values.

```
using System;

public class AssignDemo
{
   public static void Main()
   {
      double[] data = { 12.3, 4.5, 2.1 };
      double sum = 0.0;
```

```
      for(int i=0; i<data.Length; ++i)
      {
        sum += data[i];
      }

      Console.WriteLine("sum is {0}",sum);
    }
  }
```

Output

```
  sum is 18.9
```

Relational operators

Relational operators are used to compare two values with one another. They are often used in conjunction with if, while, and do-while statements.

Operator	Description
==	Equals
!=	Not equal to
<	Less than
<=	Less than or equal to
>	Greater than
>=	Greater than or equal to

For example:

```
if (x == 2.0 && y != 4.0 )
{
  // do some stuff
}
```

Logical operators

Logical operators are used to expand a conditional statement to include more than one comparison, for instance "if a is less than 2 and b is less than 3". There are also bitwise logical operators.

Operator	Description
&	Bitwise AND
|	Bitwise OR
^	Bitwise exclusive OR
&&	Logical AND
||	Logical OR
!	Not
? :	Ternary

The ternary operator performs the same operation as an `if-else` statement. For example:

```
a = b<c ? 0 : 1;
```

This statement is equivalent to the following statements:

```
if (b<c)
{
   a = 0;
}
else
{
   a = 1;
}
```

Here is a snippet of code from the example in the *Assembly class* section of Chapter 25. The ! = operator is used to determine if the return value from the `GetType()` method is non-null. If the return value is non-null, some other operations are performed.

```
Type type = Type.GetType(args[0]+", Sport");

if ( type != null )
{
   // further operations not shown.
}
```

Here is another code snippet, this one from the *FieldInfo class* section of Chapter 25. The bitwise OR operator is used to send two elements of the `BindingFlags` enumeration to the `GetField()` method.

```
Type type = hk.GetType();
FieldInfo field = type.GetField("name",BindingFlags.NonPublic|
                                BindingFlags.Instance);
```

Object operators

The object operators are used to provide information about or manipulate objects. The `sizeof` operator is only for use with code that has been marked `unsafe`. Unsafe code bypasses the C# compiler's normal type safety checking.

Operator	Description
`(<type>)`	Type cast operator.
`[]`	Accesses an element of an array or collection, or is the indexer operator.
`typeof`	Returns type of object or if the argument is a primitive the primitive type of the argument is returned.
`sizeof`	Struct size retrieval.
`.`	Member access.
`is`	Object comparison.
`as`	Performs object downcast.
`new`	Calls a constructor. For a reference type, a new object is allocated on the heap. For a value type, the fields of the value type are initialized to their default values.

The `is` operator is used to determine at runtime if an object derives from another class.

```
Mutex mutex = new Mutex();
if (mutex is WaitHandle)
{
   Console.WriteLine("mutex is a WaitHandle");
}
```

Since `Mutex` is a derived class of `WaitHandle`, the `if` expression will be true and the message will be printed.

If a downcast is performed using the `()` operator, an `InvalidCastException` is thrown if the cast fails. If the `as` operator is used to perform the downcast and the cast fails, the downcast variable is set to null and an exception is not thrown. For example, if you had defined the `Animal` class and created the `Bear` class as a derived class of `Animal`, you can downcast an `Animal` object to a `Bear` object like this.

```
Animal animal  = new Animal();

// later on in the code

Bear bear = animal as Bear;
```

Indirection and address operators

These operators are commonly used to work with pointers or to access elements of a struct. They are for use only with code that has been marked unsafe. For examples of these operators in action, see Chapter 17, *Unsafe code*.

Operator	Description
*	Value at address
&	Address at value
.	Struct member access
->	Struct pointer member access

Miscellaneous operators

These operators are important but don't fall into the previous categories.

Operator	Description
checked	Arithmetic checking turned on
unchecked	Arithmetic checking turned off

The checked operator can be applied to an expression, surrounded by parentheses, or to a block of code. It tells the compiler to generate an exception if an arithmetic overflow occurs. This can be used to prevent a garbage value from permeating its way through a program.

Operator overloading

The mathematical, assignment, and relational operators described in this chapter are only usable by predefined data types such as ints, doubles, and so on. What happens if you want to apply these operators to user-defined, reference-type variables? For instance, let's say you have defined a class named Complex that encapsulates a complex number and want to add two instances of the class using the '+' operator.

```
Complex a, b, c;

// later on in the code

c = a + b;
```

Using the standard '+' operator, this code won't compile because the standard '+' operator cannot be applied to Complex objects. It is possible to redefine the '+' operator within the Complex class definition so it will work with a Complex object. This process is called operator overloading.

To overload an operator, you simply provide a definition for the operator within the class or struct. The process is very similar to defining a method within the class or struct. The operator is designated using the operator keyword. Overloaded operators in C# must be defined as static. As such, they are associated with a class or struct rather than with an instance of the class or struct. The return value of the overloaded operator is the same as the variable type the operator will act upon.

43

The body of the operator definition should contain the logic for applying the operator to the reference type variable. For example, let us write a `Complex` class with an overloaded '+' operator.

Example: Operator overloading

```
using System;

public class Complex
{
  double a, b;

  public Complex(double d1, double d2)
  {
    a = d1;
    b = d2;
  }

  public static Complex operator + (Complex c1, Complex c2)
  {
    Complex c3 = new Complex( (c1.a+c2.a), (c1.b+c2.b) );
    return c3;
  }

  public override string ToString()
  {
    if ( b < 0 )
    {
      return a.ToString()+" - "+Math.Abs(b)+"i";
    }
    else
    {
      return a.ToString()+" + "+ b +"i";
    }
  }
}

public class OverloadDemo
{
  public static void Main()
  {
    Complex a = new Complex(3.0, 4.0);
    Complex b = new Complex(2.0, -7.0);

    Complex c = a + b;
    Console.WriteLine(c);
  }
}
```

Output:

```
5 - 3i
```

The `Complex` class contains a definition for the '+' operator. The operator takes two `Complex` objects as arguments. It returns a `Complex` object that adds the real and imaginary parts of the arguments. The `Complex` class also overrides the `ToString()` method to return a proper representation of a complex number. If you didn't overload the `ToString()` method the output when the code was run would be

```
Complex
```

You can overload the unary operators, +, -, !, ~, ++, --, true, and `false`. The overloadable binary operators are +, -, *, /, %, &, |, ^, <<, >>, ==, !=, >, <, >=, and <=. The comparison operators must be overloaded in pairs. For example, if you overload the == operator you must also overload the != operator. Overloaded comparison operators will have a return type of `bool`.

Only the operators listed above can be overloaded. In particular, it is not possible to overload member access, method invocation, or the =, &&, ||, ?:, new, typeof, is, as, checked, and unchecked operators. One final note on overloaded operators is that they are not part of the Common Language Specification (CLS). If you intend your code to be used in other languages, you should provide some other mechanism for performing the overloaded operator process.

Summary

In this chapter we've looked at all of the different types of operators available to C# programmers. Specifically, we've looked at:

- ❑ Mathematical operators and the order in which they're applied
- ❑ Assignment operators, used to assign the value of one variable to another
- ❑ Relational operators
- ❑ Logical operators
- ❑ Object operators, for when we're working with or manipulating objects
- ❑ Indirection and address operators that we use when working with structs and pointers in unsafe code
- ❑ The checked and unchecked operators
- ❑ Operator overloading

In the next chapter we'll move on to looking at program flow and exception handling.

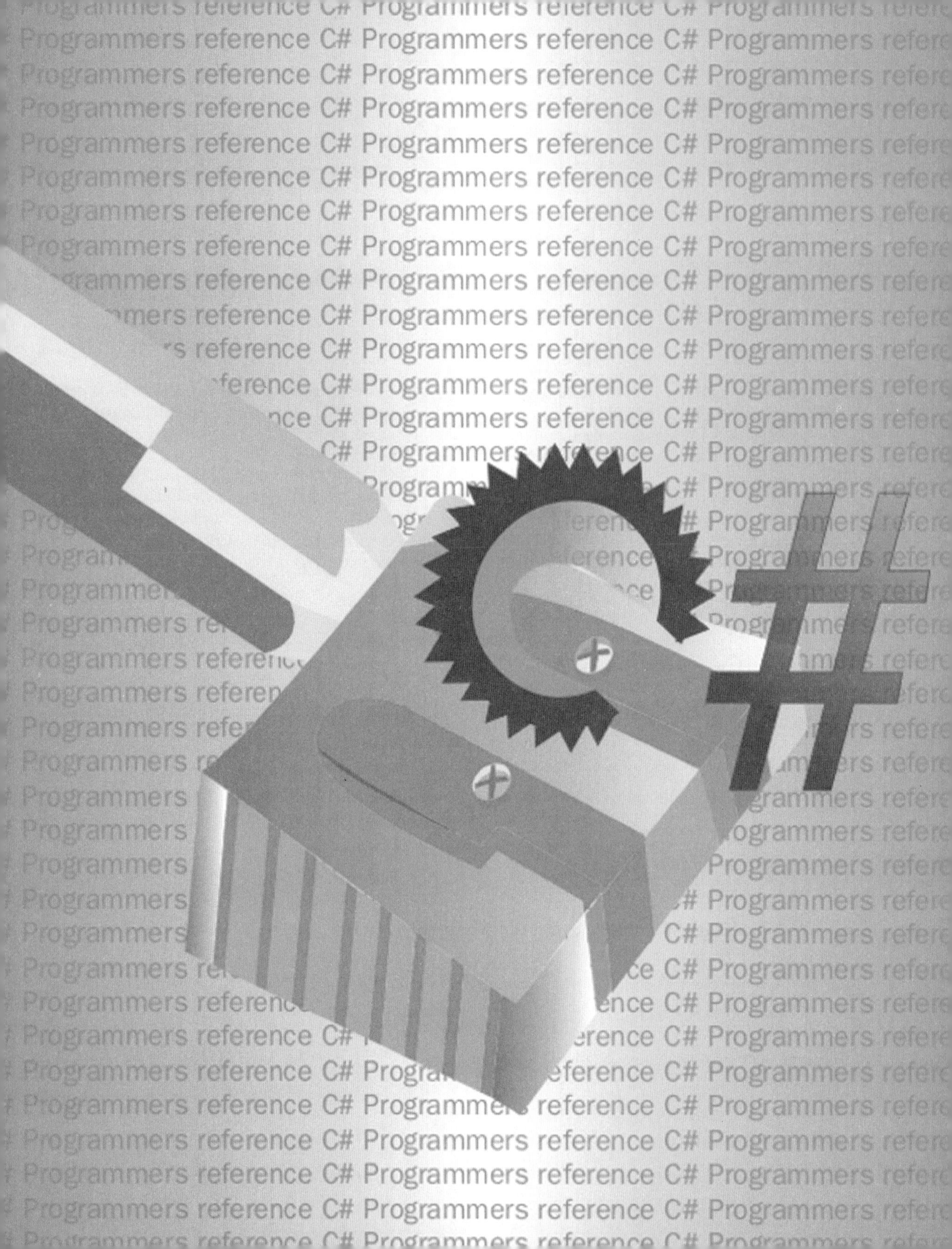
Programmers reference C#

Program flow and exception handling

A C# program, generally speaking, will not execute in a sequential, step-by-step manner. In all likelihood, it will contain conditional statements, iteration loops, and other keywords that redirect the execution point to different parts of the code. In this chapter, we will discuss all of those elements and show how they can be used.

We will also introduce the exception handling mechanism employed by C#. In an older programming language such as FORTRAN, if an error such as an attempt to divide by zero occurred you were out of luck. The program would abruptly terminate with no way to handle the error. If an error occurs in a C# program, an exception is thrown. An exception is an object containing information about what has taken place. There is also a mechanism to catch and deal with the exception. Even if an exception occurs, the program can continue running.

In this chapter we'll look at:

- ❑ Conditional statements
- ❑ Iteration loops
- ❑ Jump statements
- ❑ Exception handling

Conditional statements

A common task when developing applications is to code up statements like "if a variable is less than a certain value, do this" or "while this statement is true, do this". The C# language provides a number of expressions to deal with these situations. One category of such expressions is called the conditional statement. A conditional statement evaluates a condition and responds according to whether or not the condition is met.

if-else statement

The if-else statement evaluates one or more conditional statements in an exclusive manner. If a condition is met, the block of code following the conditional statement is executed. If a condition is met, any other conditional statements in the if-else statement will not be evaluated. You can also specify a default block of code to be executed if none of the previous conditions is met. This is the basic form of an if-else statement:

```
if (condition)
{
   // code to be executed
}
else if (condition2)
{
   // code to be executed
}
else
{
   // default code to be executed
}
```

The condition statements are logical expressions such as "x<4" that are evaluated as either true or false. Any number of else if statements can be included, or you can include none at all. The else block is optional and contains code that is executed if none of the conditions are met. If only one statement is to be executed after a condition is evaluated, the braces {} can be omitted.

Example: if-else

In this example, a Moms() method is written that consists of an if-else statement. If the input string is "Diana" a message is printed. If the input string is "Angela" another message is printed. If the input string doesn't match either condition, a string is printed saying that the input string is not in the database.

While there is only one statement after each condition is evaluated, it is a safe practice to enclose it in braces anyway. If you add additional code at some point in the future, you won't have to remember to add the braces. If you added code and forgot the braces, the code won't compile.

```
using System;

public class IfDemo
{
  public static void Main()
  {
    Moms("Diana");
    Moms("Hans");
  }

  public static void Moms(String str)
  {
    if ( str == "Diana" )
    {
Console.WriteLine(str+"'s mom is Anne");
    }
```

```
( str == "Angela" )

le.WriteLine(str+"'s mom is Carole");


le.WriteLine(str+" is not in database");
```

```
n is Anne
 in database
```

ment

ment is similar to an if-else statement in that it evaluates one or more conditional
pression is compared against one or more constant expressions contained in case
ession matches the case label, the subsequent code is executed. The default
ised to execute a block of code if the expression does not match any of the case labels.
 a switch statement is as follows:

```
ression))

stant_expression1:
de to execute

stant_expression2:
de to execute

stant_expression3:
de to execute

    //  code to execute
    break;
}
```

The expression must be a predefined integral type or a String. The case labels define constant
expressions that expression is compared against. The case labels are terminated with a colon. The code
below the case labels is executed if there is a match. This code does not need to be enclosed in braces.

There are times when you will wish to respond to different matches in the same way. You can do this by
stacking up two or more case labels.

```
   case constant_expression1:
   case constant_expression2:
   case constant_expression3:
      //  code if any of the constant expressions match
```

A match with any of the stacked constant expressions will cause the subsequent code to be executed.

Unlike the if-else statement, a switch statement is not terminated when the code after one of the case labels is executed. To exit a switch statement, a jump statement must be used. In most cases, this will be a break statement. When the break statement is reached, the code execution jumps to the statement following the switch statement. You can also use the goto statement as the jump statement although the goto statement is generally despised among computer programmers. Examples of valid goto statements are "goto default" and "goto case <constant_expression>". If you do not specify a break or another jump statement to terminate a case or default label, or if an eventuality is not covered by the case statements, the C# compiler will throw an error.

Example:

In this example, we rewrite the Moms () method from the example in the "if-else statement" section to make use of a switch statement. This makes it easy to implement the feature that a mother might have more than one child. The Moms () method takes a string as an argument. The string is used as the expression evaluated by a switch statement. The switch statement defines a number of case labels. If the expression matches one of the labels, the appropriate message is printed. If no matches are found, the default code is executed. Note the use of stacked case labels. If the expression matches "Mark", "Maria", "Scott", or "Diana", the "mom is Anne" message is printed.

```
using System;

public class SwitchDemo
{
   public static void Main()
   {
      Moms("Lisa");
      Moms("Scott");
      Moms("Cheryl");
   }

   public static void Moms(String str)
   {
      switch(str)
      {
         case("Angela"):
         case("Lisa"):
            Console.WriteLine(str+"'s mom is Carole");
            break;
         case("Mark"):
         case("Maria"):
         case("Scott"):
         case("Diana"):
```

```
            Console.WriteLine(str+"'s mom is Anne");
            break;
        default:
            Console.WriteLine(str+" is not in database");
            break;
        }
    }
  }
}
```

Output:

```
Lisa's mom is Carole
Scott's mom is Anne
Cheryl is not in database
```

Iteration loops

A common programming practice is to repeat an operation a number of times. Another is to have to iterate through an array or collection. Like any other programming language, C# provides a number of built-in constructs to efficiently model these situations.

for statement

The `for` statement is used for executing a loop as long as a specified condition holds. In this way, it is similar in function to a `while` loop. The `for` statement consists of three parts: an initial value, a conditional expression, and a way to change the value. Any or all of the three parts can be omitted. The basic syntax of a `for` statement is shown below.

```
for (initial value; conditional_expression; value_change_expression)
{
   //  code to be executed
}
```

The conditional expression is evaluated before the subsequent block of code is executed. The block executes as long as the condition is met. The condition will generally involve the value defined in the initial value expression. The final part of the `for` statement is generally used to modify the value. If the initial value does not meet the condition, the block won't execute at all.

You can omit any of the three parts of a `for` statement. For instance, to create an infinite loop you would use the syntax:

```
for (;;)
{
   //  this will run forever
}
```

It is perfectly acceptable to nest `for` statements as long as the iteration variable names are different. This is common, for instance, when iterating through the elements of a multidimensional array.

Example: for statement

In this example, two arrays of double values are created. Nested `for` statements are used to divide each element of the first array by each element of the second array.

```
using System;

public class ForDemo
{
  public static void Main()
  {
    double[] a = {12.0, 8.7, 3.2};
    double[] b = {2.0, 3.0, 4.0};

    for(int i=0; i<a.Length; ++i)
    {
      for(int j=0; j<b.Length; ++j)
      {
        Console.WriteLine(a[i]+" divided by "+b[j]+" is "+a[i]/b[j]);
      }
    }
  }
}
```

Output:

```
12 divided by 2 is 6
12 divided by 3 is 4
12 divided by 4 is 3
8.7 divided by 2 is 4.35
8.7 divided by 3 is 2.9
8.7 divided by 4 is 2.175
3.2 divided by 2 is 1.6
3.2 divided by 3 is 1.0666666667
3.2 divided by 4 is 0.8
```

foreach statement

The `foreach` statement is similar in purpose to the `for` statement and is used to iterate through the elements of an array or another collection. The collection being iterated over should implement the `IEnumerable` interface.

```
foreach( type value in IEnumerable )
{
  //  code to be executed
}
```

Inside the `foreach` block, the elements of the collection are read-only. Their values cannot be changed.

Example: foreach statement

In this example, a `foreach` statement is used to iterate through the elements of a `String` array.

```
using System;

public class ForeachDemo
{
  public static void Main()
  {
    String[] strings = {"fish", "beans", "tofu"};

    foreach(String str in strings)
    {
      Console.WriteLine(str);
    }
  }
}
```

Output:

```
fish
beans
tofu
```

while statement

A `while` statement runs through a block of code over and over as long as a specified condition is true. The condition is evaluated before the block of code is executed.

```
while (condition)
{
  // code to execute
}
```

A `while` statement is used to repeat a block of code an unknown number of times. A `while` statement is also useful for putting an execution thread into a waiting state until a condition is met. The state of the condition can be changed within the `while` loop or it can be changed externally. If there is only one statement to be executed within the `while` loop, the braces can be omitted.

Since the `while` loop remains active as long as the condition is true, the following syntax can be used to set up an infinite loop:

```
while (true)
```

Example: while statement

In this example, a while loop is used to iterate through the elements of an enumeration. A regular expression pattern is defined. The regular expression pattern will search for words in a String that begin with 'k' or 'K'. A String that will be searched is also defined. For a complete description of how C# implements regular expressions, see Chapter 27.

The Matches() method returns a MatchCollection object containing any matches that were found. The GetEnumerator() method returns an enumeration containing the matches as its elements. A while loop is used to iterate through the enumeration. The MoveNext() method moves to the next element in the enumeration and returns false if the end of the collection has been reached. The matches found in the string are printed.

```csharp
using System;
using System.Collections;
using System.Text.RegularExpressions;

public class WhileDemo
{
  public static void Main()
  {
    String pattern = @"\b([kK]\S+)";
    String str = "A kangaroo kicked a can to Kenya";

    MatchCollection matches = Regex.Matches(str,pattern);
    IEnumerator enumerator = matches.GetEnumerator();

    while( enumerator.MoveNext() )
    {
      Console.WriteLine(enumerator.Current);
    }
  }
}
```

Output:

```
kangaroo
kicked
Kenya
```

do-while statement

The do-while statement is similar in form and purpose to the while statement in that a block of code is executed an unspecified number of times. With a do-while statement, the associated block of code is executed before the conditional statement is evaluated. This means the block of code will always execute at least once. The general form of a do-while statement is shown below.

```csharp
do
{
  // code to execute
} while (condition);
```

Example: do while statement

In this example, a do-while loop is used to solve a fourth-order mathematical expression. We want to solve the equation $x^4 - 5x = 42$ using a Newton-Raphson iteration procedure. What the procedure does is start with an initial value of x. An updated value of x is obtained using the derivative of the equation with respect to x. The iteration continues until the update to x falls below a specified tolerance.

The process is facilitated using a do-while loop. You need to compute the change in the value of x at least once in order to compare it against the tolerance. When you run this program, change the value of the tolerance variable and see what happens to the output.

```
using System;

public class DoWhileDemo
{
  public static void Main()
  {
    double deltaX, f, dfdx, x=0.0, tolerance=0.01;
    int count = 0;

    //============================================
    //   The do-while loop solves the equation
    //   x**4 - 5x = 42 to a specified accuracy
    //============================================

    do
    {
      f = Math.Pow(x,4.0) - 5.0*x - 42.0;
      dfdx = 4.0*Math.Pow(x,3.0) - 5.0;
      deltaX = -f/dfdx;
      x += deltaX;
      ++count;
    }

    while ( Math.Abs(deltaX) > tolerance );

    f = Math.Pow(x,4.0) - 5.0*x;
    Console.WriteLine("solution converged in {0} steps",count);
    Console.WriteLine("x is {0} f is {1}",x,f);
  }
}
```

Output:

```
solution converged in 8 steps
x is -2.345662349  f is 42.00176672
```

Jump statements

Jump statements are used to redirect the execution to another statement in the code. They are most commonly used in conjunction with conditional statements and iteration loops, but can be used in other situations as well.

break statement

The break statement is used to exit from a do-while, for, foreach, or while loop. It is also used to exit from a switch statement. The execution point of the code is moved to the next statement after the loop or switch statement

```
break;
```

continue statement

The continue statement is used to exit the current iteration of a do-while, for, foreach, or while loop. The execution returns to the top of the loop. It cannot be used to exit a finally block.

```
continue;
```

goto statement

The goto statement causes the program to jump to another line of code. The goto statement is followed by a label name. The label will be defined somewhere else in the program followed by a colon.

```
goto <label name>;

<label name>:
//  more code to follow
```

There are restrictions on the use of the goto statement. You cannot jump into the middle of a loop statement. You can't jump out of a class or out of a finally block. The general consensus on the goto statement is similar to the feeling about global variables, namely that it should be avoided. A legitimate, although still somewhat dubious, use of the goto statement is to jump through cases in a switch statement.

return statement

The return statement is used to exit a method that has a non-void return value. Methods with a return value of void can include the return statement but it is not required. When a return statement is encountered, the execution will return to the statement after the method call. If the method definition specifies a return type, a value of that type must follow the return syntax.

```
return;
```

or

```
return value;
```

Exception handling

Exception handling allows you as a developer to anticipate, catch, and process possible run time exceptions. These might occur as a result of a mathematical exception, an out-of-bound index, an IO error, or any number of other causes. In C#, exception handling is implemented by defining blocks of code using the try, catch, and finally keywords.

```
try
{
    //  code that might throw an exception
}
catch(exception-type variable-name)
{
    //  code to process the exception
}
finally
{
    //  code to perform clean-up operations
}
```

The try block is defined by the try keyword and contains the code that might possibly throw an exception. Enclosing the code in a try block ensures that if an exception occurs it will be sent to any subsequent catch blocks and that the finally block will eventually be called. The normal scope rules apply for the try block. For instance, any local variables defined in the try block will not be accessible outside of the block.

The catch block contains the code that will be used to process or respond to the exception. When an exception is thrown, the system will check the types defined in any associated catch blocks. If it finds a match, the code inside the matching catch block is executed. You don't have to specify the exception type or variable name. Providing a variable name will give you access to an instance of that exception class. If you omit the exception type, a type of System.Exception (the base class of all exception classes) will be assumed.

A catch block will catch any exception that is below its specified type in the class hierarchy. For instance, a catch block set up to catch an IOException will catch a FileNotFoundException (a derived class of IOException) if it is thrown. If a catch block is designated to catch an Exception, it will catch all exceptions.

Multiple catch blocks can be associated with a given try block but you must place derived exception type catch blocks above base type blocks. This is because only the first matching catch block will be executed. If you place an IOException catch block below an Exception catch block, the code in the IOException catch block will never be executed.

A finally block is executed when the program control leaves a try block. This can happen at the end of the try block, after a catch block has executed, or if a try block exits as a result of a jump statement. The code inside a finally block is often used to perform any necessary clean-up operations such as releasing resources from any non-C# objects.

Example: Exception handling

I/O operations, generally speaking, are prone to generating exceptions. There are a lot of things that can go wrong when reading and writing data. Because of this, it is a good idea to place I/O operations inside try-catch blocks.

In this example, we are attempting to open a StreamWriter and write a string of text to the output stream. The StreamWriter is created inside a try block. Below the try block are two catch blocks. The first captures a FileNotFoundException and prints out a message if that type of exception occurs. The second catch block catches any other type of exception that might occur. The finally block is used to close the output stream if the open and write operations were successful. Remember that the finally block will be executed regardless of how the try block is exited.

```
using System;
using System.IO;

public class ExceptionDemo
{
  public static void Main()
  {
    StreamWriter sw = null;

    try
    {
      sw = new StreamWriter(new FileStream("Area.txt", FileMode.Open));
      sw.WriteLine("Hello there");
    }
    catch (FileNotFoundException fnfe)
    {
      Console.WriteLine("File "+fnfe.FileName+" not found");
    }
    catch (Exception e)
    {
      Console.WriteLine(e);
    }
    finally
    {
      if ( sw != null)
      {
        sw.Close();
      }
    }
  }
}
```

Output:

```
File C:\C#_Prog_Ref\Chapter04\Area.txt not found
```

Summary

In this chapter we've looked at how we can alter the flow of our C# programs and how to handle exceptions when they are thrown. Specifically, we looked at:

- ❏ Conditional statements, including `if-else` and `switch`
- ❏ Iteration loops, including `for`, `foreach`, `while`, and `do-while`
- ❏ Jump statements, including `break`, `continue`, `goto`, and `return`
- ❏ Exception handling using `try`, `catch`, and `finally`

In the next chapter we'll move on to looking at local variables.

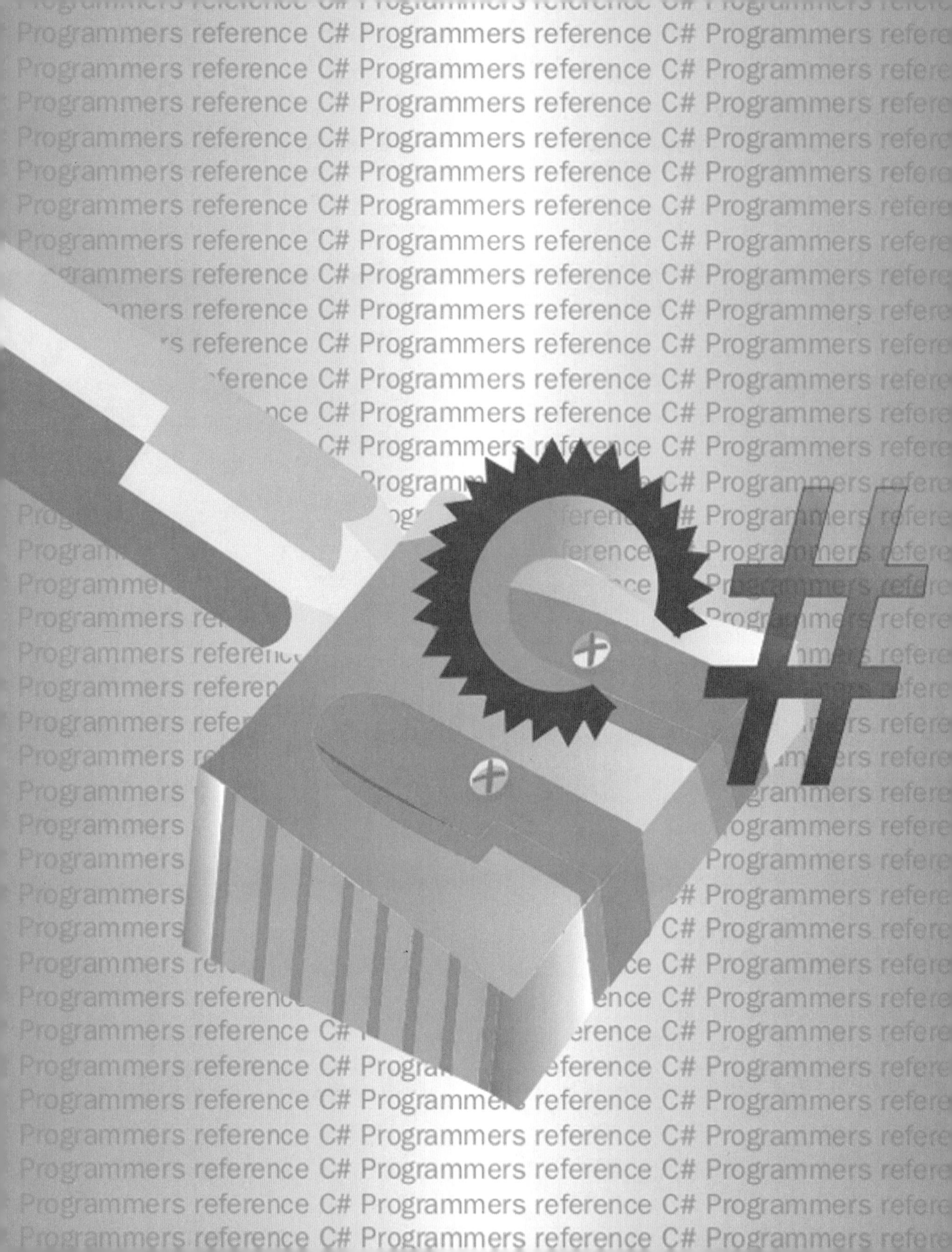
Programmers reference C#

5

Local variables

Local variables are variables defined within methods. Variables declared at type level are known as fields and are described in Chapter 11. Local variables are generally temporary entities that are created to serve a certain purpose within a method or within a block of code inside a method. Once the method or block of code exits, the local variable falls out of scope and is no longer accessible. Local variables can be either value- or reference-type.

In this chapter we will look at:

- ❑ Local variable declarations and assignations
- ❑ Permitted variable names
- ❑ The scope of local variables
- ❑ Name hiding of fields by local variables

Local variable declarations

The C# language is strongly-typed, meaning that the type of every variable must be defined when the variable is declared. Variable declarations are in the standard C-format:

```
<type> <variable_name>;
```

Access modifiers such as the `internal`, `private`, `protected`, and `public` keywords are not used with local variables, because local variables cannot be accessed outside of the method or block of code in which they are defined. Similarly, the modifiers `readonly` and `static` cannot be applied to local variables.

We can declare more than one variable of a given type in a single declaration statement:

```
int i, j, k; // all three declared as ints.
```

Local variable assignation

All variables must be assigned a value before they are used. This can happen in the declaration statement or later in the code. You can declare (and initialize) a variable anywhere in the code as long as it is done before the variable is used. An exception to this rule is that it is possible to pass an un-initialized variable to a method using the `out` keyword. See Chapter 12 for more details on the `out` keyword.

Value-type local variables (together with strings, which share many features with value types) are assigned values simply by supplying the value for the variable. This can occur either within the declaration statement or in a later statement:

```
// Declare and initialize in one statement
int i = 100;

// Separate initialization
int i;
i = 100;
```

Multiple-variable declarations can also contain assignations:

```
// i and k assigned values; j and l left unassigned
int i =20, j, k = 30, l;
```

Reference-type variables can also be initialized when they are declared, either by calling a class constructor using the `new` operator, or by providing a list of array elements (we'll look at C#'s array syntax in Chapter 6).

Example: Local variable assignation

```
int j, k;
double height = 4.0;
StringBuilder sb = new StringBuilder("hello");
double[] heights = new double[4];
```

In the first line of this example, two integer variables are declared. The second line declares a double variable and gives it an initial value of 4.0. The third and fourth lines declare and initialize a `StringBuilder` object and an array of doubles. More information on declaring class instances and arrays is provided in Chapters 6 and 7.

Identifiers

Identifiers are the names given to local variables, fields, types, namespaces, and so on. Like everything else in C#, identifiers are of course case-sensitive, so `name` and `Name` would be different variables. Identifiers can consist of almost any combination of underscores and alphanumeric characters, including non-Roman characters and characters with diacritical marks or accents, although the first character cannot be a number. Identifiers cannot, however, be one of the reserved C# keywords; these keywords are listed in Appendix A. In addition, identifiers may not be longer than 511 characters.

Although C# identifiers are permitted to contain underscores, this practice does not follow Microsoft's naming guidelines (see Appendix B), so it is not recommended.

As well as the actual characters, identifiers may contain Unicode representations of characters (preceded by \u). These are treated as identical to the actual characters, for example:

```
double π = Math.PI;
Console.WriteLine(\u03C0);
```

This code will display the value of pi in the console window (03C0 is the Unicode code for the lower-case Greek letter π). Since two variables that reside in the same scope cannot have the same name, we cannot declare variables named π and \u03C0 within the same scope.

The following are all legal variable declarations:

```
string Name = "Grant";
int øre = 50;
string _Identifier = "Identifier";
string ملك = "king";
```

The following are not legal identifiers:

```
ToB||!ToB    // Identifiers can only contain
             // alphanumeric characters and underscores

2BOrNot2B    // Identifiers can't start with a number
غ١٢٣٤        // (In right-to-left scripts, the first character
             // will obviously be on the right.)


abstract     // C# keywords can't be used as identifiers
```

There is a workaround for this last rule – we can use a C# keyword as an identifier by prefixing it with an @ symbol. We wouldn't ever want to define an identifier like this in C#, but sometimes we may want to access types written in other languages which expose members with the same name as a C# keyword. For example, we could have the following class defined in Visual Basic .NET:

```
Public Class VBNameTest
   ' A public static string field called abstract
   ' Abstract isn't a keyword in VB.NET
   Public Shared abstract As New String("a string")
End Class
```

In order to access this field from C#, we need to prefix it with the @ symbol:

```
string s = VBNameTest.@abstract;
```

Variable scope

The block of code in which a variable is recognized by the compiler and can be accessed is known as its **scope**. A local variable's scope begins at the point when it is declared, although it can't be accessed until it has been initialized with a value. Variables go out of scope once the method that defines them exits or the block of code in which they reside completes its execution. While two variables within the same scope cannot have the same name, variables in different scopes can.

We saw in Chapter 2 that variables are stored either directly on the stack or as a reference to a location on the managed heap. Reference values may be retained by passing them into another scope (for example, returning them from a method), but the variable itself will go out of scope. The fact that the stack works on a First In, Last Out basis has important implications for variable scope – the top variable on the stack will go out of scope before all the variables below it. This means that scopes are nested – any block of code defined within another will be contained entirely within the parent scope.

Example: Variable scope

In this example, an integer variable named j is declared in two different if blocks. This is perfectly acceptable because each variable only exists within the scope of its if block. What would not work is having an integer variable named j declared at the top of the Main() method. This is because the j variable defined at the top of Main() is global with respect to the if blocks.

```
using System;

public class ScopeDemo
{
  public static void Main()
  {
    int i = 4;
    // This won't work        int j;

    if (i < 5)
    {
      int j = i * i;
      Console.WriteLine("Value is {0}", j);
    }

    if (i < 5)
    {
      int j = 4 * i + i;
      Console.WriteLine("Value is {0}", j);
    }
  }
}
```

Output:

```
Value is 16
Value is 20
```

Name hiding

Since child scopes are nested entirely within the parent scope, it isn't possible to declare a variable with the same name as a local variable in the parent scope. For example, this code snippet won't compile:

```
public void DoSomething()
{
  int i = 10;
  {
    int i = 20;
  }
}
```

In this case, there would be no way to refer to the outer-scoped variable from within the inner scope. It is, however, possible for a local variable to have the same name as a field member of the type in which it is defined, so this will compile:

```
public class NameHidingDemo
{
  static int i = 10;
  public static void Main()
  {
    int i = 20;
    Console.WriteLine(i);
  }
}
```

The output from this code is 20, since the inner variable hides the name of the outer one. If we want to refer to the field, we need to prefix the name with the this keyword for an instance field, or <class_name> for a static variable:

```
public class NameHidingDemo
{
  static int i = 10;
  public static void Main()
  {
    int i = 20;
    Console.WriteLine("local i = {0}", i);
    Console.WriteLine("this.i = {0}", NameHidingDemo.i);
  }
}
```

See Chapter 11 for more information about instance and static fields.

Summary

In this chapter, we looked at local variables – temporary variables defined inside a method or block of code. We examined the syntax for declaring and initializing local variables. We also looked at the possibilities and restrictions on local variable names – names must consist only of alphanumeric characters and underscores, may not start with a number, and may not be identical to a C# keyword. We saw how we can get round this if we need to access classes written in other languages which contain identifiers which are C# keywords. Finally, we explored the scope of variables, and saw how it's possible for a field and a local variable within the same scope to have the same name, and how to refer to the field in such cases.

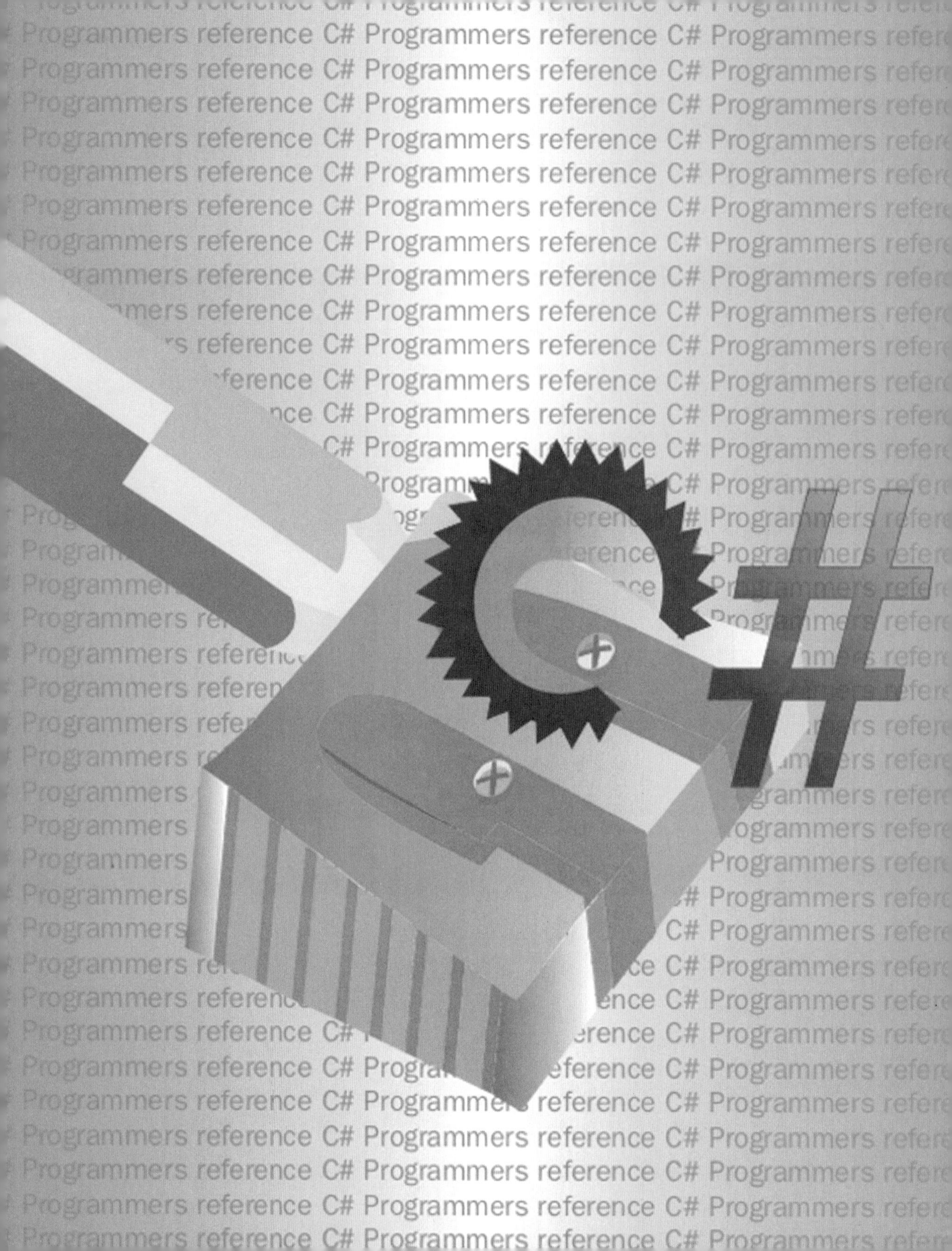
Programmers reference C# Programmers reference C#

6

Arrays

An array is a data structure that contains elements of the same data type. The elements of an array are accessed by an integer index. In C#, as in C, C++, and Java, the index of the first element is zero. In C#, arrays are defined as a distinct data type. This allows the Common Language Runtime to better manage things like out-of-bounds errors. Arrays are reference types. Even if an array contains value-type elements, the array itself is a reference type.

The .NET Framework defines two classes in the System and System.Collections namespaces that encapsulate an array. The Array class represents an immutable array of objects. It is immutable in the sense that once the length of the array has been set it cannot be changed. An Array object can be multidimensional. An ArrayList object is implemented using a one-dimensional array whose size can be increased or decreased as needed. See Chapters 22 and 23 for more details on these classes.

You can also create an array using the customary C or C++ syntax. This type of array will be described in this chapter. Since the Array class is the parent class of all arrays defined in C#, an array created using C/C++ syntax has access to the methods defined in the Array class. These methods can be used to search, sort, and modify arrays.

In this chapter we will:

- ❑ Learn how to create a one-dimensional array
- ❑ Examine the two types of multidimensional arrays
- ❑ Learn how to initialize and access array elements
- ❑ Take a brief look at the array properties and methods provided by the .NET Framework

Creating a one-dimensional array

A one-dimensional array is declared using the following syntax:

```
type[] arrayName;
```

This creates a null reference to a one-dimensional array of an indeterminate length. As with any other reference-type object, you can create the array itself using the new keyword.

```
type[] arrayName = new type[length];
```

The length of the array is provided inside square brackets. You can place the declaration and array creation parts on separate lines.

```
type[] arrayName;
arrayName = new type[length];
```

You can also specify the array length when the array is declared by provided a set of initial values. This is covered and demonstrated in the *Initializing array elements* section of this chapter.

Example: One-dimensional array

In this example, a one-dimensional, five-element, 32-bit integer array is created.

```
using System;

public class OneDDemo
{
  public static void Main()
  {
    int[] array = new int[5];

    for(int i=0; i<array.Length; ++i)
    {
      array[i] = 2*i;
      Console.WriteLine("element {0} is {1}",i,array[i]);
    }
  }
}
```

Output:

```
element 0 is 0
element 1 is 2
element 2 is 4
element 3 is 6
element 4 is 8
```

Creating a multidimensional array

There are two ways to define a multidimensional array with C#. An array where every row has the same length (the same number of columns) is referred to as a rectangular array. An array where every row can have a different length is called a jagged array. The syntax for declaring and initializing a 2-D rectangular array is:

```
type[,] arrayName = new type[numRows,numCols];
```

The number of commas inside the square brackets indicates the dimension of the array. A three-dimensional array would be declared using:

```
type[,,] arrayName = new type[dim1, dim2, dim3];
```

To create a two-dimensional jagged array that has a fixed number of rows but a variable number of columns in each row, you would use this syntax:

```
type[][] arrayName = new type[numRows][];
```

In effect, this statement has created an array of one-dimensional arrays. You would still need to initialize the length of each row.

```
arrayName[0] = new type[numCols0];
arrayName[1] = new type[numCols1];
        .
        .
        .
arrayName[numRows-1] = new type[numColsNumRowsM1];
```

A three-dimensional array would be declared in a similar way:

```
type[][][] arrayName = new type[dim1][][];
```

There are examples of how to create multidimensional arrays in the *Initializing array elements* and *Accessing array elements* sections.

Initializing array elements

There are two ways to initialize the elements of an array. The first way is to initialize the elements when the array is declared. The initial values are placed inside curly brackets after the array declaration.

```
String[] names = {"Mark", "Maria", "Scott", "Diana"};
```

The above syntax will create a one-dimensional array of length four that will contain the specified values. An equivalent syntax for the above expression is:

```
String[] names = new String[] {"Mark", "Maria", "Scott", "Diana"};
```

You can perform a similar initialization with a multidimensional array. The initialization values for each row are placed inside curly brackets.

```
String[,] names = { {"Diana","Reid"},
                    {"Cheryl","Spada"},
                    {"Scott", "Palmer"} };
```

The above expression will create a three row, two column array containing the specified values.

The second way to initialize array elements is to do it the "old fashioned" way of assigning a value to the desired array element. The advantage to this method is it can be done anywhere in the code and does not have to be performed when the array is declared. This is also the way to change an existing value of an array element.

Example: Multidimensional array

In this example, a two-dimensional, rectangular array is created. The array elements are assigned values by accessing each individual array element using the "[,]" syntax. The GetLength() method is defined in the System.Array class and returns the length of the specified dimension of an array.

```
using System;

public class MultiDemo
{
  public static void Main()
  {
    int[,] array = new int[2,3];

    for(int i=0; i<array.GetLength(0); ++i)
    {
      for(int j=0; j<array.GetLength(1); ++j)
      {
        array[i,j] = i+j;
            Console.WriteLine("element ({0},{1}) is {2}",i,j, array[i,j]);
      }
    }
  }
}
```

Output:

```
element (0,0) is 0
element (0,1) is 1
element (0,2) is 2
element (1,0) is 1
element (1,1) is 2
element (1,2) is 3
```

Accessing array elements

To access an element of a one-dimensional array, simply place the index of the desired element inside square brackets after the array name.

```
String[] names = {"Mark", "Maria", "Scott", "Diana"};
Console.WriteLine("second name is "+names[1]);
```

Keep in mind that the C# convention is the same as for C, C++, and Java, in that array indices start at 0. The runtime will provide bounds-checking of array indices. An `IndexOutOfRangeException` is thrown if you try to use an invalid index.

The manner in which you access the elements of a multi-dimensional array depends on how the array was declared. For arrays declared using the rectangular array syntax:

```
type[,] arrayName = new type[numRows,numCols];
```

you would access the array elements using the syntax:

```
value = arrayName[row,column];
```

For arrays declared using the jagged array syntax:

```
type[][] arrayName = new type[numRows][];
```

you would access the array elements using the syntax:

```
value = arrayName[row][column];
```

Example: Jagged array

Let's re-write the example at the end of the *Initializing array elements* section to use a jagged array.

A jagged two-dimensional array is created, and each row of the array is given a different number of columns. Remember that a jagged array is equivalent to an array of one-dimensional arrays. The `GetLength()` method is used to return the number of rows in the array. The `Length` property is used to return the length of each one-dimensional array. For a 1-D array the `Length` property will return the same value as `GetLength(0)`. The array elements are accessed using the "`[][]`" syntax.

```
using System;

public class JaggedDemo
{
  public static void Main()
  {
    int[][] array = new int[2][];
    array[0] = new int[2];
    array[1] = new int[4];

    for(int i=0; i<array.GetLength(0); ++i)
    {
      for(int j=0; j<array[i].Length; ++j)
      {
        array[i][j] = i+j;
        Console.WriteLine("element ({0},{1}) is {2}",i,j, array[i][j]);
      }
    }
```

```
    }
  }
```

Output:

```
element (0,0) is 0
element (0,1) is 1
element (1,0) is 1
element (1,1) is 2
element (1,2) is 3
element (1,3) is 4
```

Array properties and methods

The Array class is the parent class of all arrays in the C# language. As such, all arrays can use the properties and methods defined in the System.Array class. For example, the Rank property returns the number of dimensions in the array. The Length property returns the total number of elements in the array.

Some of the more commonly used array methods are as follows. The Reverse() method reverses the order of the elements in an array. The Sort() method arranges the array elements either alphabetically or according to some other algorithm. The Clear() method sets one or more elements of an array to zero if they are value types or null if they are reference types. Be careful using this method with jagged arrays as it will eliminate the sub-arrays. The IndexOf() and LastIndexOf() methods perform a linear search of an array for the first or last occurrence of a value. A complete description of the methods available to arrays can be found in Chapter 22.

Example: Sorted array

In this example, the Sort() method is used to alphabetically sort the elements of a 1-D array.

```
using System;

public class ArrayDemo
{
  public static void Main()
  {
    String[] names = {"Mark","Scott","Maria","Diana"};

    Array.Sort(names);

    for(int i=0; i<names.Length; ++i)
    {
      Console.WriteLine("name {0} is {1}",i,names[i]);
    }
  }
}
```

Output:

```
name 0 is Diana
name 1 is Maria
name 2 is Mark
name 3 is Scott
```

Array reference semantics

As we said at the beginning of this section, arrays are a reference type. Like all reference types, this means that a variable of an array type which has not been initialized is a null reference – it is not an empty array. A variable of type int[], for example, can hold a reference to an array of ints (of any size), or a null reference, but will hold a null reference until it has been assigned to a particular array.

This semantic distinction becomes significant when we pass an array variable to another method, particularly when it is passed by reference, or as an output variable. In particular, you should note that even when passing an array by value, the method we pass it to can alter the contents of the array to which we hold a reference.

Example: Passing array references to methods

In this example, we'll show how arrays behaved when passed by value, by reference, or as an output parameter.

```
using System;

public class ArrayReferenceDemo
{

  public static void Main()
  {
    String[] names;

    names = new String[] {"Mark","Scott","Maria","Diana"};
    PassByValue(names);

    Console.WriteLine(names[0]);

    names = new String[] {"Mark","Scott","Maria","Diana"};
    PassByReference(ref names);

    Console.WriteLine(names[0]);

    names = new String[] {"Mark","Scott","Maria","Diana"};
    PassAsOutput(out names);
```

```
        Console.WriteLine(names[0]);
    }

    public static void PassByValue(String[] names)
    {
        names[0] = "Brett";
        names = new String[] {"Julie", "Fiona", "Jack"};
    }

    public static void PassByReference(ref String[] names)
    {
        names[0] = "Brett";
        names = new String[] {"Julie", "Fiona", "Jack"};
    }

    public static void PassAsOutput(out String[] names)
    {
        // names[0] = "Brett"; // can't access an output parameter
                            // before it's assigned
        names = new String[] {"Julie", "Fiona", "Jack"};
    }
}
```

Output:

```
Brett
Julie
Julie
```

The first variable, passed by value, has its first item changed by the method, but still refers to the same array. The second variable, passed by reference, has the entire array replaced with a new one. The third variable, passed as an output variable, behaves like a pass-by-reference, but note that it is a compile-time-error to try to access an element of an output parameter within a method before it has been assigned.

Summary

In this chapter we learned how to create one-dimensional and multidimensional arrays. We learned about jagged and rectangular multidimensional arrays. The different ways of initializing array elements were explored. We saw how array elements can be accessed. Finally, some of the properties and methods available to arrays were introduced.

Programmers reference C# Programmers reference C# Programmers reference

7

Classes

The class is one of the two basic encapsulation constructs in the C# language (the other being a struct, which is described in Chapter 8). Every executable statement must be placed inside a class or struct. Classes define reference types that are the basic building blocks of most C# programs. Classes are the blueprints for the "objects" in "object-oriented programming".

A class is a composite reference type in that it can contain data members, functions, and nested types. The data members can include constants and instance and static variable fields. The function members can include methods, properties, constructors, destructors, operators, indexers, and events. A nested type is a user-defined type (a class, struct, interface, etc.) defined within another class. This is also referred to as an inner class or inner struct.

A powerful feature of C#, as in all object-oriented programming languages, is the concept of inheritance. Inheritance lets us develop a new derived class by extending the functionality of an existing base class. The derived class can be given access to constructors, methods, operators, etc., defined in the base class. This lets us reuse existing code and set up class hierarchies. The hierarchy of every class in the .NET Framework and every class that you will write derives from the Object class. This is the ultimate base class in the C# language.

This chapter will also describe special-purpose functions that classes may define. A constructor is used to initialize the data members of a class. Constructors can be inherited from a base class and can be overloaded. You can define both instance and static constructors. The C# language also provides the capability to release resources when a class instance is destroyed. The Finalize() method is used for this purpose.

In this chapter we will look at:

- ❑ Defining a class
- ❑ Creating a class instance
- ❑ Constructors
- ❑ Destructors and the Finalize() method
- ❑ Disposing of managed and unmanaged resources
- ❑ Inheritance
- ❑ Casting between user-defined types

Defining a class

Creating a user-defined class is quite simple. We define a class using the `class` keyword. The body of the class is placed inside curly brackets. As was previously stated, a class definition can contain any number of data members, function, and nested types:

```
<modifier> class <class_name>
{
  //  data members

  //  functions

  //  nested types
}
```

You have a lot of flexibility in selecting a name for a class, but there are some restrictions – for the restrictions placed on identifiers in C#, see Chapter 5.

To promote standardization and readability of C# programs, there are some class naming conventions recommended in the .NET Framework library pages: class names should be a noun or noun phrase; abbreviations should be avoided; and the first letter of the name should be capitalized (Pascal Casing).

Class modifiers

A class definition can be modified using the `abstract`, `internal`, `new`, `private`, `protected`, `public`, or `sealed` keywords. The `internal`, `private`, `protected`, and `public` keywords define the access to the class. A class declared in a namespace can only have `public` or `internal` access. A nested class (one defined inside another class) can have any of the four access types as well as `protected internal` access, which is equivalent to "protected or internal" access. You don't have to specify an access modifier, in which case the class is given `internal` access.

The other keywords concern member hiding and whether the class can be instantiated or derived from. Each of the class modifiers is described in the table below:

Modifier	Description
abstract	An instance of the class cannot be created. This usually means that the class is meant to serve as a base class. Abstract classes cannot be sealed.
internal	The class is only accessible from other classes in the same assembly. This is the default access for non-nested types. If no modifier is specified, the class will have `internal` access.
new	Used only with nested classes. It indicates that the class hides an inherited member of the same name.
private	A nested class that can only be accessed inside the class in which it is defined.
protected	A nested class that can be accessed inside the class in which it is defined and by a derived class of the class in which it is defined.
public	An instance of this class is available to all other classes that may wish to access it.
sealed	The class cannot serve as a base class for another class. In other words, the class cannot be derived from. A class cannot be both `sealed` and `abstract`.

Example: Class modifiers

Let's look at a modified version of the compilation example from Chapter 1. A class named Quad is defined in a file named Quad.cs. The Quad() method is the Quad class constructor and initializes the width and height data members. Constructors are discussed later in this chapter.

```
using System;

class Quad
{
  double width, height;

  public Quad(double w,  double h)
  {
    width = w;
    height = h;
  }

  public double GetArea()
  {
    return width * height;
  }
}
```

Note that the Quad class has the default internal access. The file is compiled into a DLL file using the compilation command:

csc /t:library Quad.cs

Another class named Test is contained in a file named Test.cs.

```
using System;

public class Test
{
  public static void Main()
  {
    Quad q = new Quad(2.0, 3.0);
    Console.WriteLine("Area is {0}", q.GetArea());
  }
}
```

The Test class uses an instance of the Quad class. To access this class, the Test class is compiled using the syntax:

csc Test.cs /r:Quad.dll

However, when you do this you will get the following error message:

Test.cs(5,7): error CS0122: 'Quad' is inaccessible due to its protection level

This is because the Quad class resides in a different assembly from the Test class. Because the Quad class has internal access, the Test class can't access it. To correct this problem, simply define the Quad class as having public access:

```
public class Quad
{
    . . .
```

The Test.cs file can now be compiled.

Output:

```
Area is 6
```

Creating a class instance

An instance of a class is a reference-type variable. As such, the object is stored on the heap. The syntax to create an instance of a class uses the new keyword:

```
class_name variable_name = new class_name(arguments);
```

What the new keyword does is to call a special function called a **constructor**. Arguments passed to the constructor are generally used to initialize the data members of the class instance, although a constructor might take no arguments, and require fields to be initialized later. Constructors are described in more detail later in this chapter.

For example, to create an instance of the Test class that was described in the previous section you might type:

```
Test mytest = new Test();
```

The syntax just described is really two statements in one. The first part of the statement:

```
Test mytest
```

creates a null reference of type Test named mytest. The second part of the syntax:

```
= new Test();
```

creates a Test object associated with the reference and initializes it by calling the no-argument Test class constructor. It is perfectly acceptable to place the two parts of the class instantiation syntax on separate lines.

```
Test mytest;
mytest = new Test();
```

Some classes may not have an accessible constructor, in which case we cannot instantiate the object in this way. Instances of these objects are typically created internally in methods in the .NET Framework, and these methods return a reference to a class instance. It is also possible to retrieve an instance of many classes that do have accessible constructors in this way. For example, the `Create()` method from the `File` class (a static method) returns a reference to a `FileStream` object. You can instantiate a `FileStream` object corresponding to a file named `data.inp` using the syntax:

```
FileStream fs = File.Create("data.inp");
```

There is one other way of instantiating an object – using reflection. We can dynamically retrieve a `ConstructorInfo` object for a specific type using the `System.Type` class, and invoke this to retrieve an instance of the class. For example, given a class `ReflectTest` with a public parameterless constructor:

```
public class ReflectTest
{
  public ReflectTest()
  {
  }
}
```

we can instantiate this class using the following code:

```
// Get the Type object for the ReflectTest class
Type t = Type.GetType("ReflectTest");

// Get the parameterless constructor for the class
ConstructorInfo ctor = t.GetConstructor(System.Type.EmptyTypes);
// Invoke the constructor with a 'null' parameter

ReflectTest test = (ReflectTest)ctor.Invoke(null);
```

Constructors

A class defines data members, functions, and nested types. A constructor is a special method that is generally used to initialize the data members of a class instance. The constructor name will always be the same as the name of the class. A constructor has no return value. A class can define any number of constructors. The runtime determines which constructor to call based on the input arguments passed to the constructor.

As with any class members, constructors can have `public`, `protected`, `internal`, `protected internal`, or `private` access. The most commonly used constructor access modifiers are `public` or `protected`. A `public` constructor has no access restrictions. It can be called anywhere. A `protected` constructor is only available to the type that defines it or to a derived type of the type that defines it. For example, a base class might contain a `protected` constructor that can be called from constructors in derived classes.

If no constructors are explicitly defined, a default `public` constructor with no parameters will be provided that will initialize the data members to their default values. If we wish to deny public access to this constructor (for example, if we only want the class to be instantiable via a factory class), we can declare this constructor with a different access level.

If we define only a `private`, parameterless constructor, we will prevent the class being instantiated (we might do this for a class with only static members, but which we can't declare as `abstract`, because we want it to be `sealed`, like the `System.Math` class).

If we want to force clients to supply arguments to the constructor (to initialize data members with specific values), we can simply define constructors which take arguments, and not supply a `public` parameterless constructor. A derived class will have access to the `public` and `protected` constructors defined in its base class or classes.

Example: Constructors

Let's re-write the `Quad` class once again, this time defining two constructors. The first represents a square where the width and height are the same. The second constructor is for a rectangle where the width and height are different.

The `ConstructorDemo` class creates two `Quad` objects. The first, representing a square, uses the one-argument constructor and the second, representing a rectangle, uses the two-argument constructor.

```csharp
using System;

public class Quad
{
   protected double width, height;

   public Quad(double d)
   {
      width = d;
      height = d;
   }

   public Quad(double w,  double h)
   {
      width = w;
      height = h;
   }

   public double GetArea()
   {
      return width * height;
   }
}

public class ConstructorDemo
{
   public static void Main()
   {
      Quad q1 = new Quad(4.0);
      Quad q2 = new Quad(2.0, 3.0);

      Console.WriteLine("Area of q1 is {0}", q1.GetArea());
      Console.WriteLine("Area of q2 is {0}", q2.GetArea());
   }
}
```

Output:

```
Area of q1 is 16
Area of q2 is 6
```

Calling a base class constructor

When an instance of a class is created, its construction includes construction of its base classes. Any data members inherited from base classes will have to be initialized. One of the things that a derived class constructor does is to call a constructor from its immediate base class. This can be either done implicitly using the base class's default (no-argument) constructor, or by having the derived class constructor make an explicit call to a base class constructor.

If the base class does not define a no-argument constructor, an explicit call to a base class constructor must be made. A base class constructor is called using the base keyword preceded by a colon. This syntax is placed after the derived class constructor name. Any arguments needed by the base class constructor are passed to it in the normal way, inside parentheses.

Example: Base constructor

This example creates a derived class of the Quad class defined in the previous example. The NamedQuad class adds a name field to the width and height data members. The NamedQuad constructor takes three arguments: a width, a height, and a string. The two-argument Quad class constructor is called using the :base syntax. The Quad class constructor initializes the width and height fields using the w and h parameters passed to the constructor. The NamedQuad constructor then initializes the name field with the input string.

```
using System;

public class NamedQuad : Quad
{
    string name;

    public NamedQuad(double w, double h, string str) : base(w, h)
    {
        name = str;
    }

    public string GetName()
    {
        return name;
    }
}
```

```
public class BaseConstDemo
{
  public static void Main()
  {
    NamedQuad nq = new NamedQuad(2.0, 3.0, "Harry");

    Console.WriteLine("Area of {0} is {1}", nq.GetName(), nq.GetArea());
  }
}
```

Output:

```
Area of Harry is 6
```

An interesting note on this example is that if we had defined the NamedQuad class constructor this way:

```
public NamedQuad(double w, double h, string str)
{
    width = w;
    height = h;
    name = str;
}
```

the program would not compile. This is because the NamedQuad constructor would try to call a no-argument constructor from the Quad class, but the Quad class does not define one. Note that this is true even if the signature of the constructor matches one of the base class's constructors.

Calling a constructor defined in the same class

We can call another overload of the constructor defined in the same class in a similar way to calling a base class constructor. The constructor is called by using the : this syntax and providing the appropriate input arguments to the constructor. One reason to do this is to avoid duplication of code between constructors.

Example: Calling other overloads

Let's rewrite our Quad class one more time. In this case, we define three constructors. The constructors take zero, one, and two arguments respectively but they all do the exact same thing, namely initialize the width and height fields:

```
public class Quad
{
  double width, height;

  public Quad()
  {
    width = 1.0;
```

```
      height = 1.0;
  }

  public Quad(double d)
  {
    width = d;
    height = d;
  }

  public Quad(double w,  double h)
  {
    width = w;
    height = h;
  }

  public double GetArea()
  {
    return width * height;
  }
}
```

Code duplication is dangerous. If you modify one constructor, you have to be sure to modify the others in exactly the same way. This is not so much an issue here where the constructors are very simple, but may be an issue with more complicated constructors. To remove the code duplication, we will modify the Quad class so the zero- and one-argument constructors initialize the data members by calling the two-argument constructor:

```
using System;

public class Quad
{
  double width, height;

  public Quad() : this(1.0, 1.0)
  {
  }

  public Quad(double d) : this(d, d)
  {
  }

  public Quad(double w,  double h)
  {
    width = w;
    height = h;
  }

  public double GetArea()
  {
    return width * height;
  }
}
```

```
public class ThisDemo
{
  public static void Main()
  {
    Quad q1 = new Quad();
    Quad q2 = new Quad(2.0);
    Quad q3 = new Quad(2.0, 3.0);

    Console.WriteLine("Area of q1 is {0}", q1.GetArea());
    Console.WriteLine("Area of q2 is {0}", q2.GetArea());
    Console.WriteLine("Area of q3 is {0}", q3.GetArea());
  }
}
```

Output:

```
Area of q1 is 1
Area of q2 is 4
Area of q3 is 6
```

Static constructors

A static constructor is designated by the static keyword and is normally used to initialize static data members. A static data member is associated with a type rather than with an instance of a type. A static constructor is not permitted to have an access modifier. We cannot explicitly call a static constructor; it is called by the runtime once, when the class is loaded – before any instance of the class is created and before any static members of the class are referenced. Static constructors are not inherited, and it is possible for classes to have both static and instance constructors.

Example: Static constructors

In this example, the Blah class defines a static field and a static constructor to initialize the field. When the field is initialized with the static constructor, its value can be accessed using the standard syntax to access a static field:

```
using System;

public class Blah
{
    public static int MaxIter;

    static Blah()
    {
        MaxIter = 50;
    }
}

public class StaticConstDemo
{
```

```
    public static void Main()
  {
        Console.WriteLine("Value of MaxIter is {0}",Blah.MaxIter);
    }
}
```

Output:

```
Value of MaxIter is 50
```

Note that the static constructor is never explicitly called. It is called by the runtime.

Destructors and the Finalize() method

A destructor is a method that is called when an object gets destroyed. In C++, destructors are used to free up memory and perform other cleanup operations. The C# language employs a garbage collector that does most of this type of thing automatically. As a general rule, unless there is a compelling reason to use one, you should forget about defining a destructor and leave the cleanup operations to the runtime.

In C#, the Finalize() method performs the functions that a standard C++ destructor would do. In fact, when you define a Finalize() method, you don't name it Finalize. Instead you use the C++ destructor syntax of placing a tilde (~) symbol before the name of the class.

```
public class Blah
{
  ~Blah()
  {
    // Perform cleanup operations
  }
}
```

This is translated into a method named Finalize() when the C# code is compiled into IL:

```
.method family hidebysig virtual instance void
        Finalize() cil managed
{
  .try
  {
    // Cleanup code
  } // end .try
  finally
  {
    IL_000c:  ldarg.0
    IL_000d:  call        instance void [mscorlib]System.Object::Finalize()
    IL_0012:  endfinally
  } // end handler
  IL_0013:  ret
} // end of method Blah::Finalize
```

89

Notice that the base class's destructor (in this case `System.Object::Finalize()`) is implicitly called by the destructor once any cleanup code has executed.

The most important point to be aware of if you supply a destructor is that we can't predict when it will be called – it won't be executed until the garbage collected runs and removes the object from memory. For this reason, if you have any expensive unmanaged resources to release when a class is destroyed, it is generally preferable to dispose of them in a `Close()` or `Dispose()` method, which can be called explicitly by the programmer when the object is no longer in use. In fact, there is no guarantee that the destructor will ever be called, since we can ask the garbage collector not to call an object's destructor by calling the `SuppressFinalize()` method of the `System.GC` class.

Destructors have no access modifiers and no return type, and they take no inputs. The body of the destructor is written to perform whatever cleanup operations are required. Destructors often work in conjunction with the `Dispose()` or `Close()` method. See the next section for an example of writing a `Finalize()` method.

Disposing of managed and unmanaged resources

There are two types of resources that can be part of a C# type. There are managed resources that are defined in the .NET Framework. There may also be unmanaged, external resources that a type may want to access. The runtime may dispose of unmanaged resources when it calls the destructor associated with the type; however, we can also implement the `IDisposable` interface to allow clients of our class to ask explicitly for resources to be released.

The `IDisposable` interface declares one method, `Dispose()`, that takes no arguments and has a return type of `void`. The `Dispose()` method is used to free up managed and/or unmanaged resources associated with an object. Every class that implements `IDisposable` must provide an implementation of the `Dispose()` method.

One way to take care of both of these disposal needs is to define a second `Dispose()` method that takes a `bool` argument. If the argument is `true`, both the managed and unmanaged resources are disposed of. If the argument is `false`, only the unmanaged resources are disposed of. This second `Dispose()` method is called by the no-argument `Dispose()` method and is called inside the destructor method.

Example: Dispose() method

In this example we define the `Blah` class that contains both managed and unmanaged resources. It actually only defines one of each and the unmanaged resource is never initialized, but it is sufficient to demonstrate clearly how `Dispose()` works. The `Blah` class implements the `IDisposable` interface and provides an implementation of the `Dispose()` method.

The second `Dispose()` method, as previously described, takes a `bool` argument and allows for the disposal of managed and/or unmanaged resources. This method is called either by the no-argument `Dispose()` method or by the destructor. If you were creating a derived class of `Blah`, you would write an overridden version of the `Dispose(bool)` method that would also dispose of any base class resources.

```
using System;
using System.IO;

public class Blah : IDisposable
{
  private IntPtr handle;
  private StreamWriter writer;
  private bool disposed = false;

  public Blah(string Filename)
  {
    writer = new StreamWriter(
                new FileStream(Filename, FileMode.OpenOrCreate));
    //  unmanaged initialization code
  }

  public StreamWriter Writer
  {
    get
    {
      return writer;
    }
  }

  public void Dispose()
  {
    Dispose(true);
    GC.SuppressFinalize(this);
  }

  protected virtual void Dispose(bool disposeManaged)
  {
    //========================================================
    //  If the object has been disposed already, do nothing
    //========================================================
    if (!this.disposed)
    {
      //=========================================================
      //  If disposeManaged is true, dispose of managed resources
      //=========================================================
      if (disposeManaged)
      {
        writer.Close();
      }

      //==========================================================
      //  Dispose of unmanaged resources and set disposed to true
      //==========================================================

      //  code to dispose of unmanaged resource here

      disposed = true;
  }
  }
```

```
    ~Blah()
    {
      Dispose(false);
    }
  }
```

The `DoSomeStuff()` method of the `UsingDemo` class creates an instance of the `Blah` class as a local variable. Inside a `using` statement, the `StreamWriter` associated with the `Blah` object writes a `string` to a file. When this operation is complete, the resources associated with the `Blah` object are disposed of. The `using` statement causes `Dispose()` to be called automatically on an object when the variable goes out of scope; we will look at this keyword in the next section.

```
using System;
using System.IO;

public class UsingDemo
{
  public static void Main()
  {
    DoSomeStuff();
  }

  public static void DoSomeStuff()
  {
    Blah b = new Blah("Blah.out");

    using(b)
    {
      b.Writer.WriteLine("Hello");
    }
  }
}
```

Output (contents of `Blah.out` file):

```
Hello
```

using statement

When the `using` statement is applied to an object, the resources associated with the object are disposed of as soon as the block of code following the `using` statement is executed. The resource disposal is facilitated by calling the object's `Dispose()` method. Don't confuse this with the `using` keyword that is used to access the contents of a namespace without using the fully qualified type names. The basic syntax of the `using` statement is as follows:

```
using(object)
{
  // code to execute
}
```

You can declare and initialize the object inside the parentheses. The using statement is really just shorthand for a try-finally block. The basic syntax shown above is equivalent to the code:

```
try
{
  // code to execute
}
finally
{
  if (object != null) ((IDisposable)object).Dispose();
}
```

The object argument must be an instance of a class that implements the IDisposable interface.

Example: using statement

In this example, we use a StringWriter to write the current date to a file. This operation is placed inside a using block, so the StringWriter is disposed of once the operation has completed:

```
using System;
using System.IO;

public class UsingDemo2
{
  public static void Main()
  {
    DoSomeStuff();
  }

  public static void DoSomeStuff()
  {
    StreamWriter writer = File.CreateText("Blah.out");
    using(writer)
    {
      writer.WriteLine(DateTime.Now.ToLongDateString());
    }

    //  method does some more stuff
  }
}
```

Output (contents of Blah.out file; this will vary):

```
Thursday, February 07, 2002
```

The `using` statement compiles to the following IL code:

```
.try
{
  IL_000d:  ldloc.0
  IL_000e:  call         valuetype [mscorlib]System.DateTime
                         [mscorlib]System.DateTime::get_Now()
  IL_0013:  stloc.2
  IL_0014:  ldloca.s     V_2
  IL_0016:  call         instance string
                         [mscorlib]System.DateTime::ToLongDateString()
  IL_001b:  callvirt     instance void
                         [mscorlib]System.IO.TextWriter::WriteLine(string)
  IL_0020:  leave.s      IL_002c
} // end .try
finally
{
  IL_0022:  ldloc.1
  IL_0023:  brfalse.s    IL_002b
  IL_0025:  ldloc.1
  IL_0026:  callvirt     instance void
                         [mscorlib]System.IDisposable::Dispose()
  IL_002b:  endfinally
} // end handler
```

Notice that the C# compiler wraps the code in the `using` block in a `try` block, and calls `Dispose()` in an associated `finally` block, so it will be called even if an error occurs.

Inheritance

Inheritance is one of the pillars of object-oriented programming, and is one of the ways that OOP encourages code reuse. Inheritance lets you develop a new derived class by extending the functionality of an existing base class. Inheritance also allows the development of class hierarchies. Common functionality can be placed in a base class and any number of specific derived classes can be created that make use of this functionality without having to duplicate it internally.

A derived class (also called a child or subclass) inherits from a base class (also called a parent or superclass). Inheritance is indicated in the class declaration by a colon followed by the name of the base class. For example, if you wanted to create a `public` class named `Eagle` that was a derived class of `Bird`, the `Eagle` class signature might be:

```
public class Eagle : Bird
```

The C# language only supports single inheritance for classes (although a class can implement multiple interfaces). A class can only have one direct base class although its base class can have a base class, and so on.

There are access restrictions for derived classes with respect to their base classes. A base class member that is given `private` access is not available to derived classes.

A base class member given `internal` access is only available to derived classes (or any classes for that matter) that reside in the same assembly. Derived classes have free access to the `protected`, `protected internal`, and `public` base class members.

Example: Inheritance

In this example, the `Coin` class defines one protected field, `Value`, and a method for accessing this field.

```
using System;

public class Coin
{
   protected int Value;

   public int GetValue()
   {
      return Value;
   }
}
```

We also have two classes, `Quarter` and `Dime`, which derive from the `Coin` class. They inherit the `Value` field and the `GetValue()` method from the `Coin` class. The only thing the `Quarter` and `Dime` classes do is to define a constructor that sets the `Value` field:

```
public class Quarter : Coin
{
   public Quarter()
   {
      Value = 25;
   }
}

public class Dime : Coin
{
   public Dime()
   {
      Value = 10;
   }
}
```

The `Main()` method of the `InherDemo` class creates a `Quarter` and a `Dime` object. These objects call the `GetValue()` method. They can do this because the `Quarter` and `Dime` classes inherit this method from the `Coin` class:

```
public class InherDemo
{
   public static void Main()
   {
      Quarter q = new Quarter();
      Dime d = new Dime();
```

```
        Console.WriteLine("Value of quarter is {0}", q.GetValue());
        Console.WriteLine("Value of dime is {0}", d.GetValue());
    }
}
```

Output:

```
Value of quarter is 25
Value of dime is 10
```

There are some restrictions on inheritance. Any private data members or methods of a base class are not accessible to a derived class. If you change the access of the `Value` field in the `Coin` class from `protected` to `private`, the program will no longer compile because the `Quarter` and `Dime` class constructors won't be able to access the `value` field.

Casting between user-defined types

In Chapter 2, we listed the permissible implicit and explicit casts allowed between predefined value types. Conversions are also allowed between certain user-defined types, such as classes, structs, and interfaces. Most of these conversions require casts to be defined within either the type to be converted or the type to be converted from, but a number of conversions are allowed implicitly, without any additional code:

From	To
Any type	`Object`
Any derived class	A base class
Any class or struct	Any interface implemented by the class or struct
`null`	Any reference type
An array type	Any other array type, so long as both arrays have the same number of dimensions, the elements of both the arrays are reference types, and an implicit conversion is possible between the element types

In addition, we can explicitly convert interface types to classes which implement this interface, and we can cast base classes back to subclasses, but only if the object is of that specific type. In other cases, we will need to define casts within our code.

Example: User-defined casts

To demonstrate how this works in practice, let's expand our shapes example. We'll define an interface IShape, two classes which implement this, Rectangle and Circle, and a third class, Square, which inherits from Rectangle:

```
using System;

public interface IShape
{
  double Area { get; }
}

public class Rectangle : IShape
{
  private double width;
  private double height;

  public Rectangle(double Width, double Height)
  {
    width = Width;
    height = Height;
  }

  public double Width
  {
    get
    {
      return width;
    }
    set
    {
      width = value;
    }
  }

  public double Height
  {
    get
    {
      return height;
    }
    set
    {
      height = value;
    }
  }

  public double Area
  {
    get
    {
      return width * height;
```

```
      }
    }
}

public class Square : Rectangle
{
  public Square(double Width) : base(Width, Width)
  {
  }
}

public class Circle : IShape
{
  private double radius;

  public Circle(double Radius)
  {
    radius = Radius;
  }

  public double Radius
  {
    get
    {
      return radius;
    }
    set
    {
      radius = value;
    }
  }

  public double Area
  {
    get
    {
      return Math.PI * (radius * radius);
    }
  }

  public double Diameter
  {
    get
    {
      return 2 * radius;
    }
  }
}
```

We can implicitly convert between any of the three shapes and the IShape interface, as they all implement this interface. We can cast this interface back to the original type, or to the base class of this type, but we can't cast an IShape of type Circle to a Square or Rectangle:

```
class CastDemo
{
  static void Main(string[] args)
  {
    Square sq = new Square(3.0);
    IShape shape = sq;              // Can implicitly cast sq to IShape

    // Can cast this IShape back to a Rectangle,
    // since Square is derived from Rectangle
    Rectangle rect = (Rectangle)shape;
    Console.WriteLine("Rectangle of area {0}", rect.Area);

    // This would give a runtime error - although Circle implements IShape,
    // we can't cast from an interface to a class unless the object
    // belongs to that class or a base class
    // Circle circ = (Circle)shape;
  }
}
```

Custom casts

If we want to cast a `Circle` to a `Square`, or vice versa, we need to define within our code exactly how we want the cast to be performed. A custom cast is defined in C# as an operator:

```
public static <implicit | explicit> operator <target_type> (<source_type> <argument>)
```

User-defined casts *must* be `public` and `static`. We also specify whether the cast is to be implicit or explicit (implicit casts can always also be made explicitly), the target type (the type we want to convert to), and the source type (the type we want to convert from).

Example: Custom casts

Coming back to our example, this is how we might define the conversion from `Square` to `Circle` (we return a new circle with the diameter the same as the square's width). We'll define this as `explicit`, as we don't want this cast to be made unless the programmer specifically requests it:

```
public static explicit operator Circle (Square Sq)
{
  return new Circle(Sq.Width / 2);
}
```

Similarly, within the `Circle` class, we define a cast to the `Square` type (this returns a square with the width of the circle's diameter):

```
public static explicit operator Square (Circle Circ)
{
  return new Square(Circ.Radius * 2);
}
```

One thing to be aware of if we provide two-way casts of this type is the danger of introducing possible errors if the two casts don't match. For example, suppose we returned the circle's "inner" square (where the circle's diameter is equal to the square's diagonal), instead of its outer square:

```
public static explicit operator Square (Circle Circ)
{
   return new Square(2 * Math.Sqrt((Circ.Radius * Circ.Radius) / 2));
}
```

Now, if we convert a square to a circle and back, we'll end up with a completely different square:

```
Square sq1 = new Square(3.0);
Console.WriteLine("Square of area {0}", sq1.Area);
Circle circ = (Circle)sq1;
Console.WriteLine("Circle of area {0}", circ.Area);
Square sq2 = (Square)circ;
Console.WriteLine("Square of area {0}", sq2.Area);
```

The output from this code is:

```
Square of area 9
Circle of area 7.06858347057703
Square of area 4.5
```

So we've unintentionally halved the area of our square!

Disallowed casts

There are certain conversions which C# will not allow us to define. We can't define any casts which are permitted by default (such as casting a class to an implemented interface), and we can't define casts to convert base types to inherited types. The full list of disallowed casts is:

From	To
Any type	The same type
Any type	object
object	Any type
Any type	Any interface
Any interface	Any type

From	To
Any derived class	A base class
A base class	Any derived class

Summary

This chapter covered one of the most important types in the C# language, the class. We learned how to define a class. The modifier keywords that can be applied to a class definition were explained. We learned how to create an instance of a class using the `new` keyword. We examined specialized functions called constructors that are used to initialize the data members of a class instance. We also looked at destructors and the `Finalize()` method, which are called when a class is destroyed by the garbage collector, and we saw how this can be used in conjunction with the `Dispose()` method to release managed and unmanaged resources. We also saw how we can use the `using` statement to call `Dispose()` automatically when an object goes out of scope. The concept of inheritance, where classes can build upon other classes, was introduced. Finally, we looked at casting between classes and other user-defined types, and saw how we can define our own casts for our classes.

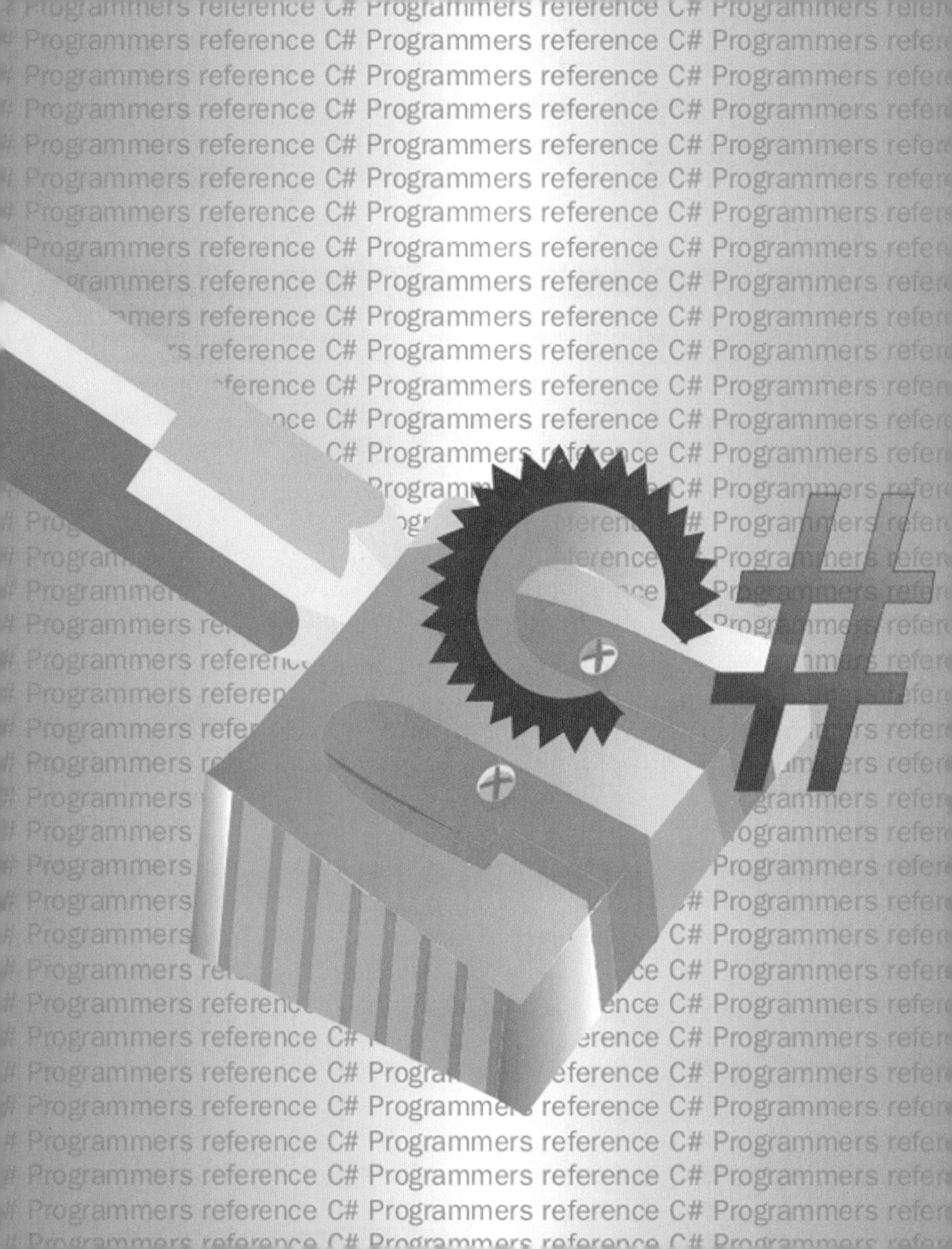
C# Programmers reference

8

Structs

A **struct** is an encapsulation construct that's similar to a class, in that it can contain data, type, and function members. Unlike a class, however, a struct is a **value type**, and as such is stored in the area of memory known as the **stack**. A struct is normally used to store a collection of simple data types – entities that have a fixed size in memory. In fact, the built-in primitive value types Int32, Int64, Double, etc., are implemented in the .NET Framework as structs.

In this chapter, we will:

❑ Examine more carefully the differences between structs and classes

❑ See how to define a struct

❑ Present the semantics for creating a struct instance

Differences between structs and classes

Because structs are stored on the stack and passed by value, they can offer a performance advantage over a comparable class object that's stored on the heap. For one thing, value types are allocated more quickly than reference types; for another, values on the stack are *immediately* de-allocated when they go out of scope. There is no waiting around for the garbage collector to do its thing.

This behavior, however, can become an issue if you're passing a struct as the argument to a method. When a reference type is passed to a method, only the reference to an object is passed. With a struct, a complete copy of the struct is made before it is passed. Compared to a reference type, the more complex the struct, the more significant the performance overhead associated with copying it. Because of this, structs should only be used to represent small data structures.

A struct implicitly inherits from the System.ValueType class, which in turn inherits from the System.Object class. The ValueType class provides some overridden versions of the Object class methods, and therefore a struct instance can invoke methods of the Object class.

Another difference between structs and classes is that a struct can define neither a no-argument constructor nor a destructor. Instead, a no-argument constructor is provided by the runtime to initialize all data members to default values, while any constructors defined by a struct must assign values to every field the struct contains.

Finally, unlike classes, structs do not support implementation inheritance, although they can provide the implementation of one or more interfaces. A struct implicitly inherits from the `ValueType` class and the `Object` class, but it's also implicitly `sealed`, meaning that it cannot serve as the base for other types.

Defining a struct

A struct is defined similarly to a class, but using the `struct` keyword. As you'd expect, then, the body of a struct is a block of code that's delimited by braces; the basic syntax of a struct definition is shown below.

```
<access_modifier> struct <struct_name>
{
    // Data members

    // Methods

    // Nested type definitions
}
```

There are a few restrictions on the definition of a struct that come as a result of the differences between structs and classes. Because a struct cannot be inherited from, no member of a struct can be declared `virtual`. Similarly, you can't define a struct as `abstract`, since this would imply that it was intended to be a base for derived types. You don't have to use the `sealed` keyword in the definition of a struct – it's implied automatically.

The rules about applying access modifiers to a struct are the same as those for classes. A struct that's declared in a namespace can be given `public` or `internal` access (where the latter is the default), while a nested struct can be given `public`, `internal`, or `private` access (where the last is the default). See the *Class modifiers* section of Chapter 7 for a description of the different access types.

Example: Defining a struct

In Chapter 3, an example defined the `Complex` class that encapsulates a complex number. However, since the `Complex` class only defines two value-type data members, it doesn't really make sense to go to the trouble of storing a `Complex` object on the heap. It's a better idea to represent the complex number as a struct, a change you can make (on this occasion) just by using the `struct` keyword in place of the `class` keyword.

The `Complex` struct defines a two-argument constructor. (Remember: you can't define a no-argument constructor, and every constructor must initialize all the data members of the struct.) The `Complex` struct also overloads the '+' operator and provides an overloaded version of the `ToString()` method.

```
public struct Complex
{
    double a;
    double b;
```

```
public Complex(double d1, double d2)
{
  a = d1;
  b = d2;
}

public static Complex operator +(Complex c1, Complex c2)
{
  Complex c3 = new Complex((c1.a + c2.a), (c1.b + c2.b));
  return c3;
}

public override string ToString()
{
  String str = "";
  if(b < 0)
  {
    str = str + a + " - " + -b + "i";
  }
  else
  {
    str = str + a + " + " + b + "i";
  }
  return str;
}
}
```

Creating a struct instance

As with creating a class instance, a struct instance is created and initialized in a two-step process. The first step is to declare the struct variable:

```
struct_name variable_name;
```

This statement allocates space on the stack for the struct – but at this point, the struct's data members are uninitialized. To initialize the data members (which you must do before using the struct instance), you can call one of the struct's constructors by using the new keyword:

```
variable_name = new struct_name(arguments);
```

The arguments are passed to the constructor and used to initialize the struct's data members. If no arguments are provided to the constructor, the default constructor is invoked. The two steps above can be combined into a single statement:

```
struct_name variable_name = new struct_name(arguments);
```

If the data members of the struct have public access (which is not usually good object-oriented programming practice), you can also initialize them by accessing them directly.

```
variable_name.member_name = value;
```

Example: Initializing a struct

The `StructDemo` class in the listing below creates two `Complex` struct instances. The first uses the default, no-argument constructor to initialize the a and b fields of the struct. The second instance calls the two-argument constructor that we defined above. A third `Complex` instance is defined as the sum of the first two, before the overloaded `ToString()` method is used to obtain a proper `String` representation of the complex number:

```
using System;

// Insert Complex struct definition

public class StructDemo
{
  public static void Main()
  {
    Complex c1 = new Complex();
    Complex c2 = new Complex(3.0, -7.0);

    Console.WriteLine(c1);

    Complex c3 = c1 + c2;
    Console.WriteLine(c3);
  }
}
```

Output:

```
0 + 0i
3 - 7i
```

Summary

In this chapter, we've looked at the value-type encapsulation construct known as a struct. We examined the ways in which a struct is similar to and different from a class, in terms of where the two are created, the members they may contain, and their relationships with other data types. Finally, you saw how to define, create, and use a struct by means of a short example.

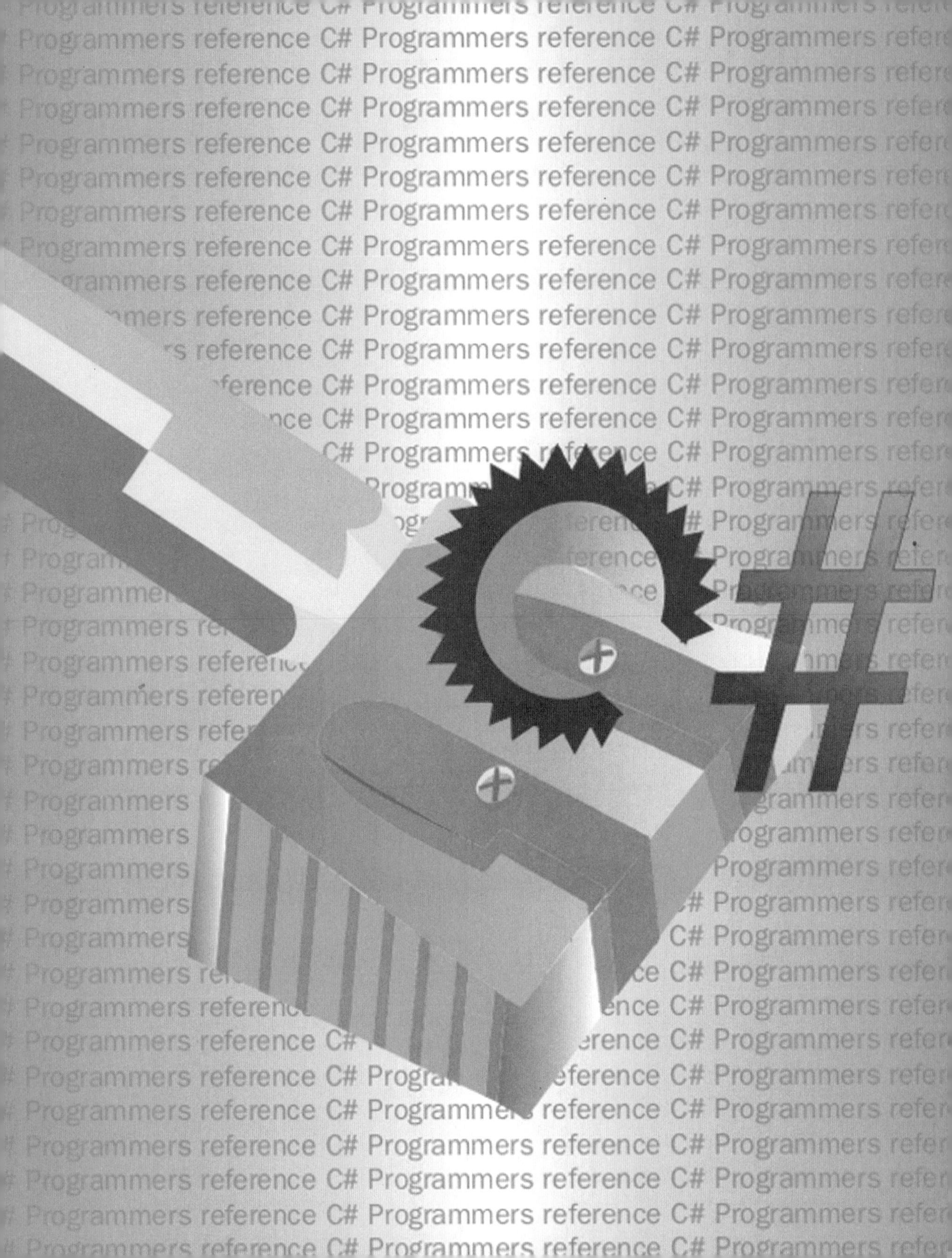
C# Programmers reference
C#

Interfaces

An interface provides a blueprint for a class or struct. It is a programming construct that can declare properties, indexers, events, and methods. It doesn't provide implementation for these members, just the definition. A data type that implements an interface must provide implementation of the interface members, but the way the members are implemented is left up to the individual needs of the type.

All members declared in an interface are implicitly `public` and `abstract`. While a class can only inherit from one base class, it can implement any number of interfaces. Structs can also implement interfaces. An interface itself can derive from multiple base interfaces.

Defining an interface

An interface is defined using the `interface` keyword according to the syntax:

```
<access> interface <name>
{
  // interface members
}
```

An interface that is declared in a namespace can be given `public` or `internal` access. A nested interface can be given `public, protected, internal, protected internal,` or `private` access. The default access is `internal`. See the *Class modifiers* section of Chapter 7 for a description of the different access types. The `new` keyword can be applied to an interface to indicate that one of its members is hiding a member from an inherited interface.

Interface members (properties, indexers, events, or methods) are implicitly `public` and `abstract`. They are declared without implementation and without an access modifier. The interface name is subject to the same restrictions as class names. The C# convention is for interface names to start with a captial 'I'.

Example: Defining an interface

An interface named `IShape` is defined to provide a specification for classes that represent a shape. The `IShape` interface declares a property named `NumSides` and a method, `GetArea()`. The interface body contains only the syntax for the property and method without any implementation.

```
public interface IShape
```

```
{
  int NumSides { get; }     // A property

  double GetArea();         // A method
}
```

Implementing an interface

A class or struct can indicate that it is implementing an interface by including the interface name preceded by a colon in the type definition statement. This is the same as the syntax to indicate inheritance. A type can implement more than one interface. In this case, the interface names are listed one after another separated by commas. When a class both inherits from a base class and implements an interface, the base class is placed first.

For example, let's say we want to write a `public` class named `Eagle` that inherits from the `Bird` class and implements two interfaces named `IAnimal` and `IRaptor`. The `Eagle` class syntax would be:

```
public class Eagle : Bird, IAnimal, IRaptor
```

Once a type implements an interface, it must provide implementation for the members declared in the interface. Members of any base interfaces, from which base classes or implemented interfaces are derived, must also be implemented. The type can implement the required members any way it sees fit as long as the implementation adheres to the member syntax declared in the interface. For example, when you implement a method you could declare it to be `virtual`, but you could not change the argument list or return type of the method.

Example: Implementing an interface

In this example, the `Triangle` class that encapsulates a triangular shape is defined. The `Triangle` class implements the `IShape` interface. As such, it must provide an implementation of the `NumSides` property and the `GetArea()` method.

```
using System;

public class Triangle : IShape
{
  double width, height;

  public Triangle(double w, double h)
  {
    width = w;
    height = h;
  }

  public int NumSides
  {
    get
    {
      return 3;
```

```
    }
  }

  public double GetArea()
  {
    return 0.5 * width * height;
  }
}
```

The Main() method of the InterfaceDemo class creates a Triangle object, accesses the NumSides property, and calls the GetArea() method.

```
public class InterfaceDemo
{
  public static void Main()
  {
    Triangle t = new Triangle(3.0, 4.0);

    Console.WriteLine("Number of sides is {0}", t.NumSides);
    Console.WriteLine("Area is {0}", t.GetArea());
  }
}
```

Output:

```
Number of sides is 3
Area is 6
```

Interface inheritance

An interface can extend another interface. The syntax is the same as for class inheritance. The derived interface syntax includes the name of the base interface preceded by a colon. A class or struct that implements the derived interface must also provide implementation for the members declared in the base interface. Interfaces support multiple inheritance in that an interface can have multiple base interfaces. For example, you could define an ICircle interface that would extend the IShape and IDisposable interfaces as:

```
public interface ICircle : IShape, IDisposable
{
  //  ICircle interface members
}
```

A type that implements the ICircle interface would have to implement the members declared in the ICircle, IShape, and IDisposable interfaces.

Interface mapping

A type must provide implementations of all interfaces that are part of its base class list. The process of connecting member implementations to interface declarations is called interface mapping.

The compiler will start with the current type and work its way up the type hierarchy. A type does not have to implement an inherited interface member if one of its base types does.

In some situations, the comparisons are simple. If a method defined in the type has the same name, return type, and parameter list as a method declared in an implemented interface, the method is recognized as an appropriate match. Similar one-to-one comparisons can be made with properties, events, and indexers.

But in some cases, the situation becomes more complicated. For instance, let's say a class implements two interfaces that declare a method of the same name and argument list but a different return type. You can't define two such methods in the same class. What you can do is use what is called an explicit interface member implementation by prefixing the member name with the name of the interface it is to be associated with. An explicitly implemented interface member has no return type and can only be accessed through an interface instance.

Example: Interface mapping

In this example, a class named `Account` implements two interfaces named `ITrans` and `IBank`. As well as declaring other unspecified members, the `ITrans` and `IBank` interfaces declare a `Deposit()` method. The `ITrans Deposit()` method returns a `double`. The `IBank Deposit()` method has no return value.

This presents a problem for the `Account` class. It must implement both methods, but if you try to do it the standard way as shown below the code won't compile. The reason is that you can't define two methods with the same name and argument list in the same class.

```
public interface ITrans
{
    double Deposit(double b);
    // other interface members
}

public interface IBank
{
    void Deposit(double b);
    //other interface members
}

public class Account : ITrans, IBank
{
    double balance;

    public Account(double b)
    {
        balance = b;
    }

    public double Deposit(double b)
    {
        balance += b;
        return balance;
```

```
    }

    public void Deposit(double b)
    {
        balance += 100.0;
    }
}
```

One solution to this problem is to use explicit implementation for the Deposit() method declared in the IBank interface. This removes the method signature conflict. However, an Account object will not be able to call the IBank.Deposit() method (although an instance of the IBank interface could).

```
using System;

public class Account : ITrans, IBank
{
    public double balance;

    public Account(double b)
    {
        balance = b;
    }

    public double Deposit(double b)
    {
        balance += b;
        return balance;
    }

    void IBank.Deposit(double b)
    {
        balance += 100.0;
    }
}

public class MapDemo
{
    public static void Main()
    {
        Account acct = new Account(500.0);

        Console.WriteLine("balance is {0}",acct.Deposit(100.0));
    }
}
```

Output:

```
balance is 600
```

There are other situations that may arise in interface mapping. If two interfaces declare a member with exactly the same name, return value, and parameter list, you can map both of these interface members onto a single class or struct member.

For example, let's say the IBank and ITrans interfaces both declared a method:

```
void GetBalance();
```

If the Account class provided a single GetBalance() method with a return type of void it would satisfy both interface implementations.

Summary

In this chapter we learned how interfaces can define a framework for a class or struct. We covered how to define and implement an interface. We explored issues concerning interface inheritance and interface mapping including explicit interface member implementations.

Programmers reference C# Programmers reference C# Programmers reference
C#

10

Enumerations

An enumeration is a convenience value type that maps words to integer values. In essence it creates a series of aliases. This can be used to make a program listing easier to understand. Another useful feature of an enumeration is that the compiler will throw an error if an attempt is made to use a value not defined in the enumeration.

In this chapter we'll look at:

- ❏ Defining an enumeration
- ❏ Using an enumeration
- ❏ Enum class methods

Defining an enumeration

An enumeration is defined using the `enum` keyword and has the following syntax:

```
<modifiers> enum <enum_name> : integer_type
{
  name1 = value1,
  name2 = value2,
      .
      .
  nameN = valueN
}
```

The access modifiers applicable to an enumeration follow the same rules as those for a class or struct. An enumeration declared as a member of a namespace can have `public` or `internal` access. If you don't specify an access modifier, the access will default to `internal`. A nested enumeration can have `public`, `protected`, `internal`, `protected internal`, or `private` access. See the *Class modifiers* section of Chapter 7 for a description of the different types of access.

An enumeration can be modified with the `new` keyword indicating that it hides an inherited member. Enumerations cannot be derived from, so the `abstract` and `sealed` modifiers are not permitted. You have the option of specifying an integer type for the enumeration. Valid integer types are `byte`, `short`, `int`, `long`, `sbyte`, `ushort`, `uint`, or `ulong`. The default integer type is a 32-bit integer, or `int`.

The body of the enumeration contains the list of enumeration names and values. The values are optional. If you don't specify values, default values of 0, 1, 2, etc. will be used. The names or name-value pairs are separated by commas (rather than semicolons). There is no punctuation mark after the last element in the list. Enumeration members implicitly have `public` access.

Example: Defining an enumeration

In this example, an enumeration named `Planet` is defined that relates names of planets to integer values:

```
public enum Planet
{
    Earth   = 1,
    Mars    = 2,
    Venus   = 3,
    Jupiter = 4
}
```

Using an enumeration

The elements of an enumeration are accessed very much like you would access a static field. You simply type the name of the enumeration, a period, and the name of the field. You can also declare a variable of an enumeration type:

```
Planet p = Planet.Earth;
```

When using an enumeration element in a conditional statement, you cannot directly compare the enumeration element with a primitive data type. For example, let's say you have defined an enumeration named Food that maps names to 32-bit integers and one of the entries is "Fish = 2". You might think the following code would be acceptable:

```
int j = 2;

if (j == Food.Fish)
{
   //  do some stuff
}
```

In fact, this code will not compile. You must first convert the integer j into a corresponding Food enumeration element. One way to do this is to cast the `int` into a `Food` enumeration instance.

```
if ( (Food)j == Food.Fish )
{
   //  do some stuff
}
```

Example: Using an enumeration

This example applies the `Planet` enumeration described in the example from the *Defining an enumeration* section. A `switch` statement attempts to match one of the `Planet` enumeration elements with an integer value. The value is hard coded in this example, but think of it as a user-selected value from a menu, GUI component, or other input mechanism. Before the integer can be compared against the enumeration elements, the integer must be converted to a `Planet` enumeration element.

```
using System;

public class EnumDemo
{
  public static void Main()
  {
    int i = 2;

    Planet p = (Planet) i;

    switch (p)
    {
      case Planet.Earth:
        Console.WriteLine("selection was " + p);
        break;
      case Planet.Mars:
        Console.WriteLine("selection was " + p);
        break;
      case Planet.Venus:
        Console.WriteLine("selection was " + p);
        break;
      case Planet.Jupiter:
        Console.WriteLine("selection was " + p);
        break;
      default:
        Console.WriteLine("planet not recognized");
        break;
    }
  }
}
```

Output:

```
selection was Mars
```

In a real life application, instead of simply writing "selection was <planet>" you might perform a computation based on the specific planet's atmosphere, display some pertinent information about the planet, and so on.

Enum class methods

The System.Enum class provides a number of static convenience methods for manipulating enumerations. These methods can be used to access the name or value of an enumeration element, determine if a value exists in an enumeration, format an enumeration value, or convert a value into an enumeration type. The System.Enum class also provides an overridden version of the ToString() method that returns a String representation of the value of an enumeration instance.

Here is a description of some of the methods defined in the System.Enum class.

```
public static string GetName(Type enumType, object value)
public static string[] GetNames(Type enumType)
public static Type GetUnderlyingType(Type enumType)
public static Array GetValues(Type enumType)
public static bool IsDefined(Type enumType, object value)
```

Method	Description
GetName()	Returns the name of the enumeration element corresponding to the specified value. You can use the typeof() operator to return the Type for a given enumeration. The method returns null if the value does not exist in the enumeration.
GetNames()	Returns a string array containing all of the names defined in the enumeration.
GetUnderlyingType()	Returns the underlying Type of the specified enumeration.
GetValues()	Retrieves an Array object containing the values of the enumeration elements.
IsDefined()	Indicates if the specified value is defined in the specified enumeration.

```
public static object Parse(Type enumType, string value)
public static object Parse(Type enumType, string value, boolean ignoreCase)
```

Method	Description
Parse()	Converts the string representation of the name or value of an enumeration element into an equivalent enumeration object. The return value will be an enumeration object of type enumType. The search can be made case-insensitive by setting ignoreCase to be true.

```
public static object ToObject(Type enumType, byte value)
public static object ToObject(Type enumType, short value)
public static object ToObject(Type enumType, int value)
public static object ToObject(Type enumType, long value)
public static object ToObject(Type enumType, object value)
public static object ToObject(Type enumType, sbyte value)
public static object ToObject(Type enumType, ushort value)
public static object ToObject(Type enumType, uint value)
public static object ToObject(Type enumType, ulong value)
```

Method	Description
ToObject()	Returns an enumeration object of type enumType corresponding to the specified value. There are overloaded versions for every integer type.

Example: Enum class methods

This example uses some of the Enum class methods in conjunction with the previously described Planet enumeration. Its purpose is to give the user a list of planets to choose from. Once a selection is made, a method is called to print out some information about the selection.

The GetValues() method is used to return an Array containing the values of the Planet enumeration. Using this Array and the GetName() method, a list of available choices is presented to the user. When the user makes a selection and hits the *Enter* key, the IsDefined() method checks to see if a valid input was entered. If the input is valid, the ToObject() method converts the integer selection into a Planet enumeration instance. This variable is then sent to the PlanetInfo() method where it calls the ToString() method to display the name of the selection.

```csharp
using System;

public class EnumDemo2
{
  public static void Main()
  {

    Array values = Enum.GetValues(typeof(Planet));

    Console.WriteLine("\nAvailable choices are:");
    for(int j=0; j<values.Length; ++j)
    {
      Object value = values.GetValue(j);
      Console.WriteLine("   "+Enum.GetName(typeof(Planet),value)+
                                        " \t= "+(int)value);
    }
    Console.Write("\nMake selection: ");
    String input = Console.ReadLine();

    int i = Int32.Parse(input);

    if ( Enum.IsDefined(typeof(Planet),i) )
    {
      PlanetInfo((Planet)Enum.ToObject(typeof(Planet),i));
    }
    else
    {
      Console.WriteLine("bad input selection");
    }
  }

  public static void PlanetInfo(Planet p)
```

```
    {
        Console.WriteLine("Planet selected was "+p.ToString());
    }
}
```

Output (sample):

```
Available choices are:

    Earth    = 1
    Mars     = 2
    Venus    = 3
    Jupiter  = 4

Make selection: 1
Planet selected was Earth
```

Summary

This chapter covered the convenience construct known as an enumeration. An enumeration maps names to integer values making a code listing easier to understand. We learned how to define and use an enumeration. We also covered some of the methods defined in the System.Enum class that can be applied to enumerations.

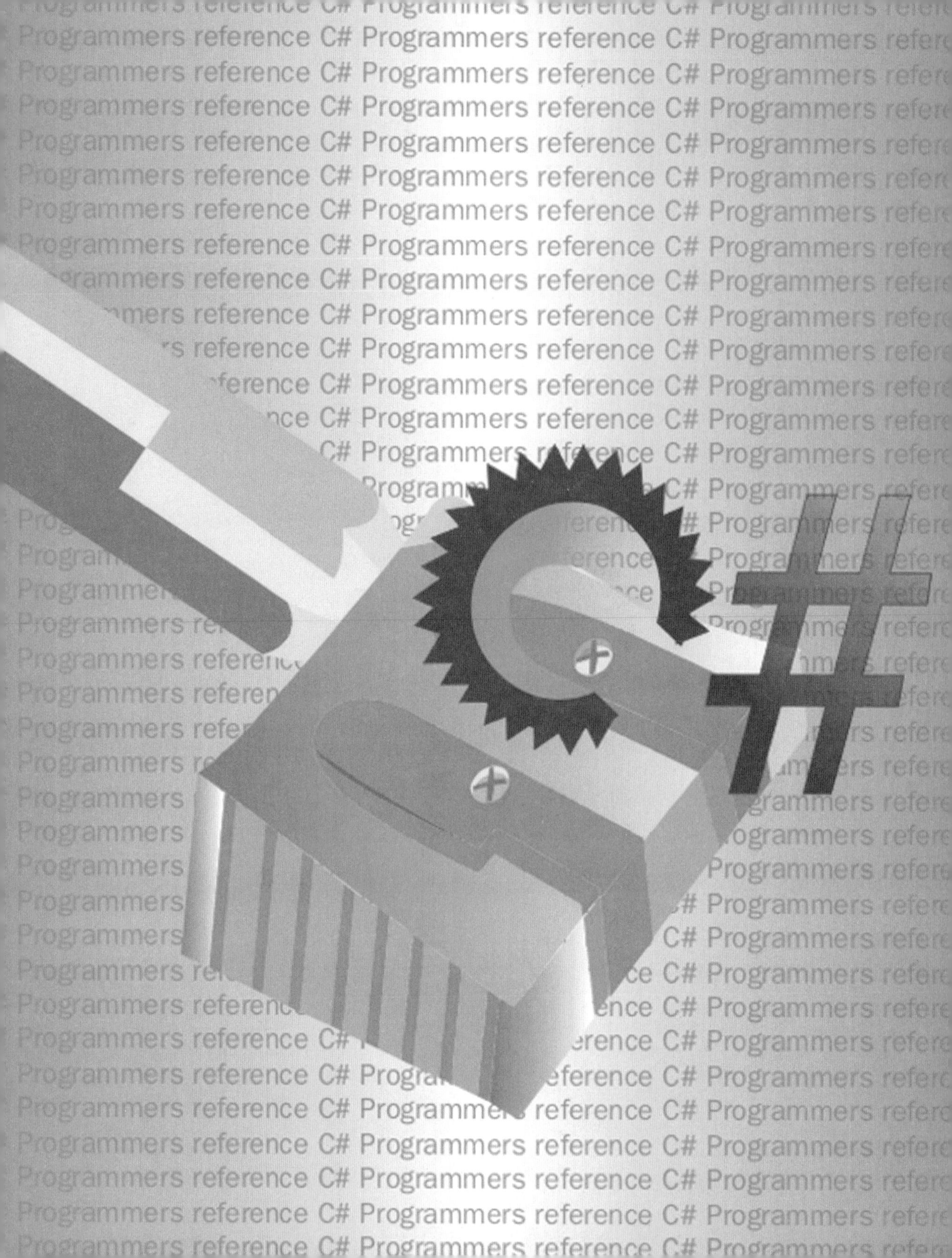
Programmers reference C#
C#

11

Fields

A **field** is a variable whose declaration appears in the definition of a class or a struct. As such, it is available to *all* the member functions (methods, constructors, etc.) of that class or struct. This differentiates a field from a local variable that's defined within (and is therefore only available to) a given function or block of code. Fields can be either value or reference types.

There are two general types of field: **instance fields** are associated with an instance of a type, while **static fields** are associated with the type itself. As we'll see, you can specify the availability of a field outside of the type in which it is defined by including an **access modifier** keyword in the field declaration. Furthermore, you can designate a field as being read-only or constant.

In this chapter, we'll look at:

- ❑   Instance fields
- ❑   Static fields
- ❑   Access modifiers
- ❑   Constant fields
- ❑   Read-only fields
- ❑   The `lock` statement

Instance fields

An instance field is associated with an instance of a type. Every instance of the type has its own copy of the field, and can manipulate that copy as it sees fit. The basic syntax for declaring and initializing an instance field is exactly the same as for a local variable:

```
<modifiers> <type> <field_name> = <value>;

<modifiers> <type> <field_name> = new <constructor_call>;
```

The first line is the syntax for declaring and initializing a value type; the second is for a reference type or a struct. Fields don't have to be initialized when they're declared, but they *do* have to be initialized before they are used.

If you wish, the declaration and initialization statements can be placed on separate lines.

```
// Value type
<modifiers> type <field_name>;
<field_name> = <value>;

// Reference type (or struct)
<modifiers> type <field_name>;
<field_name> = new <constructor_call>;
```

An instance field is always accessible *inside* the type in which it is defined, and there are three ways to arrange for a field to be accessible *outside* the type in which it is defined. The first is to use an access modifier that specifies the field to be `internal`, `protected`, `protected internal`, or `public`. (The default access for a field is `private`.)

For example, let's say that there is a class named `Bird` that defines a `public` field of type `double` named `wingspan`. Let's also say that we've created an instance of the `Bird` class named `bird1`. To access the `wingspan` field associated with `bird1`, you could use this syntax:

```
double d = bird1.wingspan;
```

However, declaring a field to be `public` (having it directly accessible outside of its type) violates the object-oriented principle of encapsulation. A preferred alternative is to define a method inside the type that will manipulate the value of the desired field. In the previous example, you might set the access of the `wingspan` field to be `private`, and define a method named `GetWingspan()` inside the `Bird` class.

```
public double GetWingspan()
{
  return wingspan;
}
```

To access the `wingspan` field associated with the `bird1` object, you would now use this syntax:

```
double d = bird1.GetWingspan();
```

The third way to access a field outside of the type in which it is defined is to associate it with a **property**. Properties are discussed in Chapter 13.

Other modifiers that can be associated with a field include the `new`, `readonly`, and `volatile` keywords. The `new` keyword indicates that the field hides a field of the same name defined in a base type, the `readonly` keyword prevents the value of the field from being changed once it has been assigned, while a field marked as `volatile` will restrict instruction-reordering optimizations performed upon it by the compiler or the runtime. This last setting is mainly used in multithreaded programs that access fields without synchronization.

Example: Using instance fields

In this example, a class named `Account` is defined to contain (among other things) two instance fields: a `double` and a `System.String`. The fields are initialized in the `Account` class constructor.

```
using System;

public class Account
{
  private double sharesOwned;
  private String ownerName;

  public Account(double d, String s)
  {
    sharesOwned = d;
    ownerName = String.Copy(s);
  }

  public double GetSharesOwned()
  {
    return sharesOwned;
  }

  public String GetOwnerName()
  {
    return ownerName;
  }
}
```

Next, the `InstanceDemo` class creates two `Account` objects, each of which has its own independent copy of the `sharesOwned` and `ownerName` fields. The two `Account` objects assign different values to the fields through the `Account` class constructor.

```
public class InstanceDemo
{
  public static void Main()
  {
    Account acct1 = new Account(123.45, "Maria Lopez");
    Account acct2 = new Account(45.67, "Hans Richter");
    Console.WriteLine("{0} has {1} shares",
                      acct1.GetOwnerName(), acct1.GetSharesOwned());
    Console.WriteLine("{0} has {1} shares",
                      acct2.GetOwnerName(), acct2.GetSharesOwned());
  }
}
```

Output:

```
Maria Lopez has 123.45 shares
Hans Richter has 45.67 shares
```

Static fields

A static field is one that's associated with a type, rather than with an instance of the type. There is only one copy of a static field, no matter how many instances of the type are created. A static field is available whenever you need it, and using one will, if necessary, cause the assembly or module that contains the associated type to be loaded into the runtime. By comparison, an instance field is available only when an instance of the type is created.

To define a field as static, you place the `static` keyword in the field's declaration statement:

```
<modifiers> static type <field_name> = <value>;
```

```
<modifiers> static type <field_name> = new <constructor_call>;
```

Static fields can be initialized when they are declared, as in the above statements, or by using a **static constructor**, as described in Chapter 7. Unlike instance fields, static fields are often given `public` access to allow them to be accessed outside of the type in which they are defined. Also, because static fields are associated with a type (rather than an instance of a type), a static field is accessed using the type name:

```
<type_name>.<field_name>
```

Example: Static fields

In this example, a class named `Gas` is defined that encapsulates a gas mixture. All gas mixtures are subject to a universal gas constant that relates the pressure, density, and temperature of the gas – it has the same value for any gas mixture, and is represented in our `Gas` class (below) as a static field. Because the field has `public` access, it can be accessed outside of the `Gas` class using the `Gas.Rgas` syntax.

```
using System;

public class Gas
{
   public static double Rgas = 8.3144;

   // Other elements of the Gas class
}

public class StaticDemo
{
   public static void Main()
   {
      Console.WriteLine("Gas constant is {0}", Gas.Rgas);
   }
}
```

Output:

```
Gas constant is 8.3144
```

Access modifiers

As we've already seen, it's possible to specify the access that will be granted to a field in the field declaration statement. The access modifier you supply will be one of the following keywords; if none is specified, `private` is the default:

❑ `public` indicates that the field is freely accessible inside and outside of the class in which it is defined.

❑ `internal` means that a field is only accessible to types defined in the same assembly. For example, an internal static field in one assembly would not be accessible to a class contained in another assembly.

❑ `protected` means that the field is accessible in the type where it is defined, and in derived types of the type where it is defined. This is used to give derived classes access to the fields defined in base classes.

❑ `protected internal` indicates that a field is accessible to types defined in the same assembly *or* to derived types. Essentially, it means "`protected` *or* `internal`" access.

❑ `private` is the most restrictive type of access. A private field is only accessible in the class in which it is defined.

Example: Access specifiers

This is a simplified version of the example from the *Inheritance* section of Chapter 7. A `Coin` class is defined as containing one field and a method to access that field. A `Quarter` class is written as a derived class of `Coin`. For the `Quarter` class to be able to access the `value` field of the `Coin` class, the `value` field must be given `protected` (rather than `private`) access.

```
using System;

public class Coin
{
   protected int value;

   public int GetValue()
   {
     return value;
   }
}

public class Quarter : Coin
{
   public Quarter()
   {
     value = 25;
   }
}

public class AccessDemo
{
```

```
public static void Main()
  {
    Quarter q = new Quarter();

    Console.WriteLine("Value of quarter is {0}", q.GetValue());
  }
}
```

Output:

```
Value of quarter is 25
```

Many programmers believe that *all* fields should be declared `private`. If you defined the `value` field as `private`, you could define a `protected` method to set the field with a value, to go alongside the existing `public` method for retrieving the value stored in the field.

Constant fields

A field that's declared to be constant is treated as a fixed value. To indicate a constant field, you place the `const` keyword in the field declaration statement:

```
<modifiers> const <type> <field_name> = <value>;
```

A constant field *must* be given a value when it is declared, and the value *must* be computable at compile time. A constant field is implicitly static and is accessed in the same way you would access a static field; you may not declare a field to be both `const` and `static`.

The `const` keyword can only be applied to one of the built-in value types (`int`, `byte`, `double`, etc.), a `String`, or an enum. Other than strings, you cannot define reference types as constant fields.

Example: Constant fields

This example revisits the example from the *Static fields* section, but defines the gas constant as a `const` field.

```
using System;

public class Gas
{
  public const double Rgas = 8.3144;

  // Other elements of the Gas class
}

public class ConstDemo
{
  public static void Main()
  {
```

```
Console.WriteLine("Gas constant is {0}", Gas.Rgas);
    }
}
```

Output:

```
Gas constant is 8.3144
```

Read-only fields

A read-only field is similar to a `const` field in that its value cannot be changed once it has been assigned. However, there are more opportunities for assignment: a read-only field can be assigned where it's declared, or in a constructor of the type to which it belongs, but nowhere else. By default, a read-only field is an instance field, meaning that it can have a different value for each instance of the type in which it is defined. A read-only field *can* be static, but it must be explicitly declared as such.

To specify a read-only field, you place the `readonly` keyword in the declaration statement:

```
<modifiers> readonly <type> <field_name>;
```

If you don't assign a value to a read-only field, it will assume its default value: zero for value types, and null for reference types. The following list summarizes the primary differences between read-only fields and constant fields:

❑ Constant fields are *always* static. Read-only fields *can* be static, but by default they're not.

❑ Constant fields must be initialized when they're declared, and the value must be computable at compile time. Read-only fields can be initialized when they are declared, or in a constructor, or not at all. The value given to a read-only field can come from a variable that's evaluated at runtime.

❑ Constant fields can be used as local variables; read-only fields cannot.

❑ Constant fields can only be built-in value types, strings, or enumerations. Any value or reference type can be defined as a read-only field.

Example: Read-only fields

A problem with the example in the *Static fields* section above is that since the `Rgas` field was declared `public`, it's possible to change the value of the field from outside of the `Gas` class. For example, if you placed the statement

```
Gas.Rgas = 4.0;
```

as the first line in the `Main()` method of the `StaticDemo` class, you'd change the value of the `Rgas` field to 4.0. To prevent this possibility, the field can be declared as being read-only.

```
using System;

public class Gas
{
  public static readonly double Rgas = 8.3144;

  // Other elements of the Gas class
}

public class ReadOnlyDemo
{
  public static void Main()
  {
    Console.WriteLine("Gas constant is {0}", Gas.Rgas);
  }
}
```

Output:

```
Gas constant is 8.3144
```

Now, if you tried to place the statement Gas.Rgas = 4.0; in the Main() method of the ReadOnlyDemo class, you'd get a compiler error to remind you that this is a field whose value should not be changed.

The lock statement

The lock statement provides synchronized access to a reference-type variable. We're describing it here in the *Fields* chapter, but in fact any reference-type variable can be locked. The basic syntax for a lock statement is:

```
lock(variable)
{
  // Code to be executed
}
```

What the lock statement does is to wrap a **mutually exclusive lock**, or **mutex**, around the specified variable. The lock remains in effect until execution leaves the block in which the lock begins. Only one thread at a time can hold the lock and access the variable; another thread that tries to access the variable will be put to sleep until the thread that has the lock releases it.

Example: Locking up

This example demonstrates using a lock statement to prevent a thread conflict. The Account class defines a balance field and a Withdraw() method that reduces the balance by a specified amount. The Withdraw() method also calls the Sleep() method to simulate some unspecified time-consuming activity.

```
using System;
using System.Threading;

public class Account
{
   private double balance;

   public Account(double b)
   {
      balance = b;
   }

   public double Withdraw(double b)
   {
      balance -= b;
      Thread.Sleep(500);
      return balance;
   }
}
```

Next, the static Main() method of the MonitorDemo class creates an instance of that class, which declares an Account object as a private field and initializes it in its instance constructor. After that, Main() starts two threads, each of which calls the Trans() method that's also defined in the MonitorDemo class. The Trans() method calls the Withdraw() method on the Account object, subtracting 100 from the balance.

```
public class MonitorDemo
{
  Account acct;

  public MonitorDemo(double b)
  {
    acct = new Account(b);
  }

  public static void Main()
  {
    double initialBalance = 500.0;
    MonitorDemo demo1 = new MonitorDemo(initialBalance);

    Thread one = new Thread(new ThreadStart(demo1.Trans));
    Thread two = new Thread(new ThreadStart(demo1.Trans));

    Console.WriteLine("Initial balance is {0}", initialBalance);
    one.Start();
    two.Start();
  }

  public void Trans()
  {
    double amount = 100.0;
    Console.WriteLine("balance after {0} withdrawal is {1}",
                      amount, acct.Withdraw(amount));
```

```
    }
    }
```

Output:

```
Initial balance is 500
balance after 100 withdrawal is 300
balance after 100 withdrawal is 300
```

That doesn't look right, does it? What's happened is that the second thread also subtracted 100 from the balance before the first thread exited the `Withdraw()` method. To prevent this confusion, we can rewrite the `Trans()` method using a `lock` statement, so that only one thread at a time will be able to execute the code between the braces.

```
public void Trans()
{
  lock(acct)
  {
    double amount = 100.0;
    Console.WriteLine("balance after {0} withdrawal is {1}",
                    amount, acct.Withdraw(amount));
  }
}
```

Output:

```
Initial balance is 500
balance after 100 withdrawal is 400
balance after 100 withdrawal is 300
```

Volatile Fields

Including the `volatile` modifier in a field declaration limits the optimizations that can be performed on operations against the field. These optimizations may be performed by the compiler or by the system when the IL code is JIT compiled and executed. Non-volatile fields may be subject to optimizations in the order in which different threads access or modify their values, and this can lead to unpredictable results if multiple threads access the field, unless we specifically synchronize it (for example, using the `lock` keyword discussed above). Marking a field as `volatile` ensures that reads and writes will occur before any reads and writes that follow them in the instruction sequence. The syntax for declaring a volatile field is:

```
<modifiers> volatile <type> <field_name>;
```

For example:

```
public static volatile bool finished;
```

Only certain types of field may be declared `volatile`:

❑ Any reference type

❑ `byte`, `sbyte`, `short`, `ushort`, `int`, `uint`, `char`, `float`, or `bool` fields

❑ Enum types with a base type of byte, sbyte, short, ushort, int or uint

> Note that **volatile** will only protect against unpredictability due to optimization, and isn't an alternative to synchronization.

Summary

This chapter discussed the type-level variables known as fields. In it, we've seen how to define a field, compared and contrasted instance and static fields, and examined the circumstances under which it's possible to access a field from outside of the type in which it is defined. Later on, we looked at constant and read-only fields, and saw the differences between those, too. Finally, we examined how a lock statement can be used to provide synchronized access to a field variable.

Programmers reference C# Programmers reference C# Programmers reference

12

Methods

A method is a function member used in the C# language to perform a computation or some other action. A method is a named block of code that is used to divide a program into smaller units. A C# program will most likely define numerous methods. Methods facilitate code reuse and code efficiency, and greatly improve the readability of a code listing. Methods are always defined within the bounds of a class or struct.

There are two general types of methods. An instance method is called on an instance of the type in which it is defined. A static method is associated with a type itself. You can declare a method to be `virtual`, `abstract`, or `sealed`. Methods can be overloaded, overridden, and hidden.

Arguments can be passed to a method as part of a parameter list. The arguments represent information the method needs to do its job. The arguments can be valuetypes or referencetypes. There are a number of keywords to customize the way arguments are passed. You can, for instance, pass a value type by reference, or pass a variable as an output parameter to a method before it has been initialized. A C# method can return at most one value, although the return value might be an array of values, a class instance, or a struct.

In this chapter we'll look at:

- ❑ How to define a method
- ❑ Exiting from a method
- ❑ Instance and static methods
- ❑ Method arguments
- ❑ Abstract, virtual, and sealed methods
- ❑ The `extern` keyword
- ❑ Method overloading, overriding, and hiding

Defining a method

The basic syntax for defining a method is shown below:

```
<modifiers> <return_type> <method_name> (<parameter_list>)
{
  // body of method
}
```

The name and parameter list of the method compose what is called the method signature. The modifiers can include a keyword that defines access to the method. A method can be assigned `public`, `protected`, `internal`, `protected internal`, or `private` access. See the *Access modifiers* section of Chapter 11 for a description of the access modifiers. If no access modifier is specified, the method will be given `private` access by default.

There are other modifying keywords that can be applied to a method. The `new` keyword indicates that the method hides a method of the same signature inherited from a base class. If a method is defined as `static` it is associated with the type in which it is defined instead of an instance of that type. A `virtual` method is one that can be overridden in a derived class. A `sealed` method, in contrast, is one that cannot be overridden. The `override` keyword indicates that the method overrides a `virtual` or `abstract` method from a base class. If a method is marked as `extern` it means that the method is implemented in another (non-.NET) programming language.

The return type is the type of the value returned by the method. If the method doesn't return anything, the return type is `void`. You can use some creativity when choosing a method name but must follow the same sorts of restrictions as when naming a class or struct. For instance, the first character of a method name can't be a number and a method name can't be one of the C# keywords (listed in Appendix A). If the method signature is the same as a method defined in a base class the current method will override or hide the base class version. Method overriding and hiding are described in detail later in this chapter.

The arguments that are to be passed to the method are defined in a parameter list surrounded by parentheses. If the method takes no parameters, you must still provide an empty set of parentheses. Curly braces surround the body of the method.

Exiting a method

A `return` statement is used to exit a method and return the execution to the point in the program following the method call. The syntax for a `return` statement is:

```
return;
```

or:

```
return value;
```

If a method has a return type of `void`, the `return` statement is optional and would contain only the `return` keyword. Methods with a non-`void` return type must include at least one `return` statement consisting of the `return` keyword followed by a value of the same type as the method return type. A method may contain more than one `return` statement.

Instance methods

As was stated before, an instance method is associated with an instance of a type. An instance method can only be called on an instance of the type in which it is defined or by a derived type. All methods are by default instance methods.

Example: Instance methods

The `Triangle` class defines two instance methods. The first, `GetArea()`, takes no input arguments and returns the area of the triangle. The second, `Scale()`, is used to scale the width and height of the triangle. This method takes a `double` as an argument and returns nothing.

The `InstanceDemo` class creates two `Triangle` objects. The first object calls the `GetArea()` method using the syntax:

```
t1.GetArea();
```

The second `Triangle` object calls the `Scale()` method to change its width and height. It then calls the `GetArea()` method. Note that since the `Scale()` method has a return type of `void`, the 'return;' syntax is optional.

```
using System;

public class Triangle
{
   double width, height;

   public Triangle(double w, double h)
   {
     width = w;
     height = h;
   }

   public double GetArea()
   {
     return 0.5 * width * height;
   }

   public void Scale(double scale)
   {
     width *= scale;
     height *= scale;
     return;
   }
}

public class InstanceDemo
{
   public static void Main()
```

```
    {
        Triangle t1 = new Triangle(2.0,3.0);
        Triangle t2 = new Triangle(5.0,6.0);

        double area1 = t1.GetArea();
        Console.WriteLine("area of t1 is {0}",area1);

        t2.Scale(0.5);
        double area2 = t2.GetArea();
        Console.WriteLine("area of t2 is {0}",area2);
    }
}
```

Output:

```
area of t1 is 3
area of t2 is 3.75
```

Static methods

A static method is associated with a type instead of with an instance of a type. Static methods are often used to provide some generic functionality that is independent of any particular type instance. The Sleep() method from the Thread class is an example of such a static method. Operator definitions (+, -, etc.) are required to be statically defined.

A static method is designated as such by placing the static keyword in the method definition. The static keyword is placed between the access modifier and the return type:

```
<modifiers> static <return_type> <method_name> (<parameter list>)
{
    // body of method
}
```

Static methods can have any of the five previously described types of access. They are rarely given private access because you generally want to access a static method outside of the class in which it is defined. A static method cannot be defined to be virtual or abstract.

Because a static method is associated with a type, you do not have to create an instance of the type to call a static method. To invoke a static method, you write the name of the type in which the method is defined, a period, and the method call syntax.

Example: Static methods

The Triangle class is written to contain a static method that computes the hypotenuse of a right triangle. The Hypotenuse() method takes two arguments representing the short sides of a triangle. The method then computes and returns the hypotenuse of the triangle.

The StaticDemo class defines the width and height of a triangle and calls the Hypotenuse() method to compute the hypotenuse. Because the Hypotenuse() method is defined in the Triangle class, the syntax for calling the method is:

```
Triangle.Hypotenuse(width, height);
```

Note that the Hypotenuse() method itself calls a static method, Sqrt(), that is defined in the Math class.

```
using System;

public class Triangle
{
  public static double Hypotenuse(double a, double b)
  {
    double c = Math.Sqrt(a*a + b*b);
    return c;
  }
}

public class StaticDemo
{
  public static void Main()
  {
    double width, height;

    width = 3.0;
    height = 4.0;

    double hypotenuse = Triangle.Hypotenuse(width, height);

    Console.WriteLine("hypotenuse is {0}", hypotenuse);
  }
}
```

Output:

```
hypotenuse is 5
```

Access modifiers

An access modifier is a keyword that specifies the access granted to a method. The access modifier is part of the method declaration syntax. If specified, the access modifier will be one of the following:

- internal
- private
- protected
- protected internal
- public

If no modifier is specified, the method is given private access. Access modifiers are discussed in Chapter 11.

Method arguments

Method arguments are variables passed to a method when the method is called. The arguments can be passed by value or by reference. Unmodified parameters are passed by value, meaning that a copy of the variable is sent to the method. Any changes to the variable inside the method will not be reflected in the original variable. However, because object variables are stored on the heap, with only a reference to this location stored on the stack, it is this memory address rather than the actual object which is passed into the method, and any changes made to the object will be reflected in the original variable.

A reference argument is passed by reference to the method. This means that a reference to the object is sent to the method. Any changes to the reference type inside the method will be reflected in the original variable. The difference between reference-type arguments passed by value and arguments passed by reference is subtle, but is very apparent when dealing with strings, and we will look at the distinction in more detail in the section on the ref keyword.

Example: Method arguments

The Blah class defines a static method named SetValues() that sets the values of elements of an integer array. The method takes two arguments. The first is a reference-type variable representing the integer array. The second argument is a value-type variable that is the value to which the array elements will be set.

The Main() method creates an integer array and defines an integer named v. The value of the first element of the array (set to the default value of 0) and the value of the integer variable are printed out. Then the SetValues() method is called. The values of the array elements are changed, is as the value of the integer variable.

When the execution returns to the Main() method, the elements of the integer array retain their new values but the value of the integer variable is the same as it was before the method call. This is because a copy of the integer variable had its value changed inside the SetValues() method rather than the original integer variable.

```
using System;

public class Blah
{
  public static void SetValues(int[] intArray, int v)
```

```
    {
      for (int i=0; i<intArray.Length; ++i)
      {
        intArray[i] = v;
      }
      v = 12;
    }

    public static void Main()
    {
      int[] intArray = new int[5];
      int v = 4;

      Console.WriteLine("value is {0}", v);
      Console.WriteLine("intArray[0] is {0}", intArray[0]);

      Blah.SetValues(intArray, v);

      Console.WriteLine("value is {0}", v);
      Console.WriteLine("intArray[0] is {0}",intArray[0]);
    }
}
```

Output:

```
value is 4;
intArray[0] is 0

value is 4;
intArray[0] is 4
```

params keyword

The params keyword indicates that an input parameter will be treated as a parameter array. A parameter array will contain a variable number of parameters of the specified type. The params keyword therefore facilitates variable argument list behavior. The params keyword can only be applied to the last parameter in the argument list.

Example: params keyword

The ParamsDemo class defines the Process() method that simply prints out an array of Strings. If the params keyword is not used, you must create and load an array of Strings before calling the method:

```
using System;

public class ParamsDemo
{
```

```
public static void Main()
{
    String[] s = new String[3];
    s[0] = "Jackson";
    s[1] = "Zachary";
    s[2] = "Erica";

    ParamsDemo.Process(s);
}

public static void Process(String[] str)
{
    for (int i=0; i<str.Length; ++i)
    {
        Console.WriteLine(str[i]);
    }
}
}
```

Now let's look at the program listing if the params keyword is used in the argument list.

```
using System;

public class ParamsDemo2
{
    public static void Main()
    {
        ParamsDemo2.Process("Jackson", "Zachary", "Erica");
    }

    public static void Process(params String[] str)
    {
        for (int i=0; i<str.Length; ++i)
        {
            Console.WriteLine(str[i]);
        }
    }
}
```

The arguments to the Process() method can now be passed directly to the method when the method is invoked. What's more, you can supply any number of arguments that you desire.

Output:

```
Jackson
Zachary
Erica
```

ref keyword

The `ref` keyword causes a value-type input parameter to be passed by reference. The reference parameter will occupy the same storage location as the variable given as the argument in the method invocation. Any changes made to the variable inside the method will also change the value of the original variable. The `ref` keyword is placed before the variable type in the argument list. The `ref` keyword must also be used when the method is called.

One way that `ref` can be used is to circumvent the restriction that a method can only return one value. With the `ref` keyword it is possible to obtain an updated value of more than one value-type variable. Reference parameters are passed both into and out of the method and must be initialized before being passed in.

Example: ref keyword

A static method named `Scale()` is defined that scales two floating-point numbers by a specified factor. The floating-point numbers (doubles) are passed to the method using the `ref` keyword. When their values are changed inside the `Scale()` method, they will retain those changes when the method returns. Note the use of the `ref` keyword when the `Scale()` method is called.

```
using System;

public class Blah
{
   public static void Scale(double scale, ref double a, ref double b)
   {
     a *= scale;
     b *= scale;
   }

   public static void Main()
   {
      double d1, d2;
      d1 = 2.0;
      d2 = 3.0;

      Blah.Scale(1.5, ref d1, ref d2);

      Console.WriteLine("d1 is {0}",d1);
      Console.WriteLine("d2 is {0}",d2);
   }
}
```

Output:

```
d1 is 3
d2 is 4.5
```

We stated earlier that reference types are passed by value, but that that value is the address in memory where the object is stored. Any changes made to the object will therefore be reflected in the variable in the calling scope. However, strings behave somewhat differently – because strings are immutable in C#, a new string object is created whenever we modify a string. This means that the original variable won't be affected – it will still reference the original String object. Similarly, if we explicitly create a new object using the new keyword and point a value parameter to that, this won't affect the original variable in the calling scope.

This is where reference parameters behave differently – reference parameters are effectively in/out parameters, and if the value of the parameter is modified in the method body, or if the parameter is made to point to a different object, the original variable outside the method will also be updated, and made to point to the new reference.

Example: Passing strings by reference

To demonstrate the difference between reference parameters and reference-type value parameters, the following code calls two methods, each of which takes a string parameter and modifies that string within the method body. The first method takes a value parameter, and the second a reference parameter using the ref keyword.

```
using System;

class StringDemo
{

    static void Main(string[] args)
    {
        string s = "A string";
        Console.WriteLine(s);
        DoSomethingByValue(s);
        Console.WriteLine(s);
        DoSomethingByReference(ref s);
        Console.WriteLine(s);
    }

    static void DoSomethingByValue(string s)
    {
        s = "A different string";
    }

    static void DoSomethingByReference(ref string s)
    {
        s = "Another string";
    }
}
```

Output:

```
A string
A string
Another string
```

Notice that the call to DoSomethingByValue() doesn't affect the value of s in the Main() method, but the call to DoSomethingByReference() does update s.

out keyword

In C#, a variable must always be initialized before it is used. If a method is defined that will assign a value to an input parameter, the input variable must still be given a dummy value before it is passed to the method. There is a way to avoid this meaningless step by using the out keyword.

An input parameter modified with the out keyword becomes an output parameter and can be passed to a method before it is initialized. The out keyword is placed before the variable type in the method declaration statement. The out keyword must also be used in the method call. An output parameter must be given a value before the method returns.

Example: out keyword

A SetString() method is defined that sets the value of a String and an int. Using the out keyword, the input arguments do not have to be initialized before they are passed to the SetString() method. Without the out keyword this example would not compile. Note how the out keyword is also used in the method call.

Note that the integer output parameter retains the value assigned to it in the SetString() method even after returning to the Main() method. This is because an output parameter uses the same storage location as the variable given as the argument in a method invocation.

```
using System;

public class OutDemo
{

    public static void SetString(out string str, out int i)
    {
        str = "Happy New Year";
        i = 4;
    }

    public static void Main()
    {
        String s;
        int i;

        OutDemo.SetString(out s, out i);

        Console.WriteLine(s);
        i += 2;
        Console.WriteLine(i);
    }
}
```

Output:

```
Happy New Year
6
```

Virtual methods

A virtual method is one that can be overridden by a derived class. A virtual method is designated as such by placing the `virtual` keyword in the method declaration statement between the access modifier and the return type. When a virtual method is called, the runtime will determine what class the invoking object is an instance of and call the appropriate overridden method. The runtime checking of overridden methods comes at a slight performance cost.

Virtual methods are overridden using the `override` keyword. Overridden methods are described in more detail later in this chapter. You cannot modify a method with both the `virtual` and `override` keywords. This is because a `virtual` method is one that has not yet been overridden. A `virtual` method cannot be declared either `static` or `abstract`.

Example: Virtual methods

This example is similar to the example in the *Abstract methods* section except in this case the `Triangle` class is written as a derived class of the `Quad` class. The `Quad` class defines a `width` and a `height` field and a method named `GetArea()` that returns the area of a quadrilateral.

The `Triangle` class makes use of the `width` and `height` fields from the `Quad` class but needs its own `GetArea()` method to compute the area of a triangle. This is accomplished by defining the `GetArea()` method in the `Quad` class as `virtual` and defining an overridden version of the method in the `Triangle` class.

```csharp
using System;

public class Quad
{
  protected double width, height;

  public Quad(double w, double h)
  {
    width = w;
    height = h;
  }

  public virtual double GetArea()
  {
    return width * height;
  }
}
```

```
public class Triangle : Quad
{

  public Triangle(double w, double h) : base(w,h) {}

  public override double GetArea()
  {
    return 0.5 * width * height;
  }
}

public class VirtualDemo
{
  public static void Main()
  {
    Quad q = new Quad(2.0, 3.0);
    Triangle t = new Triangle(2.0, 3.0);

    Console.WriteLine("area of quad is {0}", q.GetArea());
    Console.WriteLine("area of triangle is {0}", t.GetArea());
  }
}
```

Output:

```
area of quad is 6
area of triangle is 3
```

Abstract methods

An abstract method is one that must be overridden by a derived class. An abstract method can be thought of as a virtual method with no method body. If any method of a class is abstract, the class must also be declared abstract. An abstract method is designated as such by placing the abstract keyword in the method declaration statement.

```
<modifiers> abstract <return_type> <method_name> (<parameter_list>);
```

Abstract methods can only be defined in abstract classes. You cannot declare an abstract method to be static or extern.

Example: Abstract methods

In this example, an abstract class named Shape is defined with one abstract method, GetArea(). The Triangle class is written as a derived class of Shape. The Triangle class provides an overridden version of the GetArea() method.

```
using System;

public abstract class Shape
{
  public abstract double GetArea();
}

public class Triangle : Shape
{
  double width, height;

  public Triangle(double w, double h)
  {
    width = w;
    height = h;
  }

  public override double GetArea()
  {
    return 0.5 * width * height;
  }
}

public class AbstractDemo
{
  public static void Main()
  {
    Triangle t1 = new Triangle(2.0,3.0);
    Console.WriteLine("area of t1 is {0}",t1.GetArea());
  }
}
```

Output:

```
area of t1 is 3
```

Sealed methods

A sealed method, indicated by the sealed keyword, overrides an inherited virtual method with the same signature. The sealed keyword is always used in conjunction with the override keyword. When a method is sealed, it cannot be overridden in a derived class.

Example: Sealed methods

To rewrite the GetArea() method from the Triangle class in the previous example as a sealed method, simply insert the sealed keyword.

```
public sealed override double GetArea()
{
    return 0.5 * width * height;
}
```

Now a derived class of `Triangle` will not be able to override the `GetArea()` method.

Extern keyword

The `extern` keyword is used to indicate that the method will be implemented externally, in a non-.NET programming language. The `extern` keyword is placed between the access modifier and the return type. An example of using the `extern` keyword can be found in the *Void pointers* section of Chapter 17.

Method overloading

It is possible to define different versions of the same method within a given type. This process is called method overloading. This differs from method overriding where you define a new version of an inherited method. Overloaded versions of a method will have the same name but each overloaded method must have a different parameter list. Overloaded methods do not have to have the same return type.

The .NET Framework libraries contain many overloaded methods. For instance, here are the overloaded versions of the `Sort()` method defined in the `System.Array` class:

```
public static void Sort(Array array)
public static void Sort(Array keys, Array items)
public static void Sort(Array array, IComparer comparer)
public static void Sort(Array keys, Array items, IComparer comparer)
public static void Sort(Array array, int startIndex, int length)
public static void Sort(Array keys, Array items, int startIndex, int length)
public static void Sort(Array array, int startIndex, int length, IComparer
comparer)
public static void Sort(Array keys, Array items, int startIndex, int length,
IComparer comparer)
```

The runtime determines which overloaded method to call based on the arguments passed to the method. The process for determining which method to call is as follows.

First, the set of candidate methods is reduced according to the given argument list. For a candidate method to pass this test, the number of arguments in the method call statement must be the same as in the method signature. Each argument in the method call must have the same parameter passing mode as each parameter in the method parameter list. An error is passed if none of the candidate methods meet these requirements.

Of the remaining candidate methods, the closest match is determined again by examining the input argument list and the implicit conversions that must take place between the argument and parameter lists. The best matching method will be the one that is invoked. If there is not exactly one method that is a better match than all the other candidate methods, an error is thrown.

Method overriding

A derived class may have reason to provide a different implementation of a method defined in a base class for its own particular needs. This process is called overriding a method. The overridden method is designated as such by placing the `override` keyword in the method declaration statement. Only a method designated as `virtual` or `abstract` can be overridden.

The overridden method must have the same name, parameter list, and return type as the method it is overriding. You cannot declare a method to be both `virtual` and `override`. This is because a virtual method is one that has not yet been overridden. A method modified with the `override` keyword can itself be overridden if it has not been sealed.

For examples of method overriding, see the examples in the *Abstract methods* and *Virtual methods* sections of this chapter.

Method hiding

In a previous section, it was stated that only a `virtual` or `abstract` method could be overridden in a derived class. Another way to have a derived class define a method with the same signature as a non-abstract base class method is by using the `new` keyword. This process is called method hiding.

```
<modifiers> new <return_type> <method_name> (<parameter_list>);
```

One of the nice things about method hiding is that you can change the return type of the method you are hiding. Method hiding does not take part in the virtual function mechanism. The new function will never be invoked by a base class pointer. For example, if a derived type is cast upwards to a base type, the base type method will be called.

Example: Method hiding

The `Account` class defines a field representing an account balance and a method, `Deposit()`, to increase the balance. The `Deposit()` method has a return type of void.

```
using System;

public class Account
{
  protected double balance;

  public Account(double b)
  {
    balance = b;
  }

  public void Deposit(double amount)
  {
    balance += amount;
  }
}
```

Let's say you wanted to define a derived class of Account named NewAccount. You want to make use of other features of the Account class (let's pretend there were some), but you also want to rewrite the Deposit() method so it returns the updated balance. This is easily done by defining a Deposit() method in the NewAccount class with the new keyword. Because the signatures of the two methods are the same, without the new keyword this code won't compile.

```
using System;

public class NewAccount : Account
{

  public NewAccount(double b) : base(b) {}

  public new double Deposit(double amount)
  {
    balance += amount;
    return balance;
  }
}

public class HidingDemo
{
  public static void Main()
  {
    NewAccount na = new NewAccount(500.0);

    Console.WriteLine("Balance is {0}", na.Deposit(100.0));
  }
}
```

Output:

```
Balance is 600
```

Note that if we create a NewAccount object and cast it to the base type before calling the Deposit() method, it will be the base method, not the derived method, that is called.

Summary

In this chapter we learned about the most commonly used function member in the C# language, the method. We learned how to define a method and about method modifiers and return types. We revisited the return statement that is used to exit a method. We explored the differences between instance and static methods. We saw how input parameters can be modified using the params, out, and ref keywords. We learned about abstract and virtual methods. We delved into the topics of method overloading and overriding. Finally, we learned how to define a method that hides a base class method.

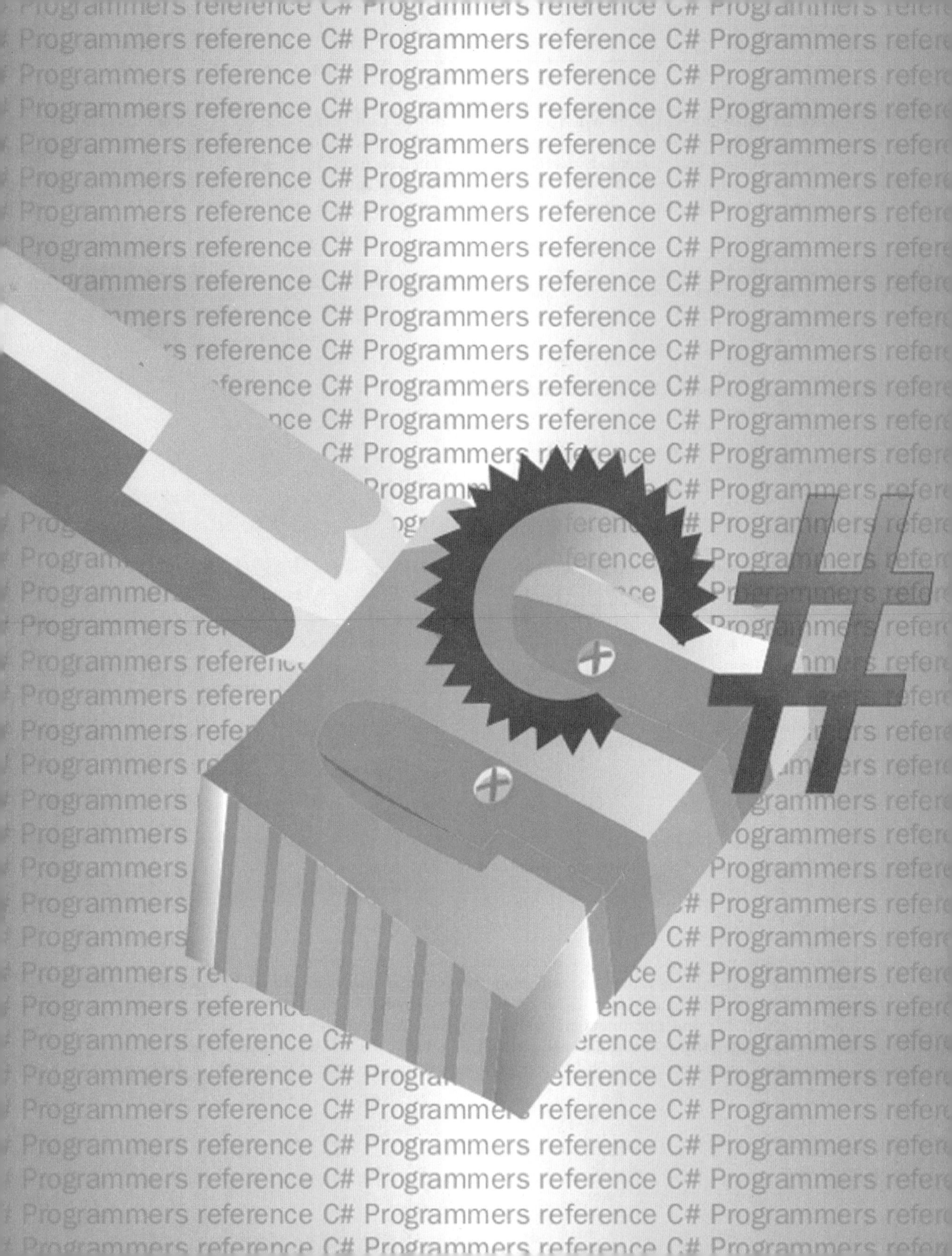
C# Programmers reference

13

Properties

A property is a function member that looks like a function internally but externally acts like a field. Access to the value of the property is facilitated by accessor methods named `get` and `set` defined by the property. The advantage of using properties is they allow you the ease of access that comes with a public field while at the same time they permit a class to control access to the property through the `get` and `set` accessors. The `set` accessor can be used to evaluate proposed changes to a property value before the property is updated.

A property can be read-only or read-write. You can access or change the value of a property very much like you would a public field. A property can be used to allow external access to the value of a `private` field.

In this chapter we will look at:

- ❑ Defining a property
- ❑ Instance properties
- ❑ Static properties

Defining a property

A property declaration statement is very much like that of a method but without an input parameter list. Properties can be defined inside classes and structs. The basic syntax for defining a property is given below:

```
<modifiers> <type> <property_name>
{
  get
  {
    //  body of get accessor
  }

  set
  {
    //    body of set accessor
  }
}
```

The declaration statement will consist of the property type and the property name. The declaration may also include an access modifier and other keywords used to define the property. As with all type members, a property can be given `public`, `protected`, `internal`, `protected internal`, or `private` access. The default access is `private`. See the *Access modifiers* section of Chapter 11 for a description of the different types of access.

In addition to the access modifiers described above, a property definition can be modified with the `new`, `static`, `virtual`, `sealed`, `override`, `abstract`, and `extern` keywords. The keywords have the same effect on properties as they would on methods. A `static` property is associated with a type rather than an instance of a type. The `new` keyword means a property hides one of the same name defined in a base class. A `virtual` property is one whose accessors can be overridden. A `sealed` property is an overridden property that cannot itself be overridden. An overridden property indicates this state using the `override` keyword. The `extern` keyword means the property was written in a non-.NET language.

The body of the property definition statement contains the definitions of the `get` and `set` accessors. You have to define at least one, but don't have to define both. A property that only defines a `get` accessor is read-only. One that defines both a `get` and a `set` accessor is read-write.

get accessor

The `get` accessor is used to return the current value of the property. It takes no input parameters and implicitly returns the same type as the property in which it is defined. It is perfectly acceptable to perform some computations inside the `get` accessor before returning the value.

The `get` accessor is defined inside the body of the property. It consists simply of the `get` keyword followed by the body of the `get` accessor enclosed in curly braces.

Example: get accessor

The `Circle` class represents a circle. It contains one private field that represents the circle radius. The `Circle` class also defines a read-only `Area` property. The `get` accessor inside the `Area` property definition computes and returns the area of the circle.

```
using System;

public class Circle
{
  double radius;

  public Circle(double r)
  {
    radius = r;
  }

  public double Area
  {
    get
    {
      return Math.PI*radius*radius;
    }
```

```
    }

    public static void Main()
    {
      Circle c = new Circle(4.0);

      Console.WriteLine("area is {0}",c.Area);
    }
  }
```

Output:

```
  area is 50.265482457
```

Note that if you didn't use a property for the area, you would have to define a GetArea() method. This is perfectly acceptable, of course, but using a property simplifies the client code used to access the area of the circle.

set accessor

The set accessor is used to change the value of a property. It implicitly takes a single argument named value that represents the new value of the property. The set accessor implicitly has a return type of void. As with the get accessor, the set accessor can perform value checking or other operations before updating the property value.

The set accessor is defined inside the body of the property. It consists simply of the set keyword followed by the body of the set accessor enclosed in curly braces. In theory you could create a write-only property by only defining a set accessor. Microsoft recommends against this practice because write-only properties may be confusing to developers writing client code.

Example: set accessor

The Account class defines a private field named balance. A property named Balance is defined that gets or sets the value of the balance field. The set accessor defined by the Balance property checks to see if the balance field will fall below zero. If it does, a warning message is printed and the balance field is not updated.

The Main() method creates an Account object and provides an initial value to the balance field. The value of the balance field is changed by invoking the set accessor with the statement.

```
  acct.Balance = 256.76;
```

If we had used a method to set the balance field, the client code might look like this.

```
  acct.SetBalance(256.76);
```

When an attempt is made to change the balance field to a value below zero, the code inside the set accessor catches this and writes an error message.

Don't spend too much time wondering whether a bank would really use this code. Its purpose is really just to demonstrate the set accessor in action.

```
using System;

public class Account
{
  private double balance;

  public Account(double d)
  {
    balance = d;
  }

  public double Balance
  {
    get
    {
      return balance;
    }

    set
    {
      if ( value < 0.0 )
      {
        Console.WriteLine("balance can't be negative");
      }
      else
      {
        balance = value;
      }
    }
  }

  public static void Main()
  {
    Account acct = new Account(456.78);

    acct.Balance = 256.76;
    Console.WriteLine("balance is {0}",acct.Balance);

    acct.Balance = -45.67;
  }
}
```

Output:

```
balance is 256.76
balance can't be negative
```

Instance properties

Properties are by default instance properties, meaning that they are associated with an instance of a type. Every instance of the type will have its own copy of the property. The syntax to access an instance property is the object name, a period, and the name of the property.

For examples of instance properties, see the examples in the *get accessor* and *set accessor* sections where instance properties are used to represent the area of a circle and an account balance.

Static properties

A static property is one that refers to static data. As with static fields and methods, a static property is associated with a type, rather than an instance of a type. To declare a property as static, place the `static` keyword in the property declaration statement. A static property cannot be declared to be `virtual` or `abstract`.

The `get` and `set` accessors are defined in the same manner with a static property as they are with an instance property. The syntax to access a static property is the type name, a period, and the property name.

Example: Static properties

The `Password` class defines a static field named `minLength` that represents the minimum acceptable length of a password. The class also defines a static property named `MinLength` that is used to set or return the current value of the field.

In the `Main()` method, the value of the `MinLength` property is set to 10. A three letter password is created and its length is compared against the `MinLength` property. The `MinLength` property is accessed using the `"Password.MinLength"` syntax.

```
using System;

public class Password
{
    private static int minLength;

    static Password()
    {
        minLength = 8;
    }

    public static int MinLength
    {
        get
        {
            return minLength;
        }
        set
        {
            minLength = value;
```

```
    }
  }

  public static void Main()
  {
      Password.MinLength = 10;
      String password = "cow";

      if ( password.Length < Password.MinLength )
      {
          Console.WriteLine("password must be {0} "+
                  "characters long",Password.MinLength);
      }
  }
}
```

Output:

```
password must be 10 characters long
```

In the preceding example, did you notice that another property was invoked? Every String object has an instance property named Length associated with it that represents the number of characters in the String. The password object accesses its Length property using the "password.Length" syntax.

Summary

A property is a programming construct that looks like a function but acts like a field. In this chapter, we learned how to define a property including the access modifiers and other keywords that can be associated with a property definition. We examined the get and set accessors that are used to return or change the value of a property. We discussed instance and static properties.

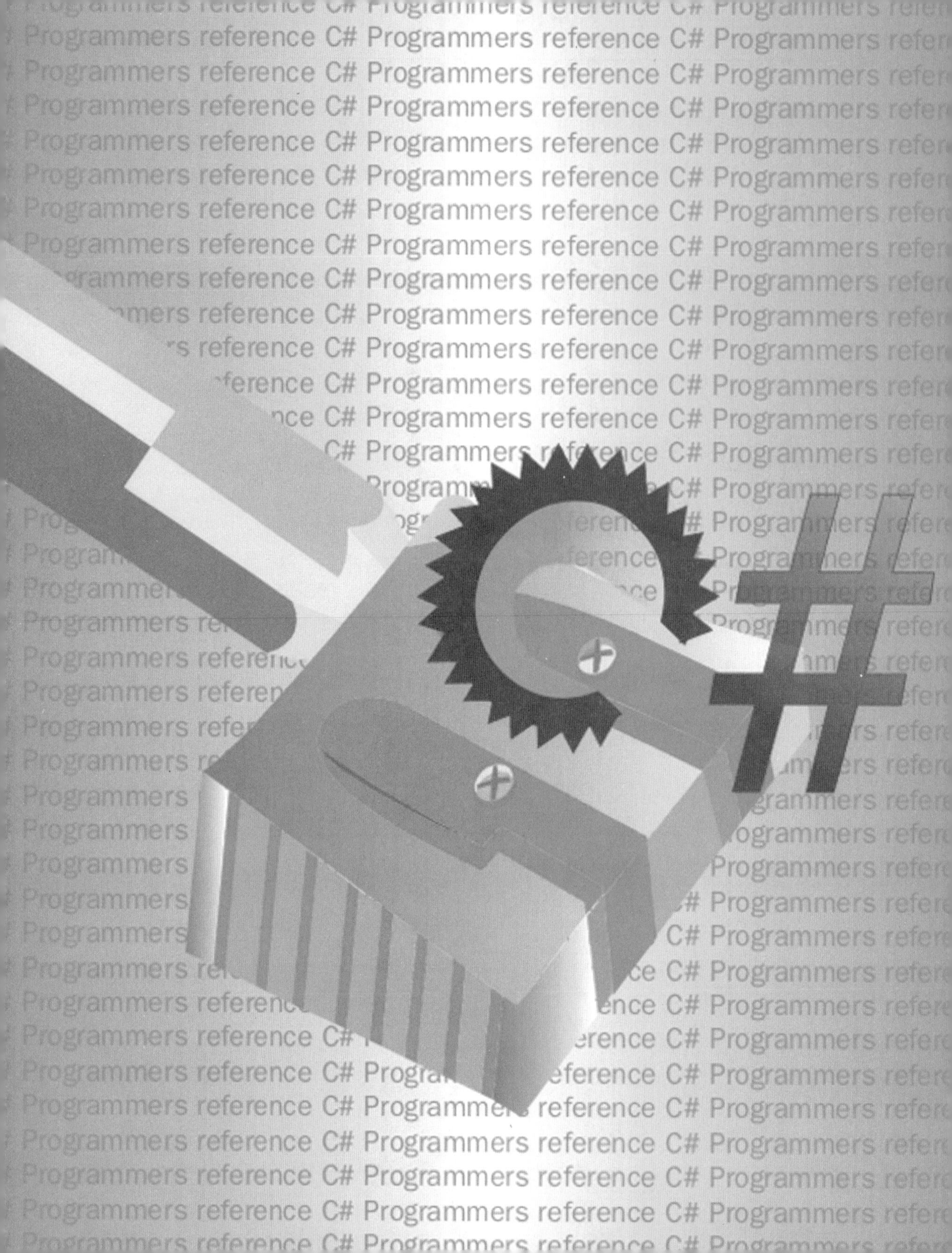
Programmers reference C#

14

Indexers

An indexer is a syntactical convenience that allows an object to be indexed as if it were an array. Indexers are usually defined in classes or structs that represent a collection of elements or in a class that has array-like behavior. An indexer allows you to access an element of the collection using the standard array syntax "[]". Many classes in the .NET Framework libraries use indexers. The indexer for the String class, for instance, returns the character at the specified index in the String.

Indexers, much like properties, are provided strictly as a convenience. They don't add any additional functionality. Everything that an indexer or property does can be performed the old-fashioned way using methods.

In this chapter we will look at:

❑ What indexers are

❑ How to define an indexer

❑ Using an indexer

Let's start with an example.

Example: Indexers

In this simple example, a String is created and the characters that make up the String are accessed using the String indexer. The String indexer is read-only (Strings are immutable), so you couldn't use the indexer to change one of the characters in the String.

```
using System;

public class StringDemo
{
  public static void Main()
  {
    String str = "Lisa";

    // Each letter in the string is printed out using the String indexer
```

```
        for(int i=0; i<str.Length; ++i)
        {
          Console.WriteLine(str[i]);
        }

        //  This won't work because the String indexer
        //  is read-only
        //
        //      str[0] = 'B';
    }
}
```

Output:

```
L
i
s
a
```

Defining an indexer

Indexers are defined in much the same manner as properties. The this keyword identifies the block of code as an indexer. Following the this keyword are square brackets containing a parameter list.

```
<modifers> <type> this[<parameter_list>]
{
  get
  {
    //  body of get accessor
  }

  set
  {
    //  body of set accessor
  }
}
```

An indexer must declare its type. The parameter list of an indexer is similar to that of a method except it must contain at least one parameter. Parameters in the list cannot be modified with the ref or out keywords. Indexers can be defined to treat multidimensional collections of objects by placing more than one argument inside the square brackets.

Indexers can be given the same type of access as properties (public, protected, internal, protected internal, or private). Indexers can be declared virtual or abstract. An indexer can override or hide an indexer defined in a base class using the override, sealed, or new keywords. You can define overloaded indexers with the same name but different parameter lists. Indexers cannot be defined as static.

The get and/or set accessor functions are defined inside the body of the indexer. These accessor functions are used to retrieve or change the value of some part of the object. The get accessor corresponds to a method with the same parameter list as the indexer.

It implicitly has a return type the same as the indexer type. The set accessor corresponds to a method with the same parameter list as the indexer plus an additional parameter named value. It implicitly has a return type of void.

If only a get accessor is provided, the indexer is read-only. Although read-only indexers are legal syntax, they offer no benefits over a method. Indexers can be write-only by defining only a set accessor. An indexer is read-write if both a get and a set accessor are defined.

Using an indexer

The [] operator is used to invoke the get or set accessor of an indexer. The arguments placed inside the square brackets must correspond to the parameter list defined by the indexer. Because indexers are always instance members, the [] operator will be preceded by the name of a class or struct instance.

Example: Using an indexer

In this example, an indexer is used to make a one-dimensional array appear to be a two-dimensional array. The TwoDim class defines a one-dimensional Array and two integers representing the size of the i and j dimensions of a two-dimensional array.

An indexer is defined that takes two integer arguments. These arguments represent an i and j index. The get and set accessors convert these indices into the corresponding index of a one-dimensional array and return or set the value at that location in the Array.

The Main() method of the IndexerDemo class creates a TwoDim object that has two "rows" and three "columns". The value of the element in the second row and column of the TwoDim object is changed by invoking the set accessor. This value is then returned using the get accessor. This behavior, of mapping a multidimensional array into a 1-D array, is essentially what takes place with the .NET Framework's built-in multidimensional arrays.

```
using System;

public class TwoDim
{
  int numI, numJ;
  Array array;

  public TwoDim(int numI, int numJ)
  {
    this.numI = numI;
    this.numJ = numJ;
    array = Array.CreateInstance(typeof(object),numI*numJ);
  }

  //===========================================================
  //  Define indexers that will access the one-dimensional
  //  array as if it were a two-dimensional array.
  //===========================================================

  public object this[int i,int j]
  {
```

```
        get
        {
            int k = i*numI + j;
            return array.GetValue(k);
        }

        set
        {
            int k = i*numI + j;
            array.SetValue(value,k);
        }
    }
}

public class IndexerDemo
{
    public static void Main()
    {
        TwoDim myArray = new TwoDim(2,3);

        myArray[1,1] = 4.5;
        Console.WriteLine(" value of element [1,1] is "+myArray[1,1]);
    }
}
```

Output:

```
value of element [1,1] is 4.5
```

Summary

In this chapter we learned how a syntactical convenience known as an indexer can be used to allow an object to be indexed as if it were an array. We discussed how to define an indexer including its get and set accessors. We learned how to use an indexer to access information about an object.

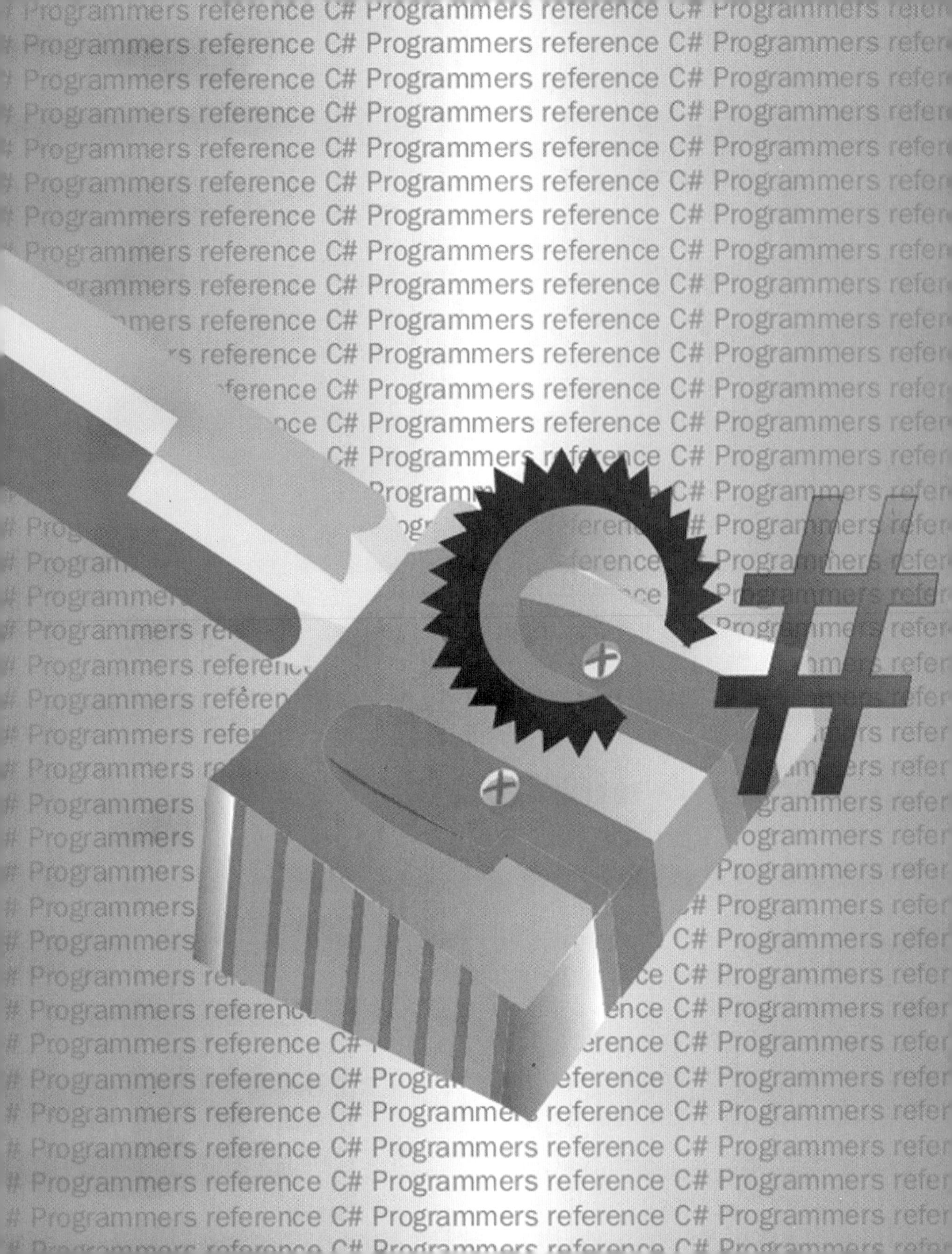
C# Programmers reference

15

Delegates

A delegate is a reference type that provides a generic reference to a method with a specific return type and argument list. It is similar in nature to a function pointer in C or C++. Unlike C++ function pointers, however, delegates are fully object-oriented – they encapsulate both a method and an object instance. Delegates are user-defined types, so when we define a delegate, we actually define a particular type of delegate, rather than a specific instance. This delegate type only specifies the return type and argument list of the method it represents – it can represent any method with the same argument list and return type. The method can have any name, it can be instance or static, and there are no restrictions on what the method actually does. In order to retrieve a delegate representing a specific method (and, if it is an instance method, the object on which it is to be invoked), we need to create an instance of our delegate.

Delegates are used in multi-threaded programming to specify the method that is called when a thread is started. They are also used as callbacks in asynchronous programming. Delegates are employed extensively in the C# event model. They indicate the method that is used to process a given event. Delegates are used in the development of generic class libraries. These classes usually define some generic process. The specifics of the process, including which methods to use, are supplied by client code at runtime.

In this chapter we will look at:

- ❑ Defining a delegate
- ❑ Creating a delegate instance
- ❑ Invoking a delegate
- ❑ Multi-cast delegates

Defining a delegate

A delegate is declared in a similar manner to declaring a method, except that the `delegate` keyword is included in the declaration statement. The declaration must include the return type and argument list of the method the delegate represents:

```
<modifiers> delegate <return_type> <delegate_name> (<argument_list>);
```

A delegate declaration may also include an access modifier. The access modifier can be `public`, `protected`, `internal`, `protected internal`, or `private`. A delegate can hide a delegate defined in a base class by including the `new` keyword in its declaration statement.

Creating a delegate instance

Although delegates are declared in a similar fashion to methods, they are implemented as instances of classes derived from the `System.Delegate` class. As with any other class, a delegate instance is created using the `new` keyword:

```
<delegate_type> <name> = new <delegate_type> (<method>);
```

The *method* argument is the name of the method to which the delegate refers. For example, let's say we had defined a delegate named `ProcessString`:

```
public delegate string ProcessString(string str);
```

Suppose further that there is a static method named `LowerCaseString()` defined in the `Blah` class that takes a `string` argument and returns a `string`. We can create an instance of the `ProcessString` delegate named `process` that is associated with the `LowerCaseString()` method with the line:

```
ProcessString process = new ProcessString(Blah.LowerCaseString);
```

To associate an instance method with the delegate instance, the syntax inside the parentheses would be:

```
<instance_name>.<method_name>
```

In both cases, only the method name is specified, without any argument list or parentheses.

Invoking a delegate

A delegate is invoked by typing the name of the delegate instance and the arguments that will be sent to the method represented by the delegate. The arguments are placed inside parentheses.

```
<delegate_name>(<argument_list>)
```

A delegate is a reference type and can be passed to a method or included in a method's parameter list like any other reference type.

Example: Invoking delegates

In this example we will use delegates to write a method for a generic class library. The `ComputeIt()` method evaluates an expression that is a function of two variables, v and T. The first part of the expression is a function of v and is performed the same for all values of T. The second part of the expression is a function of T and is meant to be evaluated differently depending on the value of T. It should be evaluated one way for low values of T and another way for high values of T.

One way to handle this situation would be to define different versions of ComputeIt(), one for low values of T and one for high values. A more compact way is to write a single, generic version applicable under all conditions using delegates.

The ComputeIt() method is written such that it takes three arguments: two doubles corresponding to the v and T parameters and a reference to a delegate instance. The method associated with the delegate is used to compute the second, T-dependent part of the expression.

```
public class GenericLibrary
{
  public static double ComputeIt(double v, double T, Equation eq)
  {
    return (0.5 * v * v) + eq(T);
  }
}
```

The Equation delegate itself is defined such that it takes a double argument and returns a double.

```
public delegate double Equation(double x);
```

The DelegateDemo class defines an Equation delegate instance as a field. It then calls the ComputeIt() method twice. The first time the delegate is associated with the LowT() method. The second time the delegate is associated with the HighT() method. In both cases, the syntax to call the ComputeIt() method is identical, but the output from the ComputeIt() method is different because different methods are called inside the ComputeIt() method.

```
using System;

public class DelegateDemo
{
  public static void Main()
  {
    double result;
    Equation eqn;

    //==========================================================
    //  First compute a result by associating the delegate
    //  with the LowT() method.
    //==========================================================

    eqn = new Equation(DelegateDemo.LowT);
    result = GenericLibrary.ComputeIt(100.0, 4000.0, eqn);
    Console.WriteLine("Result is {0}", result);

    //==========================================================
    //  Now compute the result when the delegate is associated
    //  with the HighT() method.
    //==========================================================

    eqn = new Equation(DelegateDemo.HighT);
    result = GenericLibrary.ComputeIt(100.0, 4000.0, eqn);
```

```
                Console.WriteLine("Result is {0}", result);
            }


            //=========================================================
            //   These two methods evaluate the condition-variable
            //   part of the ComputeIt() method.
            //=========================================================

            public static double LowT(double T)
            {
                return 1009.0 * T;
            }

            public static double HighT(double T)
            {
                return (1009.0 * T) + (0.1 * T * T);
            }
        }
```

Output:

```
    Result is 4041000
    Result is 5641000
```

Note that the `ComputeIt()` method is completely generic. You can pass whatever method you want to `ComputeIt()` through the delegate, as long as the method has the same argument list and return type as the delegate.

Multi-cast delegates

A multi-cast delegate is one that refers to more than one method. When the delegate is invoked, it successively calls each method. In order to combine individual delegate instances into a multi-cast delegate, the delegates must be of the same type, must have a return type of void, and may not take output parameters (but reference parameters are permitted). Other than that, they are declared and instantiated like any other delegate. Multi-cast delegates are used in the C# event model.

You can think of a multi-cast delegate as a chain of two or more standard delegates. Delegates can be chained together using the mathematical operators + and +=. A delegate can be removed from a multi-cast delegate using the − and −= operators. When a multi-cast delegate is invoked, each of the methods represented by the delegate is called in turn. If there are any arguments, these will be applied to all the methods.

Example: Multi-cast delegates

In this example, a delegate named `Message` is declared that takes no arguments. The `Messages` class defines three methods that print out various messages. The methods have a return type of void and take no arguments.

```
    using System;
```

```
public delegate void Message();

public class Messages
{
  public static void Greeting()
  {
    Console.WriteLine("Welcome to Mandolin Co.");
    return;
  }

  public static void DateAndTime()
  {
    Console.WriteLine(DateTime.Now.ToLongDateString());
    return;
  }

  public static void Maintenance()
  {
    Console.WriteLine("System maintenance will be done tonight");
    return;
  }
}
```

The `MultiDemo` class creates an instance of a `Message` delegate. A multi-cast delegate is created by chaining together three `Message` delegates. When the multi-cast delegate is invoked, the three methods are invoked in turn. One of the delegates is removed from the multi-cast delegate. When the multi-cast delegate is run again, only two methods are invoked.

```
using System;

public class MultiDemo
{
  public static void Main()
  {
    Message msg;

    //===========================================
    //  Create a multi-cast delegate that will
    //  print out a number of messages
    //===========================================

    msg = new Message(Messages.Greeting);
    msg += new Message(Messages.DateAndTime);

    Message msg2 = new Message(Messages.Maintenance);
    msg += msg2;
    msg();

    //============================================
    //  A delegate is removed from the multi-cast
    //============================================
```

```
        Console.WriteLine();

        msg -= msg2;
        msg();
    }
}
```

Output:

```
Welcome to Mandolin Co.
Thursday, January 10, 2002
System maintenance will be done tonight

Welcome to Mandolin Co.
Thursday, January 10, 2002
```

Summary

Delegates are versatile reference types which provide a generic reference to a method of a given parameter list and return type. In this chapter we saw how to:

- ❑ Define a delegate type
- ❑ Create an instance of a delegate to represent a specific method
- ❑ Invoke delegates
- ❑ Form a multi-cast delegate by chaining delegates together

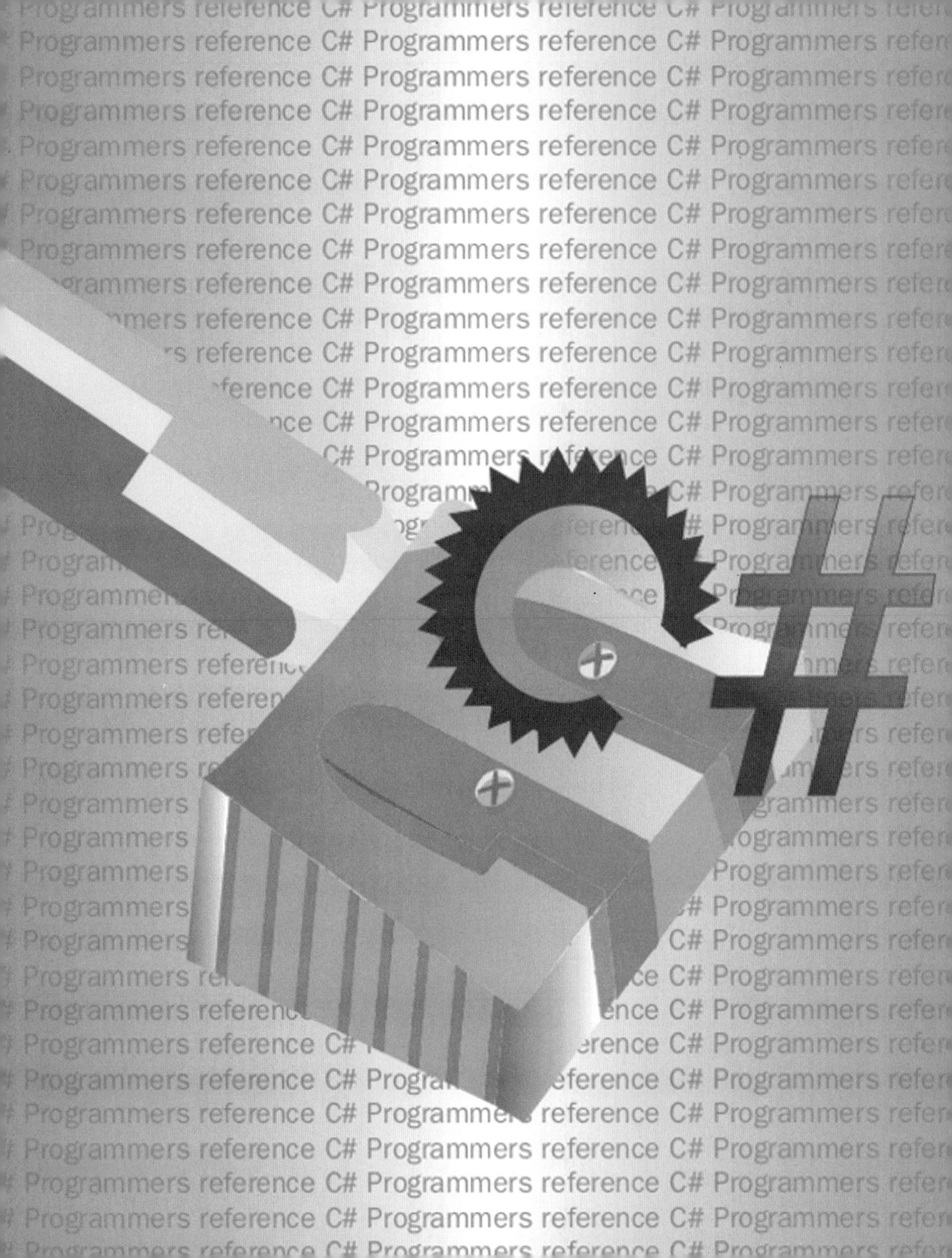
C# Programmers reference

16

Events

An event, as you might suppose, is one way C# indicates that something has happened. This is particularly important in Windows applications. If you push a button, select a menu item, or make a list selection, you expect something to happen. The component you interacted with generates an event with information about the interaction. This information is sent to another method, which processes or responds to the event.

In this chapter, we'll look at:

- ❏   The C# event model
- ❏   Event delegates
- ❏   Event-handling methods
- ❏   Firing an event
- ❏   Customizing the methods for adding and removing delegates from an event

The C# event model

The C# language uses a delegation model to implement events. The event-handling method does not have to be defined in the class that will generate the event. This system has many advantages; for example, it is both general and flexible. Suppose we have two buttons in our application, but the buttons do different things. If the event handler were tied to the event source, we might have to write two derived button classes, each having its own event handler. Under the delegation model, the button class remains general and only the event handlers must be separately defined. The event handlers can be (and usually are) placed in a different class entirely.

What is needed under the delegation model is a mechanism for connecting the event source to the event handler. This is where delegates come into the picture. A delegate provides a generic reference to a method with a specified return type and argument list. What the method does is unimportant to the delegate. These characteristics are made-to-order when dealing with events. An event-handling delegate (also referred to as simply an event delegate) can be defined as a member of the class that generates the event. The method that will be used to process the event is associated with the event-handling delegate. When the event occurs, the delegate is invoked and the event-handling method is called.

Event-handling delegates are multi-cast, so a given delegate can be associated with and can call any number of event-handling methods when an event is generated.

The basic event life cycle process is shown below. The event generator defines an instance of an event delegate as one of its members. The event consumers are those objects that wish to be notified when an event is generated. They define the event-handling methods that will be associated with the event delegate. When the event is generated, the event generator "fires" the event by invoking the event delegate. The delegate then calls the event-handling methods associated with it:

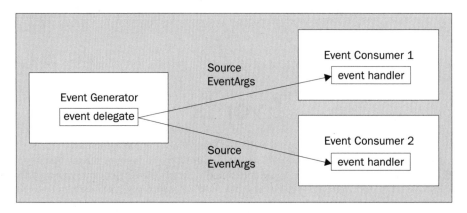

The event delegate sends two objects to every event-handling method. The first is a reference to the object that generated the event, known as the event source. The second object will be an instance of the System.EventArgs class or one of the derived classes of EventArgs. This object contains additional information about the event.

Event delegates

Delegates were introduced in Chapter 15. They are reference types that provide a generic reference to one or more methods. The general form for an event delegate is shown below.

```
<modifiers> delegate void <delegate_name>(object source, EventArgs e);
```

The access and other modifying keywords applicable to event delegates are the same as for delegates in general and are described in Chapter 15. Event delegates always have a return type of void. They will always have two parameters in their parameter list. As was previously described, the first parameter represents the event source.

The second parameter is an instance of the EventArgs class, or of a class derived from EventArgs, which contains additional information about the event. For example, the MouseEventArgs class defines the following properties:

```
public MouseButtons Button {get;}
public int Clicks {get;}
public int Delta {get;}
public int X {get;}
public int Y {get;}
```

These properties tell the event handler which button caused the event, how many clicks were associated with the event, and the location where the event occurred.

Event delegates in the .NET Framework libraries

The .NET Framework defines a large number of event-handling delegates. The built-in delegates all derive from the `System.Delegate` class. Here are a few of the event-handling delegates contained in the `System.Windows.Forms` namespace:

```
public delegate void ColumnClickEventHandler(object source,
                                             ColumnClickEventArgs args)
public delegate void DragEventHandler(object source, DragEventArgs args)
public delegate void KeyEventHandler(object source, KeyEventArgs args)
public delegate void MouseEventHandler(object source, MouseEventArgs args)
```

You can see that all of these built-in delegates follow the standard event-delegate form: return type of `void`, two parameters in their parameter lists.

User-defined event delegates

While the .NET Framework provides a large number of event delegates, there is nothing preventing you from defining your own. Simply define your delegate according to the syntax described previously. You can also define your own `EventArgs`-derived class to contain information pertinent to your delegate. For example, if you wanted to define a delegate that would respond to changes in the name of something you might define it as:

```
public delegate void NameEventHandler(object source, NameEventArgs args);
```

You would also have to define the `NameEventArgs` class. An example of doing this is provided in the *Firing an event* section below.

Creating an event delegate instance

An `event` delegate instance is created differently from a standard delegate in that you don't use the `new` keyword. Instead, you use the `event` keyword. To create an instance of the previously described `NameEventHandler` delegate you would use the syntax:

```
public event NameEventHandler handler;
```

The `event` keyword tells the compiler that this delegate instance is an event. The compiler will check to ensure that the delegate has the proper signature for an event delegate. The compiler will also restrict the operations that can be performed on the event delegate to the `+=` and `-=` operators. What the above statement has done is to create a `null` reference to an event delegate named handler. The `null` state indicates that no event handlers have been associated with the delegate.

179

Event handlers

An event handler is a method that is called by an event delegate when an event is generated. The event-handling method can be defined in a class different from the event source. Because it is associated with an event delegate, an event handler will always have the same parameter list and return type as an event delegate. The body of the event handler can do whatever is required to respond to the event. The C# event model gives you complete freedom to define (and name) the event handlers you need.

To associate an event handler with an event, the event must add a delegate associated with the method to the list of delegates that it maintains. You can add a delegate to the list using the += operator, and you can remove a delegate from the list using the -= operator. For example, if you wanted to associate an event handler named NameChange() with a NameEventHandler instance named handler you would use the syntax:

```
handler += new NameEventHandler(NameChange);
```

Firing an event

For a class to be able to fire an event, an event delegate instance should be defined as a member of the class. The event-generating class should define code to determine when to generate the event and code for generating the EventArgs object that will accompany the event.

To fire the event, simply invoke the event delegate instance. As you may recall from Chapter 15, to invoke a delegate instance, type the name of the instance followed by the arguments that are to be passed to the event-handling methods. When an event is generated, information about the event is sent to any event handlers that have been registered to the event source.

Example: User-defined events

In this example we create and apply a user-defined event. The NameList class represents an ArrayList that generates an event when a string is added to the list. An ArrayList is defined as a field. The NameList class also declares a NameListEventHandler instance as a field. Other than a constructor, the only other function member in the NameList class is the Add() method.

The Add() method adds the specified string to the ArrayList. It then checks to see if any event-handling delegates have been added to the NameListEventHandler instance. If there are any, the event delegate is invoked, calling these methods and passing them a reference to the event source and an instance of the NameListEventArgs class.

```
using System;
using System.Collections;

public class NameList
{
    ArrayList list;
    public event NameListEventHandler nameListEvent;

    public NameList()
    {
```

```
      list = new ArrayList();
   }

   //=============================================================
   //  The Add() method is used to add elements to the ArrayList.
   //  If there are any event-handling delegates associated with
   //  the NameList object, they are invoked.
   //=============================================================

   public void Add(string Name)
   {
      list.Add(Name);
      if (nameListEvent != null)
      {
         nameListEvent(this, new NameListEventArgs(Name, list.Count));
      }
   }
}
```

The NameListEventHandler delegate is shown below. It takes as its second parameter a
NameListEventArgs object:

```
public delegate void NameListEventHandler(object source,
                                          NameListEventArgs args);
```

The NameListEventArgs class encapsulates information about the event generated by the NameList
class. It defines two fields, a string representing the name that was added to the list and an integer
whose value is the current number of names in the list. The NameListEventArgs class defines a public
constructor and two properties to return the values of the fields:

```
public class NameListEventArgs : EventArgs
{
   string name;
   int count;

   public NameListEventArgs(string str, int i)
   {
      name = str;
      count = i;
   }

   public string Name
   {
      get
      {
         return name;
      }
   }

   public int Count
   {
      get
```

```
      {
        return count;
      }
    }
  }
```

The `EventDemo` class creates a `NameList` object. The event delegate of the `NameList` object adds two event-handling delegates to its list. The first refers to the `NewName()` method. The second refers to the `CurrentCount()` method. Both of these methods are defined in the `EventDemo` class.

Two names are then added to the `NameList`. Each time a name is added, an event is fired and both the `NewName()` and `CurrentCount()` methods are called. These methods print out the name that was added and the current number of names in the list:

```csharp
using System;

public class EventDemo
{
  public static void Main()
  {

    //============================================================
    //  A NameList object is created.  Two event handling methods
    //   are associated with the NameList event handling delegate.
    //   Two names are added to the NameList.
    //============================================================

    NameList names = new NameList();
    names.nameListEvent += new NameListEventHandler(NewName);
    names.nameListEvent += new NameListEventHandler(CurrentCount);

    names.Add("Flowfield");
    names.Add("Bosworth");
  }

  //========================================================
  //   The NewName() method is an event handling method
  //   that prints out the name that was added to the list.
  //========================================================

  public static void NewName(object source, NameListEventArgs args)
  {
    Console.WriteLine(args.Name + " was added to the list");
  }

  //=========================================================
  //   The CurrentCount() method is an event handling method
  //   that prints out the current number of items in the list.
  //=========================================================

  public static void CurrentCount(object source, NameListEventArgs args)
  {
    Console.WriteLine("list currently has " + args.Count + " items");
```

```
    }
    }
```

Output:

```
Flowfield was added to the list
list currently has 1 items
Bosworth was added to the list
list currently has 2 items
```

One important thing to note about this example is that the event-handling code is entirely separate from the event source. You can change the method that is called when an element is added to the NameList without changing anything about the NameList class itself.

Event accessors

If you look at the IL code generated by the C# compiler for the NameList class, you'll see that behind the scenes a private delegate field named nameListEvent and two methods for adding and removing delegates to this delegate are created:

```
.field private class NameListEventHandler nameListEvent
.method public hidebysig specialname instance void
        add_nameListEvent(class NameListEventHandler 'value') cil managed
        synchronized
{
  // ...
} // end of method NameList::add_nameListEvent

.method public hidebysig specialname instance void
        remove_nameListEvent(class NameListEventHandler 'value') cil managed
        synchronized
{
  // ...
} // end of method NameList::remove_nameListEvent
```

Because one field is declared for every event in the class, and because delegates are reference types, this means that for every instance of our class, space will be allocated on the heap for each event declared in our class. Since most of the events in a class won't be hooked into by any client, this could potentially be an expensive waste of resources.

The solution to this is to define our own storage add and remove methods, and to use these to store the delegates in a more efficient way (typically using a Hashtable). These methods are called **event accessors**, and C# allows us to define them using a syntax very similar to the get and set accessors of properties:

```
<modifiers> event <delegate_type> <instance_name>
{
  add
  {
    // Add accessor code
```

```
    }
  remove
  {
    // Remove accessor code
  }
}
```

Example: Using event accessors

```
(Delegate)instanceHash[nameListEventKey], value);
        }
      }


      // The remove event accessor - this is similar to the add accessor,
      // except that we won't need to create a new child Hashtable,
      // and we call Delegate.Remove() instead of Delegate.Combine()
      remove
      {
        lock (delegates)
        {
          Hashtable instanceHash = (Hashtable)delegates[this];
          instanceHash[nameListEventKey] = Delegate.Remove(
                  (Delegate)instanceHash[nameListEventKey], value);
        }
      }
    }

  public NameList()
  {
    list = new ArrayList();
  }

  public void Add(string name)
  {
    list.Add(name);

      // Get the delegate from the Hashtable and invoke it
      Hashtable instanceHash = (Hashtable)delegates[this];
      NameListEventHandler handler =
                  (NameListEventHandler)instanceHash[nameListEventKey];
      if (handler != null)
        handler(this, new NameListEventArgs(name, list.Count));
  }

  // Implement a Dispose() method for the class to remove the object
  // from the Hashtable; if this is called explicitly, we don't want the
  // destructor to be called, so we call GC.SuppressFinalize()
  public void Dispose()
  {
    delegates.Remove(this);
```

```
            GC.SuppressFinalize(this);
        }

        // If Dispose() hasn't already been called, call it now
        ~NameList()
        {
            Dispose();
        }
}
```

The only change we'll make to the client is to wrap up our call to NameList in a using statement, so that the Dispose() method is called when we've finished with the object:

```
using System;

public class EventDemo
{
    public static void Main()
    {
        using (NameList names = new NameList())
        {
            names.nameListEvent += new NameListEventHandler(NewName);
            names.nameListEvent += new NameListEventHandler(CurrentCount);

            names.Add("Flowfield");
            names.Add("Bosworth");
        }
    }

    public static void NewName(object source,
                               NameListEventArgs args)
    {
        Console.WriteLine(args.Name+" was added to the list");
    }

    public static void CurrentCount(object source,
                                    NameListEventArgs args)
    {
        Console.WriteLine("list currently has "+
                          args.Count+" items");
    }
}
```

The output remains the same as before:

```
Flowfield was added to the list
list currently has 1 items
Bosworth was added to the list
list currently has 2 items
```

Summary

In this chapter we learned about events. We learned that the C# language uses a delegation event model where the event-handling code is separate from the event-generating code. We explored event delegates, reference types used to connect the event generator to the event handler. We examined how to define an event delegate and how to create an event delegate instance. We discussed event-handling methods and how to fire an event. Finally, we saw how we can override the default event accessors, and provide our own means of storing the delegates in our class.

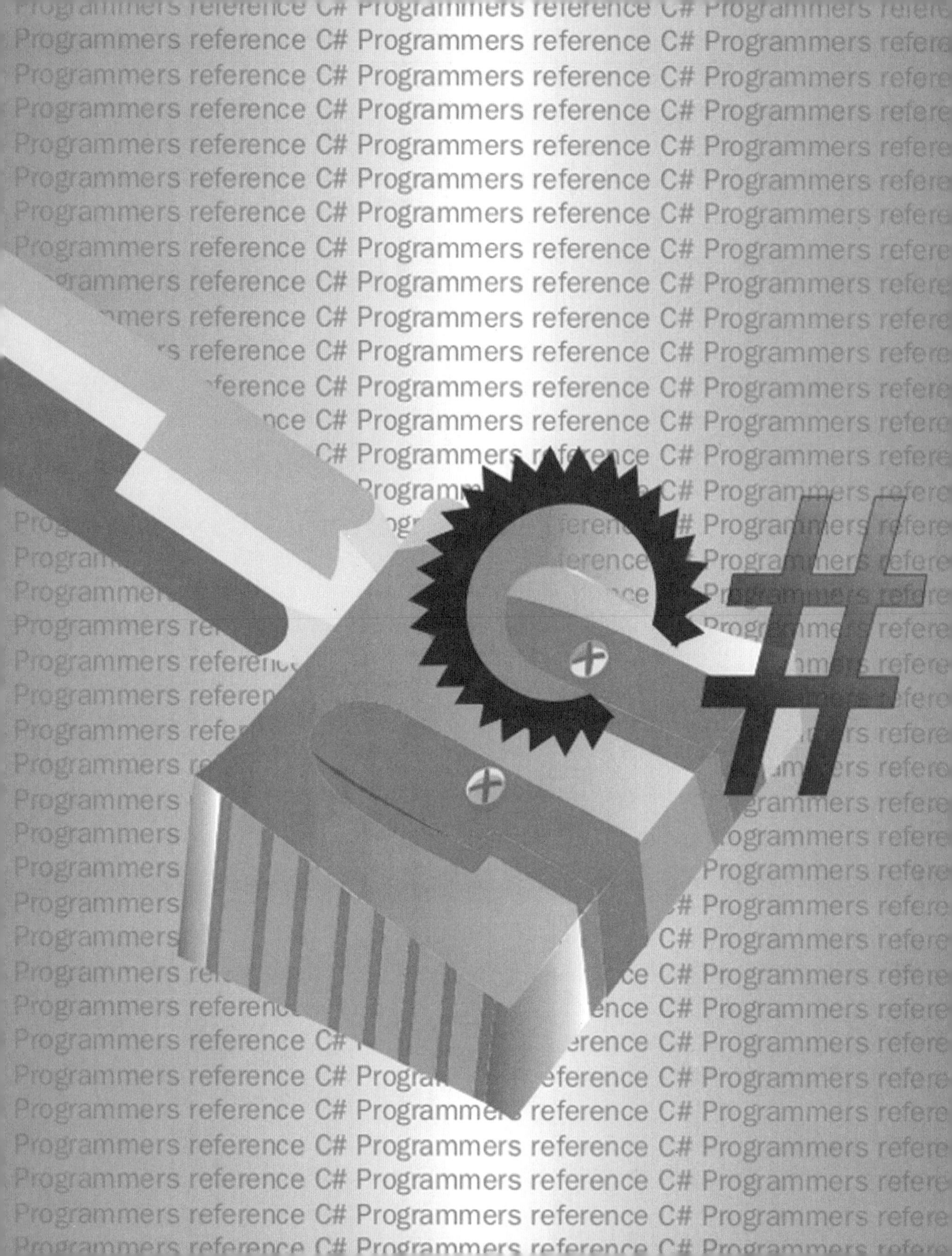
Programmers reference C#
C#

17

Unsafe code

Unsafe code is the rather scary term that's applied to the use of pointers in C#. The CLR goes to a lot of trouble to provide a secure system of memory allocation, access, and garbage collection, but by using pointers you can circumvent the system-provided checks and access and modify the contents of memory directly. If you have previous experience with C or C++, you're probably comfortable with the concept of pointers already – and with how they can get you into trouble if you're not careful!

In this chapter, we'll look at:

❑ Pointers and C#

❑ The sizeof operator

❑ Pointer arithmetic

❑ The unsafe and fixed keywords

❑ Stack arrays

Pointers and C#

By using a pointer, you can directly access a variable at its position in memory, rather than waiting for the runtime to retrieve the value on your behalf. This sounds like a great idea, but you have to remember that when you use pointers, you're circumventing .NET's rather nice system of memory management – there's nothing to prevent you from inadvertently corrupting the contents of memory.

The use of pointers is considered to be "unsafe" code in C#, and is discouraged in most cases. However, there are at least three valid reasons to use pointers in a C# program:

❑ Pointers allow you to access data in the most efficient way possible, and using them intelligently can give you a performance advantage.

❑ You may need to use pointers to make a C# program compatible with non-.NET code. For example, you may wish to incorporate some calls to Windows API functions in your code.

❑ Occasionally, there can be a need to make memory addresses available to the user – in a debugging application, perhaps.

Pointer syntax

If you're coming from a C or C++ background, you'll be familiar with pointer syntax. Every value type has a corresponding pointer type that's designated by the type name followed by an asterisk (*). The C# language does not allow explicit pointers to reference types, with the exception that pointers *can* be associated with a String or an array. For these types, the pointer will refer to the first character in the String, or to the first element in the array. A pointer can be used with a struct, as long as the struct in question doesn't contain any reference types.

The C# language defines three operators for dealing with pointers; they're the same as the operators used in C and C++.

Operator	Usage
*	Returns the value stored at the specified address. Sometimes known as the de-reference operator.
&	Returns the address of the specified variable. Sometimes known as the address-of operator.
->	A syntactic shortcut often used with structs. A->B is equivalent to (*A).B.

The unsafe keyword

Because of the pitfalls that can arise from using pointers, C# makes you jump through a couple of hoops before you can use them. Not only do you have to label any unsafe code as such in your code, but also you must tell the C# compiler that your program contains such code before it begins its work. Let's start by looking at the first of those.

The unsafe keyword can be applied to a class, a struct, a method, a field, or a block of code within a class or struct. We cannot, however, specify a local variable as being unsafe. If we want to define a pointer as a local variable, we need either to surround it with an unsafe block or to declare the method in which the pointer is declared as unsafe.

Example: The unsafe keyword

This example demonstrates how the value of a variable can be changed through a pointer to its address in memory. First, a 32-bit integer variable is declared and given an initial value. Then, an integer pointer is declared and assigned to the location in memory occupied by the integer, using the & operator. The integer pointer is then used to change the value of the integer variable, through the * operator. The entire Main() method is marked as unsafe.

```
using System;

public class PointerDemo
{
    public unsafe static void Main()
    {
        int I = 4;
        int* pI = &I;
```

```
        *pI = 2;
        Console.WriteLine("Value of I is {0}", I);
    }
  }
}
```

Output:

```
Value of I is 2
```

Actually, if you attempt to compile this example as you've done with the others in this book so far, it won't work. That's because you need to use the C# compiler's /unsafe option, which we'll discuss in the next section.

Compiling unsafe code

If you try to compile a program that contains unsafe code in the normal manner, you'll get an error. The reason for this is that you must explicitly inform the C# compiler if a program contains unsafe code. When compiling at the command line, you do this by specifying the /unsafe (or -unsafe) option:

```
csc /unsafe PointerDemo1a.cs
```

or:

```
csc -unsafe PointerDemo1a.cs
```

To do the same thing when you're using Visual Studio, you should go to the project's Property Pages dialog, select Configuration Properties | Build, and set Allow unsafe code blocks to True.

Example: Using the -> operator

This example illustrates how the -> operator can access the elements of a struct. In it, a struct named Gas is defined as having two data members, p and T. The PointerDemo class creates an instance of the Gas struct, and defines a static method named WriteContents() that takes a pointer to a Gas struct as an input argument. Inside the WriteContents() method, the -> pointer is used to access the values of the p and T fields. Since pointer syntax is used in both the Main() and WriteContents() methods, the entire PointerDemo class is declared unsafe.

```
using System;

public struct Gas
{
  internal double p;
  internal double T;

  public Gas(double p, double T)
  {
```

```
      this.p = p;
      this.T = T;
    }
  }

  public unsafe class PointerDemo
  {
    public static void Main()
    {
      Gas g = new Gas(101325.0, 300.0);
      WriteContents(&g);
    }

    public static void WriteContents(Gas* gas)
    {
      Console.WriteLine("p is {0}", gas->p);
      Console.WriteLine("T is {0}", gas->T);
    }
  }
```

Output:

```
p is 101325
T is 300
```

The fixed keyword

Generally speaking, when objects are stored on the heap, they may not reside at fixed memory locations during the lifetime of the program. As memory is allocated and de-allocated by the runtime, the garbage collector will move objects around in order to avoid memory fragmentation. This poses a problem if you want to create a pointer to a data member of a class – if an object is moved to a different memory location, a previously defined pointer will no longer point to it!

To solve this problem, the C# language provides the fixed keyword, which causes the memory location of a reference-type instance to be fixed while a block of code is executed. Syntactically, one or more pointer assignment statements are placed in parentheses between the fixed keyword and the block of code within which the location of the instance must not change. The use of fixed blocks can reduce performance, and so they should be employed sparingly.

Example: Using the fixed keyword

In this example, the FixedDemo class is defined as having a value-type data member, T. In the Main() method, an instance of the FixedDemo class is created, and a pointer is assigned to the T field of the instance. A pointer, pT, is then used to change the value of the field inside a fixed block that locks the memory location of the FixedDemo instance while this operation takes place.

```
using System;

public class FixedDemo
{
  double T;

  public FixedDemo(double T)
  {
    this.T = T;
  }

  public static void Main()
  {
    FixedDemo fd = new FixedDemo(300.0);

    unsafe
    {
      fixed(double* pT = &(fd.T))
      {
        *pT = 250.0;
      }
    }

    Console.WriteLine("Temperature is {0}", fd.T);
  }
}
```

Output:

```
Temperature is 250
```

As you can see, the assignment of the pT pointer takes place between the parentheses that follow the fixed keyword, while the value-changing statement is placed inside a block of code after the pointer assignment. If you didn't use the fixed keyword, this program wouldn't compile.

The sizeof operator

The sizeof operator returns the size of a value data type (including a struct) in bytes. To use it, the name of the data type is placed between parentheses after the sizeof keyword. The sizeof operator is used implicitly in pointer arithmetic (see the next section), and also for such things as determining I/O buffer sizes. The sizeof operator cannot be used on reference types, since their size is not fixed.

As an example, to display the size of a ulong, you can type:

```
Console.WriteLine("Size of ulong is {0} bytes", sizeof(ulong));
```

The output from this would be:

```
Size of ulong is 8 bytes
```

Pointer arithmetic

You can perform arithmetic operations on pointers using the +, =, +=, -=, ++, and – operators. These operators are always used to add or subtract integers from pointers... but they don't perform the 'standard' addition and subtraction that you'd get when working with integer value types.

Example: Using pointer arithmetic

In this example, we assign a String to a variable of type char* (pointer to char). As a result, the pointer *really* points to the first character in the String. The characters of the String are then written to the console using the * operator.

```
using System;

public class OpDemo
{
    public unsafe static void Main()
    {
        String str = "hello";

        fixed(char* pC = str)
        {
            for(int i = 0; i < str.Length; ++i)
            {
                Console.WriteLine("Element {0} is {1}", i, *(pC + i));
            }
        }
    }
}
```

Output:

```
Element 0 is h
Element 1 is e
Element 2 is l
Element 3 is l
Element 4 is o
```

Successive characters in the string are accessed using the *(pC + i) syntax. The entire operation is contained inside a fixed statement, and the Main() method is declared to be unsafe.

From the code listing, it looks as though we're adding successive integer values to the pointer (1, 2, 3...). In fact, when you add (say) 2 to a pointer, the compiler assumes that you want to refer to the memory location two places after the variable to which the pointer points. To put this more formally, if you have a pointer P of type T* and add a value N to it, the address of P will increase by the amount N times sizeof(T).

As well as the characters of a String, you can use pointer arithmetic to move a pointer through the elements of an array. The same technique is also useful for accessing values of a given type that are stored in successive memory locations. Pointer arithmetic operations are, however, prohibited on void pointers, which we'll discuss in the next section.

Casting pointers

Sometimes, it can be useful to cast a pointer to a value of some other type. Because of the unusual properties of pointers, we can identify two distinct groups of types that could find themselves the target of such an operation.

Casting pointers to integer types

A pointer stores an integer that represents an address in memory. As a result, a pointer can be cast to and from any integer type using the standard casting operator, (). One reason for wanting to do this would be to display a pointer value using `Console.Write()` and `Console.WriteLine()`. These methods don't provide an overloaded version that takes a pointer argument, but they do for integer values.

On 32-bit computer systems, an address takes up four bytes. Because of this, you should really only cast a pointer to a `UIntPtr`, a `long`, a `uint`, or a `ulong` (integer types that are at least four bytes in size). You shouldn't use a plain `int`, because while these are indeed four bytes long, their value range (-2.147e+9 to 2.147e+9) doesn't cover the entire possible range for a memory address (0 to 4.294e+9).

When C# is released for 64-bit processors, an address will require eight bytes. On such systems, a pointer should only be cast to a `ulong`.

Example: Casting pointers to integers

In this example, a pointer to an integer value is cast to a `uint`, and its value is displayed.

```
using System;

public class CastDemo
{
  public unsafe static void Main()
  {
    int I = 4;
    int* pI = &I;

    Console.WriteLine("Decimal value of pI is {0}", (uint)pI);
    Console.WriteLine("Hexadecimal value of pI is {0:X}", (uint)pI);
  }
}
```

Output:

```
Decimal value of pI is 1243476
Hexadecimal value of pI is 12F954
```

Casting pointers to other pointer types

Pointers can also be explicitly cast to other pointers. For example, to convert an `int` pointer to a `double` pointer, you might use this code:

```
int I = 4;
int* pI = &I;
double* pD = (double*)pI;
```

However, you have to be careful when performing operations like this. In the above example, if you tried to de-reference the value associated with pD:

```
double D = *pD;
Console.WriteLine("Value of D is {0}", D);
```

you would get this output (or something similar):

```
Value of d is 5.627206314-295
```

The value is garbage because the double pointer is looking at some memory that actually contains an integer but is treating it as if it were a double. In general, though, there can be good reasons for wanting to convert a pointer to another pointer type. For example, you may need to provide an argument to a Windows API method, or you might want to cast a pointer to an sbyte pointer in order to examine the individual bytes of memory.

void pointers

A void pointer is one that does not specify the type of data to which it points. That might not sound particularly useful, but it provides a way to pass values of all kinds between methods and functions – a technique that's often employed by the Windows API. To cast an int pointer to a void pointer, for example, you might use the following statement:

```
void* pV = (void*)pI;
```

Example: Calling external functions

To demonstrate the use of a void pointer, as well as a more practical example of how we might use pointers in C#, we'll call one of the functions from the Windows API. The VirtualQuery() function resides in kernel32.dll, and populates a struct with information about a location in virtual memory. In order to call functions from an external DLL, we need to define the function as an extern method, and use the DllImport attribute to specify the DLL that the function resides in. This attribute is defined in the System.Runtime.InteropServices namespace.

The VirtualQuery() function takes three parameters: a void pointer to the address that we want to get information about, a pointer to the struct that will be populated by the function, and a uint indicating the size of this struct:

```
using System;
using System.Runtime.InteropServices;

unsafe class WinApiDemo
{
    [DllImport("kernel32.dll")]
    public static extern uint VirtualQuery(void* pAddress,
                                   MemoryInfo* pBuff, uint Length);
```

We'll also need to define the struct, which has seven members:

- A void pointer to the base address of the range of pages that contain the address we want information about

- A void pointer to the base address of the allocated region in virtual memory

- A uint indicating the protection level applied when the region was originally allocated

- A uint indicating the size of the region

- A uint indicating the state of the memory – whether the memory is committed (physical memory has been allocated), free for allocation, or reserved (no physical memory has been allocated)

- A uint indicating the current protection level of the memory

- A uint indicating the type of the memory – whether it is private or mapped onto the view of a section

```
public struct MemoryInfo
{
  public void* pBaseAddress;
  public void* pAllocationBase;
  public uint AllocationProtect;
  public uint RegionSize;
  public uint State;
  public uint Protect;
  public uint Type;
}
```

Next, we'll define enums to give meaningful representations for the protection level, type, and state uints:

```
public enum Protection : uint
{
  NoAccess = 0x01,
  ReadOnly = 0x02,
  ReadWrite = 0x04,
  WriteCopy = 0x08,
  Execute = 0x10,
  ExecuteRead = 0x20,
  ExecuteReadWrite = 0x40,
  ExecuteWriteCopy = 0x80,
  Guard = 0x100,
  NoCache = 0x200,
  WriteCombine = 0x400
}

public enum MemoryState : uint
{
  Commit = 0x1000,
  Reserve = 0x2000,
```

```
    Decommit = 0x4000,
    Release = 0x8000,
    Free = 0x10000,
    Private = 0x20000,
    Mapped = 0x40000,
    Reset = 0x80000,
    TopDown = 0x100000,
    FourMbPages = 0x80000000
}
```

We can now call our `extern` method and display the results. We instantiate a new `MemInfo` struct, and retrieve a pointer to this to pass into the function. We also get a pointer to an `int` and cast this to `void*` to pass in as the address we want information about. Finally, we need to get the size of our `MemoryInfo` struct to use as the last parameter. When we call the function, our struct will be populated, and we display the information by printing out the values of the struct's fields, casting to a displayable representation as appropriate:

```
static void Main()
{
    // Define the arguments for the function call
    MemoryInfo memInfo = new MemoryInfo();
    MemoryInfo* pMemInfo = &memInfo;

    int i = 0;
    void* pAddress = (void*)&i;
    uint length = (uint)sizeof(MemoryInfo);

    // Call the extern method
    uint result = VirtualQuery(pAddress, pMemInfo, length);

    // Print out the results
    Console.WriteLine("Stats for address {0}", (uint)pAddress);
    Console.WriteLine("============================");
    Console.WriteLine("Base Address = {0}", (uint)memInfo.pBaseAddress);
    Console.WriteLine("Allocation Base = {0}",
                     (uint)memInfo.pAllocationBase);
    Console.WriteLine("Allocation Protection = {0}",
                     (Protection)memInfo.AllocationProtect);
    Console.WriteLine("Region Size = {0}", memInfo.RegionSize);
    Console.WriteLine("State = {0}", (MemoryState)memInfo.State);
    Console.WriteLine("Protection = {0}", (Protection)memInfo.Protect);
    Console.WriteLine("Type = {0}", (MemoryState)memInfo.Type);
}
}
```

Output (this may vary):

```
Stats for address 1243300
============================
Base Address = 1241088
```

```
Allocation Base = 196608
Allocation Protection = ReadWrite
Region Size = 4096
State = Commit
Protection = ReadWrite
Type = Private
```

Stack arrays

In C#, arrays are treated as objects. The good news is that as reference types, arrays have access to bounds checking and other features provided by the runtime. The bad news is that they suffer from the performance penalty that results from being stored on the heap.

Using pointers and the `stackalloc` keyword, it's possible to define temporary, one-dimensional arrays that are stored on the stack, improving code performance at the expense of the features we talked about above. Stack-based arrays are treated as local variables, and exist only for as long as the method in which they are defined.

Stack arrays are declared using the `stackalloc` keyword, rather than the `new` keyword. The left-hand side of the statement will consist of a pointer declaration and the array name, while the right-hand side consists of the `stackalloc` keyword, the type, and the size of the array. The size of the array can be evaluated at runtime, meaning that another variable can be used to define the size if required.

```
<type>* <array_name> = stackalloc <type>[<size>];
```

What the above statement does is to allocate a certain amount of memory on the stack. The pointer that's returned by `stackalloc` points to the beginning of the memory that was allocated; the total memory allocated will be equal to `size` times `sizeof(type)`. Following the rules of pointer arithmetic, to access the value of the first element in the array, you would use this syntax:

```
*(array_name)
```

To access the value of the second element in the array, you would use this syntax:

```
*(array_name + 1)
```

And so on. You can also make use of the index operator (`[ ]`) to access the elements of the array.

Example: Creating a stack array

This example demonstrates the basics of creating a stack-based array and accessing the values of its elements. An integer array of size 5 is created on the stack, and values are assigned to its elements using the * operator. The values are then accessed using the index operator.

```
using System;

public class StackDemo
{
```

199

```
public static void Main()
{
  int size = 5;

  // Create a stack-based array
  unsafe
  {
    int* intArray = stackalloc int[size];

    // Assign values to the array elements
    for(int i = 0; i < size; ++i)
      *(intArray + i) = i * i;

    // Write out the array elements using the indexer
    for(int i = 0; i < size; ++i)
      Console.WriteLine("Element {0} is {1}", i, intArray[i]);
  }
}
}
```

Output:

```
0
1
4
9
16
```

Summary

In this chapter, we examined how pointers are implemented in the C# language through special pointer syntax, along with the unsafe and fixed keywords. We looked at the operators that can be used on pointers, at pointer arithmetic, and at the sizeof operator that returns the size of a value type in bytes. Next, we saw how pointers can be cast to integer values, or to other pointer types, including the void pointer. Finally, we discussed how the stackalloc keyword can be used to create arrays that are stored on the stack rather than the heap, for better performance at the expense of run-time facilities.

Programmers reference C# Programmers reference C# Programmers reference
C#

18

Attributes

An attribute is a marker that provides the C# compiler with additional information about a code element. Attributes can be applied to any code element (class, constructor, delegate, field, etc.) or they can be applied to a program as a whole. Unlike the preprocessor directives described in Chapter 19, attributes are part of the .NET Framework and are represented by classes.

Attributes are also used to provide metadata for a code element. The metadata can be accessed at runtime via reflection or by using some other tool that reads the metadata. In addition to the built-in attributes provided in the .NET Framework libraries, you can develop your own custom attributes. All attributes, whether they're built-in or user-defined attributes, will derive either directly or indirectly from the System.Attribute class.

In this chapter we'll look at:

- ❑ Applying an attribute to a code element
- ❑ Predefined attributes
- ❑ Conditional compiling with attributes
- ❑ User-defined attributes
- ❑ Exposing attributes using reflection

Applying an attribute to a code element

An attribute is applied to a code element by placing an attribute statement before the code element. The attribute name is placed inside square brackets ([ ]). Any input arguments required by the attribute are placed inside parentheses after the attribute name. More than one attribute can be associated with a given code element. Each attribute is placed inside its own set of square brackets. Instances of a multi-instance attribute appear within the same brackets.

The naming convention for attribute classes is that the class name ends with "Attribute". When applying the attributes, the "Attribute" ending is optional. You can use "Serializable" or "SerializableAttribute" for example. The types of code elements to which an attribute can be applied depend on the definition of the attribute class. For instance, the ContextStatic attribute can only be applied to a field. The Debuggable attribute can be applied to an assembly or module.

Every attribute class in the .NET Framework has an `AttributeUsage` attribute associated with it. The `AttributeUsage` attribute includes one or more members of the `AttributeTargets` enumeration that define the attribute usage.

Example: Applying attributes

In this example, two attributes are applied to a method named `DoSomeStuff()`. The `Conditional` attribute, contained in the `System.Diagnostics` namespace, represents a conditional compilation instruction to the compiler. If `WIN95` is defined using the `#define` preprocessor statement, the `DoSomeStuff()` method will be compiled. Otherwise, the compiler will ignore the method. This process is called conditional compiling and is described in more detail later in this chapter.

The second attribute applied to the `DoSomeStuff()` method is the `Obsolete` attribute. This attribute is a tag that indicates that the method is obsolete. The `Obsolete` attribute causes a warning message when the method is compiled. There are three overloaded versions of this attribute. You can provide your own warning string as an input argument to the attribute. You can also set the attribute so an error is thrown instead of a warning.

```
#define WIN95

using System;
using System.Diagnostics;

public class BasicAttribDemo
{

  [Conditional("WIN95")]
  [Obsolete()]
  public void DoSomeStuff()
  {
    Console.WriteLine("Perform some Win95-specific task");
  }

  public static void Main()
  {
    BasicAttribDemo ad = new BasicAttribDemo();

    ad.DoSomeStuff();
  }
}
```

Output:

When the program is compiled you will get the warning message:

```
BasicAttribDemo.cs(17,7): warning CS0612: 'BasicAttribDemo.DoSomeStuff()' is
obsolete
```

When you run the program, the following is displayed

```
Perform some Win95-specific task
```

Predefined attributes

The .NET Framework contains a large number of predefined attribute classes. Here are the signatures for a few of the attribute classes defined in the System namespace.

```
[AttributeUsage(AttributeTargets.Class)]
[Serializable]
public sealed class AttributeUsageAttribute : Attribute

[AttributeUsage(AttributeTargets.Any)]
[Serializable]
public sealed class CLSCompliantAttribute : Attribute

[AttributeUsage(AttributeTargets.Field)]
[Serializable]
public sealed class ContextStaticAttribute : Attribute

[AttributeUsage(AttributeTargets.Enum)]
[Serializable]
public sealed class FlagsAttribute : Attribute
```

One thing you will notice is that each of these attribute classes has two attributes associated with it. The first, the Attributeusage attribute, indicates the types of code elements to which the attribute can be applied. For example, a ContextStaticAttribute class can only be applied to fields. A CLSCompliantAttribute can be applied to any code element. An interesting note is that an AttributeUsage attribute class is applied to the AttributeUsageAttribute class. The second attribute applied to each of these classes is the Serializable attribute. This marks the attribute class as being serializable. An instance of a type that is serializable can be saved (to disk, for instance) and restored.

For an example of predefined attributes, see the example in the section where the Conditional and Obsolete attributes are applied to a method.

Conditional compiling with attributes

The example in the section made use of the Conditional attribute. When the Conditional attribute is applied to a method, the compiler will evaluate a condition before compiling the method. If the condition is not met, the method and any statements that refer to the method will not be compiled. The method to which the Conditional attribute is applied must have a return type of void.

The Conditional attribute can be used to define different versions of an application within the same code listing. The condition associated with the attribute will generally evaluate whether a preprocessor variable has been defined in the code listing.

For example, if the "DEBUG" preprocessor variable has been defined, methods and method calls associated with the "debug" version of the code will be activated.

Use of the Conditional attribute is one way to achieve conditional compiling. The other way is via the #if, #elif, and #else preprocessor directives described in Chapter 19. The advantage to using preprocessor directives is that their conditions can contain logical expressions and they can be applied to any arbitrary section of code. The advantage of using the Conditional attribute is that it will not only affect the method, but also apply to any other reference to the method in the code listing.

Example: Conditional compilation

In this example, the Conditional attribute is used to define a "standard" and "professional" version of a program. The CondDemo class defines two methods. The StandardStuff() method performs some process that is common to both the standard and professional versions. If a customer has purchased the professional version, that customer is also to have access to some additional capability provided by the ProStuff() method.

The Conditional attribute is applied to the ProStuff() method. If the PROFESSIONAL preprocessor variable is defined at the top of the code listing, the ProStuff() method and the call to the ProStuff() method are compiled. If the PROFESSIONAL variable is not defined, the method and the method call are ignored.

```
#define PROFESSIONAL

using System;
using System.Diagnostics;

public class CondDemo
{
  public void StandardStuff()
  {
    Console.WriteLine("Perform some standard-version task");
  }

  [Conditional("PROFESSIONAL")]
  private void ProStuff()
  {
    Console.WriteLine("Perform some professional-version task");
  }

  public static void Main()
  {
    CondDemo cd = new CondDemo();
    cd.StandardStuff();
    cd.ProStuff();
  }
}
```

Output:

```
Perform some standard-version stuff
Perform some professional-version stuff
```

User-defined attributes

If the predefined attribute classes defined in the .NET Framework libraries are not sufficient for your needs, you can define your own attribute classes. As far as the compiler and runtime are concerned, user-defined attributes are for informational purposes only. They will have no effect on how code is compiled. A user-defined attribute class should derive either from the Attribute class or from a derived class of Attribute. The class should have an AttributeUsage attribute associated with it.

The AttributeUsageAttribute class constructor has the form:

```
[AttributeUsage(AttributeTargets.Class)]
[Serializable]
public AttributeUsageAttribute(AttributeTargets validOn, AllowMultiple=mult,
Inherited=inh)
```

The AllowMultiple and Inherited parameters are optional and are given true or false values. The AllowMultiple variable is a property of the AttributeUsageAttribute class. If it is true, more than one instance of the AttributeUsage attribute can be assigned to a code element. The default value is false. The Inherited variable is also a property of the AttributeUsageAttribute class. If it is true, the AttributeUsage attribute will be inherited by derived classes. The default value is true.

The AttributeTargets enumeration defines the usage limitations for the attribute. The elements of the enumeration are All, Assembly, Class, Constructor, Delegate, Enum, Event, Field, Interface, Method, Module, Parameter, Property, ReturnValue, and Struct. If you want your property available to any code element, specify All. You can specify two or more AttributeTargets enumeration elements by using the bitwise OR operator, "|".

Other than having an AttributeUsage attribute associated with it, a user-defined attribute class is like any other class. You can apply other attributes to the class. The attribute class will have data members and at least one constructor to initialize the data members. User-defined attributes are applied to code elements just like a built-in attribute. The attribute statement is placed before the code element to which the attribute will be applied.

Example: User-defined attributes

The UsageAttribute class is used to provide information about the usage of a delegate, interface, or method. The AttributeUsage attribute associated with the class defines the usage of the Usage attribute and allows for multiple Usage attributes to be associated with a given code element. The UsageAttribute class has one data member, a String containing a description of how the method is used. The class also defines a property for accessing the data member.

207

```
using System;

[AttributeUsage(AttributeTargets.Delegate |
AttributeTargets.Interface | AttributeTargets.Method,
AllowMultiple=true)]
public class UsageAttribute : Attribute
{
  private String desc;

  public UsageAttribute(String desc)
  {
    this.desc = desc;
  }

  public String Desc
  {
    get
    {
      return desc;
    }
  }
}
```

Notes:

Compile this program into a library file using the syntax:

csc /t:library UsageAttribute.cs

We'll use the UsageAttribute class in the next section.

Exposing attributes using reflection

Reflection is a way to investigate the contents of a library or executable file without looking at the original code listing. One of the things reflection allows you to do is to expose the metadata contained in attributes associated with code elements of a program. To make use of this feature, you will need to use the classes defined in the System.Reflection namespace. The main elements of this namespace are covered in Chapter 25.

The Assembly class encapsulates a reusable, versionable, and self-describing entity known as an assembly. A "dll" or "exe" file can be considered an assembly. The static GetTypes() method defined in the Assembly class can return an array of Type objects representing the types defined in the assembly. A Type object provides access to information about the constructors, methods, properties, and so on defined in the type.

The GetCustomAttributes() method can return an array consisting of the custom attributes defined for a given type or type element. This is a static method defined in the Attribute, Assembly, MemberInfo, Module, and ParameterInfo classes. The Attribute class also defines the GetCustomAttribute() method that returns a custom attribute of a given type.

Example: Exposing attributes using reflection

In this example, we will apply the `UsageAttribute` class we defined in the previous section. The `Air` class encapsulates the thermodynamic properties of air. A gas mixture has a pressure, temperature, and density associated with it. The three variables are mutually dependent. You can calculate the density, for instance, if you know the pressure and temperature.

The `Air` class defines the `GetDensity()` method to compute the density of air. The method has a `Usage` attribute associated with it. This attribute provides a description of the `GetDensity()` method.

```csharp
using System;

public class Air
{
   private double p,t;

   public Air(double p, double t)
   {
     this.p = p;
     this.t = t;
   }

   //=============================================
   //  These properties return the value of the
   //  p and t fields.
   //=============================================
   public double P
   {
     get {return p;}
   }

   public double T
   {
     get {return t;}
   }

   //=================================================
   //  The GetDensity() method has a Usage attribute
   //  associated with it.
   //=================================================

   [Usage("Computes the density of air")]
   public double GetDensity()
   {
     return p*0.02885/(8.3144*t);
   }
}
```

As we did with the `UsageAttribute` class, the `Air` class is contained in a separate file and is compiled as a library using the syntax:

```
csc /t:library /r:UsageAttribute.dll Air.cs
```

We next define a program that will look inside an assembly and print out the names and return types of the methods for every type defined in the assembly. The program also checks to see if any of the methods have `Usage` attributes attached to them. If any method does, the `String` associated with the `Usage` attribute is printed. This program is compiled with the syntax:

```
csc /r:UsageAttribute.dll ReflDemo.cs
```

```csharp
using System;
using System.Reflection;

public class ReflDemo
{
  public static void Main()
  {

    //=======================================================
    //  Load the assembly corresponding to the Air.dll
    //  file and extract the types defined in the file.
    //=======================================================

    Assembly assembly = Assembly.Load("Air");
    Type[] types = assembly.GetTypes();

    //=============================================================
    //  Go through each type in the assembly and extract a
    //  MethodInfo object for each method defined in each type.
    //=============================================================

    foreach (Type type in types)
    {
      Console.WriteLine("Methods defined in "+type.Name+"\n");
      MethodInfo[] methods = type.GetMethods();

      //=============================================================
      //  The GetCustomAttributes() method returns any Usage
      //  attributes associated with a method. The method name
      //  and return type are printed. If there are any Usage
      //  attributes, the descriptive String associated with the
      //  attribute is also printed.
      //=============================================================

      foreach (MethodInfo method in methods)
      {
        object[] attributes = method.GetCustomAttributes(
                        typeof(UsageAttribute), false);
```

```
              Console.WriteLine("  "+method.ReturnType+" "+method.Name+"()");
              foreach ( UsageAttribute att in attributes )
              {
                Console.WriteLine("        Description: "+att.Desc);
              }
              Console.WriteLine();
          }
      }
    }
  }
```

Output:

```
Methods defined in Air

System.Int32 GetHashCode()
System.Boolean Equals()
System.String ToString()
System.Double get_P()
System.Double get_T()

System.Double GetDensity()
     Description:  Computes the density of air

System.Type GetType()
```

Summary

In this chapter we covered attributes: markers used by the C# language to give the compiler additional information about a code element. The syntax for applying an attribute to a code element was outlined. We learned about predefined and user-defined attributes. We detailed how attributes can be used for conditional compiling and how they can be exposed via reflection.

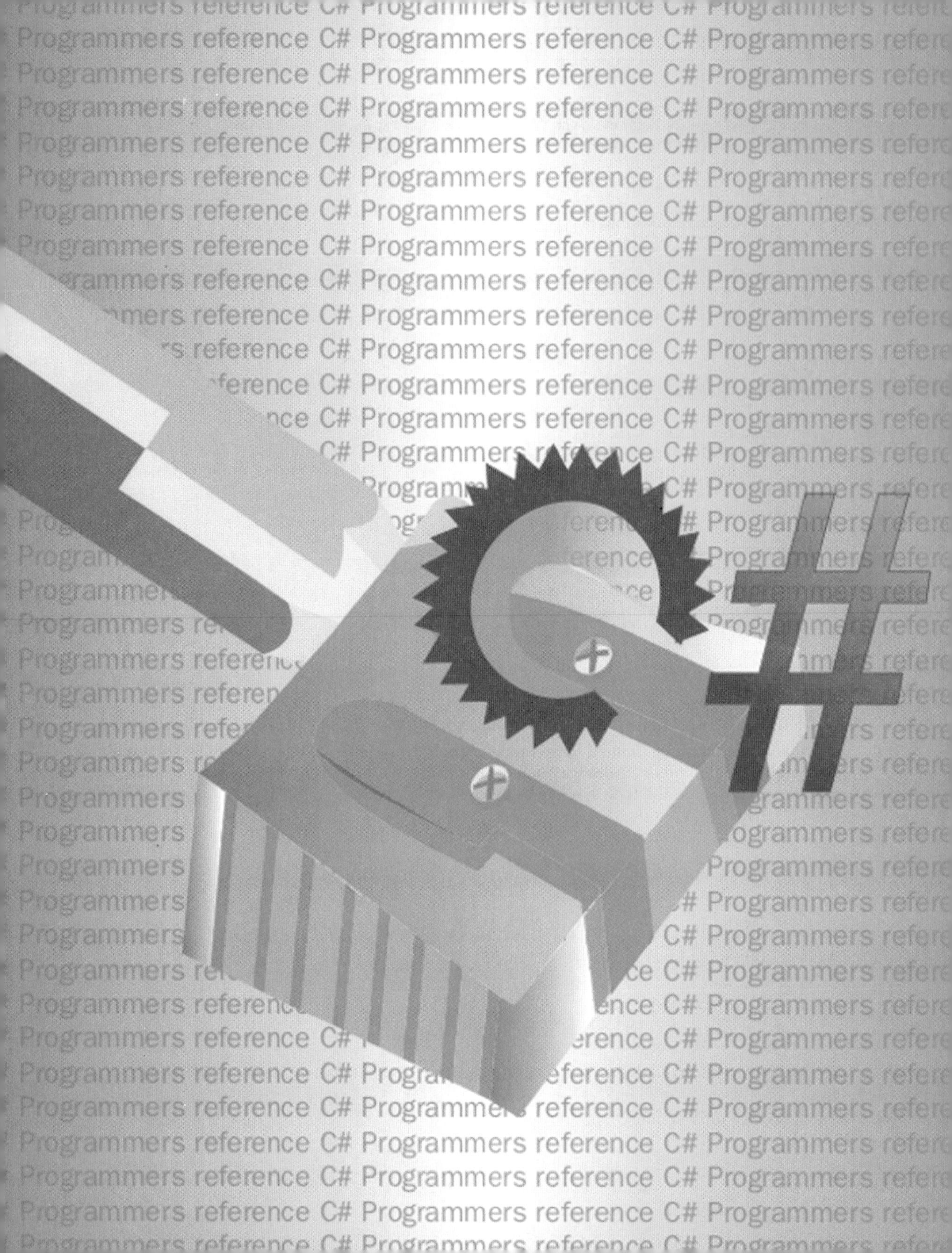
Programmers reference C#

19

Preprocessor directives

Preprocessor directives are program statements that provide the compiler with instructions on how to compile the code. They are not, strictly speaking, executable statements. For that matter, C# actually doesn't use a separate preprocessor. The preprocessor directives are handled by the compiler. They are mainly included in the C# language as a convenience for those with a C or C++ background who want to continue to use preprocessor directives in their C# programs.

One use for preprocessor directives is to enable conditional compilation, where sections of a program may only be compiled if a preprocessor variable has been defined. This allows you to develop different versions of an application within the same code listing. This is an alternative to conditional compiling using attributes that was described in Chapter 18. Preprocessor directives can do other useful things such as provide warning statements when the program is compiled or tag certain blocks of code within a program.

There are many developers who consider preprocessor directives archaic with no place in a modern programming language. Whether you agree with this or not, care should be exercised when using them. Overuse of preprocessor directives can lead to code that is difficult to read, and if misused they can do things such as inadvertently make portions of source code write-only.

Preprocessor directives

The following is a listing of the C# preprocessor directives and a brief description of what they do. When they are used in a program, preprocessor directives are not terminated by semicolons, or any other punctuation mark.

Directive	Description
#define	Defines a preprocessor variable. This statement is placed at the top of a source file before any executable statements. Once a preprocessor variable is defined it is available throughout the rest of the source file.
#undef	Undefines a preprocessor variable. The variable will no longer be recognized inside the program. As with the #define statement, an #undef statement is placed at the top of a source file.

Directive	Description
#if	Conditional `if` statement. The condition following the `#if` is evaluated. If the condition is met, the subsequent lines of code are executed. The preprocessor conditional statements allow you to customize the compilation of a program based on the definition of preprocessor variables. This process is called conditional compilation. For example: ``` #if DEMO // demo version code #elif STANDARD // standard version code #else // professional version code #endif ``` You can use the `==`, `!=`, `!`, `&&`, and `||` operators as part of the condition to be evaluated. The conditions can be placed inside parentheses to isolate them if you wish. ``` #if STANDARD && (DEBUG == false) ``` You can nest `#if`, `#if-#else`, or `#if-#elif-#else` statements.
#elif	The preprocessor version of the conditional `else if` statement. As with the `#if` statement, you can use the `==`, `!=`, `!`, `&&`, and `||` operators as part of the condition to be evaluated. The conditions can be placed inside parentheses to isolate them if you wish.
#else	The "else" in an `if-else` conditional statement. The code following this statement is executed if the preceding conditions are not met.
#endif	Terminates an `#if`, `#if-#else`, or `#if-#elif-#else` conditional statement.
#region	Places a name on, or marks, a region of code. Marked regions are used by some editors, Visual Studio .NET for instance, to display the marked region of code on the screen.
#endregion	Used in conjunction with the `#region` directive to indicate the end of a marked region of code.
#line	The `#line` directive lets you pin a line number to a given line. This directive is most commonly used as a meta-language that "compiles" to C# as an intermediate language. For debugging purposes, it's easier to associate code to the lines of the original source rather than the intermediate one.
#line default	Used after a `#line` statement to return to the default line numbering.
#error	Causes an error to be displayed when the code is compiled and the compilation is terminated. One use of the `#error` directive is to prevent a preprocessor directive conflict. ``` #if DEMO && STANDARD #error "DEMO and STANDARD cannot be defined simultaneously" #endif ```

Directive	Description
`#warning`	Causes a warning to be displayed when the program is compiled. This is generally used to remind the developer of something concerning the program.

```
#if DEBUG
    #warning "Debug mode is on"
#endif
```

Example: Preprocessor directives

This example shows some of the preprocessor directives in action. It demonstrates a common situation where one program actually represents three different versions of an application. At the top of the code listing are defined two preprocessor variables. The first indicates whether the debug parts of the code are active. The second identifies the program as the demo, standard, or professional version.

A little later in the program, the `DoSomeStuff()` method is defined. An `#if-#endif` statement contains a `#warning` directive. This reminds the developer if the debug option is active. You would want to be sure to turn off the annoying diagnostic messages before shipping the application to customers. An `#if-#elif-#else` conditional statement compiles different versions of the code depending on which preprocessor variable is defined. Inside the `Main()` method is an example of defining a region; in this case, it surrounds the `DoSomeStuff()` method call.

This example essentially does the same thing as the example in the *Conditional compiling with attributes* section of Chapter 18 in that it defines different code versions. In the Chapter 18 example, attributes were used. In this example, preprocessor directives are used.

```
#define DEBUG
#define DEMO

using System;

public class PPDemo
{
  public void DoSomeStuff()
  {

    #if DEBUG
      #warning "Debug mode is on"
    #endif

    #if DEMO
      Console.WriteLine("Demo version code");
    #elif STANDARD
      Console.WriteLine("Standard version code");
    #else
      Console.WriteLine("Professional version code");
    #endif
```

```
      }

   public static void Main()
   {
     PPDemo ppd = new PPDemo();

     #region DoSomeStuff Call
       ppd.DoSomeStuff();
     #endregion
   }
}
```

Output:

When you compile this program you will get the message:

```
PPDemo.cs(13,22): warning CS1030: #warning: '"Debug mode is on"'
```

This is the output when the code is executed.

```
Demo version code
```

Summary

In this chapter we learned about the preprocessor directives available in the C# language. We learned what each of them does and how they can be used to perform conditional compilation and other activities.

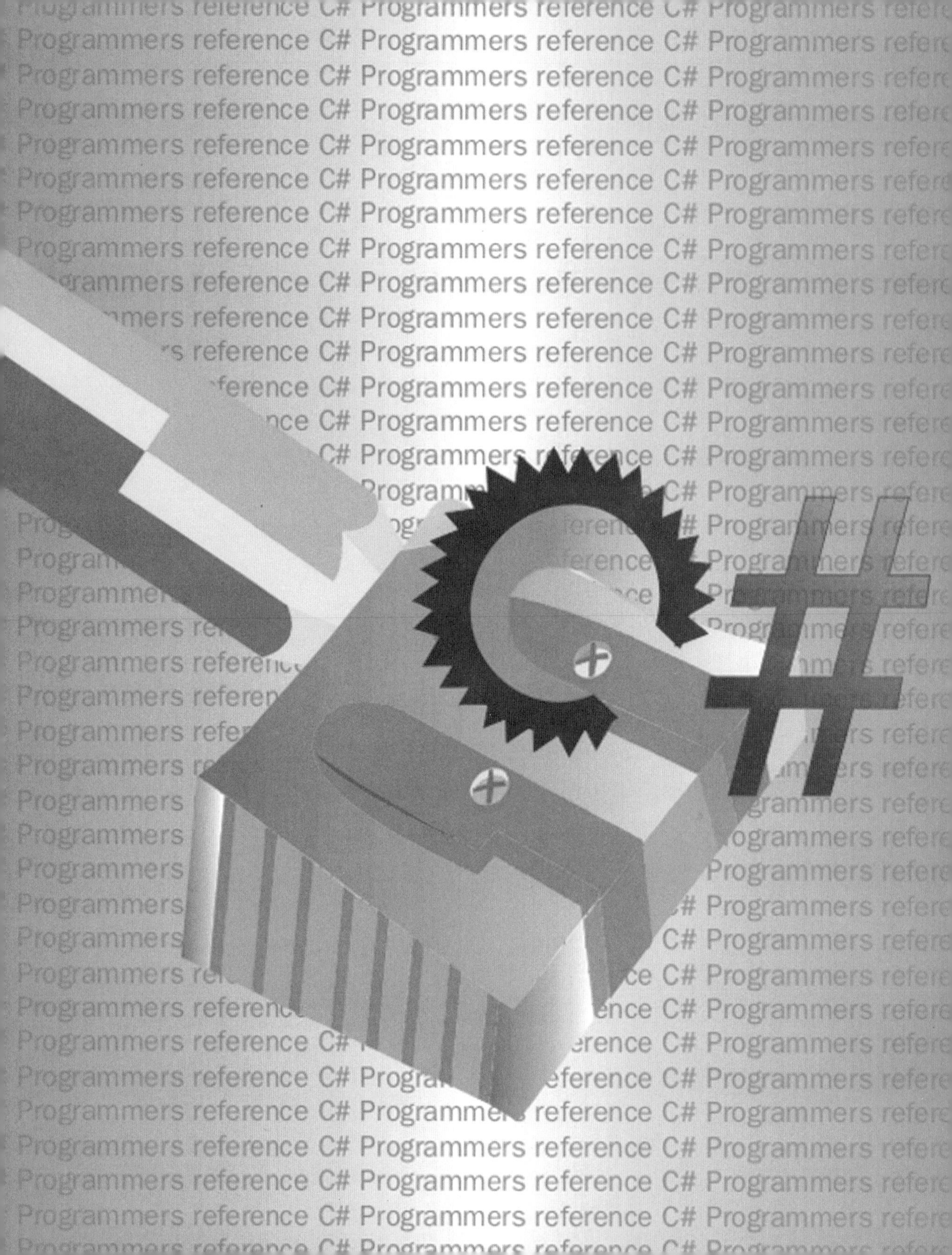
Programmers reference C#
C#

20

XML documentation

The C# language supports three types of comment statements. The first two are the "standard" comment types used in C, C++, and Java. The `//` syntax precedes a single-line comment. A multi-line comment starts with the characters `/*` and ends with the characters `*/`. The standard-type comments can be examined in the source code listing only.

C# supports a third type of comment statement with a very useful feature. The `///` syntax denotes a single-line comment that can be incorporated into an XML document when the program is compiled. These comments are called XML documentation comments. Unlike standard comments, documentation comments can be viewed external to the source code listing by processing the XML file in which they are placed.

In this chapter we'll look at:

❑ Creating XML documentation comments

❑ Extracting an XML documentation file

Creating XML documentation comments

Documentation comments start with `///` and contain one line of text. They can define a standard plain-text comment, but documentation comments can also have XML tags embedded in them. XML tags specify information about the types and type members in a program. The following predefined XML tags can be incorporated into documentation comments. Note that any tag that ends in `"/>"` does not have a corresponding closing tag. For example, there is no `</include>` tag. We'll take a look at these comments in use in the example later in this chapter.

Tag	Description
`<c>`	Marks the text within a single line of a description as code. The text would be placed between the `<c>` tag and the `</c>` tag.
`<code>`	Marks multiple lines of text in a description as code.
`<example>`	Typically contains the `<c>` and/or `<code>` tags and lets you specify an example of how to use a method or other library member.

Table continued on following page

Tag	Description
`<exception [cref="type"]>`	Describes the exceptions a method might throw. The optional `cref` attribute specifies the exception type. The type name must be enclosed in double quotes.
`<include file='filename' path='tagpath [@name="id"]'/>`	Includes comments from another documentation file that describe the types and members in the current source code. The `filename` is the name of the file containing the documentation and is enclosed in single quotation marks. The `tagpath` is the path of the tags in `filename` that leads to the tag `name`. The `name` will have an `id` for the tag that precedes the comments.
`<list type="bullet" | "number" | "table">`	Inserts a list into the documentation. The list may include `<listheader>` and `<item>` tags, each of which then contain `<term>` and `<description>` elements. The `type` indicates whether it will be a bulleted list, a numbered list, or a table. The `<listheader>` tag defines the heading row of a table. The `<item>` tag defines an item in the list.
`<para>`	Defines a paragraph within a tag such as a `<remarks>` or `<returns>` tag.
`<param name='name'>`	Defines a description of a method parameter. The `name` attribute is required. It represents the name of the parameter and must be enclosed in single quotes. If you apply the `<param>` tag to one parameter of a method you must apply a `<param>` tag to all the parameters. The description of the parameter will lie between the opening and closing `<param ...>` tags.
`<paramref name="name"/>`	Marks a word as being a method parameter. The XML file can be processed to format this parameter in some specified way.
`<permission [cref="type."]>`	Describes the access permission of a member. The optional `cref` attribute indicates the type that represents the set of permissions given to the member. The type name must be enclosed in double quotes. The text after the `<permission>` tag describes the permission given to the member.
`<remarks>`	Allows you to specify overview information about a class or type.
`<returns>`	Details the return value of a method.
`<see cref="reference"/>`	Provides a cross-reference to another code element. The `reference` is a member or field available to the current compilation environment and must be enclosed in double quotes. The `<see>` tag lets you specify a link from within the text.
`<seealso cref="reference"/>`	Similar to the `<see>` tag except the `<seealso>` tag creates a separate "see also" section in a description.
`<summary>`	Provides a short summary of a member of a type. The `<remarks>` tag is used to provide information about the type itself.
`<value>`	Gives you the ability to add a description to a property.

The compiler will verify the syntax of an `<exception>`, `<include>`, `<param>`, `<paramref>`, `<permission>`, `<see>`, or `<seealso>` tag. The compiler will also expand any references to (names of) code elements into fully qualified type IDs. The first part of the ID string identifies the type of member. The letter 'N' is for namespace, 'T' is for type, 'F' is for field, 'M' is for method, 'P' is for parameter, and 'E' is for event.

The second part of the ID string is the fully qualified name of the element including the namespace, type, and name of the item, separated by periods. Any periods in the name of the item are replaced by the hash sign, '#'. If a method or property has a parameter list, the elements of the list are included inside parentheses. If there are no parameters, there are no parentheses.

For example, in the next section there is an example that defines a class named DocCommentDemo in a namespace named CSharpProgRef. The fully qualified IDs for the namespace and class are.

```
N:CSharpProgRef
T:CSharpProgRef.DocCommentDemo
```

The DocCommentDemo class defines a Main() method that takes no arguments. It also defines a GetAirDensity() method that takes two doubles as arguments. The IDs for these methods are

```
M:CSharpProgRef.DocCommentDemo.Main
M:CSharpProgRef.DocCommentDemo.GetAirDensity(System.Double,System.Double)
```

Along with the predefined XML tags, you can also incorporate user-defined tags into your documentation comments; however, the compiler won't perform any consistency checks on a user-defined tag, and they will be brought into the XML documentation file verbatim.

We'll see an example in the next section where documentation comments with built-in and user-defined XML tags are embedded inside a code listing.

Extracting an XML documentation file

An XML documentation file is generated by the compiler when the following compile option is used:

/doc:<filename>

A skeleton XML file containing <?xml>, <doc>, and <members> tags will be generated automatically. The name of the assembly in which the type resides is indicated by <assembly> and <name> tags. Every code element preceded by a documentation comment in the code listing will be described in the XML file with a <member> tag. Any other pre- or used-defined XML tags embedded in documentation comments will also be translated into the XML file.

Example: Creating an XML documentation file

The CSharpProgRef namespace contains two classes. The DocCommentDemo class defines the static GetAirDensity() method that computes the density of air based on its pressure and temperature. The Main() method calls GetAirDensity() and prints the results to the console. Documentation comments are placed before the DocCommentDemo, Main(), and GetAirDensity() code listings.

```
using System;

namespace CSharpProgRef
```

```
{
   /// <remarks>
   /// The DocCommentDemo class shows document comments
   /// in action.
   /// </remarks>
   public class DocCommentDemo
   {
      /// <summary>
      /// The Main() method simply calls the GetAirDensity()
      /// method and prints out the result
      /// </summary>
      public static void Main()
      {
         Console.WriteLine("density is {0}",GetAirDensity(101325.0, 300.0));
      }

      ///<summary>
      /// The GetAirDensity() method computes and returns the
      /// density of air based on its temperature and pressure
      /// The molecular weight of air is 0.02885 kg/mole.
      /// The <paramref name="p"/> parameter is the pressure.
      /// </summary>
      ///
      /// <param name="p"> pressure in N/m^2 </param>
      /// <param name="T"> temperature in K </param>
      /// <returns> density in kg/m^3 </returns>
      /// <permission cref="System.Security.PermissionSet"> public access
                                                        </permission>
      public static double GetAirDensity(double p, double T)
      {
         return p*0.02885/(8.3144*T);
      }
   }
}
```

The second class defined in the `CSharpProgRef` namespace is named N2. This class uses the `<include>` tag to reference documentation comments contained in another file.

```
///<include file='species.txt' path='SpcDocs/SpeciesTags[@name="N2"]/*'/>
class N2
{
   string name;

   public N2(string str)
   {
      name = str;
   }
}
```

Here are the contents of the species.txt file.

```
<SpcDocs>

<SpeciesTags name="N2">
<remarks> This is data for diatomic nitrogen </remarks>
</SpeciesTags>

</SpcDocs>
```

The DocCommentDemo and SpcDocs classes are contained in a file named DocCommentDemo.cs. This file is compiled using the syntax:

```
csc /doc:DocCommentDemo.xml DocCommentDemo.cs
```

Output:

```
density is 1.17195317761955
```

When the DocCommentDemo.cs code is compiled using the above syntax, a file named DocCommentDemo.xml is created. The listing of this file is given below. Notice the fully qualified ID string for the code element in each <member> tag.

```
<?xml version="1.0"?>
<doc>
  <assembly>
    <name>DocCommentDemo</name>
  </assembly>
  <members>
    <member name="T:CSharpProgRef.DocCommentDemo">
      <remarks>
        The DocCommentDemo class shows document comments
        in action.
      </remarks>
    </member>
    <member name="M:CSharpProgRef.DocCommentDemo.Main">
      <summary>
        The Main() method simply calls the GetAirDensity()
        method and prints out the result
      </summary>
    </member>
    <member name="M:CSharpProgRef.DocCommentDemo.GetAirDensity
                                      (System.Double,System.Double)">
      <summary>
        The GetAirDensity() method computes and returns the
        density of air based on its temperature and pressure
        The molecular weight of air is 0.02885 kg/mole.
        The <paramref name="p"/> parameter is the pressure.
      </summary>
```

```
                <param name="p"> pressure in N/m^2 </param>
                <param name="T"> temperature in K </param>
                <returns> density in kg/m^3 </returns>
                  <permission cref="T:System.Security.PermissionSet"> public access
                  </permission>
            </member>
            <member name="T:CSharpProgRef.N2">
                <remarks> This is data for diatomic nitrogen </remarks>
            </member>
        </members>
    </doc>
```

The resulting XML file can then be displayed in a more user-friendly format simply by formatting it using XSLT:

```
<?xml version="1.0"?>
<xsl:stylesheet version="1.0" xmlns:xsl="http://www.w3.org/1999/XSL/Transform">
  <xsl:template match="doc">
    <html>
      <head>
        <title>XSLT Generated Documentation</title>
      </head>
      <body>
        <xsl:apply-templates/>
      </body>
    </html>
  </xsl:template>

  <xsl:template match="assembly">
    <h1><xsl:value-of select="name"/></h1>
  </xsl:template>

  <xsl:template match="members">
    <table border="2" bordercolor="white" bgcolor="white">
      <xsl:apply-templates/>
    </table>
  </xsl:template>

  <xsl:template match="member[starts-with(@name, 'T:')]">
    <tr>
      <td colspan="2" bgcolor="silver"><b>
        <xsl:value-of select="substring-after(@name, 'T:')"/></b></td>
    </tr>
    <tr>
      <td colspan="2" bgcolor="gainsboro"><xsl:value-of select="remarks"/></td>
    </tr>
  </xsl:template>

  <xsl:template match="member[starts-with(@name, 'M:')]">
    <tr>
      <td bgcolor="silver">
        <b><xsl:value-of select="substring-after(@name, 'M:')"/></b></td>
```

```
        <td bgcolor="gainsboro"><xsl:apply-templates/></td>
      </tr>
    </xsl:template>

    <xsl:template match="summary/text()">
      <xsl:value-of select="."/>
    </xsl:template>

    <xsl:template match="summary/paramref">
      <code><xsl:value-of select="@name"/></code>
    </xsl:template>
  </xsl:stylesheet>
```

Producing the following output:

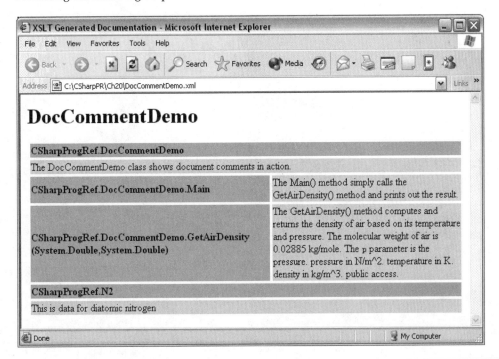

Summary

In this chapter we learned how XML documentation comments can be placed inside a code listing and then extracted into a separate XML file when the program is compiled.

Programmers reference C# Programmers reference C# Programmers reference

21

.NET classes roadmap

Let's say you're an art student who walks into the Louvre museum in Paris without a map or tourguide. You know there is a lot of great art in this vast museum, but you don't know where it all is or where to start looking for what you want to see. A C# developer might feel very much the same way when faced with the .NET Framework class libraries.

This chapter is intended to give you a top-level roadmap of the .NET libraries to provide some orientation to this vast library. Each namespace will be described: what's in it, what's covered in detail in this book, and what is not. When you look through these descriptions, keep in mind that this book focuses on namespace elements that represent core elements of the generic developer libraries provided by the .NET Framework.

Namespaces contained in the .NET Framework

We'll look through the namespaces according to their general function. Some of them will be covered in more detail in later chapters in this book and will have a note to indicate this.

Compiler classes

The .NET Framework contains a namespace for each of the three compilers that are shipped with the .NET SDK.

```
Microsoft.CSharp
Microsoft.JScript
Microsoft.VisualBasic
```

Installing additional languages, for example, J#, can add more namespaces to this list. In the case of J#, this would be Microsoft.JSharp.

Namespace	Description
Microsoft. CSharp	Contains code generation and compilation classes for the C# programming language. Included are classes that represent a managed wrapper for the C# compiler, an error or diagnostic message generated by the compiler, and a class that provides access to an instance of the C# code generator and compiler.
Microsoft. JScript	Provides access to the JScript code compiler and code generator.
Microsoft. VisualBasic	Contains the Visual Basic .NET runtime for use with the Visual Basic .NET language. It also contains a class that is used to access instances of the Visual Basic compiler and code generator.

Other namespaces that include classes for creating or working with compilers include:

```
System.CodeDom
System.CodeDom.Compiler
System.Reflection.Emit
System.Runtime.CompilerServices
```

Interacting with the Windows OS

One namespace is supplied for working with the Windows operating system:

Microsoft.Win32

Namespace	Description
Microsoft. Win32	Contains classes and delegates that are used to handle events generated by the operating system. It also contains classes that are used to manipulate the system registry. The Microsoft.Win32 namespace also defines several enumerations that deal with various system-level operations.

Core classes

The core base types (including primitive types such as Int32 and Boolean) are defined in one of the namespaces in the .NET class libraries:

System

Namespace	Description
System	The System namespace contains fundamental base classes including the Object, EventArgs, and Exception classes. The System namespace provides the String and Math classes that supply the basic text and mathematical functions used in all types of applications. It also contains the Convert class that is used to convert one data type into another. Other classes represent basic system-level operations such as garbage collection and remote and local program invocation. Interfaces that define the basic functionality of certain types of classes are also found in the System namespace. The methods declared in these interfaces allow an object to be copied, compared, converted, and disposed. Among the more important interfaces are the ICloneable, IComparable, IConvertible, and IDisposable interfaces. The System namespace is covered in Chapter 22. This namespace is quite large and a complete coverage of its members is beyond the scope of this book. Specifically, the classes relating to application domains, application environment management, the supervision of managed and unmanaged applications, and the specific exception classes are not covered.

CodeDOM classes

```
System.CodeDom
System.CodeDom.Compiler
```

Namespace	Description
System. CodeDom	Contains classes used when working with the Code Document Object Model (CodeDOM) source code model. These classes represent the elements and structure of a source code. These classes can be used to represent and generate source code. Examples of these classes include the CodeArgumentReferenceExpression, CodeComment, and CodeObject classes. The description and use of CodeDOM to dynamically generate code is beyond the scope of this book.
System. CodeDom. Compiler	Contains classes that provide the source code generation and compilation aspects of a CodeDOM source code model.

Other classes for working with compilers and emitting IL code can be found in the following namespaces:

```
Microsoft.CSharp
Microsoft.JScript
Microsoft.VisualBasic
System.Reflection.Emit
System.Runtime.CompilerServices
```

Collections

```
System.Collections
System.Collections.Specialized
```

Namespace	Description
System. Collections	Collections of data are important to virtually every type of programming application. The System.Collections namespace contains classes that encapsulate the basic types of collections: arrays, lists, dictionaries, hashtables, stacks, and queues. A description of the ArrayList, CollectionBase, DictionaryBase, Hashtable, Queue, SortedList, and Stack classes can be found in Chapter 20. Collection classes in general have a considerable amount of common functionality and this functionality is defined by various interfaces contained in the System.Collections namespace. The ICollection, IComparer, IDictionary, IDictionaryEnumerator, IEnumerable, IEnumerator, and IList interfaces are all described in Chapter 20.
System. Collections. Specialized	Contains classes that define special-purpose and strongly-typed collections. Examples of this include the ListDictionary and StringCollection classes.

Component behavior

```
System.ComponentModel
System.ComponentModel.Design
System.ComponentModel.Design.Serialization
System.EnterpriseServices
```

Namespace	Description
System. ComponentModel	Provides classes that encapsulate the run-time and design-time behavior of components and controls. These include core component, component licensing, attribute, descriptor, persistence, and type converter classes.
System. ComponentModel. Design	Contains classes that are part of the .NET Framework designer architecture. They can be used to define custom logic and behavior for components at design time.
System. ComponentModel. Design. Serialization	Provides support for developing custom component serialization. This refers to the persistent storage of objects.
System. EnterpriseServices	Component services (such as transactions and message queuing) are implemented using the classes in the System.EnterpriseServices namespace.

Configuration

```
System.Configuration
System.Configuration.Assemblies
System.Configuration.Install
```

Namespace	Description
System. Configuration	Contains classes and interfaces that allow you to access and manipulate .config files including error handling.
System. Configuration. Assemblies	Contains one structure and two enumerations that are used to configure an assembly. An assembly is a reusable, versionable, self-describing collection of libraries and executable files.
System. Configuration. Install	Provides support for writing custom component installers. It includes the Installer class that is the base class for all installers in the .NET Framework.

Data access

```
System.Data
System.Data.Common
System.Data.OleDb
System.Data.SqlClient
System.Data.SqlTypes
```

Namespace	Description
System. Data	The ADO.NET architecture enables the development of components that can efficiently manage data from multiple data sources. The classes that make up the ADO.NET architecture are contained in the System.Data namespace.
System. Data. Common	Contains classes shared by .NET data providers. A data provider accesses a database or other data source in the managed space.
System. Data. OleDb	Contains classes that serve as the OLE DB .Net data provider. The ODBC provider is available as a separate download.
System. Data. SqlClient	Supplies classes that act as the SQL Server .NET data provider
System. Data. SqlTypes	Defines classes for native data types within a SQL Server. Using these classes can help to minimize conversion errors when using a SQL server.

Data access and the System.Data namespaces are covered in depth in *Professional ADO.NET Programming, Wrox Press, ISBN: 1-861005-27-X,* and the *ADO.NET Programmer's Reference, Wrox Press, ISBN: 1-861005-58-X.*

Debugging

```
System.Diagnostics
System.Diagnostics.SymbolStore
```

Namespace	Description
System.Diagnostics	Provides classes that facilitate application debugging and code execution tracing. The namespace also contains classes that allow you to start system processes, monitor system performance, and access event logs.
System.Diagnostics.SymbolStore	Provides the capability to read, write, and debug symbol information. An example of where this would be useful would be manipulating Microsoft intermediate language (MSIL) maps.

Directory services

```
System.DirectoryServices
```

Namespace	Description
System.DirectoryServices	The classes contained in the System.DirectoryServices class provide access to an Active Directory service provider including Internet Information Services (IIS), Lightweight Directory Access Protocol (LDAP), Novell NetWare Directory (NDS), and WinNT.

Graphics

The graphics functionality of .NET is provided by GDI+, the successor to GDI. GDI+ is a very large topic, which we can't cover in this book, but for more information, you may wish to look at *Professional Windows Forms, Wrox Press, ISBN: 1-861005-54-7*:

```
System.Drawing
System.Drawing.Drawing2D
System.Drawing.Imaging
System.Drawing.Printing
System.Drawing.Text
```

Namespace	Description
System.Drawing	Provides access to the basic GDI+ graphics functionality. Included in this namespace are the Graphics, Brush, Font, and Icon classes. The members of the System.Drawing namespace allow the developer to extend the built-in design-time user interface (UI) logic and drawing. Examples of UI extensions include custom type-specific editors or toolbox items.

Namespace	Description
System. Drawing. Drawing2D	Contains classes and enumerations that have more sophisticated two-dimensional and graphics capability than the basic classes contained in the System.Drawing namespace.
System. Drawing. Imaging	Provides more advanced GDI+ imaging functionality than the basic classes contained in the System.Drawing namespace. This namespace also contains the Metafile class that is used for recording and saving metafiles.
System. Drawing. Printing	Facilitates customized printing processes. The namespace includes the PrintDocument, PrinterSettings, and PrintingPermission classes.
System. Drawing. Text	Allows you to create and use collections of fonts. This more advanced typography functionality is in addition to the typography classes provided by the System.Drawing namespace.

Component services

System.EnterpriseServices

Namespace	Description
System. EnterpriseServices	Provides support for server-based applications including COM+ and MSMQ queue support.

Globalization

System.Globalization

Namespace	Description
System. Globalization	When developing applications, it is helpful if they can be quickly modified for different language and cultural environments. The System.Globalization namespace contains classes and enumerations that define culture-specific information such as language, calendars, text orientation, and currency.

Culture-specific resources for an application can be configured using the following namespace:

```
System.Resources
```

Input/Output

System.IO
System.IO.IsolatedStorage

Namespace	Description
System. IO	Contains classes, delegates, enumerations, and structures used to read and write data. Included are the `Stream`, `TextReader`, and `TextWriter` base classes and the classes that derive from them. Classes are also provided to read and write binary data and to read and write data to a file. The major elements of the `System.IO` namespace are detailed in Chapter 24. The class also defines various I/O exception classes that are not covered in detail in this book.
System. IO. IsolatedStorage	The classes provided by this namespace can be used to isolate data from a less trusted source from sensitive information stored in another part of the system.

These namespaces are covered in more detail in Chapter 24.

WMI

System.Management

Namespace	Description
System. Management	Provides support for Windows Management Instrumentation (WMI). Allows applications and services the ability to query for such information as available disk space and current CPU utilization.

Message queuing

System.Messaging

Namespace	Description
System. Messaging	Contains classes that can be used to access message queues on the network. You can connect to message queues, send messages to the queues, or receive messages from the queues. The primary classes that provide this functionality are the `MessageQueue` and `Message` classes.

Networking

System.Net
System.Net.Sockets

Namespace	Description
System. Net	This namespace provides a basic programming interface for creating network connections. Classes in the namespace allow HTTP protocol, cookie, socket permission, and authentication functionality. The `System.Net` namespace provides a sort of generic capability to develop Internet applications without having to specify a particular network protocol to use.

Namespace	Description
System. Net. Sockets	Provides an implementation of the Windows Sockets interface. This interface is used by developers who want a tightly-controlled connection between client and server. The primary classes for creating TCP and UDP connections to the Internet are the `TcpClient`, `TcpListener`, and `UdpClient` classes.

Reflection

System.Reflection
System.Reflection.Emit

Namespace	Description
System. Reflection	The namespace contains classes that mirror the assemblies, types, methods, and fields that make up an application. It also provides for the capability for the dynamic creation of run-time objects. The key elements of this namespace are covered in Chapter 25.
System. Reflection. Emit	The namespace contains classes that permit a compiler or other tool to emit metadata and MSIL. They can also be used to generate a portable executable (PE) file on disk. The classes in this namespace are generally used by script engines and compilers.

Resource management

System.Resources

Namespace	Description
System. Resources	The `System.Resources` namespace is part of the collection of namespaces that allow developers to create, store, and manage any culture-specific resources used by an application including culture-specific objects and strings.

Other namespaces for handling internationalization include:

```
System.Globalization
```

Compiler services

System.Runtime.CompilerServices

Namespace	Description
System. Runtime. CompilerServices	Contains classes that help compiler writers specify attributes in metadata. These attributes are used to modify the run-time behavior of the Common Language Runtime.

COM interoperability

```
System.Runtime.InteropServices
System.Runtime.InteropServices.Expando
```

Namespace	Description
System. Runtime. InteropServices	Provides classes that can be used to access COM objects and native APIs from .NET. Subjects covered in this namespace include attributes, exceptions, managed definitions of COM types, wrappers, the Marshal class, and type converters.
System. Runtime. InteropServices. Expando	The namespace has a funny name and defines one interface that declares methods to modify an object by adding or removing MemberInfo objects.

Remoting

```
System.Runtime.Remoting
System.Runtime.Remoting.Activation
System.Runtime.Remoting.Channels
System.Runtime.Remoting.Channels.Http
System.Runtime.Remoting.Channels.Tcp
System.Runtime.Remoting.Contexts
System.Runtime.Remoting.Lifetime
System.Runtime.Remoting.Messaging
System.Runtime.Remoting.Metadata
System.Runtime.Remoting.MetadataServices
System.Runtime.Remoting.Proxies
System.Runtime.Remoting.Services
```

Namespace	Description
System. Runtime. Remoting	Contains classes and interfaces used to develop distributed applications. This namespace contains the RemotingConfiguration class that allows the use of XML formatted configuration files, the RemotingServices class that assists in using and publishing remote objects, and the ObjRef class that contains information used to activate and communicate with a remote object.
System. Runtime. Remoting. Activation	Provides classes, interfaces, and enumerations that enable client-server activation of remote objects.
System. Runtime. Remoting. Channels	Contains classes that support channels and channel sinks. These are used to transport information when a client makes a remote method call.
System. Runtime. Remoting. Channels. Http	This namespace supplies HTTP channels that use the SOAP protocol to transport information between remote objects.

Namespace	Description
System. Runtime. Remoting. Channels. Tcp	This namespace defines channels that use the TCP protocol to transport objects in binary format to a remote location.
System. Runtime. Remoting. Contexts	Provides support for objects that are intended when activated to contain certain automatic services such as synchronization, transactions, just-in-time activation, and security.
System. Runtime. Remoting. Lifetime	Contains classes that manage the life cycle of remote objects. This includes the lease associated with the remote object as well as the lease sponsor.
System. Runtime. Remoting. Messaging	Contains classes and interfaces that are used to control the passing of messages between message sinks.
System. Runtime. Remoting. Metadata	Contains classes that are used to provide information to the SOAP serializer when it outputs SOAP. The classes are also used when SOAP is generated from a URL.
System. Runtime. Remoting. MetadataServices	This namespace provides support to the SOAPSUDS utility when it converts metadata to and from XML Schema.
System. Runtime. Remoting. Proxies	Enables the creation of local images of a remote object. These proxies allow clients to access remote objects across remoting boundaries.
System. Runtime. Remoting. Services	Contains support classes for creating a remoting network. These include the `RemotingService` and `TrackingService` classes.

More information on remoting can be found in *C# Web Services – Building Web Services with .NET Remoting and ASP.NET, Wrox Press, ISBN: 1-861004-39-7.*

Serialization

```
System.Runtime.Serialization
System.Runtime.Serialization.Formatters
System.Runtime.Serialization.Formatters.Binary
System.Runtime.Serialization.Formatters.Soap
```

Namespace	Description
System. Runtime. Serialization	Contains classes used to serialize and deserialize objects. Serialization refers to converting an object to a series of bytes that can be transmitted or stored. Deserialization is the reconfiguring of an object from a stored series of bytes.
System. Runtime. Serialization. Formatters	Provides classes, interfaces, and enumerations that are common to the serialization formatter classes.

Table continued on following page

Namespace	Description
System. Runtime. Serialization. Formatters. Binary	Contains the `BinaryFormatter` class that is used to serialize or deserialize objects in binary format.
System. Runtime. Serialization. Formatters. Soap	This namespace contains the `SoapFormatter` class that is used to serialize or deserialize objects in SOAP format.

Security and cryptography

```
System.Security
System.Security.Cryptography
System.Security.Cryptography.X509Certificates
System.Security.Cryptography.Xml
System.Security.Permissions
System.Security.Policy
System.Security.Principal
```

Namespace	Description
System. Security	Provides the basic functionality of the Common Language Runtime security system. Included in this namespace are the `SecurityManager` and `Permission` classes.
System. Security. Cryptography	Contains classes that provide secure coding and decoding of data. The namespace also contains classes for random number generation, hashing, and message authentication.
System. Security. Cryptography. X509Certificates	Contains classes that represent the Common Language Runtime implementation of the Authenticode X.509 v.3 certificate. This certificate is used to provide a unique identification of the holder of the certificate.
System. Security. Cryptography. Xml	This namespace provides the means to provide a digital signature to XML objects. These objects can then be used in conjunction with the .NET Framework security system.
System. Security. Permissions	The namespace contains classes that encapsulate various types of permissions.
System. Security. Policy	Contains classes that define rules used by the Common Language Runtime security policy system. The policy hierarchy includes code groups, membership conditions, and evidence.
System. Security. Principal	Provides classes that define the principal security context under which the code is running.

Windows services

```
System.ServiceProcess
```

Namespace	Description
System. ServiceProcess	Contains classes that allow services to be installed and run. A service is a long-running program that runs without a user interface. They are often set up to be started whenever the host computer is started or restarted.

Text manipulation

System.Text
System.Text.RegularExpressions

Namespace	Description
System. Text	Contains classes that encapsulate ASCII, Unicode, UTF-7, and UTF-8 character encodings. It also contains abstract base classes for character to byte and byte to character conversions. This namespace also provides the StringBuilder class that can be used to modify an existing string without creating a new string instance. The components of this namespace are described in detail in Chapter 26.
System. Text. RegularExpressions	The namespace contains classes that allow the generation of regular expression by providing access to the .NET Framework regular expression engine. The classes from this namespace are covered in Chapter 26.

Threading

System.Threading

Namespace	Description
System. Threading	Provides the classes, structures, delegates, and enumerations that facilitate multi-threaded programming. Included in the namespace are classes to enable thread synchronization, classes to manage groups of threads, and a timer that calls a delegate after a specified amount of time. A full discussion of the elements of this namespace can be found in Chapter 27.

Timer

System.Timer

Namespace	Description
System. Timer	This namespace contains the classes needed to create a server-based timer component that causes an event to be raised after a recurring interval. The Timer class itself is designed to work in a multi-threaded environment.

Web programming

```
System.Web
System.Web.Caching
System.Web.Configuration
System.Web.Security
```

Namespace	Description
System. Web	Provides classes that enable browser/server communication using the HTTP protocol. There are classes that support client requests, server responses, cookie manipulation, file transfer, exception information, and output cache control.
System. Web. Caching	Provides the ability to cache on a server resources such as ASP.NET pages, web services, and user controls. There are also classes to provide information about the current state of items stored in the cache.
System. Web. Configuration	This namespace contains classes and enumerations that are used to create an ASP.NET configuration.
System. Web. Security	Contains the authorization, authentication, and identity classes that are used to implement the ASP.NET security feature in web-based applications.

Web services

```
System.Web.Services
System.Web.Services.Description
System.Web.Services.Discovery
System.Web.Services.Protocols
```

Namespace	Description
System. Web. Services	Enables the development and use of web services. A web service is an application that resides on a web server that can be accessed using standard Internet protocols. This namespace defines the WebService class that serves as the base class for ASP.NET web services.
System. Web. Services. Description	Contains classes used to create a Web Service Description Language (WSDL) that describes a web service.
System. Web. Services. Discovery	Provides classes that are used to locate available Web Services.
System. Web. Services. Protocols	Contains the classes that define protocols used to transmit data between ASP.NET web services and clients using those services.

Web forms

```
System.Web.UI
System.Web.UI.Design
```

```
System.Web.UI.Design.WebControls
System.Web.UI.Design.HtmlControls
System.Web.UI.WebControls
```

Namespace	Description
System. Web. UI	Contains classes, interfaces, delegates, and enumerations that are used to develop controls and pages that appear in a web application. These elements appear as a user interface on a web page.
System. Web. UI. Design	Provides classes that can be used to extend binding, editing, and other support functions for web forms.
System. Web. UI. Design. WebControls	Contains classes used to extend the functionality of web controls.
System. Web. UI. Design. HtmlControls	Supplies classes that can create HTML server controls on a web page. The server controls map to standard HTML tags supported by all browsers.
System. Web. UI. WebControls	Contains classes used to create web server controls. These controls run on the server allowing you to programmatically control elements on a web page.

For more information on all aspects of programming Web Forms with ASP.NET, see *Professional ASP.NET 1.0, Wrox Press, ISBN: 1-861007-03-5.*

Windows forms

```
System.Windows.Forms
System.Windows.Forms.Design
```

Namespace	Description
System. Windows. Forms	Contains classes that are designed for developing Windows-based applications taking advantage of features available under the Windows operating system.
System. Windows. Forms. Design	Provides classes that extend the capabilities of Windows forms.

Windows forms are covered in detail in *Professional Windows Forms, Wrox Press, ISBN: 1-861005-54-7.*

XML

```
System.Xml
System.Xml.Schema
System.Xml.Serialization
System.Xml.XPath
System.Xml.Xsl
```

Namespace	Description
System. Xml	This namespace is the base namespace for XML classes that provide standards-based processing of XML.
System. Xml. Schema	Contains classes that provide standards-based support for XML schemas. Standards are supported for both structures and data types.
System. Xml. Serialization	Contains classes that are used to serialize objects into XML format documents or streams and to deserialize those documents or streams back into objects. Both processes use the SOAP protocol.
System. Xml. XPath	Contains the XPath XML parser and evaluation engine.
System. Xml. Xsl	Contains classes that provide support for XSL/T transformations.

A detailed look at these namespaces can be found in *Professional XML for .NET Developers, Wrox Press, ISBN: 1-861005-31-8.*

Summary

In this chapter we've taken a very brief look at the .NET Framework class libraries. While it's impossible to detail all of these classes in this book, some of these libraries are looked at in depth in the upcoming chapters.

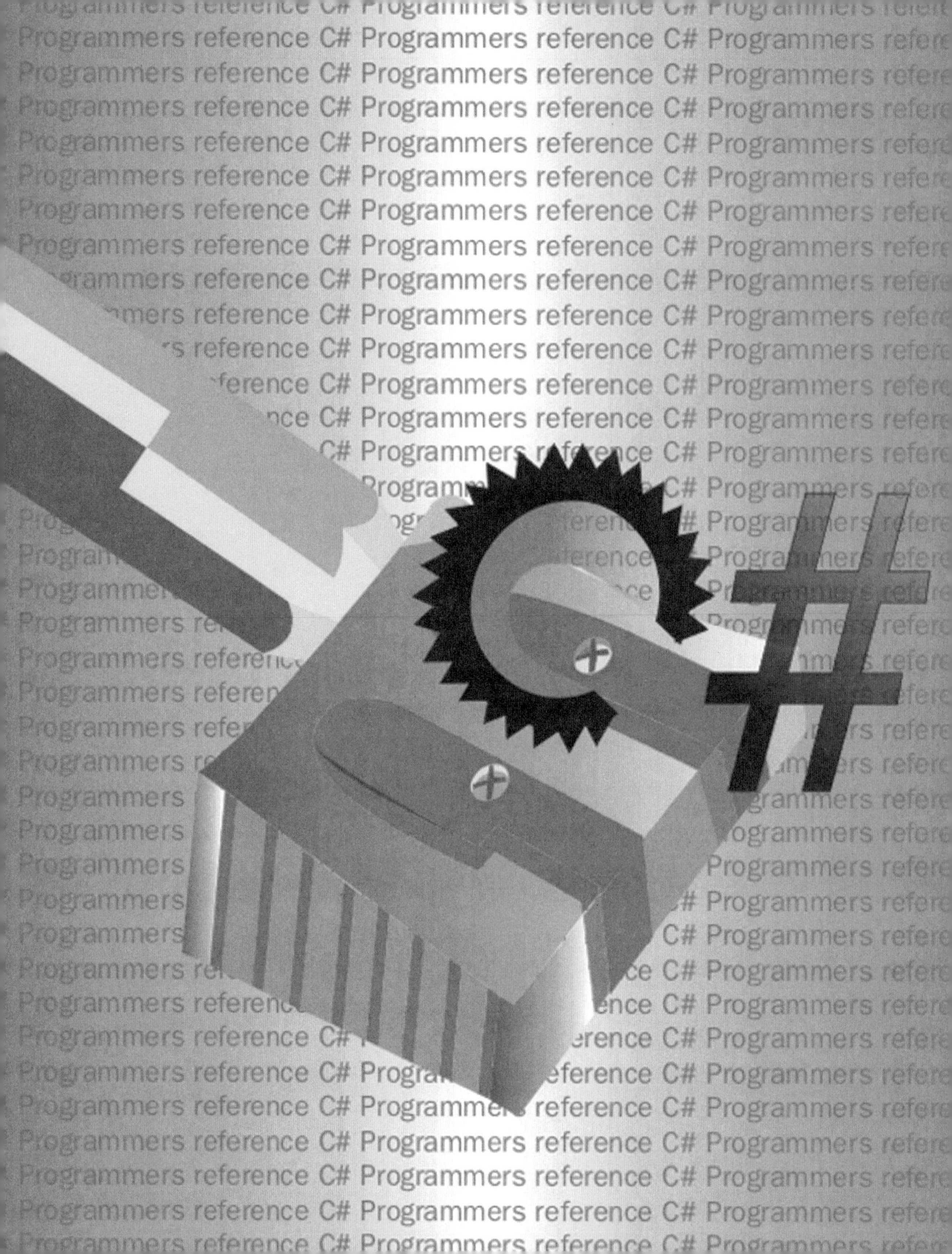
Programmers reference C#

System classes

In this chapter, we'll look in detail at some of the classes in the System namespace, which is something of a catch-all for generic functionality. Its contents include:

- ❑ The fundamental Object and Type classes that form the base for so much of the .NET Framework's functionality.

- ❑ General-purpose classes like Array, Console, and String, which are used in many different types of applications.

- ❑ Important base classes such as EventArgs, Exception, and MarshalByRefObject. These classes define properties and methods that are common to a wide variety of derived classes.

- ❑ The Math class, which is a self-contained library of mathematical functions and constants, and the Convert class, which provides conversion functions.

Type class

The Type class encapsulates a type. Instances of this class can provide information about the data and function members defined in a given type; they can also be used to invoke methods, properties, and any other members of a class or struct. Type objects are used extensively in reflection, and are commonly seen as input parameters for .NET Framework functions.

There are two ways to acquire a Type object: you can use one of the GetType() methods, or you can use the typeof operator. For example, either of the following statements would provide a Type object representing the String class:

```
Type type1 = Type.GetType("System.String");
Type type2 = typeof(string);
```

If the type isn't in the same assembly as the calling code, or one of the core system assemblies, we need to specify the assembly where it resides. For example, to get a Type named Wrox.MyClass in a private assembly called Wrox.dll we use:

```
Type t = Type.GetType("Wrox.MyClass, Wrox");
```

If the assembly is shared, we also need to supply version and culture information and the public key code (these can be found by looking in the Global Assembly Cache):

```
Type t = Type.GetType("Microsoft.Data.Odbc.OdbcConnection," +
                      "Microsoft.Data.Odbc, Version=1.0.3300.0," +
                      "Culture=neutral, PublicKeyToken=b77a5c561934e089");
```

Syntax

```
public abstract class Type : MemberInfo, IReflect
```

The Type class is abstract, and defines no public constructors. To get a Type instance, you can use the GetType() method defined in the Object and Type classes, or you can use the typeof operator.

Hierarchy

```
Object --- MemberInfo --- Type
```

Constructors

```
protected Type()
```

Type() is a protected constructor that can be used by derived classes of Type.

Fields

```
public static readonly char Delimiter
public static readonly Type[] EmptyTypes
public static readonly MemberFilter FilterAttribute
public static readonly MemberFilter FilterName
public static readonly MemberFilter FilterNameIgnoreCase
public static readonly object Missing
```

Delimiter is a read-only character that's used to separate the nested namespaces when the full name of the Type's namespace is displayed (by default, a period, as in System.Type).

EmptyTypes returns an empty array of type Type. This can be used when we want to retrieve a constructor that takes no arguments via reflection:

```
Type t = Type.GetType("System.Object");
ConstructorInfo ctor = t.GetConstructor(Type.EmptyTypes);
```

FilterAttribute holds a reference to a delegate of type MemberFilter that can be used with the FindMembers() method. This delegate refers to a method with a return type of bool, and with two parameters: a MemberInfo object, and an object representing the filter criteria. The method returns true if the MemberInfo object matches these criteria; in this case, the object can be any of the FieldAttributes, MethodAttributes, or MethodImplAttributes enum values, and will return true if the member is associated with the specified attribute.

FilterName holds a reference to a MemberFilter delegate that can be used with the FindMembers() method. In this case, the criterion object is a string, and the method will return true if the member name matches this string. The string may contain the wildcard character (*).

FilterNameIgnoreCase holds a reference to a MemberFilter delegate that can be used with the FindMembers() method. This is identical to the method represented by the FilterName delegate, except that the match is case-insensitive.

Missing represents an unspecified value. This can be used with reflection to invoke a method which has optional arguments. Optional arguments are not supported by C#, but are supported by Visual Basic .NET, and allow us to call a method without specifying a value for every parameter, instead using default values supplied in the method definition. (They serve much the same purpose in the world of VB as method overloading does in the C# universe.)

For example, suppose we have a VB.NET class defined like this:

```
Namespace MissingDemo
   Public Class VBClass

      ' A static method with an optional parameter. If no value is supplied
      ' for this parameter when the method is called, the default value
      ' "Boo!" will be used instead.
      Public Shared Sub DoSomething(Optional ByVal s As String = "Boo!")
        Console.WriteLine(s)
      End Sub

   End Class
End Namespace
```

Normally, we would need to specify a value for the parameter if calling the static DoSomething() method from C#. However, we can invoke this method via reflection passing in Type.Missing as the argument to take advantage of the default value:

```
Type t = Type.GetType("MissingDemo.VBClass, MissingDemo");
MethodInfo meth = t.GetMethod("DoSomething");
meth.Invoke(null, new object[] { Type.Missing });
```

This will output Boo! to the console window.

Properties

```
public abstract Assembly Assembly {get;}
public abstract string AssemblyQualifiedName {get;}
public TypeAttributes Attributes {get;}
public abstract Type BaseType {get;}
```

```
public override DeclaringType {get;}
public static Binder DefaultBinder {get;}
public abstract string FullName {get;}
public abstract Guid GUID {get;}
public bool HasElementType {get;}
```

`Assembly` returns an `Assembly` object representing the assembly in which the `Type` resides.

`AssemblyQualifiedName` returns the fully qualified name of the `Type`, including the name of the assembly from which the `Type` was loaded, plus the version, culture, and public key token information (for example, `"Microsoft.Data.Odbc.OdbcConnection, Microsoft.Data.Odbc, Version=1.0.3300.0, Culture=neutral, PublicKeyToken=b77a5c561934e089"`).

`Attributes` obtains the attributes associated with the `Type`.

`BaseType` returns the `Type` from which the current `Type` inherits (or `null` if the `Type` represents the `Object` class).

`DeclaringType` retrieves a `Type` object for the class that declares this member.

`DefaultBinder` returns the default binder used by the system.

`FullName` obtains the fully qualified name of the `Type`, including the namespace in which it resides (for example, `"Microsoft.Data.Odbc.OdbcConnection"`).

`GUID` returns the GUID associated with the `Type`.

`HasElementType` returns `true` if the current `Type` is an array, a pointer, or passed by reference.

```
public bool IsAbstract {get;}
public bool IsAnsiClass {get;}
public bool IsArray {get;}
public bool IsAutoClass {get;}
public bool IsAutoLayout {get;}
public bool IsByRef {get;}
public bool IsClass {get;}
public bool IsCOMObject {get;}
public bool IsContextful {get;}
public bool IsEnum {get;}
public bool IsExplicitLayout {get;}
public bool IsImport {get;}
public bool IsInterface {get;}
public bool IsLayoutSequential {get;}
public bool IsMarshalByRef {get;}
public bool IsNestedAssembly {get;}
public bool IsNestedFamANDAssembly {get;}
public bool IsNestedFamily {get;}
public bool IsNestedFamORAssembly {get;}
public bool IsNestedPrivate {get;}
public bool IsNestedPublic {get;}
public bool IsNotPublic {get;}
public bool IsPointer {get;}
public bool IsPrimitive {get;}
```

```
public bool IsPublic {get;}
public bool IsSealed {get;}
public bool IsSerializable {get;}
public bool IsSpecialName {get;}
public bool IsUnicodeClass {get;}
public bool IsValueType {get;}
```

These properties return a `true` or `false` value depending on whether the current `Type` has the specified characteristic. Some of the not-so-self-explanatory ones are the `IsAutoClass`, `IsAutoLayout`, and `IsLayoutSequential` properties that determine if the `AutoClass`, `AutoLayout`, and `SequentialLayout` attributes are associated with the `Type`.

```
public override MemberTypes MemberType {get;}
public abstract Module Module {get;}
public abstract string Namespace {get;}
public override Type ReflectedType {get;}
public abstract RuntimeTypeHandle TypeHandle {get;}
public ConstructorInfo TypeInitializer {get;}
public abstract Type UnderlyingSystemType {get;}
```

`MemberType` returns a bitmask of `MemberTypes` values describing the type of a member. `MemberTypes` is an enumeration which indicates whether the member is a type, a method, and so on. It can be one or more of:

❑   `All` – All members.

❑   `Constructor` – The member is a constructor.

❑   `Custom` – The member is a custom member type.

❑   `Event` – The member is an event.

❑   `Field` – The member is a field.

❑   `Method` – The member is a method.

❑   `NestedType` – The member is a nested type.

❑   `Property` – The member is a property.

❑   `TypeInfo` – The member is a type.

`Module` retrieves a `Module` representing the module in which the `Type` is defined.

`Namespace` returns the name of the namespace in which the `Type` resides.

`ReflectedType` is used with reflection and returns the `Type` through which a `MemberInfo` object was obtained. For example, if the `MemberInfo` represents a method, `ReflectedType` will return the `Type` to which that method belongs.

`TypeHandle` returns the handle for the current `Type`. This is a pointer to an internal structure representing the type, and can be passed into the `Type.GetTypeFromHandle()` static method to retrieve the corresponding `Type` object.

TypeInitializer retrieves a ConstructorInfo object representing the static constructor for the current Type. Static constructors are called ".cctor" in IL, so this will be the name of the ConstructorInfo object.

UnderlyingSystemType returns the underlying CLR system type for the current type.

Static methods

```
public static Type GetType(string typeName)
public static Type GetType(string typeName, bool throwOnError)
public static Type GetType(string typeName, bool throwOnError,
                           bool ignroreCase)
public static Type[] GetTypeArray(object[] args)
public static TypeCode GetTypeCode(Type type)
```

GetType() returns a Type object according to the specified name. If ignoreCase is true or unspecified, the name-to-Type conversion is case in sensitive. If throwOnError is true, a TypeLoadException will be thrown if an error occurs while loading the Type. The typeName parameter can be a simple type name, a type name that includes a namespace, or a fully qualified type name that includes an assembly name specification. An ArgumentNullException is thrown if type name is a null reference.

GetTypeArray() returns an array of Type objects representing the types of the objects in the input array. An ArgumentNullException is thrown if args is a null reference.

GetTypeCode() returns the underlying type code of the specified Type. TypeCode is an enumeration which indicates the general type of an object. It can be one of:

- ❑ Boolean
- ❑ Byte
- ❑ Char
- ❑ DateTime
- ❑ DBNull (a database null column)
- ❑ Decimal
- ❑ Double
- ❑ Empty (a null reference)
- ❑ Int16 (a short value)
- ❑ Int32 (an int value)
- ❑ Int64 (a long value)
- ❑ Object (any type not represented by any of the other TypeCode values)
- ❑ SByte
- ❑ Single (a float value)
- ❑ String

- ❑   UInt16 (a ushort value)

- ❑   UInt32 (a uint value)

- ❑   UInt64 (a ulong value)

```
public static Type GetTypeFromCLSID(Guid classID)
public static Type GetTypeFromCLSID(Guid classID, bool throwOnError)
public static Type GetTypeFromCLSID(Guid classID, string server)
public static Type GetTypeFromCLSID(Guid classID, string server,
                                    bool throwOnError)
```

GetTypeFromCLSID() retrieves a Type instance based on the specified class identifier (CLSID). If throwOnError is true, a TypeLoadException will be thrown if an error occurs while loading the Type. You can specify the server from which to load the type.

```
public static Type GetTypeFromProgID(string progID)
public static Type GetTypeFromProgID(string progID, bool throwOnError)
public static Type GetTypeFromProgID(string progID, string server)
public static Type GetTypeFromProgID(string progID, string server,
                                     bool throwOnError)
```

GetTypeFromProgID() returns a Type instance based on the specified program identifier (ProgID). If throwOnError is true, a TypeLoadException will be thrown if an error occurs while loading the Type. You can specify the server from which to load the type. A SecurityException can also be thrown if the caller lacks the required permission.

```
public static Type GetTypeFromHandle(RuntimeTypeHandle handle)
public static RuntimeTypeHandle GetTypeHandle(object obj)
```

GetTypeFromHandle() creates and returns a Type reference based on the specified type handle. An ArgumentNullException is thrown if handle is a null reference.

GetTypeHandle() returns the handle for the Type of the specified object (a pointer to an internal structure which represents the type).

Instance methods

```
public override bool Equals(Type type)
public override bool Equals(object obj)
public override int GetHashCode()
public override string ToString()
```

Equals() returns true if the invoking Type object has the same underlying system type as that of the specified Type or Object.

GetHashCode() retrieves the hash code for the Type.

ToString() returns a String representation of the current Type.

```
public virtual Type[] FindInterfaces(TypeFilter filter,
                                     object filterCriteria)
```

```
public virtual MemberInfo[] FindMembers(MemberTypes memberType,
        BindingFlags bindingAttr, MemberFilter filter, object filterCriteria)
public virtual MemberInfo[] GetDefaultMembers()
```

FindInterfaces() returns an array of Type objects representing the interfaces implemented or inherited by the invoking Type object. The list is filtered using a TypeFilter delegate, and an object that contains the search criteria. If no interfaces meet the criteria, an empty array is returned. The method will throw an ArgumentNullException if filter is a null reference.

FindMembers() returns an array of MemberInfo objects of the specified member type that are associated with the invoking Type object. The list is filtered using a MemberFilter delegate, according to search criteria defined in filterCriteria. The bindingAttr also specifies how the search should be conducted; this is a bitmask of BindingFlags enumeration members (the BindingFlags enumeration is covered in Chapter 25). An ArgumentNullException is thrown if filter is a null reference.

GetDefaultMembers() retrieves an array of MemberInfo objects representing the default members for the invoking Type.

```
public virtual int GetArrayRank()
protected abstract TypeAttributes GetAttributeFlagsImpl()
public abstract Type GetElementType()
```

GetArrayRank() returns the number of dimensions in the array represented by the current Type. An ArgumentException is thrown if the Type does not represent an array.

GetAttributeFlagsImpl() returns a bitmask of TypeAttributes enumeration values which contain information about the type, such as its access level, whether it is abstract or sealed, whether it is serializable, and so on. This method is abstract, so can't be called on the Type itself, but can be overridden in derived classes.

GetElementType() is overridden in a derived class to return the Type of the object or objects associated with an array, pointer, or reference type. For example, if called on an array of ints, this method will return a Type object representing the System.Int32 type.

```
public ConstructorInfo GetConstructor(Type[] types)
public ConstructorInfo GetConstructor(BindingFlags bindingAttr,
        Binder binder, Type[] types, ParameterModifier[] modifiers)
public ConstructorInfo GetConstructor(BindingFlags bindingAttr,
        Binder binder, CallingConvention convention, Type[] types,
        ParameterModifier[] modifiers)

public ConstructorInfo[] GetConstructors()
public ConstructorInfo[] GetConstructors(BindingFlags bindingAttr)
```

GetConstructor() searches the Type for a constructor whose parameters match the types in the specified array. The bindingAttr parameter defines how the search is conducted – the default is to search for public instance constructors. The Binder object defines properties that enable binding; this argument can be null, in which case the default binder is used. The types array contains objects representing any parameters to be passed into the constructor. The ParameterModifier array contains objects representing the modifiers applied to each element in the types array; this parameter is only used for parameters passed by reference, and only when calling a method through COM interoperability. A custom Binder object must be written to handle modifiers. The CallingConvention parameter defines a set of rules for how the arguments are presented and used (such as CallingConventions.Standard – the default calling convention in .NET – or CallingConventions.VarArgs for methods with variable arguments). An exception is thrown if types is a null reference, if either types or modifiers is a multidimensional array, or if types and modifiers don't have the same length.

GetConstructors() returns an array of constructors defined by the Type. The bindingAttr parameter defines how the search is conducted. The default is to search for public instance constructors.

```
public EventInfo GetEvent(string name)
public abstract EventInfo GetEvent(string name, BindingFlags bindingAttr)
public virtual EventInfo[] GetEvents()
public abstract EventInfo[] GetEvents(BindingFlags bindingAttr)
```

GetEvent() returns an EventInfo object corresponding to the specified event. A bindingAttr parameter can be provided to define the search. An ArgumentNullException is thrown if name is a null reference.

GetEvents() retrieves an array of EventInfo objects corresponding to the events declared or inherited by the invoking Type. The bindingAttr parameter defines how the search is conducted. The default is to search for public events.

```
public FieldInfo GetField(string name)
public abstract FieldInfo GetField(string name, BindingFlags bindingAttr)
public virtual FieldInfo[] GetFields()
public abstract FieldInfo[] GetFields(BindingFlags bindingAttr)
```

GetField() returns a FieldInfo object corresponding to the specified field. A bindingAttr parameter can be provided to refine the search (for example, to retrieve only static fields or instance fields, or fields with a specific access level). An ArgumentNullException is thrown if name is a null reference.

GetFields() retrieves an array of FieldInfo objects corresponding to the fields declared or inherited by the invoking Type. Again, the bindingAttr parameter can be used to refine the search – the default is to search for public fields.

```
public Type GetInterface(string name)
public abstract Type GetInterface(string name, bool ignoreCase)
public virtual InterfaceMapping GetInterfaceMap(Type interfaceType)
public abstract Type[] GetInterfaces()
```

GetInterface() searches for an interface of the specified name in the invoking Type. The return value is null if the interface is not found. If ignoreCase is true, the search is case-insensitive. The default is for the search to be case-sensitive. An ArgumentNullException is thrown if name is a null reference.

GetInterfaceMap() returns an object that provides a mapping of the specified interface type. This object provides access to information about the methods defined in one of the interfaces implemented by the type, and about the type's implementations of those methods. The GetInterfaceMap() method throws an exception if interfaceType does not refer to an interface or is a null reference.

GetInterfaces() is an abstract method that can be overridden by derived classes to return all of the interfaces implemented or inherited by the invoking Type object.

```
public MemberInfo[] GetMember(string name)
public virtual MemberInfo[] GetMember(string name, BindingFlags bindingAttr)
public virtual MemberInfo[] GetMember(string name, MemberTypes type,
                                      BindingFlags bindingAttr)
public MemberInfo[] GetMembers()
public abstract MemberInfo[] GetMembers(BindingFlags bindingAttr)
```

GetMember() allows us to retrieve objects representing specific members of the type; an array of MemberInfo objects is returned containing an object for each member with the specified name. (This is an array rather than a single object because overloaded methods, for example, have the same name but are represented by different MemberInfo objects.) A bindingAttr parameter can be provided to define the search; the default search will return only public members. You can further limit the search by specifying a member type for which to search. An ArgumentNullException is thrown if name is a null reference.

GetMembers() retrieves an array of MemberInfo objects representing all of the members of the invoking Type. The bindingAttr parameter can be used to limit the search. The default is to search for public members.

```
public MethodInfo GetMethod(string name)
public MethodInfo GetMethod(string name, BindingFlags bindingAttr)
public MethodInfo GetMethod(string name, Type[] types)
public MethodInfo GetMethod(string name, Type[] types,
                            ParameterModifier[] modifiers)
public MethodInfo GetMethod(string name, BindingFlags bindingAttr,
                            Binder binder, Type[] types,
                            ParameterModifier[] modifiers)
public MethodInfo GetMethod(string name, BindingFlags bindingAttr,
                            Binder binder, CallingConvention convention,
                            Type[] types, ParameterModifier[] modifiers)
protected MethodInfo GetMethodImpl(string name, BindingFlags bindingAttr,
                            Binder binder, CallingConvention convention,
                            Type[] types, ParameterModifier[] modifiers)
public MethodInfo[] GetMethods()
public abstract MethodInfo[] GetMethods(BindingFlags bindingAttr)
```

GetMethod() returns a MethodInfo object containing information about the specified method. The bindingAttr parameter is used to define the search. The default search is for public instance methods.

A `Type` array can be provided with the types of the input arguments to the method. Information about the modifiers can be supplied with an array of `ParameterModifiers`. This information is used only for input arguments passed by reference and when the method is called using COM interoperability. The `Binder` object defines properties that enable binding. This argument can be `null`, in which case the default binder is used. The `CallingConvention` parameter defines a set of rules for how the arguments are presented and used. This method will throw an exception if more than one method is found matching the input arguments, if `name` or `types` is a `null` reference, if `types` or `modifiers` is multidimensional, or if `types` and `modifiers` have different lengths.

`GetMethodImpl()` is overridden in a derived class to search for the specified method under the specified constraints.

`GetMethods()` returns an array of `MethodInfo` objects containing information about the methods defined by the `Type`. The `bindingAttr` parameter defines how the search is conducted. The default is to search for public methods.

```
public Type GetNestedType(string name)
public abstract Type GetNestedType(string name, BindingFlags bindingAttr)
public Type[] GetNestedTypes()
public abstract Type[] GetNestedTypes(BindingFlags bindingAttr)
```

`GetNestedType()` returns a `Type` object representing a member with the specified name which is a nested type of the invoking `Type`. A `bindingAttr` parameter can be provided to refine the search. An `ArgumentNullException` is thrown if `name` is a `null` reference.

`GetNestedTypes()` retrieves an array of `Type` objects representing the nested types within the invoking `Type`. The `bindingAttr` parameter can be used to define the search; the default is to search for public members only.

```
public PropertyInfo GetProperty(string name)
public PropertyInfo GetProperty(string name, BindingFlags bindingAttr)
public PropertyInfo GetProperty(string name, Type returnType)
public PropertyInfo GetProperty(string name, Type[] types)
public PropertyInfo GetProperty(string name, Type returnType, Type[] types)
public PropertyInfo GetProperty(string name, Type returnType, Type[] types,
                      ParameterModifier[] modifiers)
public PropertyInfo GetProperty(string name, BindingFlags bindingAttr,
                      Binder binder, Type returnType, Type[] types,
                      ParameterModifier[] modifiers)
public PropertyInfo GetPropertyImpl(string name, BindingFlags bindingAttr,
                      Binder binder, Type returnType, Type[] types,
                      ParameterModifier[] modifiers)
public PropertyInfo[] GetProperties()
public abstract PropertyInfo[] GetProperties(BindingFlags bindingAttr)
```

`GetProperty()` returns a `PropertyInfo` object containing information about the specified property. As with other methods which return members of the type, the `bindingAttr` parameter can be used to define the search; the default search is for public properties. A `Type` array can be provided with the types of the input arguments to the property. Although C# doesn't support parameterized properties, VB.NET does, so this could be used when calling a class defined in VB.NET. It can also be used with a C# indexer. The return type of the property can also be specified. Information about the modifiers for the input arguments can be supplied with an array of `ParameterModifiers`. The `Binder` object defines properties that enable binding. This argument can be `null`, in which case the default binder is used. This method will throw an exception if more than one property is found matching the input arguments, if name or `types` is a `null` reference, if `types` or `modifiers` is multidimensional, or if `types` and `modifiers` have different lengths.

`GetPropertyImpl()` is overridden in a derived class to search for the specified property under the specified constraints.

`GetProperties()` returns an array of `PropertyInfo` objects containing information about the properties defined by the `Type`. The `bindingAttr` parameter defines how the search is conducted. The default is to search for public properties.

```
protected abstract bool HasElementTypeImpl()
protected abstract bool IsArrayImpl()
protected abstract bool IsByRefImpl()
protected abstract bool IsCOMObjectImpl()
protected virtual bool IsContextfulImpl()
protected virtual bool IsMarshalByRefImpl()
protected abstract bool IsPointerImpl()
protected abstract bool IsPrimitiveImpl()
protected virtual bool IsValueTypeImpl()
```

These methods are overridden in a derived class to implement their associated property. For instance, the `IsArrayImpl()` method is overridden to implement the `IsArray` property, since the `IsArray` property isn't virtual.

```
public object InvokeMember(string name, BindingFlags invokeAttr,
                           Binder binder, object target, object[] args)
public object InvokeMember(string name, BindingFlags invokeAttr,
                           Binder binder, object target, object[] args,
                           CultureInfo info)
public object InvokeMember(string name, BindingFlags invokeAttr,
                           Binder binder, object target, object[] args,
                           ParameterModifier[] modifiers, CultureInfo info,
                           string[] namedParameters)
```

InvokeMember() invokes the specified member on a specified object according to the specified binding constraints, modifiers, cultural information, and argument list. The name parameter is the name of the constructor, method, property or field member to invoke. The invokeAttr parameter can define the search for the member. The Binder object defines properties that enable binding. This argument can be null, in which case the default binder is used. The target is the object on which to invoke the member. The args array contains the input arguments that will be passed to the member. Information about the modifiers for the input arguments can be supplied with an array of Parameter Modifiers. The CultureInfo object represents the globalization locale to use. The namedParameters array contains the names of the parameters to which the values in the args array are passed. The return value is an Object representing the return value of the member. This method will throw an exception if any of the input parameters are invalid, if the member cannot be found, if the member match is ambiguous, if the member cannot be invoked on target, or if there is a permission failure.

```
public virtual bool IsAssignableType(Type c)
public virtual bool IsInstanceOfType(object obj)
public virtual bool IsSubClassOf(Type c)
```

IsAssignableType() returns true if the c parameter and the invoking Type represent the same type, if the invoking Type is in the inheritance hierarchy of c, or if the invoking Type is an interface that c supports. Otherwise, the method returns false.

IsInstanceOfType() returns true if obj is an instance of the current Type, if the current Type is in the inheritance hierarchy of obj, or if the invoking Type is an interface that obj supports.

IsSubClassOf() returns true if the invoking Type and the input parameter c both represent classes and the class associated with the current Type derives from the class associated with c.

Example: Using the Type class

In this example, we'll show just a few of the many methods and properties of the Type object by instantiating a DateTime object and invoking a couple of its members. We start off by getting a reference to the Type object from its fully qualified name:

```
using System;
using System.Reflection;

class TypeDemo
{
    static void Main(string[] args)
    {
        // Get a Type object for the DateTime struct
        string typeName = "System.DateTime";
        Type t = Type.GetType(typeName);
```

Next, we'll call the `Type` object's `FindMembers()` method to find all the static public properties of the type. We use the `MemberTypes` enumeration to specify that we want properties, we use an OR operation on two values of the `BindingFlags` enumeration (`BindingFlags.Static` and `BindingFlags.Public`) to specify we want only public static properties, and we use a name filter with the value set to the wild card (`*`) to state that we want to retrieve all members that meet these criteria. This returns an array of `MemberInfo` objects, and we loop through this, casting each `MemberInfo` to a `PropertyInfo` object, and displaying the data type, name, and current value of each property. The value for the properties is obtained by calling the `PropertyInfo` object's `GetValue()` method. We pass two parameters into this – `null` for the instance of the object we want to invoke the property on (because we only got the static properties), and an empty `Type` array for the parameters to the property:

```
// Call FindMembers to find all public static properties of the type
MemberInfo[] members = t.FindMembers(MemberTypes.Property,
                        BindingFlags.Static | BindingFlags.Public,
                                Type.FilterName, "*");

// Print out the type, name, and current value of these properties
Console.WriteLine("Public static properties of type {0}:", t.Name);
foreach (MemberInfo member in members)
{
   PropertyInfo prop = (PropertyInfo)member;
   Console.WriteLine("{0} {1}   Value -> {2}", prop.PropertyType,
                   prop.Name, prop.GetValue(null, Type.EmptyTypes));
}
```

Next, we get a reference to the constructor overload which takes three `int` arguments (for the year, month, and day to initialize the object with), and invoke this to retrieve an instance of the `DateTime` struct:

```
// Invoke the constructor for the type to create an instance
// We pass in three ints, for the year, month, and day
Console.WriteLine("\nCalling constructor...");
ConstructorInfo ctor = t.GetConstructor(
              new Type[] { typeof(int), typeof(int), typeof(int) });
object dt = ctor.Invoke(new object[] { 2002, 2, 1 });
```

Now we've got an object instance, we can invoke a couple of properties and methods on it. First, we find the seconds component of the `DateTime` by accessing its `Second` property; then we call the `AddSecond()` method, which returns a new `DateTime` object object with the specified number of seconds added to the value of the original `DateTime`. This takes one `double` argument (the number of seconds to add). Finally, we display the seconds component of the new object:

```
// Invoke the Second property on our late-bound object
// and display its value
PropertyInfo secondProp = t.GetProperty("Second");
Console.WriteLine("Seconds of original DateTime: {0}",
                  secondProp.GetValue(dt, Type.EmptyTypes));

// Invoke the AddSeconds() method to add 30 seconds to the DateTime
```

```
        // The result is returned as a new DateTime object
        Console.WriteLine("Adding 30 seconds...");
        MethodInfo addMeth = t.GetMethod("AddSeconds");
        object newDT = addMeth.Invoke(dt, new object[] { 30.0d });

        // Display the Second property of this new object
        Console.WriteLine("Seconds part of new DateTime: {0}",
                      secondProp.GetValue(newDT, Type.EmptyTypes));
    }
}
```

Output:

```
Public static properties of type DateTime:
System.DateTime Now    Value -> 28/02/2002 16:39:27
System.DateTime UtcNow    Value -> 28/02/2002 16:39:27
System.DateTime Today    Value -> 28/02/2002 00:00:00

Calling constructor...
Seconds of original DateTime: 0
Adding 30 seconds...
Seconds part of new DateTime: 30
```

Object class

The `Object` class is the ultimate parent of all other classes in the .NET Framework. It provides low-level service methods that are common to all other classes, although many will override them to suit their individual needs. Because all other classes derive from `Object`, inheritance from `Object` is assumed and does not have to be declared.

> The C# language provides the **object** keyword as an alias for an instance of the **Object** class, and you can use it in any expression that requires an **Object**.

Syntax

```
public class Object
```

Hierarchy

```
Object
```

Constructors

public Object()

`Object()` is a no-argument constructor that's used by derived classes. The `Object` class is not declared `abstract`, so if you needed to, you could use this constructor to create an instance of the `Object` class itself.

259

Static methods

```
public static bool Equals(object objA, object objB)
public static bool ReferenceEquals(object objA, object objB)
```

The implementations of these two methods in the Object class are identical: they both return true if the object *references* that are passed as arguments are equal – that is, they refer to the same object, or are both null. In derived types, it's possible to override the Equals() method so that it performs a value, rather than a reference, comparison. This is what happens in the ValueType class, for instance, so that while this code will return False:

```
int i = 4;
int j = 4;
Console.WriteLine(Object.ReferenceEquals(i, j));
```

this code will return True:

```
int i = 4;
int j = 4;
Console.WriteLine(Object.Equals(i, j));
```

Instance methods

```
public virtual bool Equals(object obj)
public virtual int GetHashCode()
public Type GetType()
public virtual string ToString()
```

This version of Equals() does the same thing as the static version, but in this case the invoking object is compared to the input parameter, obj. Again, if the references are equal, the method returns true.

GetHashCode() returns the hash code for the invoking object. This implementation returns an index for the object determined by the Common Language Runtime.

GetType() returns the Type of the invoking object.

ToString() returns a String representation of the invoking object. The default implementation returns the fully qualified name of the object, but this method is often overridden by derived classes to provide more detailed information.

Protected instance methods

```
protected virtual void Finalize()
protected object MemberwiseClone()
```

Finalize() tells the system to attempt to free any resources allocated to the invoking object, and to perform other cleanup operations before the object is reclaimed by garbage collection. This method is called automatically by the system after the object becomes inaccessible, unless the GC.SuppressFinalize() method has been used. The version defined in the Object class does nothing, but it can be overridden by derived classes to perform whatever cleanup processes are desired.

MemberwiseClone() creates a shallow copy of the invoking object. If the original object contains any reference-type data members, the shallow copy will contain references to (instead of copies of) those data members. This method cannot be overridden.

Example: Using the Object class

This example shows some of the uses of the ToString(), Equals(), and GetType() methods, as implemented in derived classes.

```
using System;

public class ObjectDemo
{
  public static void Main()
  {
    Console.WriteLine("The date is " + DateTime.Now.ToString());

    String str = "bear";
    if(Object.Equals(str, "Bear"))
    {
      Console.WriteLine("Strings are equal");
    }
    else
    {
      Console.WriteLine("Strings are not equal");
    }

    if(str.GetType() == typeof(string))
    {
      Console.WriteLine("str is of type {0}", str.GetType());
    }
  }
}
```

Output:

```
The date is 11/7/2001 7:11:02 PM
Strings are not equal
str is of type System.String
```

String class

The String class encapsulates an immutable string of characters. Once a String object is created, its contents cannot be changed. In this way, Strings, which are reference types, have some value-type behavior. Methods that are used to 'modify' a String actually return a new String instance.

Two strings can be compared by using the Compare() and Equals() methods, or by using the equality and inequality relational operators that are defined in the String class. You can't, however, use the > or < operators on Strings. Like Object and object, C# allows you to use the string keyword as an alias for an instance of the String class.

Syntax

```
public sealed class String : IComparable, ICloneable,
                             IConvertible, IEnumerable
```

Hierarchy

```
Object --- String
```

Constructors

```
unsafe public String(char* value)
public String(char[] value)
unsafe public String(sbyte* value)
public String(char c, int count)
unsafe public String(char* value, int startIndex, int length)
public String(char[] value, int startIndex, int length)
unsafe public String(sbyte* value, int startIndex, int length)
unsafe public String(sbyte* value, int startIndex, int length, Encoding enc)
```

String() initializes a new instance of the String class, and there are various options for defining the contents of the string. The versions that take a pointer argument are not Common Language Specification (CLS) compliant; those that accept startIndex and length arguments initialize the string with a subset of a char or sbyte array. If value is null or a null pointer, a reference to String.Empty is returned.

In addition to creating a String using one of the String class constructors, you can also use a string literal. Here, a reference to a String object is set equal to a sequence of characters surrounded by double quotes, for example String str = "hello";

Fields

```
public static readonly string Empty
```

Empty is a read-only String that represents the empty string " ".

Properties and indexers

```
public char this[int index] {get;}
public int Length {get;}
```

this[] is the indexer for the String class. It returns the character at the specified character position in the string.

Length returns the number of characters in the invoking String.

Static methods

```
public static int Compare(string strA, string strB)
public static int Compare(string strA, string strB, bool ignoreCase)
public static int Compare(string strA, string strB, bool ignoreCase,
                          CultureInfo culture)
```

```
public static int Compare(string strA, int indexA, string strB,
                          int indexB, int length)
public static int Compare(string strA, int indexA, string strB,
                          int indexB, int length, bool ignoreCase)
public static int Compare(string strA, int indexA, string strB,
                          int indexB, int length, bool ignoreCase,
                          CultureInfo culture)
```

Compare() compares two String objects – it returns a negative integer if strA is less than strB, zero if the Strings are equal, and a positive integer if strA is greater than strB. (The terms "less than" and "greater than" are used in a lexicographical sense, and the comparison is also affected by the character set defined by the current locale. A CultureInfo object can be specified to provide culture-specific information.) If one of the String arguments is a null reference, it will be "less than" any other type of String. If index arguments are provided, the comparison is made on substrings of strA and strB. Compare() will throw an exception if culture is a null reference, or if the index or length arguments are invalid.

```
public static int CompareOrdinal(string strA, string strB)
public static int CompareOrdinal(string strA, int indexA,
                                 string strB, int indexB, int length)
```

CompareOrdinal() compares two String objects without considering the local language or culture. The method returns a negative integer if strA is less than strB, zero if the strings are equal, and a positive integer if strA is greater than strB. You can compare whole strings, or a subset of them. An ArgumentOutOfRangeException is thrown if the index or length arguments are invalid.

```
public static string Concat(object obj)
public static string Concat(object objA, object objB)
public static string Concat(string strA, string strB)
public static string Concat(object objA, object objB, object objC)
public static string Concat(string strA, string strB, string strC)
public static string Concat(string strA, string strB,
                            string strC, string strD)
public static string Concat(params object[] args)
public static string Concat(params string[] args)
```

Concat() concatenates a collection of strings (or the String representations of objects) and returns the result as a String. If objects are specified as input arguments, the method uses the ToString() method to generate a String representation. You can also use the + operator to concatenate strings.

```
public static string Copy(string str)
```

Copy() creates a new instance of a String with the same value as the specified String.

```
public static bool Equals(string strA, string strB)
```

Equals() returns true if the *value* of strA is the same as the *value* of strB. The comparison is case-sensitive.

```
public static string Format(string format, object obj)
public static string Format(string format, object objA, object objB)
public static string Format(string format, object objA,
                            object objB, object objC)
public static string Format(string format, params object[] args)
public static string Format(IFormatProvider provider,
                            string format, params object[] args)
```

Format() replaces any format specifications in the specified String with the textual equivalent of a corresponding object's value. The Object arguments represent an object or objects that will be formatted and placed in the string. An IFormatProvider can be used to supply culture-specific formatting information. This method will throw an exception if format or any of the Object arguments is a null reference, or if the format specification is invalid.

The format string will contain zero or more format specifications of the form {N, W:F} where N is a zero-based integer indicating the argument to be formatted, W is optional and defines the width of the formatted value, and F is a formatting code. Some valid formatting codes are described in the *Console class* section of this chapter.

```
public static string Intern(string str)
public static string IsInterned(string str)
```

Intern() retrieves the system's internal reference for the specified String. An internal reference table called the **intern pool** is managed by the Common Language Runtime as a way to conserve string storage. If several String objects are assigned with the same string literal, each String object will be set to reference the same constant in the pool. If the string str does not exist in the intern pool, this method will add str to the pool, and a reference to str is returned. An ArgumentNullException is thrown if str is a null reference.

IsInterned() returns the intern pool reference to the specified input String if it exists as part of the pool, or null if the input String does not exist in the pool. Again, an ArgumentNullException is thrown if str is a null reference.

```
public static string Join(string separator, string[] strArray)
public static string Join(string separator, string[] strArray,
                          int startIndex, int count)
```

Join() creates a new concatenated string by placing the specified separator between the elements of the specified String array. The new combined String is returned. You can do this to the whole array, or to a subset of it defined by the startIndex and count parameters. An ArgumentOutOfRangeException is thrown if the sum of startIndex and count exceeds the size of the array.

Instance methods

```
public object Clone()
```

Clone() returns a reference to the invoking String object. The return value is not an independent object, but rather a duplicate reference to the same object.

```
public int CompareTo(object value)
public int CompareTo(string str)
```

CompareTo() compares the input argument to the invoking String object. The method returns a negative integer if the invoking String is less than str, zero if the strings are equal, and a positive integer if the invoking String is greater than str. In these and other senses, this method is similar to the static Compare() method.

```
public void CopyTo(int sourceIndex, char[] destination,
                   int destIndex, int count)
```

CopyTo() transfers the characters of the invoking String starting from position sourceIndex to the specified char array starting at index destIndex. An exception is thrown if the destination array is a null reference, or if sourceIndex, destIndex, or count is out of bounds.

```
public bool EndsWith(string str)
public bool StartsWith(string str)

public override bool Equals(object obj)
public bool Equals(string str)
```

EndsWith() returns true if the invoking String object ends with the specified String, or false if it does not. StartsWith() does the same, but examines the character at the start of the string. Both throw an ArgumentNullException if str is a null reference.

The two Equals() methods above are single-parameter versions of the static methods defined by String and Object. A NullReferenceException is thrown if the instance that calls this method is a null reference.

```
public CharEnumerator GetEnumerator()
public override int GetHashCode()
public TypeCode GetTypeCode()
```

GetEnumerator() retrieves an object that can be used to iterate through the characters that make up the invoking String object.

GetHashCode() is an overridden version of the method defined in the Object class. It returns the hash code for the invoking String object.

GetTypeCode() returns the TypeCode for the invoking String.

```
public int IndexOf(char c)
public int IndexOf(string str)
public int IndexOf(char c, int startIndex)
public int IndexOf(string str, int startIndex)
public int IndexOf(char c, int startIndex, int count)
public int IndexOf(string str, int startIndex, int count)

public int LastIndexOf(char c)
public int LastIndexOf(string str)
public int LastIndexOf(char c, int startIndex)
public int LastIndexOf(string str, int startIndex)
public int LastIndexOf(char c, int startIndex, int count)
public int LastIndexOf(string str, int startIndex, int count)
```

IndexOf() returns the index in the invoking String of the first occurrence of the specified character or String, or -1 if the character or String was not found. You can search through the entire invoking String, start the search at position startIndex, or search between startIndex and startIndex + count. An exception is thrown if the input String is a null reference, if either startIndex or count is negative, or if A is greater than the length of the invoking String.

LastIndexOf() behaves identically to IndexOf(), except that it returns the index in the invoking String of the *last* occurrence of the specified character or String.

```
public int IndexOfAny(char[] chars)
public int IndexOfAny(char[] chars, int startIndex)
public int IndexOfAny(char[] chars, int startIndex, int count)

public int LastIndexOfAny(char[] chars)
public int LastIndexOfAny(char[] chars, int startIndex)
public int LastIndexOfAny(char[] chars, int startIndex, int count)
```

IndexOfAny() returns the index in the invoking String of the first occurrence of any of the characters in the specified character array, or -1 if none of the characters in chars is found. Apart from the change in the number of characters being examined, its behavior is the same as that of IndexOf(). Predictably, LastIndexOfAny() does the same for the last occurrence of one of the characters.

```
public string Insert(int startIndex, string str)
```

Insert() creates and returns a new String by inserting the specified string into the invoking String at position startIndex. An exception is thrown if the str is a null reference, if startIndex is negative, or if startIndex is larger than the length of the invoking String.

```
public string PadLeft(int totalWidth)
public string PadLeft(int totalWidth, char paddingChar)

public string PadRight(int totalWidth)
public string PadRight(int totalWidth, char paddingChar)
```

PadLeft() right-aligns the characters in the invoking String object by placing blank spaces or a repeated character at the beginning of the string to make it the specified length, while PadRight() performs left-alignment by inserting characters at the end. In both case, a new, padded String is returned. An ArgumentException is thrown if totalWidth is less than zero.

```
public string Remove(int startIndex, int count)
```

Remove() deletes count characters from the invoking String, starting from position startIndex. A new, truncated String is returned. An ArgumentOutOfRangeException is thrown if either startIndex or count is negative, or the sum of them is greater than the length of the invoking String.

```
public string Replace(char oldChar, char newChar)
public string Replace(string oldString, string newString)
```

Replace() replaces all instances of the specified character or String in the invoking String with the specified replacement character or String. A new String with the modified character sequence is returned.

```
public string[] Split(params char[] separators)
public string[] Split(params char[] separators, int maxElements)
```

Split() separates the invoking String into substrings. The substring delimiters are the elements contained in the separators array, while the substrings themselves are placed in a String array that's the return value of the method. You can also specify the maximum number of elements to return. If the separators array is empty, the invoking String is returned intact. If the separators array is set to the null reference, whitespace is used as the delimiter. An ArgumentOutOfRangeException is thrown if maxElements is negative.

```
public string Substring(int startIndex)
public string Substring(int startIndex, int length)
```

Substring() returns a new String object that contains a substring of the invoking String object. You can specify a starting index and a range from which to make the substring. An ArgumentOutOfRangeException is thrown if either startIndex or length is negative, or if the sum of them is greater than the length of the invoking String.

```
public char[] ToCharArray()
public char[] ToCharArray(int startIndex, int length)
```

ToCharArray() copies the characters that make up the invoking String object into a character array. You can do this with the entire String, or a substring of it. An ArgumentOutOfRangeException is thrown if either startIndex or length is negative, or if the sum of them is greater than the length of the invoking String.

```
public string ToLower()
public string ToLower(CultureInfo info)

public string ToUpper()
public string ToUpper(CultureInfo info)
```

ToLower() returns a copy of the invoking String with all the characters changed to lowercase, while ToUpper() will change them to uppercase. A CultureInfo object that supplies culture-specific formatting information can be specified. An ArgumentNullException is thrown if info is a null reference.

```
public override string ToString()
public string ToString(IFormatProvider provider)
```

The first ToString() method here is an artifact of the String class's inheritance from Object – it simply returns the invoking String. No modification of the original String is performed. The second accepts a reference to an implementation of IFormatProvider that can supply culture-specific formatting information.

```
public string Trim()
public string Trim(params char[] trimChars)
public string TrimEnd(params char[] trimChars)
public string TrimStart(params char[] trimChars)
```

`Trim()` removes all occurrences of the specified characters from the beginning and end of the invoking `String`, `TrimEnd()` removes them only from the end, and `TrimStart()` removes them only from the beginning. If you fail to pass an argument (or pass a `null` one), whitespace is removed. A new, trimmed `String` object is returned.

Operators

```
public static bool operator ==(string a, string b)
public static bool operator !=(string a, string b)
```

`==` returns `true` if the strings a and b have the same value. Otherwise, it returns `false`.
`!=` returns `true` if the strings a and b do not have the same value. Otherwise, it returns `false`.

Example: Using the String class

In this example, we use some of the methods from the `String` class to parse lines read from an input file that contains the data necessary to determine the volume of a particular geometric shape. The first line in the input file is the type of shape, and the inequality operator defined in the `String` class is used to compare this string against the word "cylinder".

The next two lines of the file contain radius and height data. Each line has the form "name = value" and is read into the program as a single `String`. The `Split()` method is used to parse each line into substrings, using the "=" character as the delimiter.

Finally, the program writes the results to standard output in a structured format, using the `PadLeft()` method. This causes the output to be right-aligned.

```csharp
using System;
using System.IO;

public class StringDemo
{
  public static void Main()
  {
    String line;
    String[] strings;
    double radius;
    double height;
    double volume;

    StreamReader sr = new StreamReader(
                    new FileStream("StringDemo.inp", FileMode.Open));

    if(sr.ReadLine() != "cylinder")
    {
      Console.WriteLine("Shape type must be cylinder");
      return;
    }

    char[] delimiter = {'='};
```

```
            strings = sr.ReadLine().Split(delimiter);
            radius = Convert.ToDouble(strings[1]);

            strings = sr.ReadLine().Split(delimiter);
            height = Convert.ToDouble(strings[1]);

            volume = Math.PI * radius * radius * height;

            line = "Cylinder radius =";
            Console.WriteLine(line.PadLeft(17) + " {0}", radius);

            line = "Height =";
            Console.WriteLine(line.PadLeft(17) + " {0}", height);

            line = "Volume =";
            Console.WriteLine(line.PadLeft(17) + " {0}", volume);
         }
      }
```

Input file:

```
   cylinder
   radius = 4.0
   height = 5.0
```

Output:

```
   cylinder radius = 4
            height = 5
            volume = 251.327412287
```

Array class

The Array class is the parent class for *all* arrays in the Common Language Runtime. It defines methods to create, search, sort, and modify arrays. Arrays created using the 'standard' C and C++ syntax described in Chapter 6 are otherwise identical to the array created using the Array class, and they can therefore utilize the methods and properties that it provides. It's worth noting here that C# arrays are safe, in that the runtime will prevent you from doing such things as using an out-of-bounds index.

Syntax

```
   public abstract class Array : ICloneable, IList, ICollection, IEnumerable
```

Hierarchy

```
   Object --- Array
```

Constructors

The `Array` class is abstract and doesn't define any public constructors (only the system and compilers can derive explicitly from the `Array` class). Instead, you can use the static, overloaded `CreateInstance()` method to generate one- or multidimensional `Array` objects; or you can use language features such as those we looked at in Chapter 6.

The number of dimensions in an `Array` is called its **rank**, the total number of elements in an `Array` is called its **length**, and every element in an `Array` has a **value** that can be `null`.

An `Array` object is immutable in that once its length is initialized, elements cannot be added to or removed from it. For a one-dimensional array whose length *can* be modified, see the `ArrayList` class that's described in the next chapter.

Public instance properties

```
public virtual bool IsFixedSize {get;}
public virtual bool IsReadOnly {get;}
public virtual bool IsSynchronized {get;}
public int Length {get;}
public int Rank {get;}
public virtual object SyncRoot {get;}
```

`IsFixedSize` is `true` if the `Array` represents a fixed-size array. You can't change the dimensions of a fixed-size `Array`, but you *can* modify its existing elements. The `IsFixedSize` property is `true` by default, but can be overridden in a derived class.

`IsReadOnly` is `true` if the associated `Array` is read-only. By default this property is `false`, but it can be overridden in a derived class.

`IsSynchronized` indicates whether access to the `Array` is synchronized and therefore thread-safe. This property is `false` unless overridden in a derived class. A synchronized version of an `Array` can be obtained by using the `SyncRoot` property.

`Length` is the total number of elements in the `Array`, across all dimensions.

`Rank` represents the number of dimensions in the `Array`. A two-dimensional `Array` would have a `Rank` property equal to 2.

`SyncRoot` returns an object that can be used to synchronize access to an `Array`. Synchronized operations are performed on the `SyncRoot` of the `Array`, rather than on the `Array` itself. This ensures proper synchronization with any threads that may be trying to modify the `Array` simultaneously.

Public static methods

The `Array` class defines a number of static methods that implement the basic operations of creating, copying, clearing, sorting, or searching an `Array`. In many cases, the methods are overloaded, allowing them to be applied to different types of `Array` objects for different purposes.

```
public static int BinarySearch(Array array, object value)
public static int BinarySearch(Array array, object value,
                    IComparer comparer)
```

```
public static int BinarySearch(Array array, int startIndex, int length,
                               object value)
public static int BinarySearch(Array array, int startIndex, int length,
                               object value, IComparer comparer)
```

BinarySearch() searches a one-dimensional, sorted Array for the specified value using a binary search algorithm. Each element of the Array and the object to be searched for must implement the IComparable interface in order to allow the search to proceed. The method returns the index where value is located in the Array, or a negative number if the value was not found in the Array. If you wish, you can specify your own implementation of IComparer to be used during the search; if you don't provide startIndex and length parameters, the entire Array is searched.

The BinarySearch() method will throw an exception if array is a null reference or multidimensional, or if the startIndex or length arguments are invalid. It will also throw an exception if either value or the elements in array don't implement the IComparable interface.

```
public static void Clear(Array array, int startIndex, int length)
```

Clear() sets the values of the specified elements of Array to null (if they are reference types) or to zero (if they are value types). The startIndex is the starting index of the range of elements to be cleared, and length is the number of elements to clear. This method will throw an exception if array is a null reference, or if the startIndex or length parameters are out of bounds.

```
public static void Copy(Array sourceArray,
                Array destinationArray, int length)
public static void Copy(Array sourceArray, int sourceStartIndex,
                Array destinationArray, int destinationStartIndex, int length)
```

Copy() copies a range of elements from sourceArray into destinationArray, which must have equal numbers of dimensions. You can copy the elements of a reference-type array into a value-type array (and vice versa), as long as appropriate conversions are possible. If a reference-type array is copied into another reference-type array, a shallow copy will occur, meaning that the new array will contain references to the elements of the original array. For a value-type-to-value-type copy, either the two arrays must be of the same type, or the copy must not involve a narrowing conversion. (A copy from a 64-bit integer array to a 32-bit integer array, for instance, is not allowed.)

The starting indices define where copying will start in the sourceArray, and where the copied elements will be placed in the destinationArray. If starting indexes are not provided, copying will be performed from and to the start of each Array.

This method will throw an exception if either Array is a null reference, if the Arrays have different ranks, or if they are of incompatible types. An exception is also thrown if the starting indices are less than zero, or greater than the size of the Array.

```
public static Array CreateInstance(Type elementType, int length1)
public static Array CreateInstance(Type elementType, int length1,
                               int length2)
public static Array CreateInstance(Type elementType, int length1,
                               int length2, int length3)
```

```
public static Array CreateInstance(Type elementType, int[] lengths)
public static Array CreateInstance(Type elementType, int[] lengths,
                                   int[] lowerBounds)
```

As we suggested at the start of this section, CreateInstance() returns an Array of the specified Type. Array elements will be initialized to null (for reference-type Arrays) or to zero (for value-type Arrays). The first three versions create one-, two-, and three-dimensional arrays respectively, while the fourth and fifth versions create a multidimensional Array with dimension sizes set according to the values in the lengths array. The lowerBounds array can be used to specify the starting index for each dimension in the Array, which is zero by default. This method will throw an exception if elementType is null or does not represent a valid type. An exception will also be thrown if any of the length parameters are less than zero.

```
public static int IndexOf(Array array, object value)
public static int IndexOf(Array array, object value,
                          int startIndex)
public static int IndexOf(Array array, object value,
                          int startIndex, int length)

public static int LastIndexOf(Array array, object value)
public static int LastIndexOf(Array array, object value,
                              int startIndex)
public static int LastIndexOf(Array array, object value,
                              int startIndex, int length)
```

IndexOf() performs a forward search of the specified Array looking for the first occurrence of the specified value, as matched using the Object.Equals() method. The method returns the index of the first occurrence of the object, or the lower bound of the array minus one (usually -1) if the object is not found. The startIndex and length parameters can be used to define the range of the search; if they are not provided, the entire Array will be searched. This method will throw an exception if the specified Array is a null reference, or if it is multidimensional. An exception is also thrown if the startIndex or length parameters are invalid.

LastIndexOf() performs the same search, but returns the index of the last occurrence of the specified value.

```
public static void Reverse(Array array)
public static void Reverse(Array array, int startIndex, int length)
```

Reverse() reverses the order of the elements of a one-dimensional Array. The startIndex and length parameters can be used to define the range of reversal; if they are not provided, the entire Array is reversed. This method will throw an exception if the specified Array is a null reference, or if it is multidimensional. An exception is also thrown if the startIndex or length parameters are invalid.

```
public static void Sort(Array array)
public static void Sort(Array keys, Array items)
public static void Sort(Array array, IComparer comparer)
public static void Sort(Array keys, Array items, IComparer comparer)
public static void Sort(Array array, int startIndex, int length)
public static void Sort(Array keys, Array items, int startIndex, int length)
public static void Sort(Array array, int startIndex, int length,
                        IComparer comparer)
```

```
public static void Sort(Array keys, Array items, int startIndex, int length,
                        IComparer comparer)
```

Sort() sorts the elements of a one-dimensional array according to either the IComparable interface implemented by each element of the Array, or an implementation of the IComparer interface that you provide. If two Arrays are specified, they should represent an array of keys and an array of items. If a key element is repositioned, the corresponding item element will also be repositioned. If a starting index and a length are not specified, the entire array (or arrays) will be sorted.

This method will throw an exception if keys is a null reference, or if either the keys or items Array is multidimensional. An exception is also thrown if the comparer throws an exception, if the comparer is a null reference, or if the elements of the keys Array do not implement the IComparable interface. Lastly, an exception will be thrown if the startIndex and length parameters are invalid.

Public instance methods

The Array class also defines a number of public instance methods for performing array operations. In general, these methods are used to access or change the elements of an Array.

```
public virtual object Clone()
public virtual void CopyTo(Array destinationArray, int index)
```

Clone() returns a shallow copy of the invoking Array object. If the original Array contained reference types, the new Array will be the same Type, and will contain references to the elements of the original Array.

CopyTo() shallow-copies all of the elements of the invoking one-dimensional Array into the specified destination array, starting at the specified index. (The index is relative to the lower bound of the destination array.) This method will throw an exception if the specified Array is a null reference, or if it is multidimensional. An exception is also thrown if the index parameter is invalid.

```
public virtual IEnumerator GetEnumerator()
```

GetEnumerator() returns an IEnumerator object that can be used to read data from the invoking Array.

```
public int GetLength(int dimension)
public int GetLowerBound(int dimension)
public int GetUpperBound(int dimension)
```

GetLength() returns the number of elements in the specified dimension, which is zero-based – if you wanted the number of elements in the first dimension of an Array, you would call GetLength(0). Similarly, GetLowerBound() returns the lower bound of the specified dimension, while GetUpperBound() returns the upper bound of the specified dimension. All three methods will throw an exception if dimension is less than zero, or greater than the rank of the Array.

```
public Object GetValue(int index)
public Object GetValue(int index1, int index2)
public Object GetValue(int index1, int index2, int index 3)
```

```
public Object GetValue(int[] indices)

public void SetValue(object value, int index)
public void SetValue(object value, int index1, int index2)
public void SetValue(object value, int index1, int index2, int index 3)
public void SetValue(object value, int[] indices)
```

GetValue() returns the element at the specified index of the invoking Array as an Object. The first three versions are for one-, two-, and three-dimensional Arrays respectively; the fourth is for returning an element of a multidimensional array, where the indices array contains the location of the element. This method will throw an exception if an index value is out of bounds.

SetValue() changes the value of an element at the specified index of the invoking Array, subject to the same guidelines as for GetValue() above. This method will throw an exception if the rank of the invoking Array does not match the number of index parameters, if the index parameters are out of bounds, or if value cannot be converted into the same type as the Array.

Example: Using the Array class

In this example, we'll look at the general process of creating and manipulating an Array object. A one-dimensional Array is created, and values are assigned to the array elements. The Array is then sorted, and its contents are printed out.

```csharp
using System;

public class ArrayDemo
{
  public static void Main()
  {
    // A one-dimensional Array object is created
    Array array = Array.CreateInstance(typeof(string), 4);
    array.SetValue("Jackson", 0);
    array.SetValue("Lisa", 1);
    array.SetValue("Zachary", 2);
    array.SetValue("Bailey", 3);

    // The Array is sorted and its contents are printed out
    Array.Sort(array);
    int index = Array.IndexOf(array, "Jackson");
    if(index >= 0)
    {
      Console.WriteLine("Jackson is at index {0}", index);
    }

    for(int i = 0; i < array.GetLength(0); ++i)
    {
      Console.WriteLine("Element {0} is {1}", i, array.GetValue(i));
    }
    Console.WriteLine();
```

```
        // Array class methods also work on arrays created with C# syntax
        int[] intArray = new int[5]{14, 3, 27, 123, 8};
        Array.Sort(intArray);
        Array.Reverse(intArray);

        foreach(int i in intArray)
        {
          Console.WriteLine("Element {0} is {1}",
                            Array.IndexOf(intArray, i), i);
        }
      }
    }
```

Output:

```
Jackson is at index 1
Element 0 is Bailey
Element 1 is Jackson
Element 2 is Lisa
Element 3 is Zachary

Element 0 is 123
Element 1 is 27
Element 2 is 14
Element 3 is 8
Element 4 is 3
```

Console class

The Console class provides static methods and properties to access the standard input, output, and error streams for console applications. Included in the class definition are the standard I/O streams and methods to read from and write to the console. If these methods are used in a Windows application where the console does not exist, they do nothing, but no exception is thrown.

Syntax

```
public sealed class Console
```

Hierarchy

```
Object --- Console
```

Properties

The properties defined in the Console class represent the standard input, output, and error streams. They are all static properties, which means that they can be accessed at any time, without the explicit creation of an instance of the Console class. If necessary, the standard streams can be changed using the SetError(), SetIn(), and SetOut() methods.

```
public static TextWriter Error {get;}
public static TextReader In {get;}
public static TextWriter Out {get;}
```

Error returns a reference to a TextWriter object that represents the standard error stream. In returns a reference to a TextReader object that represents the standard input stream. Out returns a reference to a TextWriter object that represents the standard output stream.

Static methods

```
public static void SetError(TextWriter newError)
public static void SetIn(TextReader newIn)
public static void SetOut(TextWriter newOut)
```

As described above, these methods are used to change from standard streams to specified streams. If a StreamReader/Writer that encapsulates a FileReader/Writer is used, text can be retrieved from or sent to a file. If the argument you pass is null, an exception of type ArgumentNullException is thrown.

```
public static Stream OpenStandardError()
public static Stream OpenStandardError(int bufferSize)
public static Stream OpenStandardInput()
public static Stream OpenStandardInput(int bufferSize)
public static Stream OpenStandardOutput()
public static Stream OpenStandardOutput(int bufferSize)
```

These methods are used to reacquire the standard streams after they have been changed by the SetError(), SetIn(), and SetOut() methods respectively. As you can see, the return value is a reference to a Stream object in all three cases, for which you can specify a buffer size if you wish. An ArgumentOutOfRangeException is thrown if bufferSize is less than or equal to zero.

```
public static int Read()
public static string ReadLine()
```

Read() returns the next character from the standard input stream, or -1 if no more characters are available. This method will not return until the read operation is terminated – usually, when the user presses the *Enter* key. The resulting input stream will contain whatever was typed on the command line, with carriage return and linefeed characters appended to the end. An IOException is thrown if an I/O error occurs during the read.

ReadLine() returns the next line from the standard input stream, or null if no more characters are available. The method does not return until a carriage return character followed by a linefeed character is detected. The return string will not include the carriage return or linefeed characters. Once again, an IOException is thrown if an I/O error occurs during the read.

```
public static void Write(bool value)
public static void Write(char value)
public static void Write(char[] buffer)
public static void Write(char[] buffer, int startIndex, int count)
public static void Write(decimal value)
```

```
public static void Write(double value)
public static void Write(int value)
public static void Write(long value)
public static void Write(object value)
public static void Write(float value)
public static void Write(string value)
public static void Write(uint value)
public static void Write(ulong value)
public static void Write(string format, object obj)
public static void Write(string format, object object1, object object2)
public static void Write(string format, object object1, object object2,
                         object,3)
public static void Write(string format, object object1, object object2,
                         object,3, object 4)
public static void Write(string format, object[] objects)
```

Write() writes the specified input value to the standard output stream, and as you can see, it's overloaded to support all types of values, strings, and other objects. It's permissible to provide a format string of the form {N, W:F} where N is a zero-based integer indicating the argument to be formatted, W is optional and defines the width of the formatted value, and F is a formatting code. Valid formatting codes include "C" (local currency), "D" (decimal), "E" (exponential), "F" (fixed-point), "G" (general), "N" (number), "P" (percent), and "X" (hexadecimal), and are case-insensitive. This method will throw an IOException if an I/O error occurs during the write.

```
public static void WriteLine()
public static void WriteLine(bool value)
public static void WriteLine(char value)
public static void WriteLine(char[] buffer)
public static void WriteLine(char[] buffer, int startIndex, int count)
public static void WriteLine(decimal value)
public static void WriteLine(double value)
public static void WriteLine(int value)
public static void WriteLine(long value)
public static void WriteLine(object value)
public static void WriteLine(float value)
public static void WriteLine(string value)
public static void WriteLine(uint value)
public static void WriteLine(ulong value)
public static void WriteLine(string format, object obj)
public static void WriteLine(string format, object object1, object object2)
public static void WriteLine(string format, object object1, object object2,
                             object object3)
public static void WriteLine(string format, object[] objects)
```

WriteLine() writes the specified input value to the standard output stream, followed by a line terminator. Like Write(), the method is overloaded to support all types of values, strings, and other objects, and a format string can be provided. The no-argument version simply writes a line terminator to standard output. This method will throw an IOException if an I/O error occurs during the write.

Example: Using the Console class

Of course, we've been using the `Console` class for output throughout the book, so we'll do something a little different here. In this example, the standard output stream is redirected to a file named `ConsoleDemo.out` by using the `SetOut()` method. When you run this application, a file with this name will be created in the current directory, containing the text "This will be written to a file".

```
using System;
using System.IO;

public class ConsoleDemo
{
  public static void Main()
  {
    // The standard output stream is set to write data to a file
    StreamWriter sw = new StreamWriter(
                 new FileStream("ConsoleDemo.out", FileMode.Create));
    Console.SetOut(sw);

    Console.WriteLine("This will be written to a file");
    sw.Close();
  }
}
```

Output (contents of `ConsoleDemo.out`):

```
This will be written to a file
```

Convert class

The `Convert` class is really a kind of library that provides the ability to convert base data types to other base data types. Most type conversions are supported – even narrowing conversions – but care must be taken. For example, if a `double` is converted to a `float`, but the `double` is too large to be represented by the `float`, an `OverflowException` will be thrown.

Syntax

```
public sealed class Convert
```

Hierarchy

```
Object --- Convert
```

Fields

```
public static readonly object DBNull
```

`DBNull` is a constant representing a database column with no data (also known as a **database null**).

Static methods

```
public static object ChangeType(object value, Type newType)
public static object ChangeType(object value, Type newType,
                                IFormatProvider provider)
public static object ChangeType(object value, TypeCode newTypeCode)
public static object ChangeType(object value, TypeCode newTypeCode,
                                IFormatProvider provider)
```

ChangeType() takes the specified object value and converts it to a new type of object. The converted object is returned. The conversion may be defined by specifying a new Type or TypeCode. An IFormatProvider can be specified that provides culture-specific information, such as calendar and date formatting, sorting strings, numeric formatting, and so on. The value parameter must be an instance of a class that implements the IConvertible interface; this method will throw an InvalidCastException if this is not the case.

```
public static byte[] FromBase64CharArray(char[] inputArray,
                                         int offset, int length)
public static byte[] FromBase64String(string str)

public static int ToBase64CharArray(byte[] inputArray, int offsetIn,
                         int length, char[] outputArray, int offsetOut)
public static string ToBase64String(byte[] inputArray)
public static string ToBase64String(byte[] inputArray, int offset,
                                                        int length)
```

FromBase64CharArray() converts part of an array of Unicode characters consisting of base-64 digits to an array of 8-bit unsigned integers. The offset and length parameters define the range of characters to be converted. An exception is thrown if the array is a null reference, if the array length is not an even multiple of four, or if the offset or length parameters are out of bounds.

FromBase64String() converts a String representation of a value consisting of base-64 digits to an equivalent array of 8-bit unsigned integers. An exception is thrown if the String is a null reference, or if the String length is not an even multiple of four.

ToBase64CharArray() and ToBase64String() perform these conversions in the opposite direction. In the former, the return value is a 32-bit signed integer containing the number of bytes in the output array. In both, an exception is thrown if inputArray is a null reference, or if the offset or length parameters are out of bounds.

```
public static TypeCode GetTypeCode(object value)
public static bool IsDBNull(object value)
```

GetTypeCode() returns the TypeCode for the specified object. The value parameter must be an instance of a class that implements the IConvertible interface.

IsDBNull() returns true if the input object is of type DBNull.

```
public static bool ToBoolean(bool value)
public static bool ToBoolean(byte value)
public static bool ToBoolean(char value)
```

```
public static bool ToBoolean(DateTime value)
public static bool ToBoolean(decimal value)
public static bool ToBoolean(double value)
public static bool ToBoolean(short value)
public static bool ToBoolean(int value)
public static bool ToBoolean(long value)
public static bool ToBoolean(object value)
public static bool ToBoolean(sbyte value)
public static bool ToBoolean(float value)
public static bool ToBoolean(string value)
public static bool ToBoolean(ushort value)
public static bool ToBoolean(uint value)
public static bool ToBoolean(ulong value)
public static bool ToBoolean(object value, IFormatProvider provider)
public static bool ToBoolean(string value, IFormatProvider provider)
```

ToBoolean() converts the specified input parameter to an equivalent Boolean value. For numerical types, the method will return true if value is non-zero, and false if it is zero. It will throw an InvalidCastException if the cast is not supported (say, if you tried to convert a DateTime to a bool). Again, an implementation of IFormatProvider can be used to provide culture-specific information.

```
public static byte ToByte(<type> value)
public static char ToByte(<type> value)
public static DateTime ToDateTime(<type> value)
public static decimal ToDecimal(<type> value)
public static double ToDouble(<type> value)
public static short ToInt16(<type> value)
public static int ToInt32(<type> value)
public static long ToInt64(<type> value)
public static sbyte ToSByte(<type> value)
public static float ToSingle(<type> value)
public static string ToString(<type> value)
public static ushort ToUInt16(<type> value)
public static uint ToUInt32(<type> value)
public static ulong ToUInt64(<type> value)
```

The Convert class also provides methods to perform conversions to all other value types. The generic form of these methods is shown above. Each method is overloaded similarly to the ToBoolean() method, such that *any* value type, string, or object can be used as an input parameter. The ToString() method includes additional overloaded versions that take an IFormatProvider as a second input parameter. Keep in mind that some conversions may not be supported, and then an attempt to perform such a conversion will cause an InvalidCastException to be thrown.

Example: Convert class

This example demonstrates a common use of the Convert class's methods – namely, converting a String read from an input file to a value type. The ConvertDemo class reads data from an input file that consists of the name of a shape and its principal dimensions. The volume of each shape is computed and written to standard output. The dimension data is read from the input file as a String, and converted to type double using the ToDouble() method. The ToInt32() method is also used to convert the number of shapes read from the input file to a 32-bit integer value.

```
using System;
using System.IO;

public class ConvertDemo
{
  public static void Main()
  {
    String str;
    int numShapes;
    int i;

    double radius;
    double width;
    double length;
    double height;

    // An input stream is opened to read data from a file.
    StreamReader sr = new StreamReader(
                new FileStream("ConvertDemo.inp", FileMode.Open));

    // The first line of the input file is an integer representing the
    // number of volumes to be computed. The value is read from the input
    // file as a String and converted to an int using the ToInt32() method.
    numShapes = Convert.ToInt32(sr.ReadLine());
    for(i = 0; i < numShapes; ++i)
    {
      sr.ReadLine();

      // Read blank line
      str = sr.ReadLine();
      if(str.Equals("cylinder"))
      {
        // If the shape is a cylinder, the next two lines contain the
        // radius and height. These values are initially read as Strings
        // and are converted to doubles using the ToDouble() method.
        radius = Convert.ToDouble(sr.ReadLine());
        height = Convert.ToDouble(sr.ReadLine());
        Console.WriteLine("Shape is " + str);
        Console.WriteLine("Radius is {0}", radius);
        Console.WriteLine("Height is {0}", height);
        Console.WriteLine(
                "Volume is {0}", radius * radius * Math.PI * height);
        Console.WriteLine();
      }

      if(str.Equals("cuboid"))
      {
        // If the shape is a cuboid, the next three lines contain the
        // width, length, and height. These values are initially read as
        // Strings and converted to doubles using the ToDouble() method.
        width = Convert.ToDouble(sr.ReadLine());
        length = Convert.ToDouble(sr.ReadLine());
```

```
            height = Convert.ToDouble(sr.ReadLine());

            Console.WriteLine("Shape is " + str);
            Console.WriteLine("Width is {0}", width);
            Console.WriteLine("Length is {0}", length);
            Console.WriteLine("Height is {0}", height);
            Console.WriteLine("Volume is {0}", width * length * height);
            Console.WriteLine();
        }
      }
    }
  }
```

The contents of the `ConvertDemo.inp` file are as follows:

```
2

cylinder
2.0
4.0

cuboid
3.0
4.0
5.0
```

The output of this program is:

```
Shape is cylinder
Radius is 2
Height is 4
Volume is 50.2654822457

Shape is cuboid
Width is 3
Length is 4
Height is 5
Volume is 60
```

DateTime struct

The `DateTime` struct encapsulates an instant in time – usually, a date and a time of day. The time value is measured in 100-nanosecond intervals since 12:00 AM, January 1 (Gregorian calendar) 1 CE (Common Era). The time defined by the `DateTime` stack will also depend on the time zone it represents, although it's up to the developer to keep track of the time zone associated with a `DateTime` instance. The `DateTime` structure includes methods and properties for accessing and modifying every aspect of the data it contains.

Syntax

```
public struct DateTime : IComparable, IFormattable, IConvertible
```

Hierarchy

```
Object --- ValueType --- DateTime
```

Constructors

```
public DateTime(long ticks)
public DateTime(int year, int month, int day)
public DateTime(int year, int month, int day, Calendar calendar)
public DateTime(int year, int month, int day, int hour, int minute,
                int second)
public DateTime(int year, int month, int day, int hour, int minute,
                int second, Calendar calendar)
public DateTime(int year, int month, int day, int hour, int minute,
                int second, int millisecond)
public DateTime(int year, int month, int day, int hour, int minute,
                int second, int millisecond, Calendar calendar)
```

DateTime() creates a new DateTime instance that's initialized with parameters that pinpoint a date and time. If the DateTime object is initialized with a year, month, and day, its time will be set to 12:00 midnight. Examples of Calendars defined in the System.Globalization namespace are the GregorianCalendar and JulianCalendar classes.

Fields

```
public static readonly DateTime MaxValue
public static readonly DateTime MinValue
```

MaxValue represents the largest possible value of a DateTime object. It corresponds to a date and time of 11:59:59 PM, December 31, 9999 CE.

MinValue represents the smallest allowable value of a DateTime object. It corresponds to a date and time of 12:00:00 AM, January 1, 0001 CE.

Public static properties

```
public static DateTime Now {get;}
public static DateTime Today {get;}
public static DateTime UtcNow {get;}
```

Now returns a DateTime object that contains the date and time values according to the current local time on the computer.

Today retrieves a DateTime object corresponding to the current date, with the time set to midnight.

UtcNow gets a DateTime object that represents the current local time on the computer in terms of the coordinated universal time (UTC).

Public instance properties

```
public DateTime Date {get;}
public int Day {get;}
public DayOfWeek DayOfWeek {get;}
public int DayOfYear {get;}
public int Hour {get;}
public int Millisecond {get;}
public int Minute {get;}
public int Month {get;}
public int Second {get;}
public long Ticks {get;}
public TimeSpan TimeOfDay {get;}
public int Year {get;}
```

Date returns a DateTime object containing the date of the invoking DateTime object with the time value set to midnight.

Day returns the day value of the invoking DateTime object as an integer between 1 and 31.

DayOfWeek returns an enumerated constant that indicates the day of the week. The return values range from zero (Sunday) to six (Saturday).

DayOfYear returns an integer value between 1 and 366 indicating the day of the year.

Hour returns an integer value representing the hour of the day. The value can range from 0 to 23.

Millisecond gets the millisecond component of the time represented by the invoking DateTime. The value will range from 0 to 999.

Minute returns an integer value representing the minute component of the DateTime, ranging from 0 to 59.

Month returns an integer between 1 and 12 corresponding to the month.

Second gets the seconds component of the invoking DateTime object. This will be a number between 0 and 59.

Ticks retrieves the number of 100-nanosecond ticks since 12:00:00 AM, January 1, 0001 CE represented by the invoking DateTime object.

TimeOfDay returns a TimeSpan object that corresponds to the fraction of the day since midnight.

Year returns an integer corresponding to the year component of the invoking DateTime.

Public static methods

```
public static int Compare(DateTime dt1, DateTime dt2)
public static int DaysInMonth(int year, int month)
public static bool Equals(DateTime dt1, DateTime dt2)
public static DateTime FromFileTime(long fileTime)
public static DateTime FromOADate(double d)
public static bool IsLeapYear(int year)
```

`Compare()` returns -1 if dt1 is less than dt2, zero if dt1 is equal to dt2, and 1 if dt1 is greater than dt2.

`DaysInMonth()` returns the number of days in the specified month in the specified year. An `ArgumentOutOfRangeException` is thrown if month is less than 1 or greater than 12.

`Equals()` compares two `DateTime` objects and returns true if they are equal.

`FromFileTime()` returns a `DateTime` object that's initialized with the specified Windows file timestamp. An `ArgumentOutOfRangeException` is thrown if `fileTime` is not valid.

`FromOADate()` returns a `DateTime` object corresponding to the specified OLE Automation `Date` value. The input argument must be number between -657435.0 and 2958466.0. An `ArgumentException` is thrown if the input parameter is out of bounds.

`IsLeapYear()` returns true if the specified year is a leap year.

```
public static DateTime Parse(string str)
public static DateTime Parse(string str, IFormatProvider provider)
public static DateTime Parse(string str, IFormatProvider provider,
                            DateTimeStyles styles)
public static DateTime ParseExact(string str, string format,
                            IFormatProvider provider)
public static DateTime ParseExact(string str, string format,
                            IFormatProvider provider, DateTimeStyles styles)
public static DateTime ParseExact(string str, string[] formats,
                            IFormatProvider provider, DateTimeStyles styles)
```

`Parse()` creates a `DateTime` object by parsing a `String` that contains a date and a time. The `String` can't contain leading, inner, or trailing whitespace characters, but an `IFormatProvider` can be used to specify culture-specific information such as calendar and date formatting, sorting strings, numeric formatting, and so on. Furthermore, a `DateTimeStyles` object can be used to indicate the permitted format of the input `String`. This method will throw an exception if the input `String` is a `null` reference, or if it doesn't represent a valid date and time.

`ParseExact()` does the same thing as `Parse()`, except that the `String` representation of the date and time must match the specified `format` pattern or patterns *exactly*.

Public instance methods

```
public DateTime Add(TimeSpan timeInterval)
public DateTime AddDays(double days)
public DateTime AddHours(double hours)
public DateTime AddMilliseconds(double msecs)
public DateTime AddMinutes(double min)
public DateTime AddMonths(int months)
public DateTime AddSeconds(double secs)
public DateTime AddTicks(long ticks)
public DateTime AddYears(int years)
```

These methods, which all create a new `DateTime` object by applying a modification to the current object, will throw an `ArgumentOutOfRangeException` if the input argument is invalid. Integer arguments can be positive or negative, while floating-point arguments are also allowed to be fractional.

```
public int CompareTo(object value)
public override bool Equals(object value)
```

CompareTo() compares the invoking DateTime object with the specified DateTime object. The method returns a negative integer if the invoking DateTime is less than value, zero if the two DateTime objects are equal, and a positive integer if the invoking DateTime is greater than value (or value is a null reference).

Equals() compares the specified DateTime object with the invoking DateTime object, and returns true if they are equal.

```
public string[] GetDateTimeFormats();
public string[] GetDateTimeFormats(char formatSpecifier);
public string[] GetDateTimeFormats(IFormatProvider provider);
public string[] GetDateTimeFormats(char formatSpecifier,
                                   IFormatProvider provider);
```

GetDateTimeFormats() obtains one or more String representations of the invoking DateTime object. If no format specifier is provided, it retrieves all possible representations, according to the standard DateTime format specifiers. You can also specify a Unicode character containing a format specifier, and an implementation of IFormatProvider can be used to specify culture-specific information.

```
public override int GetHashCode()
public TypeCode GetTypeCode()
```

GetHashCode() is an overridden version of the method defined in the Object class. It returns a 32-bit signed integer hash code for the invoking DateTime object.

GetTypeCode() returns an enumerated constant that is the TypeCode for the DateTime type.

```
public TimeSpan Subtract(DateTime value)
public DateTime Subtract(TimeSpan value)
```

Subtract() subtracts the time interval corresponding to the specified DateTime or TimeSpan object from the invoking DateTime object. The method returns a TimeSpan or DateTime object containing the modified values. An ArgumentOutOfRangeException is thrown if the result is less than MinValue.

```
public long ToFileTime()
public long ToLocalTime()
public string ToLongDateString()
public string ToLongTimeString()
public double ToOADate()
public string ToShortDateString()
public string ToShortTimeString()
public override string ToString()
public string ToString(IFormatProvider provider)
public string ToString(string format)
public string ToString(string format, IFormatProvider provider)
public DateTime ToUniversalTime()
```

`ToFileTime()` converts the values contained in the invoking `DateTime` object to the local system's file time. This is the number of ticks since January 1, 1601, 12:00 AM.

`ToLocalTime()` converts the current universal time (UTC) of the invoking `DateTime` object to a `DateTime` object with values corresponding to local time.

`ToLongDateString()` takes the date contained by the invoking `DateTime` object and returns an equivalent long date `String` representation. The `String` will contain the name of the day, the name of the month, the numeric day of the month, and the year.

`ToLongTimeString()` takes the time values of the invoking `DateTime` object and returns an equivalent long time `String` representation. The `String` will contain the numeric values of the hours, minutes, and seconds, as well as AM or PM.

`ToOADate()` converts the values of the invoking `DateTime` object into an equivalent OLE Automation `Date` value. The OLE Automation `Date` is the number of days, or fractions thereof, from midnight, December 30, 1899.

`ToShortDateString()` takes the date contained by the invoking `DateTime` object and returns an equivalent short date `String` representation. The `String` will contain the numeric values of the month, date, and year.

`ToShortTimeString()` takes the time values of the invoking `DateTime` object and returns an equivalent short time `String` representation. The `String` will contain the numeric values of the hours and minutes, as well as AM or PM.

`ToString()` returns a generic `String` representation of the values contained in the invoking `DateTime.object` You can optionally modify the default return `String` with a format specifier or `IFormatProvider` implementation.

`ToUniversalTime()` takes the values of the invoking `DateTime` object in terms of local time and converts them to coordinated universal time. The method returns a new `DateTime` object with the modified values.

Example: Using a DateTime object

In this example, a `DateTime` object is used to keep track of the last time a bank account was accessed. The `Account` class we'll write here consists of an account number and the `DateTime` object mentioned above.

```
using System;

public class DateTimeDemo
{
    private Account acct;
    private DateTime currentDate;

    // Current date stored in a DateTime by accessing static Now property.
    public DateTimeDemo(Account account)
```

```
    {
      acct = account;
      currentDate = DateTime.Now;
    }

    // The CheckAccessDate() method compares the access date of an Account.
    public void CheckAccessDate()
    {
      // The number 864000000000 is the number of ticks in a day.
      long maxDays = 180;
      long maxTicks = maxDays * 864000000000;

      // If it's more than 180 days since the account was accessed, warn.
      if((currentDate.Ticks - acct.GetAccessDate().Ticks) > maxTicks)
      {
        Console.Write("It has been more than {0} days ", maxDays);
        Console.WriteLine("since account {0} was accessed.",
                          acct.GetAcctNumber());
        Console.WriteLine("Last date of access was {0}",
                          acct.GetAccessDate().ToLongDateString());
      }
      else
      {
        Console.WriteLine("Welcome. Your account is still active.");
      }
    }

    public static void Main()
    {
      Account ac = new Account(1998, 10, 12, 12345678);
      DateTimeDemo dtd = new DateTimeDemo(ac);
      dtd.CheckAccessDate();
    }
}

// The Account class represents a very simplistic type of account
public class Account
{
  private int acctNumber;
  private DateTime accessDate;

  // The account access date is represented by a DateTime object.
  public Account(int year, int month, int day, int number)
  {
    accessDate = new DateTime(year, month, day);
    acctNumber = number;
  }

  public int GetAcctNumber()
  {
    return acctNumber;
  }
```

```
    public DateTime GetAccessDate()
    {
      return accessDate;
    }
}
```

The `DateTimeDemo` class constructor is passed a reference to an `Account` object. It also creates a `DateTime` object representing the current date and time using the `Now` property. The `CheckAccessDate()` method then compares the `Ticks` property of the current `DateTime` object and the one associated with the `Account`. If they differ by more than 180 days, a warning message is written to the screen.

The `Account` object that's created in the `Main()` method will certainly be more than 180 days older than the one created using `DateTime.Now()` (unless your system clock is set to an unusual value). You can try changing the date so it's less than 180 days if you wish.

Output:

```
It has been more than 180 days since account 12345678 was accessed
Last date of access was Monday, October 12, 1998.
```

Exception class

The `Exception` class is the base class for all other exception classes, defining properties and methods that will be common to all derived classes. An `Exception`-derived class encapsulates an abnormal occurrence that takes place during code execution – an index might be out of bounds, an improper type conversion may have been attempted, a requested file wasn't found, and so on.

Syntax

```
public class Exception : ISerializable
```

Hierarchy

```
Object --- Exception
```

Constructors

```
public Exception()
public Exception(string message)
public Exception(string message, Exception innerException)
protected Exception(SerializationInfo info, StreamingContext context)
```

`Exception()` creates an `Exception` object; the no-argument version creates an instance with default properties (`InnerException` is equal to `null`, and `Message` is set to an empty string). The other constructors allow you to supply your own error message and inner exception, where the inner exception is used to chain exceptions together (a `FileNotFoundException` might cause an `IOException`, for example, so the former would be the inner exception for the latter).

289

The protected constructor is called during de-serialization to re-form an Exception object transmitted over a stream.

Properties

The Exception class defines a number of properties that can be used to determine the location, type, and cause of the exception:

```
public virtual string HelpLink {get; set;}
protected int HResult {get; set;}
public Exception InnerException {get;}
public virtual string Message {get;}
public virtual string Source {get; set;}
public virtual string StackTrace {get;}
public MethodBase TargetSite {get;}
```

HelpLink returns or specifies a String that represents the Uniform Resource Name (URN) or Uniform Resource Locator (URL) of a help file.

HResult retrieves or sets a 32-bit integer value that includes a severity code, a facility code, and an error code. This value helps any COM client or runtime to manage the exception.

InnerException returns the Exception (if any) that caused the current Exception. This property will be set to null if a causal Exception doesn't exist.

Message returns a String that contains an error message – usually some information about the type of exception, or why it was thrown. These messages are primarily intended for human consumption. User-defined exception classes can define the exception message as they see fit.

Source returns or sets a String identifying the application or object that caused the exception.

StackTrace returns a String containing the stack trace, which is a listing of the methods that were called leading up to the exception. This helps you to identify where the exception occurred.

TargetSite retrieves a MethodBase object that represents the method in which the exception was thrown.

Instance methods

```
public virtual Exception GetBaseException()
public virtual void GetObjectData(SerializationInfo info,
                                  StreamingContext context)
public override string ToString()
```

Sometimes, an exception can be part of a cascading sequence of exceptions. GetBaseException() returns a reference to the Exception that was the root cause of the invoking Exception – it determines the original exception using the InnerException property. If the invoking Exception stands alone, a reference to itself is returned.

GetObjectData() is used to load contextual information about the invoking Exception into a SerializationInfo object. An ArgumentNullException is thrown if info is a null reference.

ToString() is an overridden version of the method defined in the Object class. This ToString() method provides the fully qualified name of the invoking Exception, as well as (possibly) the error message, the inner exception information, and the stack trace.

See the general discussion on exception handling in Chapter 4 for an example of how to use the methods and properties defined in the Exception class.

GC class

The GC class represents the system's garbage collector. This is the mechanism that automatically reclaims memory allocated to objects for which there are no valid references, thus avoiding the dreaded memory leak. The GC class defines methods that influence when an object is garbage collected, and when resources allocated to the object are released. The GC class defines properties that contain information about the total amount of memory available to the system, and information about the memory allocated to a given object.

Syntax

```
public sealed class GC
```

Hierarchy

```
Object --- GC
```

Properties

```
public static int MaxGeneration {get;}
```

MaxGeneration returns the maximum number of **generations** the system supports – the current C# garbage collector supports three of them. A generation refers to the relative age of each block of allocated memory, where the newest is generation zero. The garbage collector assumes that more recently allocated memory is more likely to be eligible for garbage collection than older memory.

Static methods

```
public static void Collect()
public static void Collect(int generation)
```

Collect() causes the garbage collector to attempt to reclaim inaccessible memory. If a generation parameter is specified, collection will be performed from the most recently allocated memory up to the specified generation. If no generation is specified, all memory will be garbage collected. Note that there's a performance penalty associated with manually calling for garbage collection – in most cases, it's a better idea to let the runtime decide when it needs to initiate garbage collection.

```
public static int GetGeneration(object obj)
public static long GetTotalMemory(bool forceFullCollection)
public static void KeepAlive(object obj)
```

GetGeneration() returns the generation associated with an object. You can provide either a reference to the object itself or a WeakReference for that object.

`GetTotalMemory()` returns the number of bytes of memory currently allocated. If `forceFullCollection` is true, the system will perform garbage collection and finalization procedures first.

`KeepAlive()` marks the specified object as being ineligible for garbage collection. The object is protected from the start of the routine until the point in the execution order that the method is called. The method call should be placed at the *end* of the block of code in which `obj` should be available.

```
public static void ReRegisterForFinalize(object obj)
public static void SuppressFinalize(object obj)
public static void WaitForPendingFinalizers()
```

`ReRegisterForFinalize()` asks the system to call the finalizer method for the specified object. This is usually done to overrule the effect of a previous call to the `SuppressFinalize()` method. A finalizer can also use this method to resurrect itself. This method *doesn't* guarantee, however, that the garbage collector will call the object's finalizer. An exception is thrown if the input object is a `null` reference, or if the method is not called within a constructor, method, or property.

`SuppressFinalize()` asks the system to not call the finalizer method for the specified object. An exception is thrown if the input object is a `null` reference, or if the method is not called within a constructor, method, or property.

`WaitForPendingFinalizers()` suspends the current thread until any finalizers have run – which they do on a separate thread. You must be careful with this method, because there's a chance that it won't return (it may wait forever). You can set up a separate thread that will interrupt the one that's running this method after a certain amount of time.

Example: Using the GC class

This example demonstrates how the `Collect()` method can be called to clean up unused memory. The `WasteResources()` method creates an instance of the `UselessObject` class as a local variable (it just defines an integer array). When `WasteResources()` returns, the current memory usage is displayed using the `GetTotalMemory()` method. Garbage collection is then requested by calling the `Collect()` method. After that, the current memory usage is again displayed.

```
using System;

public class GCDemo
{
  public static void Main()
  {
    WasteResources();
    Console.WriteLine("Current memory usage is {0}",
                  GC.GetTotalMemory(false));
    GC.Collect();
    Console.WriteLine("Current memory usage is {0}",
                  GC.GetTotalMemory(false));
  }
```

```
    private static void WasteResources()
    {
      UselessObject useless = new UselessObject();
    }
}

public class UselessObject
{
  public int[] waste;

  public UselessObject()
  {
    waste = new int[5000];
  }
}
```

Output:

```
Current memory usage is 34864
Current memory usage is 20740
```

Guid structure

A Guid is a 128-bit integer that represents a globally unique identifier (GUID). It is intended for use across all computer systems and networks, whenever a unique identifier is needed. (Every Active Directory object, for example, will have an associated Guid.) You can apply Guids to your own classes and interfaces as well.

Syntax

```
public struct Guid : IFormattable, IComparable
```

Hierarchy

```
Object --- ValueType --- Guid
```

Constructors

```
public Guid(byte[] b)
public Guid(string str)
public Guid(int a, short b, short c, byte[] d)
public Guid(int a, short b, short c, byte d, byte e,
          byte f, byte g, byte h, byte i, byte j, byte k)
public Guid(uint a, ushort b, ushort c, byte d, byte e,
          byte f, byte g, byte h, byte i, byte j, byte k)
```

Guid() creates a Guid object. It can be initialized using a 16-element byte array, a String representation of a series of 32 hexadecimal digits, or a collection of ints, shorts, and bytes that define the ID constant. The variety of constructors is due to the multiple ways that GUIDs can be formatted.

Fields

```
public static readonly Guid Empty
```

`Empty` represents a predefined instance of the `Guid` structure that contains nothing but zeros.

Static methods

```
public static Guid NewGuid()
```

`NewGuid()` is a convenience method that creates a (theoretically) unique `Guid` object. It provides an alternative to using one of the `Guid` constructors.

Instance methods

```
public int CompareTo(object obj)
public override bool Equals(object obj)
```

`CompareTo()` compares the invoking `Guid` object with the specified object. It returns a negative integer if the invoking `Guid` is less than `obj`, zero if it is equal, and a positive integer if it is greater than `obj`. If the `obj` parameter is neither a `Guid` object nor a `null` reference, an `ArgumentException` will be thrown.

`Equals()` is a overridden version of the method defined in the `Object` class. It returns `true` if the input parameter `obj` is a `Guid` object that has the same value as the invoking `Guid` object, and `false` otherwise.

```
public override int GetHashCode()
public byte[] ToByteArray()
```

`GetHashCode()` is an overridden version of the method defined in the `Object` class. It returns the hash code for the invoking `Guid` object.

`ToByteArray()` returns a 16-element byte array that contains the value of the invoking `Guid` object.

```
public override string ToString()
public string ToString(string format)
public string ToString(string format, IFormatProvider provider)
```

`ToString()` returns a `String` representation of the value of the invoking `Guid` object. The first version overrides the `ToString()` method defined in the `Object` class. It returns a `String` in registry format, where hexadecimal digits in groups of 8, 4, 4, and 12 represent the value of the `Guid`. You can provide an alternative format if you wish.

Operators

The `Guid` class defines two static operators for comparing the value of `Guid` objects.

```
public static bool operator ==(Guid a, Guid b)
public static bool operator !=(Guid a, Guid b)
```

`==` returns `true` if the values of a and b are equal. It returns `false` otherwise.

!= returns `true` if the values of a and b are not equal. It returns `false` otherwise.

Example: Using GUIDs

In this example, the `MyObject` class consists of a `String` and a `Guid` that's used to provide each `MyObject` instance with a unique identifier. The `GuidDemo` class defines the `Compare()` method that uses the equality operator to compare two `Guids`. A message is written out to indicate whether the two values are equal.

The `MyObject` constructor uses the `NewGuid()` method to provide each `MyObject` instance with a unique `Guid`. Even though two of the `MyObject` instances have the same name value, their `guids` will be different.

```
using System;

public class GuidDemo
{
    // The Compare() method uses the "==" operator to compare two Guids.
    public static void Compare(MyObject mo1, MyObject mo2)
    {
        Guid guid1 = mo1.GetGuid();
        Guid guid2 = mo2.GetGuid();

        if(guid1 == guid2)
        {
            Console.WriteLine("Guids of " + mo1.GetName() + " and " +
                               mo2.GetName() + " are equal.");
        }
        else
        {
            Console.WriteLine("Guids of " + mo1.GetName() + " and " +
                               mo2.GetName() + " are not equal.");
        }
    }

    // Three MyObjects are created. Each will have its own Guid value.
    public static void Main()
    {
        MyObject obj1 = new MyObject("Zachary");
        MyObject obj2 = new MyObject("Lisa");
        MyObject obj3 = new MyObject("Zachary");

        GuidDemo.Compare(obj1, obj2);
        GuidDemo.Compare(obj1, obj1);
        GuidDemo.Compare(obj1, obj3);
    }
}

// The MyObject class consists of a String and a Guid.
public class MyObject
{
```

```
    private String name;
    private Guid guid;

    // The static NewGuid() method generates a Guid for every instance
    public MyObject(string str)
    {
      name = str;
      guid = Guid.NewGuid();
    }

    public Guid GetGuid() { return guid; }
    public String GetName() { return name; }
}
```

Output:

```
Guids of Zachary and Lisa are not equal
Guids of Zachary and Zachary are equal
Guids of Zachary and Zachary are not equal
```

ICloneable interface

The ICloneable interface is implemented by classes that support cloning – that is, the creation of copies of an existing object. The ICloneable interface declares just one method.

Syntax

```
public interface ICloneable
```

Methods

object Clone()

Clone() returns an object that's a copy of the invoking object. A class that implements this method may implement it as either a deep or a shallow copy. A deep copy is a complete, independent duplication of the invoking object; with a shallow copy, only the top-level objects are duplicated. A shallow copy will contain references to any lower-level objects (reference-type data members) from the original object.

IComparable interface

Classes whose objects may be compared with others of the same type implement the IComparable interface. (An example of this would be the String class.) The interface declares one method that is meant to provide a type-specific comparison.

Syntax

```
public interface IComparable
```

Methods

```
int CompareTo(object obj)
```

CompareTo() compares the invoking object with the input parameter obj. The return integer will be less than zero if the invoking object is less than obj, zero if it is equal to obj, and a positive integer if the invoking object is greater than obj. The meanings of the terms "less than", "equal to", and "greater than" will depend on the class that provides the implementation of this method.

Example: Implementing the IComparable interface

In this code, the Student class defines two fields representing a student's name and the grade that he or she received. We want to be able to sort an array of Student objects by the value of the grade field. The way to do this is to have the Student class implement the IComparable interface, and then provide an appropriate implementation of the CompareTo() method. In this case, we write CompareTo() to place the Students with the highest grades first in the array, and those with the lowest grades last.

```csharp
using System;
using System.Collections;

public class Student : IComparable
{
  string grade;
  string name;

  private Student() {}

  public Student(string name, string grade)
  {
    this.name = name;
    this.grade = grade;
  }

  public string Grade
  {
    get
    {
      return grade;
    }
  }

  public string Name
  {
    get
    {
      return name;
    }
  }
```

```
   public int CompareTo(object x)
   {
     Student y = (Student)x;
     string grade1 = this.Grade;
     string grade2 = y.Grade;

     if(grade1 == grade2)
     {
       return 0;
     }
     else if(grade1.ToUpper().CompareTo(grade2.ToUpper()) < 0)
     {
       return -1;
     }
     else
     {
       return 1;
     }
   }
 }
}
```

The CompareDemo class creates an array of Student objects. The array is sorted using the Sort() method, and the sorted array elements are printed out.

```
public class CompareDemo
{
  public static void Main()
  {
    Student[] students = { new Student("Ben","B"),
                           new Student("Bob","D"),
                           new Student("Jackson","A"),
                           new Student("Kimmy","B") };

    Comparer gradeComparer = Comparer.Default;
    Array.Sort(students, gradeComparer);

    foreach(Student s in students)
    {
      Console.WriteLine(s.Name + "   " + s.Grade);
    }
  }
}
```

Output:

```
Jackson  A
Kimmy  B
Ben  B
Bob  D
```

IConvertible interface

The IConvertible interface declares generalized type conversion and convenience methods. Classes that implement the IConvertible interface will provide type-specific implementations of these methods.

Syntax

```
public interface IConvertible
```

Methods

```
TypeCode GetTypeCode()
bool ToBoolean(IFormatProvider provider)
byte ToByte(IFormatProvider provider)
char ToChar(IFormatProvider provider)
DateTime ToDateTime(IFormatProvider provider)
decimal ToDecimal(IFormatProvider provider)
double ToDouble(IFormatProvider provider)
short ToInt16(IFormatProvider provider)
int ToInt32(IFormatProvider provider)
long ToInt64(IFormatProvider provider)
sbyte ToSByte(IFormatProvider provider)
float ToSingle(IFormatProvider provider)
string ToString(IFormatProvider provider)
object ToType(Type conversionType, IFormatProvider provider)
ushort ToUInt16(IFormatProvider provider)
uint ToUInt32(IFormatProvider provider)
ulong ToUInt64(IFormatProvider provider)
```

The IConvertible interface declares these general-purpose conversion methods. They convert a value or object to the specified type, and return the converted value or object. They will throw an exception if the conversion is invalid. The IFormatProvider is used to provide culture-specific information; a class that implements this interface would likely provide overloaded versions of these methods.

IDisposable interface

The IDisposable interface declares one method that's used to initiate a resource clean-up procedure.

Syntax

```
public interface IDisposable
```

Methods

```
void Dispose()
```

Dispose() is a method intended to release resources to an object immediately when the object is no longer needed. This is in contrast to releasing resources using the garbage collector or Finalize() method, where it is not known exactly when the resources will be released.

MarshalByRefObject class

The MarshalByRefObject class is the base class for objects that need to marshal data between application domains. These are objects that may need to be accessed remotely – for example, when an object is part of the argument list for a remote method call, a reference to the object is passed from its home AppDomain to the target AppDomain. Derived classes of MarshalByRefObject include the Component, Stream, and AppDomain classes.

Syntax

```
public abstract class MarshalByRefObject
```

Hierarchy

```
Object --- MarshalByRefObject
```

Constructors

```
protected MarshalByRefObject()
```

MarshalByRefObject() is a no-argument constructor that's intended for use by derived classes of MarshalByRefObject.

Instance methods

```
public virtual ObjRef CreateObjRef(Type requestedType)
public object GetLifetimeService()
public virtual object InitializeLifetimeService()
```

CreateObjRef() creates an object reference of the specified Type. A RemotingException is thrown if requestedType is not a valid remoting object.

GetLifetimeService() returns an object that will be used to control the lifetime service of the invoking object. The default lifetime service is of type ILease.

InitializeLifetimeService() is used by objects that want to provide their own lease, and thus control their own lifetime. Such a class would do this by overriding the InitializeLifetimeService() method.

Example: Using the MarshalByRefObject class

This is a modified version of an example that appears in Chapter 23 of *Professional C#* (which, by the way, is an excellent resource for finding out more about developing distributed applications with .NET). In it, the Hello class represents a remote object – it is designated as such by having it derive from the MarshalByRefObject class. The Hello class defines a Greeting() method that returns a friendly message.

Compile the Hello.cs source code into a DLL file using the following at the command line.

```
csc /t:library Hello.cs
```

```
using System;

public class Hello : MarshalByRefObject
{
  public Hello() {}

  public string Greeting(string name)
  {
    return "Hello " + name;
  }
}
```

Next, the HelloServer class encapsulates a simple server. First, a TcpServerChannel is created and assigned to port 8086. Then, the channel and remote object type are registered. The text "Hi" is the URI that will be used by the client; SingleCall mode indicates that a new remote object instance is created for every method call. Compile the HelloServer.cs source code into an executable with this syntax:

```
csc /r:Hello.dll HelloServer.cs
```

```
using System;
using System.Runtime.Remoting;
using System.Runtime.Remoting.Channels;
using System.Runtime.Remoting.Channels.Tcp;

public class HelloServer
{
  public static void Main()
  {
    TcpServerChannel channel = new TcpServerChannel(8086);
    ChannelServices.RegisterChannel(channel);
    RemotingConfiguration.RegisterWellKnownServiceType(
                typeof(Hello), "Hi", WellKnownObjectMode.SingleCall);

    Console.WriteLine("Hit any key to exit");
    Console.ReadLine();
  }
}
```

The HelloClient class represents a client application. A TcpClientChannel object is created and registered with ChannelServices. The GetObject() method is used to return a proxy to the remote object. Every time the proxy calls the Greeting() method, a new instance of the Hello class is created on the remote server. The HelloClient.cs source code is compiled using the syntax:

```
csc /r:Hello.dll HelloClient.cs
```

```
using System;
using System.Runtime.Remoting.Channels;
using System.Runtime.Remoting.Channels.Tcp;

public class HelloClient
{
  public static void Main()
  {
    ChannelServices.RegisterChannel(new TcpClientChannel());
    Hello obj = (Hello)Activator.GetObject(
                  typeof(Hello), "tcp://localhost:8086/Hi");

    if(obj == null)
    {
      Console.WriteLine("Could not locate server");
      return;
    }

    Console.WriteLine(obj.Greeting("Zachary"));
  }
}
```

To run this example, first run the `HelloServer` executable. To simulate 'remoteness' better, you can put the `HelloServer.exe` file and a copy of the `Hello.dll` file in another directory. (You need to copy the `Hello.dll` file because the `HelloClient` and `HelloServer` executables both need it.) Open another console window and run the `HelloClient` executable.

Output (in the client console window):

```
Hello Zachary
```

Math class

The `Math` class provides a library of constants and methods to perform the basic math functions of addition, multiplication, subtraction, and division. Methods are also provided for trigonometric, exponential, and transcendental functions. All of the methods defined in this class are static.

Syntax

```
public sealed class Math
```

Hierarchy

```
Object --- Math
```

Fields

```
public const double E
public const double PI
```

E is the constant e, the natural logarithmic base. It has a value of 2.7182818284590452354.

PI is the trigonometric constant π. It has a value of 3.14159265358979323846.

Absolute value methods

```
public static decimal Abs(decimal d)
public static double Abs(double d)
public static short Abs(short d)
public static int Abs(int d)
public static long Abs(long d)
public static sbyte Abs(sbyte d)
public static float Abs(float d)
```

Abs() returns the absolute value of the specified value. The method is overloaded to accept various input types.

Exponential and logarithmic methods

```
public static double Exp(double d)
public static double Log(double d)
public static double Log(double d, double base)
public static double Log10(double d)
```

Exp() returns the constant e raised to the power d.

Log() returns the logarithm of the input parameter d using the specified base. If no base is specified, the natural logarithm (base e) is computed.

Log10() returns the logarithm in base 10 of the specified value.

IEEERemainder method

```
public static double IEEERemainder(double x, double y)
```

IEEERemainder() returns a value equal to x – (y * Q), where Q is x / y rounded to the nearest integer.

Minimum and maximum methods

```
public static byte Max(byte value1, byte value2)
public static decimal Max(decimal value1, decimal value2)
public static double Max(double value1, double value2)
public static short Max(short value1, short value2)
public static int Max(int value1, int value2)
public static long Max(long value1, long value2)
public static sbyte Max(sbyte value1, sbyte value2)
public static float Max(float value1, float value2)
public static ushort Max(ushort value1, ushort value2)
public static uint Max(uint value1, uint value2)
public static ulong Max(ulong value1, ulong value2)
```

Max() returns the larger of two input arguments. The method is overloaded to accept various types of input.

```
public static byte Min(byte value1, byte value2)
public static decimal Min(decimal value1, decimal value2)
public static double Min(double value1, double value2)
public static short Min(short value1, short value2)
public static int Min(int value1, int value2)
public static long Min(long value1, long value2)
public static sbyte Min(sbyte value1, sbyte value2)
public static float Min(float value1, float value2)
public static ushort Min(ushort value1, ushort value2)
public static uint Min(uint value1, uint value2)
public static ulong Min(ulong value1, ulong value2)
```

Min() returns the smaller of two input arguments. The method is overloaded to accept various types of input.

Rounding methods

```
public static double Ceiling(double d)
public static double Floor(double d)
public static decimal Round(decimal d)
public static double Round(double d)
public static decimal Round(decimal d, int decimals)
public static double Round(double d, int decimals)
```

Ceiling() returns the smallest whole number greater than or equal to the specified number.

Floor() returns the largest whole number less than or equal to the specified number.

Round() returns the nearest number to the specified number. The decimals parameter indicates the number of decimal places to which the number will be rounded. If the decimals parameter is not provided, whole numbers will be returned. If, for integer rounding, the input parameter is halfway between two numbers, the nearest even number will be returned.

Sign methods

```
public static int Sign(decimal d)
public static int Sign(double d)
public static int Sign(short d)
public static int Sign(int d)
public static int Sign(long d)
public static int Sign(sbyte d)
public static int Sign(float d)
```

Sign() returns an integer indicating the sign of the specified value. If the input parameter d is less than zero, -1 is returned. If d is equal to zero, 0 is returned. If d is greater than zero, 1 is returned.

Square root and power methods

```
public static double Pow(double x, double y)
public static double Sqrt(double d)
```

Pow() returns the value of x raised to the power of y.

`Sqrt()` returns the square root of the specified value.

Trigonometry methods

```
public static double Acos(double d)
public static double Asin(double d)
public static double Atan(double d)
public static double Atan2(double y, double x)
public static double Cos(double d)
public static double Cosh(double d)
public static double Sin(double d)
public static double Sinh(double d)
public static double Tan(double d)
public static double Tanh(double d)
```

These methods behave largely as you'd expect them to. You need to know that all the angles, input and output, are specified in radians (360 degrees equals 2π radians), while `Atan2()` returns the angle whose tangent has the value `y` / `x`. The parameters `x` and `y` define a point in the x-y plane, and the angle is measured relative to the origin (0, 0).

Summary

In this chapter we've looked at some of the core classes that reside in the `System` namespace that are used on a frequent basis in any .NET application. In particular, we've looked at:

❑   The `Object` and `Type` classes

❑   The `Array`, `Console`, and `String` classes

❑   The `EventArgs`, `Exception`, and `MarshalByRefObject` classes

❑   The `Math` and `Convert` classes

In the next few chapters, we'll continue our look at core classes in some specific .NET namespaces, starting with classes that are used when working with collections.

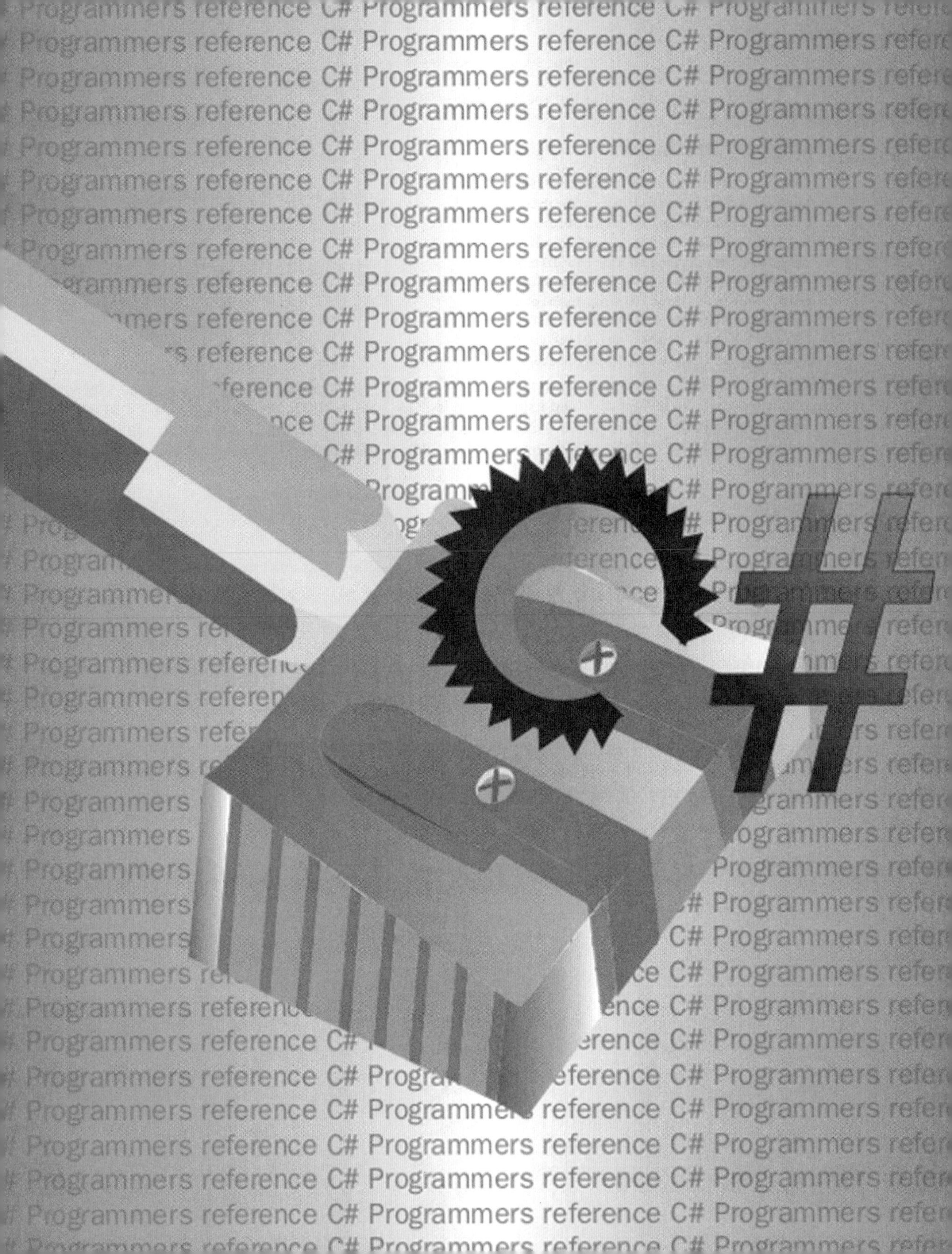
C# Programmers reference

23

Collections

The C# language provides many ways to implement collections. We discussed the standard C# array syntax in Chapter 6, and the `Array` class, the base class for all arrays in the CLR, was described in Chapter 22. In this chapter, we will examine the interfaces and classes contained in the `System.Collections` namespace. These encompass a wide range of collection types.

We start off by examining the key interfaces contained in the `System.Collections` namespace. These interfaces define the framework for all collection types in C#. Following this we will discuss the collection classes defined in the namespace. We'll cover the `ArrayList` class that encapsulates a weakly-typed one-dimensional array whose size can grow or shrink as required, the `CollectionBase` and `DictionaryBase` classes which serve as the base classes for strongly-typed collections and dictionaries, and collections that represent a series of key-value pairs such as the `HashTable` and `SortedList` class. Simple first-in-first-out and last-in-first-out collection classes named `Queue` and `Stack` are also presented.

ICollection interface

The `ICollection` interface defines properties and methods that are common to all collection classes. `ICollection` is inherited by the `IList` and `IDictionary` interfaces and implemented by the `ArrayList`, `CollectionBase`, `DictionaryBase`, `Hashtable`, `Queue`, `SortedList`, and `Stack` classes.

Syntax

```
public interface ICollection : IEnumerable
```

Hierarchy

```
IEnumerable  ---  ICollection
```

Public instance properties

```
int Count {get;}
bool IsSynchronized {get;}
object SyncRoot {get;}
```

`Count` returns the number of elements contained in the `ICollection`.

IsSynchronized returns true if access to the ICollection is synchronized.

SyncRoot returns an object that can be used to synchronize access to the ICollection. Most collection classes also provide a Synchronized() method that can place a synchronized wrapper around an ICollection.

Public instance methods

```
void CopyTo(Array array, int arrayIndex)
```

CopyTo() is implemented by a class to copy the elements of a ICollection into a one-dimensional array. Copying into the array begins at a specified arrayindex.

IComparer interface

The IComparer interface declares a method that is used to compare two objects. This interface is implemented by the Comparer, CaseSensitiveComparer, and KeysConverter classes. The difference between the IComparer interface and the System.IComparable interface is that IComparable defines the framework for a comparable object, whereas the IComparer interface defines the framework for an object used to make a comparison.

Syntax

```
public interface IComparer
```

Hierarchy

```
IComparer
```

Public instance methods

```
int Compare(object x, object y)
```

Compare() is used to compare two objects. The method of comparison depends on how classes implement this method. The method should return a negative integer if object x is less than object y, zero if the two objects are equal, and a positive integer if x is greater than y.

Example: IComparer

In this example we will write a simple IComparer. The MyComparer class implements the Compare() method declared in the IComparer interface. The method converts the input arguments to strings. It then compares the uppercase versions of the two strings. If the first string is lower lexically than the second string the number 1 is returned. If not, the number –1 is returned. The net effect of this is that a string array will be sorted in reverse alphabetical order.

```
using System;
using System.Collections;

public class MyComparer : IComparer
```

```
{
  public int Compare(object a, object b)
  {
    string strA = a.ToString();
    string strB = b.ToString();

    if (strA == strB)
    {
      return 0;
    }
    else if (strA.ToUpper().CompareTo(strB.ToUpper()) < 0 )
    {
      return 1;
    }
    else
    {
      return -1;
    }
  }
}
```

The `ComparerDemo` class defines a `string` array. It then sorts the array using a `MyComparer` instance as the comparer, and the elements of the sorted array are printed out.

```
using System;
using System.Collections;

public class ComparerDemo
{
  public static void Main()
  {
    string[] names = {"Omar", "Ben", "Betty", "Zachary"};

    Array.Sort(names, new MyComparer());

    foreach(String name in names)
    {
      Console.WriteLine(name);
    }
  }
}
```

Output:

```
Zachary
Omar
Betty
Ben
```

IDictionary interface

The IDictionary interface provides properties and methods that are used by classes that encapsulate a collection of associated keys and values (name-value pairs). The collection can be read-only, fixed-size, or variable-size. Among the classes that implement this interface are the DictionaryBase, Hashtable, and SortedList classes.

Syntax

```
public interface IDictionary : ICollection, IEnumerable
```

Hierarchy

```
IEnumerable  ---  ICollection  ---  IDictionary
```

Public instance properties

```
bool IsFixedSize {get;}
bool IsReadOnly {get;}
object this[object key] { get; set; }
ICollection Keys {get;}
ICollection Values {get;}
```

IsFixedSize indicates whether the IDictionary has a fixed size. The default is false.

IsReadOnly returns true if IDictionary is read-only. The default is false.

this[] is the indexer for the IDictionary. The object key is the key whose value will be retrieved or set.

Keys returns an ICollection containing the keys in the IDictionary.

Values returns an ICollection containing the values in the IDictionary.

Public instance methods

```
void Add(object key, object value)
void Clear()
bool Contains(object key)
IDictionaryEnumerator GetEnumerator()
void Remove(object key)
```

Add() adds an entry with the specified key and value to the invoking IDictionary.

Clear() removes all entries from the invoking IDictionary.

Contains() returns true if the specified key exists in the invoking IDictionary.

GetEnumerator() returns an IDictionaryEnumerator object that can be used to read data from the invoking IDictionary. The IDictionaryEnumerator is good only for the current state of the collection. If elements in the IDictionary are added, deleted, or modified, the IDictionaryEnumerator becomes invalid.

Remove() removes the entry with the specified key from the invoking IDictionary. When an element is removed from collections that are indexed by integer, the positions of the remaining elements are adjusted to occupy the vacant spot.

IDictionaryEnumerator interface

The IDictionaryEnumerator interface is implemented by classes that can enumerate the elements of a dictionary. The IDictionaryEnumerator is used to read data from the dictionary.

The IDictionaryEnumerator interface derives from IEnumerator and inherits the properties and methods declared in that interface. What makes the IDictionaryEnumerator particularly useful for iterating through dictionaries (Hashtables, SortedLists, etc.) is that an IDictionaryEnumerator has access to the keys and values of each element of the IDictionary it is associated with. For an example of an IDictionaryEnumerator in action, see the *Hashtable class* section of this chapter.

Syntax

```
public interface IDictionaryEnumerator : IEnumerator
```

Hierarchy

```
IEnumerator  ---  IDictionaryEnumerator
```

Public instance properties

```
DictionaryEntry Entry {get;}
object Key {get;}
object Value {get;}
```

Entry returns a DictionaryEntry object containing the key and value of the current dictionary entry.

Key retrieves the key of the current element in the enumeration.

Value returns the value of the current element in the enumeration.

IEnumerable interface

The IEnumerable interface declares one method that supports a simple iteration over a collection. Most classes (including the String class) that represent a sequence or collection of elements will implement this interface.

Syntax

```
public interface IEnumerable
```

Hierarchy

```
IEnumerable
```

Public instance methods

```
IEnumerator GetEnumerator()
```

GetEnumerator() returns an enumerator that can be used to iterate through the elements in a collection. The enumerator is intended only to read data from the collection and represents a snapshot view of the collection. If the collection is subsequently altered in some way, the enumerator becomes invalid, and an exception is thrown if a subsequent attempt is made to use the IEnumerator. Among many other uses, the GetEnumerator() method is called behind the scenes to implement the foreach construct.

IEnumerator interface

The IEnumerator interface defines properties and methods that allow an enumerator to perform a simple iteration through a collection. Any class used as an enumerator will implement this interface.

Syntax

```
public interface IEnumerator
```

Hierarchy

```
IEnumerator
```

Public instance properties

```
object Current {get;}
```

Current returns the current element in the collection, the one being accessed by the enumerator.

Public instance methods

```
bool MoveNext()
void Reset()
```

MoveNext() advances the enumerator to the next element in the collection. This method returns true if the enumerator successfully moved to the next element and false if it reached the end of the collection.

Reset() moves the enumerator back to its initial position, which is before the first element.

IHashCodeProvider interface

The IHashCodeProvider interface is implemented by classes that are designed to generate integer hash codes for objects. These hash codes are used as the keys for entries in a Hashtable.

Syntax

```
public interface IHashCodeProvider
```

Hierarchy

```
IHashCodeProvider
```

Public instance methods

```
int GetHashCode(object obj)
```

GetHashCode() returns the hash code for the specified object.

IList interface

The IList interface declares properties and methods for a collection containing elements that can be individually indexed. Classes that implement this interface include the Array and ArrayList classes.

Syntax

```
public interface IList : ICollection, IEnumerable
```

Hierarchy

```
IEnumerable   ---   ICollection   ---   IList
```

Public instance properties

```
bool IsFixedSize {get;}
virtual bool IsReadOnly {get;}
object this[int index] { get; set; }
```

IsFixedSize returns true if the IList has a fixed size and does not allow the addition or removal of elements.

IsReadOnly returns true if the IList is read-only.

this[] is the indexer for the IList object. It gets or sets the element at the specified index in the IList.

Public instance methods

```
int Add(object value)
void Clear()
bool Contains(object item)
int IndexOf(object value)
void Insert(int index, object value)
void Remove(object obj)
void RemoveAt(int index)
```

Add() is used to add the specified object to the invoking IList. The method returns the index at which the object was placed.

Clear() removes all elements from the invoking IList object. The size of the IList will be zero.

Contains() determines if the invoking IList contains the specified object, and returns true if the object is found.

IndexOf() searches the IList for the specified object. If the object is found, its index is returned. If the object is not found, -1 is returned.

Insert() places the specified object into the invoking IList at the specified index. Existing elements are shifted down to accommodate the new element.

Remove() removes the first occurrence of the specified object in the invoking IList.

RemoveAt() removes the element at the specified index.

Stack class

Perhaps the simplest of the ready-made collection classes provided by the .NET Framework is the Stack class. This models a simple last-in-first-out (LIFO) collection. The Stack class is similar in nature to its close cousin, the Queue class.

Syntax

```
public class Stack : ICollection, IEnumerable, ICloneable
```

Hierarchy

```
Object   ---   Stack
```

Constructors

```
public Stack()
public Stack(ICollection c)
public Stack(int capacity)
```

Stack() creates a Stack object. The no-argument constructor initializes the Stack object with no elements and an initial capacity of 10. You can specify a collection to be added to the Stack or another initial capacity if you like.

Properties

```
virtual int Count {get;}
virtual bool IsReadOnly {get;}
virtual bool IsSynchronized {get;}
virtual object SyncRoot {get;}
```

Count retrieves the number of elements contained in the Stack.

IsReadOnly returns true if the Stack is read-only. The default is false.

IsSynchronized specifies whether access to the Stack is synchronized. The default is false.

SyncRoot provides synchronized access to the Stack. A Stack object by default is not thread-safe. Synchronized operations should be performed on the SyncRoot of the Stack rather than on the Stack object itself.

Public static methods

```
public static Stack Synchronized(Stack stack)
```

`Synchronized()` places a synchronized (thread-safe) wrapper around the specified `Stack` and returns the wrapped version. Note that, whereas the `SyncRoot` property provides synchronized access to the `Stack` itself, the `Synchronized()` method returns a reference to a separate wrapper object. An `ArgumentNullException` is thrown if `stack` is a null reference.

Public instance methods

```
public virtual void Clear()
public virtual object Clone()
public virtual bool Contains(object obj)
public virtual void CopyTo(Array array, int arrayIndex)
public virtual IEnumerator GetEnumerator()
public virtual object Peek()
public virtual object Pop()
public virtual void Push(object obj)
public virtual object[] ToArray()
```

`Clear()` removes all entries from the invoking `Stack` and sets the `Count` property to zero.

`Clone()` returns a shallow copy of the invoking `Stack`. Rather than containing copies of the `Stack` elements, the shallow copy will contain references to the elements of the original `Stack`.

`Contains()` returns `true` if the specified object exists in the invoking `Stack`. A linear search method is used to look for the object.

`CopyTo()` copies the elements of the invoking `Stack` into the specified one-dimensional array. The `Index` parameter is the index in `array` where the copying begins. The elements are copied to the array in a last-in-first-out order. An exception is thrown if `array` is a null reference, if `array` is multi dimensional, if `arrayIndex` is out of range, or if the `Stack` element type cannot be cast implicitly into the type of the destination array.

`GetEnumerator()` returns an `IEnumerator` object that can be used to read data from the invoking `Stack`. If elements in the `Stack` are added, deleted, or modified, the `IEnumerator` becomes invalid.

`Peek()` returns a reference to the object at the top of the invoking `Stack` without removing it. An `InvalidOperationException` is thrown if the `Stack` is empty.

`Pop()` removes and returns the object at the top of the `Stack`. This method throws an `InvalidOperationException` if the `Stack` is empty.

`Push()` adds the specified object to the top of the `Stack`.

`ToArray()` copies the elements contained in the invoking `Stack` object to an object array. The elements are copied in a last-in-first-out order.

Example: Stack class

In this example, a `Stack` is used to store log files of when an account was accessed. The `EventLog` class is a simple event log that contains a description of the transaction and when the transaction occurred. `EventLog`s are added to the `Stack` using the `Push()` method. Methods are also defined to examine the most recent transaction (using the `Peek()` method) and the three most recent transactions (using the `GetEnumerator()` method).

```
using System;
using System.Collections;

public class StackDemo
{
  private Stack stack;

  public StackDemo()
  {
    stack = new Stack();
  }

  //=========================================================
  //  The AddActivity() method places an EventLog onto the
  //  top of the Stack using the Push() method.
  //=========================================================

  public void AddActivity(EventLog evt)
  {
    stack.Push(evt);
  }

  //=========================================================
  //  The MostRecent() method uses the Peek() method to return
  //  a reference to the EventLog on top of the Stack. This
  //  will be the most recently added EventLog.
  //=========================================================

  public void MostRecent()
  {
    EventLog e = (EventLog)stack.Peek();
    Console.WriteLine("Last account activity was ");
    Console.WriteLine("{0} on {1} {2}\n", e.GetDesc(),
                                 e.GetDate().ToLongDateString(),
                                 e.GetDate().ToLongTimeString());
  }

  //=========================================================
  //  The LastThree() method writes out information on the last
  //  three account transactions. It first accesses the Count
  //  property to see if the Stack contains at least three
  //  EventLogs. It then calls the GetEnumerator() method to
  //  get an IEnumerator that can access the Stack elements.
  //=========================================================

  public void LastThree()
  {
    int maxI = Math.Max(3, stack.Count);

    Console.WriteLine("Last {0} transactions were ", maxI);

    IEnumerator enumerator = stack.GetEnumerator();
```

```
      for (int i=0; i<maxI; ++i)
      {
        enumerator.MoveNext();
        EventLog e = (EventLog)enumerator.Current;
        Console.WriteLine("{0} on {1} {2}", e.GetDesc(),
                                  e.GetDate().ToLongDateString(),
                                  e.GetDate().ToLongTimeString());
      }
      Console.WriteLine();
    }

    public static void Main()
    {
      StackDemo sd = new StackDemo();

      EventLog log1 = new EventLog("balance check",
                              new DateTime(2001, 11, 3, 15, 15, 15));
      sd.AddActivity(log1);

      EventLog log2 = new EventLog("deposit",
                              new DateTime(2001, 11, 8, 6, 45, 1));
      sd.AddActivity(log2);

      EventLog log3 = new EventLog("fund transfer", DateTime.Now);
      sd.AddActivity(log3);

      sd.MostRecent();
      sd.LastThree();
    }
}

//================================================================
//  The EventLog class contains a String that describes the
//  type of account activity and a DateTime object representing
//  the date and time of the account access.
//================================================================

public class EventLog
{
  private string desc;
  private DateTime date;

  public EventLog(string str, DateTime dt)
  {
    desc = str;
    date = dt;
  }

  public string GetDesc() { return desc; }
  public DateTime GetDate() { return date; }
}
```

Output:

```
Last account activity was
fund transfer on Sunday, November 11, 2001  6:19:59 PM

Last 3 transactions were
fund transfer on Sunday, November 11, 2001 6:19:59 PM
deposit on Thursday, November 08, 2001 6:45:01 AM
balance check on Saturday, November 03, 2001 3:15:15 PM
```

Queue class

The Queue class encapsulates a first-in-first-out (FIFO) collection. Queues are useful for storing objects in the order in which they were received for subsequent processing. Every Queue object has a capacity that is automatically increased if the number of elements stored reaches the capacity. A Queue object also has a growth factor which specifies the factor that the capacity will be increased by when the Queue becomes full. This factor can be set in the Queue's constructor, and is by default 2.0 (that is, the capacity will double when the Queue becomes full).

Syntax

```
public class Queue : ICollection, IEnumerable, ICloneable
```

Hierarchy

```
Object   ---   Queue
```

Constructors

```
public Queue()
public Queue(ICollection c)
public Queue(int capacity)
public Queue(int capacity, float growthFactor)
```

Queue() creates a Queue object. The no-argument constructor initializes the Queue object with no elements, an initial capacity of 32, and a growth factor of 2.0. You can specify a collection to be added to the Queue or another initial capacity or growth factor if you like.

Properties

```
virtual int Count {get;}
virtual bool IsReadOnly {get;}
virtual bool IsSynchronized {get;}
virtual object SyncRoot {get;}
```

Count returns the number of elements contained in the Queue.

IsReadOnly indicates true if Queue is read-only. The default is false.

IsSynchronized specifies whether access to the Queue is synchronized. The default is false.

SyncRoot provides synchronized access to the Queue. A Queue object by default is not thread-safe. Synchronized operations should be performed on the SyncRoot of the Queue rather than on the Queue object itself.

Public static methods

```
public static Queue Synchronized(Queue queue)
```

Synchronized() places a synchronized (thread-safe) wrapper around the specified Queue and returns the wrapped version. Note that, whereas the SyncRoot property provides synchronized access to the Queue itself, the Synchronized() method returns a reference to a separate wrapper object. An ArgumentNullException is thrown if queue is a null reference.

Public instance methods

```
public virtual void Clear()
public virtual object Clone()
public virtual bool Contains(object obj)
public virtual void CopyTo(Array array, int arrayIndex)
public virtual object Dequeue()
public virtual void Enqueue(object obj)
public virtual IEnumerator GetEnumerator()
public virtual object Peek()
public virtual object[] ToArray()
public virtual void TrimToSize()
```

Clear() removes all entries from the invoking Queue and sets the Count property to zero.

Clone() returns a shallow copy of the invoking Queue. Rather than containing copies of the Queue elements, the shallow copy will contain references to the elements of the original Queue.

Contains() returns true if the specified object exists in the invoking Queue. A linear search method is used to look for the object.

CopyTo() copies the elements of the invoking Queue into the specified one-dimensional array. The Index parameter is the index in array where the copying begins. The elements are copied to the array in the same order that an enumerator would iterate through the Queue. An exception is thrown if array is a null reference, if array is multi dimensional, if arrayIndex is out of range, or if the Queue element type cannot be cast implicitly into the type of the destination array.

Dequeue() removes and returns the object at the beginning of the Queue. An InvalidOperationException is thrown if the Queue is empty.

Enqueue() adds the specified object to the end of the Queue.

GetEnumerator() returns an IEnumerator object that can be used to read data from the invoking Queue. If elements in the Queue are added, deleted, or modified, the IEnumerator becomes invalid and any subsequent attempts to use it will cause an InvalidOperationException to be thrown.

Peek() returns a reference to the object at the beginning of the invoking Queue without removing it. An InvalidOperationException is thrown if the Queue is empty.

`ToArray()` copies the elements contained in the invoking `Queue` object to an object array. The elements are copied in a first-to-last order.

`TrimToSize()` sets the capacity of the `Queue` to the actual number of elements in the `Queue`. A `NotSupportedException` is thrown if the `Queue` is read-only.

Example: Queue class

In this example, four elements are placed into a `Queue`. The `Queue` is "processed" by removing the elements one by one and printing out their contents. The elements are removed according to the system first-in-first-out.

```
using System;
using System.Collections;

public class QueueDemo
{
  public static void Main()
  {
    String str;
    Queue queue = new Queue();

    //====================================
    //  Add some objects to the Queue.
    //====================================

    queue.Enqueue("transaction 1");
    queue.Enqueue("transaction 2");
    queue.Enqueue("transaction 3");
    queue.Enqueue("transaction 4");

    //=========================================================
    //  "Process" the elements in the Queue by removing
    //  them and printing out their contents.
    //=========================================================

    while(queue.Count != 0)
    {
      str = (String)queue.Dequeue();
      Console.WriteLine(str);
    }
  }
}
```

Output:

```
transaction 1
transaction 2
transaction 3
transaction 4
```

ArrayList class

An `ArrayList` represents a one-dimensional array whose size is dynamically increased as required. This is in contrast to the `System.Array` class that is of fixed size. `ArrayLists` are weakly-typed – they can contain elements of any managed type, and there is no requirement for all the elements to be of the same type. They are useful when you need to model an array of objects but don't know how many objects there will be. An `ArrayList` starts off with an initial capacity; as elements are added, the size of the `ArrayList` and its capacity are automatically increased. The capacity can be decreased if elements are removed using the `TrimToSize()` method or by explicitly changing the `Capacity` property.

The instance methods of the `ArrayList` class are not thread-safe. Two threads could, for instance, attempt to add a range of elements to the `ArrayList` simultaneously. The `Synchronized()` method or `SyncRoot` property must be used to guarantee thread safety:

```
ArrayList al = new ArrayList();
lock (al.SyncRoot)
{
    // Write to al
}
```

Alternatively, using the `Synchronized()` method to create a thread-safe wrapper for the `ArrayList`:

```
ArrayList al = new ArrayList();
ArrayList syncList = ArrayList.Synchronized(al);
lock (syncList)
{
  // Write to syncList
}
```

> Notice that synchronizing collection objects doesn't eliminate the need to lock objects that could be accessed by multiple threads simultaneously.

Syntax

```
public class ArrayList : IList, ICollection, IEnumerable, ICloneable
```

Hierarchy

```
Object   ---   ArrayList
```

Constructors

```
public ArrayList()
public ArrayList(ICollection c)
public ArrayList(int initialCapacity)
```

`ArrayList()` creates an `ArrayList` object. The default initial capacity is 16. If the number of elements reaches the value of the capacity, the capacity is doubled. You can set your own initial capacity if you like. The reason you might want to set your own capacity is to minimize the number of subsequent resize operations. The initial elements will be copied from the specified `ICollection`, or the `ArrayList` will be empty if no `ICollection` is specified.

Properties and indexers

```
public virtual int Capacity { get; set; }
public virtual int Count {get;}
public virtual bool IsFixedSize {get;}
public virtual bool IsReadOnly {get;}
public virtual bool IsSynchronized {get;}
public virtual object SyncRoot {get;}
public virtual object this[int index] { get; set; }
```

`Capacity` retrieves or sets the number of elements that an `ArrayList` can hold.

`Count` returns the number of elements currently contained by the `ArrayList`.

`IsFixedSize` returns `true` if the `ArrayList` has a fixed size and does not allow the addition or removal of elements. The `ArrayList` class implementation returns `false`.

`IsReadOnly` returns `true` if the `ArrayList` is read-only. The `ArrayList` class implementation returns `false`.

`IsSynchronized` indicates whether access to the `ArrayList` is synchronized (thread-safe). The `ArrayList` class implementation returns `false`.

`SyncRoot` provides synchronized access to the `ArrayList`. An `ArrayList` object by default is not thread-safe. Synchronized operations are performed on the `SyncRoot` of the `ArrayList` rather than on the `ArrayList` itself.

`this[]` is the indexer for the `ArrayList` class. It is used to get or set the element at the specified index in the `ArrayList`.

Public static methods

```
public static ArrayList Adapter(IList list)
public static ArrayList FixedSize(ArrayList list)
public static ArrayList FixedSize(IList list)
public static ArrayList ReadOnly(ArrayList list)
public static ArrayList ReadOnly(IList list)
public static ArrayList Repeat(object value, int count)
public static ArrayList Synchronized(ArrayList list)
public static ArrayList Synchronized(IList list)
```

`Adapter()` creates an `ArrayList` wrapper for any object which implements the `IList` interface. The wrapped object can then access `ArrayList` class methods such as `Reverse()`, `Sort()`, and `BinarySearch()`. An `ArgumentNullException` is thrown if `list` is a null reference.

`FixedSize()` returns an `ArrayList` wrapper with a fixed-size restriction. If the input argument is an `IList` object, the wrapped object can access `ArrayList` class methods but elements cannot be added to or removed from it. An `ArgumentNullException` is thrown if `list` is a null reference.

ReadOnly() returns an ArrayList wrapper with a read-only restriction. If the input argument is an IList object, the wrapped object can use ArrayList class methods that do not modify the contents of the collection. An ArgumentNullException is thrown if list is a null reference.

Repeat() returns an ArrayList object that has been loaded with count number of elements. Each element is a shallow copy of value. An ArgumentOutOfRangeException is thrown if count is less than zero.

Synchronized() facilitates synchronized access to an ArrayList object by placing a synchronized wrapper around the specified ArrayList or IList object. An ArgumentNullException is thrown if list is a null reference.

Instance Methods

```
public virtual int Add(object value)
public virtual void AddRange(ICollection c)
```

Add() adds the specified object to the end of the invoking ArrayList. The method returns the index at which the object was placed. A NotSupportedException is thrown if the ArrayList is read-only or fixed-size.

AddRange() adds the elements of the specified ICollection object to the end of an ArrayList. The ICollection type does not have to be the same as the types currently stored in the ArrayList. An exception is thrown if c is a null reference or if the ArrayList is read-only or fixed-size.

```
public virtual int BinarySearch(object value)
public virtual int BinarySearch(object value, IComparer comparer)
public vitrual int BinarySearch(int startIndex, int count, object value,
                                                 IComparer comparer)
```

BinarySearch() performs a binary search of the invoking ArrayList for the specified object. The input parameter value must be of the same type as the elements of the ArrayList, and the list must be sorted for the search to execute successfully. If an IComparer object is not specified, the default comparer is used. The return value is the zero-based index in the ArrayList at which the object was found. If the object is not found, -1 is returned. You can search the entire ArrayList or a subset denoted by startIndex and count. An exception is thrown if comparer is a null reference, if the ArrayList elements or value don't implement the IComparer interface, or if the integer arguments are out of range.

```
public virtual void Clear()
public virtual object Clone()
public virtual bool Contains(object item)
```

Clear() removes all elements from the invoking ArrayList object. The Count property is set to zero, but the capacity of the ArrayList remains unchanged. A NotSupportedException is thrown if the ArrayList is read-only or fixed-size.

Clone() produces a shallow copy of the invoking ArrayList. The elements themselves are not copied – the elements of the copied ArrayList will be references to the original elements.

Contains() determines if the invoking ArrayList contains the specified object by performing a linear search of the elements in the ArrayList. If the object is found, the method returns true. Unlike BinarySearch(), this method doesn't use an IComparer object to compare the objects in the ArrayList.

```
public virtual void CopyTo(Array array)
public virtual void CopyTo(Array array, int arrayIndex)
public virtual void CopyTo(int sourceIndex, Array array, int arrayIndex,
                                                         int count)
```

CopyTo() copies all or some of the elements of an ArrayList into a one-dimensional array using zero-based indexing. The array must be of a compatible type with the ArrayList elements. The arrayIndex parameter refers to the index in the array at which the first copied element will be placed, sourceIndex is the index of the ArrayList at which copying begins, and count is the number of elements to be copied. An exception is thrown if array is a null reference, if array is multi dimensional, if the types of the ArrayList and Array are incompatible, or if any of the integer arguments is out of range

```
public virtual IEnumerator GetEnumerator()
public virtual IEnumerator GetEnumerator(int startIndex, int count)
```

GetEnumerator() returns an IEnumerator object that can be used to iterate through the invoking ArrayList. The IEnumerator is good only for the current state of the collection. If elements in the ArrayList are added, deleted, or modified, the IEnumerator becomes invalid. You can acquire an IEnumerator for the entire ArrayList or a subset defined by the startIndex and count parameters. An exception is thrown if startIndex or count is less than zero or if they don't specify a valid range.

```
public virtual ArrayList GetRange(int startIndex, int count)
```

GetRange() returns an ArrayList object containing count elements of the invoking ArrayList, starting at the element with the index startIndex. The new ArrayList does not contain copies of the original elements; it is a view window into the original ArrayList. Any changes made to the original ArrayList will cause any operations on the view window version to throw an InvalidOperationException.

```
public virtual int IndexOf(object value)
public virtual int IndexOf(object value, int startIndex)
public virtual int IndexOf(object value, int startIndex, int length)
```

IndexOf() performs a forward search of the invoking ArrayList looking for the first occurrence of the specified object. The method returns the index of the first occurrence of the object or −1 if the object is not found. You can search entire ArrayList, or a subset defined by the startIndex and length parameters. An ArgumentOutOfRangeException is thrown if the integer arguments are out of range.

```
public virtual void Insert(int index, object value)
public virtual void InsertRange(int index, ICollection c)
```

Insert() places the specified object into the invoking ArrayList at the specified index. Existing elements are shifted over to accommodate the new element. An exception is thrown if index is less than zero, if index is greater than Count, or if the ArrayList is read-only or fixed-size.

`InsertRange()` inserts the specified collection into the invoking `ArrayList` starting at the specified index. Existing elements are shifted over to accommodate the new elements. An exception is thrown if c is a null reference, if `index` is less than zero, if `index` is greater than `Count`, or if the `ArrayList` is read-only or fixed-size.

```
public virtual int LastIndexOf(object value)
public virtual int LastIndexOf(object value, int startIndex)
public virtual int LastIndexOf(object value, int startIndex, int length)
```

`LastIndexOf()` performs a backward search of the invoking `ArrayList` looking for the last occurrence of the specified object. The method returns the index of the last occurrence of the object or −1 if the object is not found. You can search the entire `ArrayList` or a subset defined by the `startIndex` and `length` parameters. An `ArgumentOutOfRangeException` is thrown if the integer arguments are out of range.

```
public virtual void Remove(object obj)
public virtual void RemoveAt(int index)
public virtual void RemoveRange(int startIndex, int  count)
```

`Remove()` removes the first occurrence of the specified object in the invoking `ArrayList`. It finds the object by performing a linear search. Subsequent objects in the `ArrayList` are moved back one place to fill up the released position. The `Count` decreases by one, but the `Capacity` stays the same. A `NotSupportedException` is thrown if the `ArrayList` is read-only or fixed-size.

`RemoveAt()` removes the element at the specified `index`. The `Count` decreases by one, but the `Capacity` stays the same. An exception is thrown if `index` is less than zero, if `index` is greater than `Count`, or if the `ArrayList` is read-only or fixed-size.

`RemoveRange()` removes the specified range of elements from the invoking `ArrayList`. The `Capacity` of the `ArrayList` remains the same. An exception is thrown if `index` or `count` is less than zero, if `index` and `count` do not specify a valid range, or if the `ArrayList` is read-only or fixed-size.

```
public virtual void Reverse()
public virtual void Reverse(int startIndex, int count)
```

`Reverse()` reverses the order of the elements in the invoking `ArrayList`. You can reverse the entire `ArrayList` or a subset of it. An exception is thrown if `index` or `count` is less than zero, if `index` and `count` do not specify a valid range, or if the `ArrayList` is read-only.

```
public virtual void SetRange(int startIndex, ICollection c)
```

`SetRange()` copies the elements of the specified collection into the `ArrayList` starting at the specified index. This will overwrite the current elements in the `ArrayList`. An exception is thrown if `index` is less than zero, if c is a null reference, if `index` plus the length of c is greater than `Count`, or if the `ArrayList` is read-only.

```
public virtual void Sort()
public virtual void Sort(IComparer comparer)
public virtual void Sort(int startIndex, int count, IComparer comparer)
```

Sort() sorts the elements of the invoking ArrayList object using an IComparer object to compare the values of the objects. If an IComparer is not provided as an input argument, the method uses the IComparer implementation of each element. You can sort the entire ArrayList or a subset of it defined by startIndex and count. An exception is thrown if index or count is less than zero, if index and count do not specify a valid range, or if the ArrayList is read-only.

```
public virtual object[] ToArray()
public virtual Array ToArray(Type type)
```

ToArray() copies the elements of the invoking ArrayList into either an Object array or an Array of the specified Type. An exception is thrown if type is a null reference or if the ArrayList type cannot be cast into type.

```
public virtual void TrimToSize()
```

TrimToSize() reduces the capacity of the invoking ArrayList to be equal to the number of elements in the ArrayList. A NotSupportedException is thrown if the ArrayList is read-only or fixed-size.

Example: ArrayList class

The ArrayListDemo class is used to demonstrate the basic creation and use of an ArrayList. An empty, synchronized ArrayList is created and four elements are added to it. The ArrayList is sorted. The ArrayList is searched for a specified object and the contents of the ArrayList are printed out.

```
using System;
using System.Collections;

public class ArrayListDemo
{
  public static void Main()
  {
    int i;

    //=======================================================
    //  A synchronized ArrayList is created using the
    //  Synchronized() method.
    //=======================================================

    ArrayList list = ArrayList.Synchronized(new ArrayList());

    //=======================================================
    //  Elements are added to the list and the list is sorted.
    //=======================================================

    list.Add("Maria");
    list.Add("Angela");
    list.Add("Diana");
    list.Add("Alicia");
```

```
        list.Sort();

        //=========================================================
        //   The BinarySearch() method is used to search the
        //   elements of the ArrayList for a string.
        //=========================================================

        String str = "Alicia";

        if ((i = list.BinarySearch(str)) < 0)
          Console.WriteLine("{0} was not found",str);
        else
          Console.WriteLine("{0} is at index {1}",str,i);

        //===========================================
        // The ArrayList elements are printed out.
        //===========================================

        Console.WriteLine("\nList elements are \n");
        IEnumerator enumerator = list.GetEnumerator();
        while (enumerator.MoveNext())
          Console.WriteLine(enumerator.Current);
    }
}
```

Output:

```
Alicia is at index 0

List elements are

Alicia
Angela
Diana
Maria
```

Hashtable class

The Hashtable class encapsulates a collection of key-value pairs that are organized based on the hash code of the keys. A hash code for an object can be obtained using an implementation of the IHashCodeProvider interface. The keys themselves must have access to the GetHashCode() and Equals() methods. They can define these methods themselves or inherit them from a parent class. Each element in the Hashtable will be a DictionaryEntry struct, regardless of the types of the keys and values.

When a key-value pair is added to the Hashtable, it is placed into a "bucket" based on the hash code of the key. This speeds up the process of accessing the key-value pair because the lookup mechanism only has to search for the key in one bucket. A Hashtable will have a load factor which is the maximum ratio of entries to buckets. Smaller load factors speed up lookup time at the cost of increased memory usage. The capacity of the Hashtable is used to compute the optimal number of buckets to be used based on the load factor. As elements are added to the Hashtable, the number of buckets is increased as needed.

A Hashtable will give you better performance than a SortedList, because Hashtable elements are not sorted. However, because they are not sorted, you cannot access a Hashtable value through an index.

Syntax

```
public class Hashtable : IDictionary, ICollection, IEnumerable,
                         ISerializable, IDeserializationCallback, ICloneable
```

Hierarchy

```
Object  ---  Hashtable
```

Constructors

```
public Hashtable()
public Hashtable(IDictionary d)
public Hashtable(int capacity)
public Hashtable(IDictionary d, float loadFactor)
public Hashtable(IHashCodeProvider hcp, IComparer comparer)
public Hashtable(int capacity, float loadFactor)
public Hashtable(IDictionary d, IHashCodeProvider hcp,
                                               IComparer comparer)
public Hashtable(int capacity, IHashCodeProvider hcp, IComparer comparer)
public Hashtable(IDictionary d, float loadFactor, IHashCodeProvider hcp,
                                               IComparer comparer)
public Hashtable(int capacity, float loadFactor, IHashCodeProvider hcp,
                                               IComparer comparer)
```

Hashtable() creates a Hashtable object. The Hashtable can be initialized with a collection of elements and an initial capacity and load factor. You can also specify a hash code provider and comparer for the Hashtable. The no-argument constructor creates an empty Hashtable with a default initial capacity, load factor, hash code provider, and comparer. The default capacity is zero and the default load factor is 1.0.

Public instance properties

```
public virtual int Count {get;}
public virtual bool IsFixedSize {get;}
public virtual bool IsReadOnly {get;}
public virtual bool IsSynchronized {get;}
public virtual ICollection Keys {get;}
public virtual object SyncRoot {get;}
public virtual ICollection Values {get;}
public virtual object this[object key] { get; set; }
```

Count retrieves the number of key-value pairs contained in the Hashtable.

IsFixedSize indicates whether the Hashtable has a fixed size. The default is false.

IsReadOnly returns true if Hashtable is read-only. The default is false.

IsSynchronized specifies whether access to the Hashtable is synchronized. The default is false.

Keys returns an ICollection implementation containing the keys in the Hashtable. The ICollection will contain references to the original Hashtable. If the elements in the Hashtable are changed, they will change inside the ICollection as well.

SyncRoot provides synchronized access to the Hashtable. A Hashtable object by default is not thread-safe. Synchronized operations are performed on the SyncRoot of the Hashtable rather than on the Hashtable itself.

Values retrieves an ICollection containing the values in the Hashtable. The ICollection will contain references to the original Hashtable. If the values in the Hashtable are changed, they will change inside the ICollection as well.

this[] is the indexer for the Hashtable class. It gets or sets the value of the specified key.

Protected instance properties

```
protected IComparer Comparer { get; set; }
protected IHashCodeProvider Hcp { get; set; }
```

Comparer is the comparer object used with the Hashtable.

Hcp is the object associated with the Hashtable that is used to generate hash codes.

Public static methods

```
public static Hashtable Synchronized(Hashtable table)
```

Synchronized() places a synchronized (thread-safe) wrapper around the specified Hashtable and returns the wrapped version. This method should be used if you want a given Hashtable to support multiple writers. An ArgumentNullException is thrown if table is a null reference.

Public instance methods

```
public virtual void Add(object key, object value)
```

Add() adds an entry with the specified key and value to the invoking Hashtable. An exception is thrown if key is a null reference, if an element with the same key already exists in the Hashtable, or if the Hashtable is read-only or fixed-size.

```
public virtual void Clear()
```

Clear() removes all entries from the invoking Hashtable and sets the Count property to zero. A NotSupportedException is thrown if the Hashtable is read-only or fixed-size.

```
public virtual object Clone()
```

Clone() returns a shallow copy of the invoking Hashtable. The elements of the Hashtable are not copied. The shallow copy will contain references to the elements of the original Hashtable.

```
public virtual bool Contains(object key)
public virtual bool ContainsKey(object key)
public virtual bool ContainsValue(object value)
```

`Contains()` returns `true` if the specified key exists in the invoking `Hashtable`. An `ArgumentNullException` is thrown if key is a null reference.

`ContainsKey()` does the same thing as `Contains()`.

`ContainsValue()` returns `true` if the specified `value` exists in the invoking `Hashtable`.

> **`public virtual void CopyTo(Array array, int arrayIndex)`**

`CopyTo()` copies the elements of the invoking `Hashtable` into the specified one-dimensional array. The `Index` parameter is the index in `array` where the copying begins. You can copy only the keys or only the values into an array by having the `Keys` or `Values` property call this method. An exception is thrown if `array` is a null reference, if `array` is multi dimensional, if `arrayIndex` is out of range, or if the `Hashtable` element type cannot be cast implicitly into the type of the destination array.

> **`public virtual IDictionaryEnumerator GetEnumerator()`**
> **`IEnumerator IEnumerable.GetEnumerator()`**

`GetEnumerator()` returns an `IDictionaryEnumerator` object that can be used to read data from the invoking `Hashtable`. If elements in the `Hashtable` are added, deleted, or modified, the `IDictionaryEnumerator` becomes invalid and will throw an exception if used.

`IEnumerable.GetEnumerator()` returns an `Enumerator` object (as compared to the `IDictionaryEnumerator` returned by the previous method) that can iterate through the `HashTable`.

> **`public virtual void GetObjectData(SerializationInfo info,`**
> **`                                   StreamingContext context)`**
> **`public virtual void OnDeserialization(object sender)`**

`GetObjectData()` places the data needed to serialize the `Hashtable` into the specified `SerializationInfo` and `StreamingContext` objects. An `ArgumentNullException` is thrown if `info` is a null reference.

`OnDeserialization()` gets a callback function to issue a deserialization event with `sender` as its source when deserialization of the invoking `Hashtable` is complete.

> **`public virtual void Remove(object key)`**

`Remove()` removes the entry with the specified key from the invoking `Hashtable`. If the key is not found, nothing happens. An exception is thrown if `key` is a null reference or if the `Hashtable` is read-only or fixed-size.

Protected instance methods

> **`protected virtual int GetHash(object key)`**
> **`protected virtual bool KeyEquals(object item, object key)`**

`GetHash()` returns the hash code for the specified key. If the `Hashtable`'s implementation uses the default hash code provider, this method will have key call its `GetHashCode()` method.

KeyEquals() compares the input arguments item and key. If the objects are equal, the method returns true. An ArgumentNullException is thrown if either item or key are null references.

Example: Using hashtables

In this example, a Hashtable is used to store some information about an account. The keys represent the account holder's name, the account number, and the account balance. Elements are added to the Hashtable using the Add() method. The keys of the Hashtable are written out to a separate Array, and the Hashtable is searched for a specified value.

```csharp
using System;
using System.Collections;

public class HashtableDemo
{
  public static void Main()
  {

    //==========================================================
    //  A Hashtable instance is created. Four key-value pairs
    //  are added to it.
    //==========================================================

    Hashtable table = new Hashtable();

    table.Add("name", "Lisa");
    table.Add("account number", 123456);
    table.Add("balance", 470.82);

    //============================================================
    //  The keys of the Hashtable are copied into a one-dimensional
    //  Array using the Keys property of the Hashtable class and
    //  the CopyTo() method. The keys are then written out.
    //============================================================

    object[] array = new object[table.Count];

    table.Keys.CopyTo(array, 0);
    IEnumerator e = array.GetEnumerator();
    Console.WriteLine("Keys: ");
    while ( e.MoveNext() )
    {
      Console.WriteLine( "    {0}", e.Current);
    }
    Console.WriteLine();

    //============================================================
    //  The Hashtable is searched for a specified value using the
    //  ContainsValue() method. If the value is found, the elements
    //  of the Hashtable are written out. The order of the elements
    //  stored in the Hashtable may be different from the order in
```

```
      //  which they were added to the Hashtable.
      //================================================================

      string name = "Lisa";

      if (table.ContainsValue(name))
      {
        IDictionaryEnumerator enumerator = table.GetEnumerator();
        while (enumerator.MoveNext())
        {
          Console.WriteLine( "{0} = {1}", enumerator.Key, enumerator.Value);
        }
      }
    }
  }
```

Output:

```
Keys:

    balance
    name
    account number

balance = 470.82
name = Lisa
account number = 123456
```

Notice in the output that the order of the elements in the Hashtable is different from the order in which they were added to the Hashtable. This is because a Hashtable stores its elements according to the hash code of the keys rather than by an alphabetical or first-in type sorting.

SortedList class

The SortedList class encapsulates a collection of key-value pairs, sorted according to the keys. The elements can be accessed by key or by index. A SortedList uses two arrays to store the elements of the list: one for the keys and another for the values. A SortedList has a capacity which is the number of elements the list can hold. The capacity is automatically reallocated as the list size increases.

Quite often the keys are strings and will be sorted alphabetically. If the keys are user-defined objects, the sorting of the list can be performed either by a specified IComparer object or by the IComparer objects associated with the keys themselves. Access to the elements of a SortedList is slower than for a Hashtable because of the sorting, but the SortedList elements can be accessed by index, whereas the Hashtable elements cannot.

Syntax

```
public class SortedList : IDictionary, ICollection, IEnumerable, ICloneable
```

Hierarchy

```
Object   ---   SortedList
```

Constructors

```
public SortedList()
public SortedList(IComparer comparer)
public SortedList(IDictionary d)
public SortedList(int capacity)
public SortedList(IComparer comparer, int capacity)
public SortedList(IDictionary d, IComparer comparer)
```

SortedList() creates a SortedList object. The SortedList can be initialized with a collection of elements and an initial capacity. You can also provide a comparer that is used to sort the SortedList. The no-argument constructor creates an empty SortedList with an initial capacity of 16. The list is sorted using the IComparer interface implemented by each key in the SortedList.

Public instance properties

```
virtual int Capacity { get; set; }
virtual int Count {get;}
virtual bool IsFixedSize {get;}
virtual bool IsReadOnly {get;}
virtual bool IsSynchronized {get;}
virtual ICollection Keys {get;}
virtual object SyncRoot {get;}
virtual ICollection Values {get;}
virtual object this[object key] { get; set; }
```

Capacity is used to get or set the number of elements the SortedList can contain. The system will automatically double the capacity if the number of elements in the SortedList equals the capacity.

Count returns the number of elements contained in the SortedList.

IsFixedSize indicates whether the SortedList has a fixed size. The default is false.

IsReadOnly returns true if SortedList is read-only. The default is false.

IsSynchronized specifies whether access to the SortedList is synchronized. The default is false.

Keys retrieves an ICollection containing the keys in the SortedList.

SyncRoot provides synchronized access to the SortedList. A SortedList object by default is not thread-safe. Synchronized operations should be performed on the SyncRoot of the SortedList rather than on the SortedList object itself.

Values returns an ICollection implementation containing the values in the SortedList.

this[] is the indexer for the SortedList class. It is used to get or set the value associated with the specified key.

Static methods

```
public static SortedList Synchronized(SortedList list)
```

Synchronized() places a synchronized (thread-safe) wrapper around the specified SortedList and returns the wrapped version. Note that, whereas the SyncRoot property provides synchronized access to the SortedList itself, the Synchronized() method returns a reference to a separate wrapper object. An ArgumentNullException is thrown if list is a null reference.

Public instance methods

```
public virtual void Add(object key, object value)
public virtual void Clear()
public virtual object Clone()
```

Add() adds an entry with the specified key and value to the invoking SortedList. An exception is thrown if key is a null reference, if an element with the same key already exists in the SortedList, or if the SortedList is read-only or fixed-size.

Clear() removes all entries from the invoking SortedList and sets the Count property to zero. A NotSupportedException is thrown if the SortedList is read-only or fixed-size.

Clone() returns a shallow copy of the invoking SortedList. Rather than containing copies of the SortedList elements, the shallow copy will contain references to the elements of the original SortedList.

```
public virtual bool Contains(object key)
public virtual bool ContainsKey(object key)
public virtual bool ContainsValue(object value)
```

Contains() returns true if the specified key exists in the invoking SortedList. A binary search method is used. An ArgumentNullException is thrown if key is a null reference.

ContainsKey() does the same thing as Contains().

ContainsValue() returns true if the specified value exists in the invoking SortedList. The method uses a linear search of the SortedList elements.

```
public virtual void CopyTo(Array array, int arrayIndex)
```

CopyTo() copies the elements of the invoking SortedList into the specified one-dimensional array. The Index parameter is the index in array where the copying begins. You can copy only the keys or only the values into an array by having the Keys or Values property call this method. An exception is thrown if array is a null reference, if array is multi dimensional, if arrayIndex is out of range, or if the SortedList element type cannot be cast implicitly into the type of the destination array.

```
public virtual IDictionaryEnumerator GetEnumerator()
IEnumerator IEnumerable.GetEnumerator()
```

GetEnumerator() returns an IDictionaryEnumerator object that can be used to read data from the invoking SortedList. If elements in the SortedList are added, deleted, or modified, the IDictionaryEnumerator becomes invalid.

`IEnumerable.GetEnumerator()` returns an Enumerator object (as compared to the `IDictionaryEnumerator` returned by the previous method) that can iterate through the `SortedList`.

```
public virtual object GetByIndex(int index)
public virtual object GetKey(int index)
public virtual IList GetKeyList()
public virtual IList GetValueList()
```

`GetByIndex()` returns the value corresponding to the element at the specified index of the `SortedList`. An `ArgumentOutOfRangeException` is thrown if index is outside the valid range for the `SortedList`.

`GetKey()` returns the key corresponding to the element at the specified index of the `SortedList`. An `ArgumentOutOfRangeException` is thrown if index is outside the valid range for the `SortedList`.

`GetKeyList()` returns an `IList` containing the keys of the invoking `SortedList`. This is a read-only view of the keys. If the keys in the original `SortedList` are modified, the changes will be reflected in the `IList` returned by this method.

`GetValueList()` returns an `IList` containing the values of the invoking `SortedList`. This is a read-only view of the values. If the values in the original `SortedList` are modified, the changes will be reflected in the `IList` returned by this method.

```
public virtual int IndexOfKey(object key)
public virtual int IndexOfValue(object value)
```

`IndexOfKey()` returns the zero-based index of the specified key or –1 if the key is not found. An `ArgumentNullException` is thrown if key is a null reference.

`IndexOfValue()` returns the zero-based index of the specified value or –1 if the value is not found.

```
public virtual void Remove(object key)
public virtual void RemoveAt(int index)
```

`Remove()` removes the entry with the specified key from the invoking `SortedList`. If the key is not found, nothing happens. An `ArgumentNullException` is thrown if key is a null reference.

`RemoveAt()` removes the element at the specified index. An exception is thrown if index is outside the valid range for the `SortedList`, or if the `SortedList` is read-only or fixed-size.

```
public virtual void SetByIndex(int index, object value)
```

`SetByIndex()` replaces the value at the specified index in the invoking `SortedList` with the specified value. An `ArgumentOutOfRangeException` is thrown if index is outside the valid range for the `SortedList`.

```
public virtual void TrimToSize()
```

TrimToSize() reduces the capacity to the actual number of elements in the invoking SortedList. A NotSupportedException is thrown if the SortedList is read-only or fixed-size.

Example: Sorted lists

In this example, a SortedList is created and three key-value pairs are added to it. The key-value pairs are printed using an IDictionaryEnumerator. The value corresponding to the "age" key is changed using the indexer. The value corresponding to the "weight" key is changed using the SetByIndex() method. The updated key-value pairs are then printed out by accessing their index. Note that the key-value pairs have been sorted alphabetically according to their keys.

```csharp
using System;
using System.Collections;

public class SortedListDemo
{
  public static void Main()
  {
    SortedList list = new SortedList();

    //=====================================
    //  Add some elements to the SortedList
    //=====================================

    list.Add("name", "Bailey");
    list.Add("age", 10);
    list.Add("weight", 25.6);

    //===========================================================
    //  Print out the elements using an IDictionaryEnumerator
    //===========================================================

    Console.WriteLine("\nList elements are \n");
    IDictionaryEnumerator enumerator = list.GetEnumerator();
    while (enumerator.MoveNext())
    {
      Console.WriteLine("key: " + enumerator.Key +
                        "   value: " + enumerator.Value);
    }

    //===========================================================
    //  Make some changes to the values, first by using the
    //  indexer and then by using the SetByIndex() method
    //===========================================================

    list["age"] = 11;
    list.SetByIndex(2, 26.3);

    //===================================
    //  Print out the elements by index
    //===================================
```

```
            Console.WriteLine("\nList elements are \n");
            for(int i=0; i<list.Count; ++i)
            {
               Console.WriteLine("key: " + list.GetKey(i) +
                                 "   value: " + list.GetByIndex(i));
            }
        }
    }
```

Output:

```
List elements are

key: age value: 10
key: name value: Bailey
key: weight value: 25.6

List elements are

key: age value = 11
key: name value = Bailey
key: weight value = 26.3
```

CollectionBase class

This is a class that we can use as a base for a strongly-typed collection. Classes derived from CollectionBase have access to a protected ArrayList field, which is used to store the actual members of the collection. We need to define methods ourselves to add and remove objects in this list (this is necessary if the collection is to be strongly-typed), but other methods and properties (such as RemoveAt() and Count) are implemented by the CollectionBase itself.

The CollectionBase class defines a number of protected methods that can be overridden by derived classes to provide procedures that are performed before an element is added to the collection, removed from the collection, accessed, or modified. Derived classes in the .NET library include the AccessControlList class that defines access to a securable object. CollectionBase derived classes represent modifiable collections.

Syntax

```
public abstract class CollectionBase : IList, ICollection, IEnumerable
```

Hierarchy

```
Object  ---  CollectionBase
```

Constructors

```
protected CollectionBase()
```

CollectionBase() is a no-argument constructor for use by derived classes of CollectionBase.

Properties

```
public int Count {get;}
protected ArrayList InnerList {get;}
protected IList List {get;}
```

Count returns the number of elements contained in the collection.

InnerList gives us access to the ArrayList object which is used to store the elements in the CollectionBase. We add and remove elements in the CollectionBase by calling the Add() and Remove() methods of this ArrayList.

List retrieves an IList object containing the elements of the CollectionBase. An IList represents a general type of collection that can access the methods defined in the IList interface.

Public instance methods

```
public void Clear()
public void RemoveAt(int index)
```

Clear() removes all objects from the invoking CollectionBase and sets the Count property to zero.

RemoveAt() removes the element at the specified index from the CollectionBase. An ArgumentOutOfRangeException is thrown if index is less than zero or greater than Count.

```
public IEnumerator GetEnumerator()
```

GetEnumerator() returns an IEnumerator object that can be used to read data from the invoking CollectionBase. The IEnumerator is good only for the current state of the collection. If elements in the CollectionBase are added, deleted, or modified, the IEnumerator becomes invalid.

```
void ICollection.CopyTo(Array array, int index)
```

ICollection.CopyTo() copies the contents of a CollectionBase into a one-dimensional Array starting at the specified index of the target array. The copying is performed using the Array.Copy() method. An exception is thrown if array is a null reference, if array is multidimensional, if index is out of range, or if the CollectionBase type cannot be cast into the type of the target array.

The CollectionBase also implements a number of methods derived explicitly from the IList interface:

```
int IList.Add(object value)
bool IList.Contains(object value)
int IList.IndexOf(object value)
void IList.Insert(int index, object value)
void IList.Remove(object value)
```

IList.Add() adds an object to the end of the CollectionBase. A NotSupportedException is thrown if the CollectionBase is read-only or fixed-size.

IList.Contains() returns true if the invoking CollectionBase contains the specified value.

`IList.IndexOf()` returns the zero-based index of the first occurrence of `value` or –1 if `value` is not found.

`IList.Insert()` inserts the specified object into the invoking `CollectionBase` at the specified `index`. Existing elements are shifted down to accommodate the new element. An exception is thrown if `index` is less than zero, if `index` is greater than `Count`, or if the `CollectionBase` is read-only or fixed-size.

`IList.Remove()` removes the first occurrence of the specified `object` from the invoking `CollectionBase`. The remaining elements are shifted up to fill the vacant spot. A `NotSupportedException` is thrown if the `CollectionBase` is read-only or fixed-size.

Protected instance methods

The `CollectionBase` class provides a number of protected methods which are called when certain events occur, such as inserting or removing an item, or clearing the list. These methods are paired – the first method, named `On...()`, is called before the operation is carried out, and the second, `On...Complete()`, is called after the operation. We can cancel the operation by throwing an exception in the first of these methods.

```
protected virtual void OnClear()
protected virtual void OnClearComplete()
```

`OnClear()` is a method that is invoked when the `Clear()` method is called. The `OnClear()` method executes before any elements of the `CollectionBase` are cleared. The default implementation (which does nothing) should be overridden by a derived class if there is a need to perform some action before the collection is cleared, such as event notifications via delegates.

`OnClearComplete()` is similar to the `OnClear()` method except it is called after the `CollectionBase` elements are cleared. The default implementation should be overridden by a derived class if there is a need to perform some post-clearing activity.

```
protected virtual void OnInsert(int index, object value)
protected virtual void OnInsertComplete(int index, object value)
```

`OnInsert()` is a method that is called before the specified object is inserted at the specified index in the `CollectionBase`. This method is overridden to allow for a pre-insertion activity to take place.

`OnInsertComplete()` is similar to the `OnInsert()` method, except that it is called after the specified object is inserted at the specified index. This method is overridden if some post-insertion procedure is required.

```
protected virtual void OnRemove(int index, object value)
protected virtual void OnRemoveComplete(int index, object value)
```

`OnRemove()` is called before the specified object is removed from the specified index in the `CollectionBase`. This method is overridden to allow for some pre-removal activity to occur.

`OnRemoveComplete()` is similar to the `OnRemove()` method except it is called after the specified object is removed from the specified index. This method is overridden if some post-removal procedure is required.

```
protected virtual void OnSet(int index, object oldValue, object newValue)
protected virtual void OnSetComplete(int index, object value)
```

`OnSet()` performs some user-defined processes before setting a value in the invoking `CollectionBase`. A derived class can override this method to perform some action before the value is set.

`OnSetComplete()` is similar to the `OnSet()` method except it is called before the specified value is changed. This method is overridden if some procedure is desired after the value has been set.

```
protected virtual void OnValidate(object value)
```

`OnValidate()` allows for processes to be defined that take place when an object in the `CollectionBase` is being validated (before it is added or removed). The default implementation validates an object by determining if it is a null reference. If it is, an `ArgumentNullException` is thrown. This method can be overridden to place additional restrictions on the type of elements that will be accepted into the collection.

Example: Implementing a typed collection

This example illustrates how we can derive a class from `CollectionBase` to create a strongly-typed collection which can only contain elements of one type. To demonstrate that this can be any kind of object, we'll create a collection that holds Windows metafile images. We need to provide implementations of the `Add()` and `Remove()` methods, and the indexer `this[]`. These simply add, remove, return, or set an element within the collection's `InnerList`. We'll also provide an override of the `OnClear()` method. We don't want just anyone going around clearing the collection, so we'll check the name of the currently logged on user (using the `UserName` property of the `System.Environment` class), and if it isn't `"Administrator"`, we'll throw an `InvalidOperationException` to stop the collection being cleared. The `Clear()` method itself is implemented by `CollectionBase`, so we don't need to code that ourselves.

```csharp
using System;
using System.Collections;
using System.Drawing.Imaging;

public class ImageCollection : CollectionBase
{
  public ImageCollection()
  {
  }

  public void Add(Metafile value)
  {
    InnerList.Add(value);
  }

  public void Remove(Metafile value)
  {
    InnerList.Remove(value);
  }

  public Metafile this[int index]
  {
    get
```

```
      {
        return (Metafile)InnerList[index];
      }
      set
      {
        InnerList[index] = value;
      }
    }

    protected override void OnClear()
    {
      if (Environment.UserName != "Administrator")
        throw new InvalidOperationException(
                     "Only Administrator can clear the collection");

    }
  }
```

In the client code, we'll just create an instance of our collection class, and add a few images to it. Then we'll display the number of elements in the collection, attempt to clear it, and print out the Count again to see whether the Clear() method has executed. Whether Clear() succeeds depends on whether you're running Windows as Administrator.

```
public class TypedCollectionDemo
{
  public static void Main()
  {
    string path = "C:\\Program Files\\Microsoft Visual Studio .NET\\" +
                   "Common7\\Graphics\\metafile\\business\\";
    ImageCollection images = new ImageCollection();
    Metafile img1 = new Metafile(path + "Calcultr.wmf");
    Metafile img2 = new Metafile(path + "Computer.wmf");
    Metafile img3 = new Metafile(path + "LapTop1.wmf");

    images.Add(img1);
    images.Add(img2);
    images.Add(img3);
    Console.WriteLine(images.Count);
    try
    {
      images.Clear();
    }
    catch (InvalidOperationException e)
    {
      Console.WriteLine(e.Message);
    }
    Console.WriteLine(images.Count);
  }
}
```

Output if run as Administrator:

```
3
0
```

Output if not run as Administrator:

```
3
Only Administrator can clear the collection
3
```

DictionaryBase class

The DictionaryBase class is the base class for a strongly-typed collection of key-value pairs. Just as the CollectionBase class internally uses an ArrayList to store its elements, the DictionaryBase uses a Hashtable. It also defines a number of protected methods that can be overridden by derived classes to provide procedures that are performed before an element is added to the collection, removed from the collection, accessed, or modified.

Syntax

```
public abstract class DictionaryBase : IDictionary, ICollection, IEnumerable
```

Hierarchy

```
Object  ---  DictionaryBase
```

Constructors

```
protected DictionaryBase()
```

DictionaryBase() is a no-argument constructor for use by derived classes of DictionaryBase.

Properties

```
public int Count {get;}
protected IDictionary Dictionary {get;}
protected Hashtable InnerHashtable {get;}
```

Count returns the number of elements contained in the DictionaryBase.

Dictionary retrieves an IDictionary containing the elements of the DictionaryBase (or one of its derived classes).

InnerHashtable allows us to access the Hashtable object which contains the elements of the DictionaryBase. A Hashtable is a specific type of IDictionary that stores its elements based on the hash code of the key.

Public instance methods

```
public void Clear()
public void CopyTo(Array array, int index)
public IDictionaryEnumerator GetEnumerator()
```

Clear() removes all objects from the invoking DictionaryBase and sets the Count property to zero.

CopyTo() copies the elements of the invoking DictionaryBase into the specified one-dimensional Array. The index parameter is the index in array where the copying begins. An exception is thrown if array is a null reference, if array is multidimensional, if index is out of range, or if the DictionaryBase type cannot be cast implicitly into the type of the destination array.

GetEnumerator() returns an IDictionaryEnumerator object that can be used to read data from the invoking DictionaryBase. If elements in the DictionaryBase are added, deleted, or modified, the IDictionaryEnumerator becomes invalid.

As well as these methods, there are four explicit interface method implementations, which cannot be called directly against the DictionaryBase, but can be called if the object is cast to IDictionary or IEnumerable:

```
void IDictionary.Add(object key, object value)
bool IDictionary.Contains(object key)
void IDictionary.Remove(object key)
IEnumerator IEnumerable.GetEnumerator()
```

IDictionary.Add() adds an element with the specified key and value to the DictionaryBase. An exception is thrown if key is a null reference, if an element with the same key already exists, or if the DictionaryBase is read-only or fixed-size.

IDictionary.Contains() returns true if the DictionaryBase contains an element with the specified key. An ArgumentNullException is thrown if key is a null reference.

IDictionary.Remove() removes the element corresponding to the specified key from the DictionaryBase. If the key is not found, the DictionaryBase is unchanged. An exception is thrown if key is a null reference or if the DictionaryBase is read-only or fixed-size.

IEnumerable.GetEnumerator() returns an IEnumerator that can be used to iterate through the contents of the DictionaryBase.

Protected instance methods

Like the CollectionBase class, DictionaryBase provides a set of paired methods that are called before and after certain operations take place. By throwing an exception in the first method of the pair, we can cancel the operation.

```
protected virtual void OnClear()
protected virtual void OnClearComplete()
```

OnClear() is a method that is invoked when the Clear() method is called. The OnClear() method executes before any elements of the DictionaryBase are cleared. The default implementation (which does nothing) should be overridden by a derived class if there is a need to perform some action before the collection is cleared such as event notifications via delegates.

OnClearComplete() is similar to the OnClear() method except it is called after the DictionaryBase elements are cleared. The default implementation should be overridden by a derived class if there is a need to perform some post-clearing activity.

```
protected virtual void OnGet(object key, object currentValue)
```

OnGet() is a method whose default implementation simply returns the object (currentValue) corresponding to the specified key. This method can be overridden to perform additional operations that are intended to occur when an object is returned using a standard Get() method.

```
protected virtual void OnInsert(object key, object value)
protected virtual void OnInsertComplete(object key, object value)
```

OnInsert() is a method that is called before a key-value pair is inserted into the DictionaryBase. This method is overridden to allow for a pre-insertion activity to take place.

OnInsertComplete() is similar to the OnInsert() method except it is called after the specified key-value pair has been added to the DictionaryBase. This method is overridden if some post-insertion procedure is required.

```
protected virtual void OnRemove(object key, object value)
protected virtual void OnRemoveComplete(object key, object value)
```

OnRemove() is a method that is called before the specified key-value pair is removed from the DictionaryBase. This method is overridden to allow for some pre-removal activity to occur.

OnRemoveComplete() is similar to the OnRemove() method except it is called after the specified key-value pair is removed from the DictionaryBase. This method is overridden if some post-removal procedure is required.

```
protected virtual void OnSet(object key, object oldValue,
                                         object newValue)
protected virtual void OnSetComplete(object key, object value)
```

OnSet() performs some user-defined operation before setting a value in the invoking DictionaryBase. A derived class can override this method to perform some action before the value is set.

OnSetComplete() is similar to the OnSet() method except it is called before the specified value is changed. This method is overridden if some procedure is desired after the value has been set.

```
protected virtual void OnValidate(object key, object value)
```

OnValidate() allows for processes to be defined that take place when an object in DictionaryBase is being validated. The default implementation validates an object by determining if it is a null reference. If it is, an ArgumentNullException is thrown. This method can be overridden to place additional restrictions on the type of elements that will be accepted into the collection.

DictionaryEntry struct

The DictionaryEntry struct defines a key-value pair that can be added to or removed from an IDictionary.

Syntax

```
public struct DictionaryEntry
```

Hierarchy

```
Object   ---   ValueType   ---   DictionaryEntry
```

Constructors

```
public DictionaryEntry(object key, object value)
```

DictionaryEntry() creates a DictionaryEntry object and initializes it with the specified key-value pair.

Properties

```
public object Key { get; set; }
public object Value { get; set; }
```

Key gets or sets the key for this entry.

Value gets or sets the value for this entry.

Summary

The .NET Framework provides a number of different ways to group together objects into collections. The simplest of these is the Array class, which we looked at in Chapter 22. We began this chapter by looking at the interfaces which define the methods and properties that collections should implement, before looking at the classes themselves. The .NET Framework provides a number of different classes which implement ready-made, weakly-typed collections, but it also provides the CollectionBase and DictionaryBase classes, which we can use as base classes for our own strongly-typed collections and dictionaries.

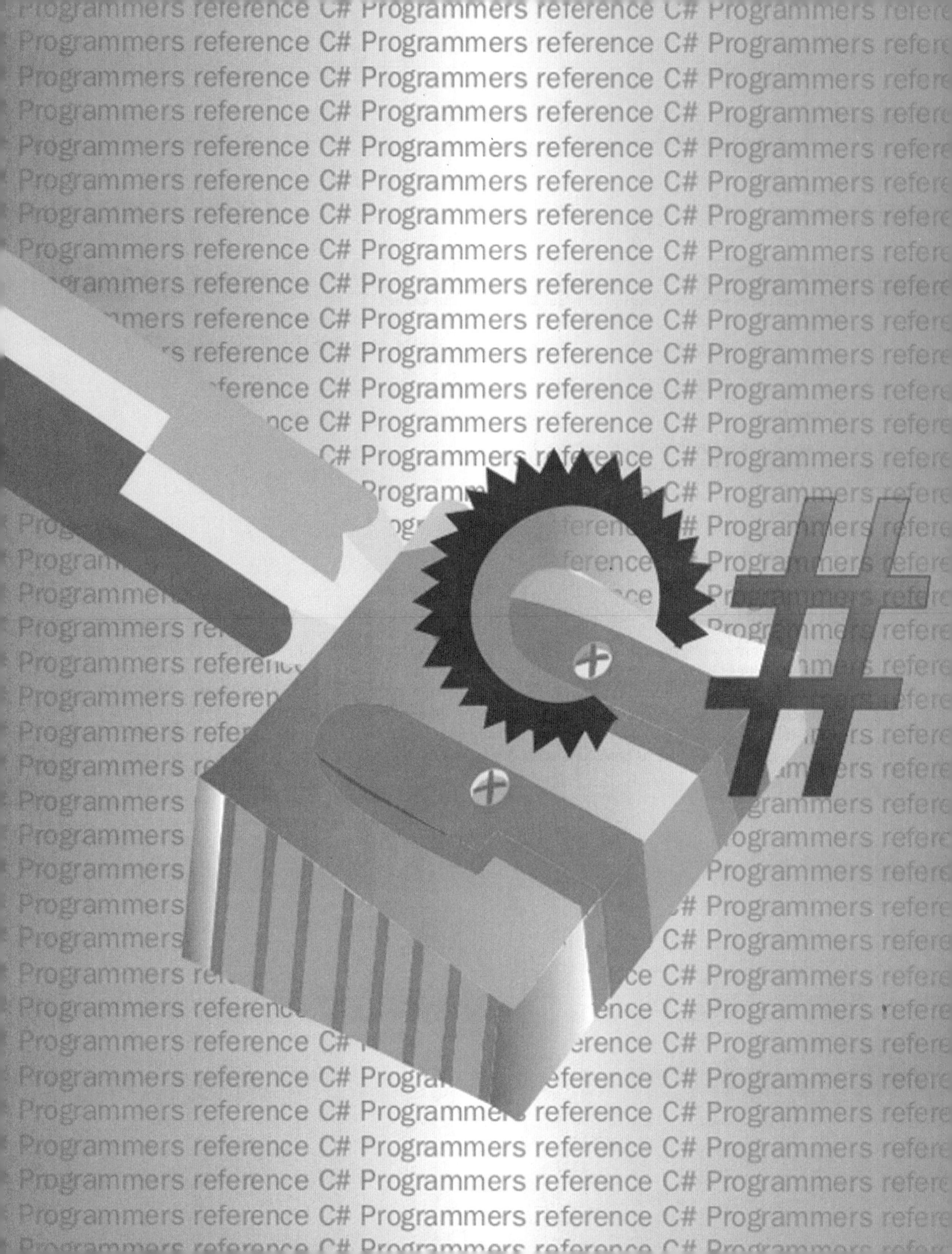
Programmers reference C#

24

Input/Output

This chapter describes the input/output facilitities provided by the .NET Framework. As with C++ and Java, the .NET Framework makes use of data streams to implement its input/output functionality. A stream is an abstraction representing a series of bytes or characters. This abstraction might represent a file, a pipe, a socket, a block of memory, or an input/output device. The stream classes contained in the `System.IO` namespace provide a generic view of data sources and storehouses. This allows the developer to focus on high-level I/O issues without worrying about the specific details of the operating system or underlying devices.

There are two main types of stream classes used by C#: those representing byte streams and those representing character streams. The byte stream classes derive from the `Stream` class. Derived classes include the `BufferedStream`, `FileStream`, and `MemoryStream` classes. These classes read and write data as a sequence of bytes. There are also binary I/O classes that can be wrapped around byte streams. The second general type of stream class is intended to read and write character data. Character stream classes include the `StreamReader`, `StreamWriter`, `StringReader`, `StringWriter`, `TextReader`, and `TextWriter` classes.

There are basically five things you can do with a stream. You can open it, read from it, write to it, change the current position of it, or close it. Access to a stream can be asynchronous or synchronous depending on how the stream object was created. Some of the stream classes use buffering to improve performance.

One of the I/O classes detailed in this chapter, the `Console` class, is contained in the `System` namespace. All other classes and enumerations described in this chapter come from the `System.IO` namespace.

Console class

The `Console` class encapsulates the standard input, output, and error streams. This class is described in Chapter 22.

Byte streams

Byte streams are the most "primitive" kind of I/O stream in that they only read and write bytes. The bytes themselves have no information about the type of object that they represent. Binary and character data streams are often wrapped around an underlying byte stream. The byte stream class hierarchy is shown below.

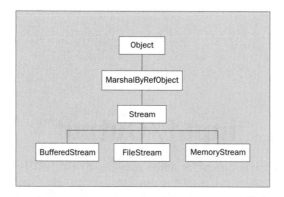

All byte stream classes inherit from the Object and MarshalByRefObject classes. The inheritance from MarshalByRefObject indicates that a byte stream instance can be used as a remote object. It can be used, for instance, to transfer data in a distributed application. The Stream class is the abstract base class for the byte stream classes. It provides the basic methods to read or write either a single byte or the contents of a byte buffer. These I/O operations can be done in a synchronous or asynchronous manner.

The BufferedStream, FileStream, and MemoryStream classes extend the Stream class and build in some additional functionality. The BufferedStream class wraps a buffer around another byte stream. Data is read or written into the buffer before it is sent to its ultimate destination. Buffered I/O can reduce the number of calls made to the operating system. The FileStream class associates an input or output stream with a file allowing you to read from or write to the file. The MemoryStream allows you to read and write directly from memory rather than from the disk or a remote connection.

Character encoding schemes are often used in conjunction with byte streams to make it easier to convert bytes into characters and vice versa. The character encoding schemes provided in the System.Text namespace are described in Chapter 26.

Stream class

The Stream class is the base class for all byte streams. It defines the basic methods for reading and writing byte data. The I/O functionality includes support for both synchronous and asynchronous data transfer. The Stream class defines methods that when overridden by a derived class let you change the current position of an I/O stream and change the length of the stream. Because Stream derives from MarshalByRefObject, a byte stream can be used as a remote object.

Syntax

```
public abstract class Stream : MarshalByRefObject, IDisposable
```

Hierarchy

```
Object  ---  MarshalByRefObject  ---  Stream
```

Constructors

```
protected Stream()
```

Stream() is a protected constructor used by derived classes of the Stream class.

Fields

```
public static readonly Stream Null
```

Null represents a Stream with no backing store. If you attempt to read from or write to the Stream.Null, nothing happens.

Properties

```
public abstract bool CanRead {get;}
public abstract bool CanSeek {get;}
public abstract bool CanWrite {get;}
public abstract long Length {get;}
public abstract long Position {get; set;}
```

CanRead returns true if the current stream supports reading or false if the stream is closed or only supports writing.

CanSeek returns true if the stream supports seeking. When you seek, you attempt to change the current position of a stream.

CanWrite returns true if the stream can be written or false if the stream is closed or is read-only.

Length retrieves the length of the stream in bytes.

Position is used to get or set the current position in the stream.

Public instance methods

```
public virtual IAsyncResult BeginRead(byte[] array, int offset,
          int numBytes, AsyncCallback userCallBack, object stateObject)
public virtual IAsyncResult BeginWrite(byte[] array, int offset,
          int numBytes, AsyncCallback userCallBack, object stateObject)
```

BeginRead() begins an asynchronous read operation. The method attempts to read the specified number of bytes into a byte array beginning at the designated offset. The userCallBack parameter refers to a method that is called when the asynchronous read operation is complete. The stateObject parameter is an object that is used to identify this read operation from other requests. The return value is a reference to the asynchronous read. An exception is thrown if an attempt is made to read past the end of file, if any of the arguments are invalid, if this method was called after the stream was closed, or if the stream does not support the read operation.

BeginWrite() is similar to BeginRead() except it performs an asynchronous write operation.

```
public virtual void Close()
public virtual WaitHandle CreateWaitHandle()
```

Close() closes the invoking Stream and releases any resources associated with it. The current implementation of this method calls the protected Dispose() method passing it a true value. This means that both managed and unmanaged resources associated with the Stream are released.

CreateWaitHandle() returns a WaitHandle object that can be used as a way of blocking inside the EndRead() or EndWrite() methods until the asynchronous read or write is complete.

```
public virtual int EndRead(IAsyncResult result)
public virtual void EndWrite(IAsyncResult result)
```

EndRead() waits (and will block) until a pending asynchronous read operation is complete. The return value is the number of bytes read from the stream. The result parameter is a reference to the asynchronous read. An exception is thrown if result is a null reference or if result did not originate from a BeginRead() method on the current stream.

EndWrite() waits for an asynchronous write operation to complete and blocks until it does. The result parameter is a reference to the asynchronous write. An exception is thrown if result is a null reference or if result did not originate from a BeginWrite() method on the current stream.

```
public abstract void Flush()
void IDisposable.Dispose()
```

Flush() empties all buffers used by the Stream. Any buffered data is written to the underlying device. An IOException is thrown if an I/O error occurs during the flush.

IDisposable.Dispose() is required since the Stream class implements the IDisposable interface. The MSDN docs state that this method is not intended to be called explicitly by your code.

```
public abstract int Read(out byte[] array, int offset, int count)
public virtual int ReadByte()
```

Read() reads a sequence of bytes from the invoking stream and places the data into the specified byte array. The offset parameter is the point in the array at which to start copying. The count parameter is the number of bytes to be read. The return value is the total number of bytes that were actually read into the array. The position of the stream is advanced by the number of bytes that were read. An exception is thrown if array is a null reference, if offset or count are out of range, if the stream does not support reading, if this method was called after the stream was closed, or if some other I/O error occurred.

ReadByte() reads a byte from the underlying stream and returns the byte cast into a 32-bit integer value. The method will return –1 if the end of the stream has been reached. The position of the stream is advanced by one byte. An exception is thrown if the stream does not support reading or if this method was called after the stream was closed.

```
public abstract long Seek(int offset, SeekOrigin origin)
public abstract void SetLength(long value)
```

`Seek()` sets the current position within the stream according to the specified byte offset relative to the specified origin. The return value is the new position of the stream. An exception is thrown if the stream does not support seeking or if this method was called after the stream was closed.

`SetLength()` sets the length of the stream in bytes to the specified value. If `value` is less than the current length of the stream, the stream will be truncated. An exception is thrown if the stream does not support both writing and seeking or if this method was called after the stream was closed.

```
public override void Write(byte[] array, int offset, int count)
public override void WriteByte(byte value)
```

`Write()` writes data from the specified byte array to the current stream. The `offset` parameter is the point in the buffer at which to begin extracting data. The `count` parameter is the number of bytes to be written to the current stream. If the write is successful, the position of the stream is advanced by the number of bytes written. An exception is thrown if `array` is a null reference, if the `offset` or `count` parameters are out of range, if this method was called after the stream was closed, or if the stream does not support writing.

`WriteByte()` writes the specified byte to the output stream and advances the stream position by one byte. An exception is thrown if the stream does not support writing or if the method was called after the stream was closed.

Protected instance methods

```
protected virtual void Dispose(bool disposing)
```

`Dispose()` immediately releases the resources allocated to the `Stream`. If `disposing` is true, both the managed and the unmanaged resources are released. If it is false, only the unmanaged resources are released.

BufferedStream class

The `BufferedStream` class provides an internal buffer for the read and write operations of other I/O streams. A buffer is a block of bytes in memory that can be used for the temporary storage of data. Buffering is already provided when data is read from or written to a file. The `BufferedStream` class is intended for I/O operations with a device that isn't automatically buffered. Use of a buffer can improve performance compared to unbuffered I/O by reducing the number of calls to the operating system. A `BufferedStream` can be wrapped around certain other types of I/O streams and provides methods for reading and writing bytes to the underlying stream.

Syntax

```
public sealed class BufferedStream : Stream
```

Hierarchy

```
Object  ---  MarshalByRefObject  ---  Stream  ---  BufferedStream
```

Constructors

```
public BufferedStream(Stream stream)
public BufferedStream(Stream stream, int bufferSize)
```

`BufferedStream()` creates a `BufferedStream` object that is wrapped around the specified underlying stream. The default buffer size is 4096 bytes or you can specify another buffer size if you like. The buffer size (obviously) must be greater than zero.

Properties

```
public override bool CanRead {get;}
public override bool CanSeek {get;}
public override bool CanWrite {get;}
public override long Length {get;}
public override long Position {get; set;}
```

`CanRead` returns true if the current stream supports reading or false if the stream is closed or only supports writing.

`CanSeek` returns true the stream supports seeking. This will be false if the stream was created from an operating system handle such as a pipe or was output to the console.

`CanWrite` returns true if the stream can be written or false if the stream is closed or is read-only.

`Length` retrieves the length of the stream in bytes. This is the length of the data to be read or written not the buffer size.

`Position` is used to get or set the current position in the stream.

Public instance methods

```
public override void Close()
public override void Flush()
```

`Close()` is used to close the invoking `BufferedStream` and releases any resources associated with it. Any data written to the buffer is sent to the underlying repository or underlying data source before the stream is closed. This method calls the protected `Dispose()` method passing it a `true` value. This means that both managed and unmanaged resources associated with the `BufferedStream` are released. An `IOException` is thrown if an I/O error occurs while the stream is closing.

`Flush()` empties all buffers used by the `BufferedStream`. Any buffered data is written to the underlying device. An `IOException` is thrown if an I/O error occurs during the flush.

```
public override int Read(out byte[] array, int offset, int count)
public override int ReadByte()
```

`Read()` copies bytes from the current buffered stream into the specified byte array. The `offset` parameter is the point in the buffer at which to start copying. The `count` parameter is the number of bytes to be read. The return value is the total number of bytes that were actually read into the array. An exception is thrown if `array` is a null reference, if `offset` or `count` are out of range, if the stream does not support reading, if this method was called after the stream was closed, or if some other I/O error occurred.

`ReadByte()` reads a byte from the underlying stream and returns the byte cast into a 32-bit integer value. The method will return –1 if the end of the stream has been reached. An exception is thrown if the stream does not support reading or if the stream was closed before this method was called.

```
public override long Seek(int offset, SeekOrigin origin)
public override void SetLength(long value)
```

Seek() attempts to set the position of the current stream according to the specified byte offset relative to the specified origin. The return value is the new position of the stream. An exception is thrown if the stream does not support seeking or if the stream was closed before this method was called.

SetLength() sets the length of the buffered stream in bytes to the specified value. If the specified value is less than the current stream length, the stream is truncated. An exception is thrown if the stream does not support both writing and seeking or if this method was called after the stream was closed.

```
public override void Write(byte[] array, int offset, int count)
public override void WriteByte(byte value)
```

Write() writes the contents of the specified byte array to the output stream and advances the position of the stream by the number of bytes written. The offset parameter is the point in the buffer at which to begin copying to the buffered stream. The count parameter is the number of bytes to be written to the stream. An exception is thrown if array is a null reference, if the offset or count parameters are out of range, if this method was called after the stream was closed, or if the stream does not support writing.

WriteByte() writes the specified byte to the current position in the buffered stream and advances the position of the stream by one byte. An exception is thrown if value is a null reference or if the method was called after the stream was closed.

Protected instance methods

```
protected override void Dispose(bool disposing)
```

Dispose() immediately releases the resources allocated to the BufferedStream. If disposing is true, both the managed and the unmanaged resources are released. If it is false, only the unmanaged resources are released.

Example: BufferedStream class

This example demonstrates some basic functionality of a BufferedStream. A BufferedStream is wrapped around a FileStream that is connected to a text file. The contents of the file are read byte-by-byte until the end of the stream is reached. The bytes are converted to characters and appended to a StringBuilder.

This example is somewhat redundant since buffering is already provided when data is read from or written to a file. The concepts demonstrated here can be applied to data from other types of devices as well.

```
using System;
using System.IO;
using System.Text;

public class BufferedDemo
```

```
public static void Main()
{
  int c;
  StringBuilder sb = new StringBuilder();

  //============================================================
  //  A BufferedStream is wrapped around a FileStream that is
  //  connected to a file named "duck.txt".
  //============================================================

  BufferedStream b = new BufferedStream(
          new FileStream("duck.txt", FileMode.Open));

  //============================================================
  //  The bytes are read from the input file until the end of
  //  the stream. The ReadByte() method returns the byte cast
  //  to a 32-bit integer which is then cast to a char and
  //  appended to a StringBuilder. When the reading is done,
  //  the string is written out.
  //============================================================

  while ( (c = b.ReadByte()) != -1 )
  {
    sb.Append((char)c);
  }

  Console.WriteLine(sb.ToString());

  b.Close();
  }
}
```

Output:

```
Five little ducks went out to play
over the fields and far away
The mother duck said with a quack, quack, quack
four little ducks came waddling back
```

FileStream class

The FileStream class represents an I/O stream that has access to a file. It allows data to be written to or read from the file. The FileStream class supports both synchronous and asynchronous file access. A FileStream is often used as the underlying stream for a binary or character stream. For instance, if you want to write character data to a file you might wrap a StreamWriter around a FileStream. A FileStream by itself is still a byte stream and can only read and write byte data.

Syntax

```
public class FileStream : Stream
```

Hierarchy

```
Object  ---  MarshalByRefObject  ---  Stream  ---  FileStream
```

Constructors

```
public FileStream(IntPtr handle, FileAccess access)
public FileStream(IntPtr handle, FileAccess access, bool ownsHandle)
public FileStream(IntPtr handle, FileAccess access, bool ownsHandle, int
                  bufferSize)
public FileStream(IntPtr handle, FileAccess access, bool ownsHandle, int
                  bufferSize, bool isAsync)
public FileStream(string path, FileMode mode)
public FileStream(string path, FileMode mode, FileAccess access)
public FileStream(string path, FileMode mode, FileAccess access, FileShare share)
public FileStream(string path, FileMode mode, FileAccess access, FileShare share,
                  int bufferSize)
public FileStream(string path, FileMode mode, FileAccess access, FileShare share,
                  int bufferSize, bool isAsync)
```

FileStream() creates a FileStream object. The versions that take an IntPtr argument are used for interacting with Win32 API calls. The handle parameter is a file handle for the file associated with the FileStream. You can also specify whether the FileStream object will own the file handle. The file handle will be closed when the Close() method is called. The path parameter is the path to the file that will be opened. The file mode, access type, and sharing convention can be provided as input parameters. The defaults are for the file to be opened with read/write access and to have read sharing. The size of the buffer used by the FileStream can be specified. The default buffer size is 8192 bytes. The isAsync parameter determines whether the file handle will be opened asynchronously. The default is false.

Properties

```
public override bool CanRead {get;}
public override bool CanSeek {get;}
public override bool CanWrite {get;}
public virtual IntPtr Handle {get;}
public virtual bool IsAsync {get;}
public override long Length {get;}
public override string Name {get;}
public override long Position {get; set;}
```

CanRead returns true if the current stream supports reading or false if the stream is closed or only supports writing.

CanSeek returns true if the stream supports seeking. This will be false if the stream is closed or was created from an operating system handle such as a pipe or was output to the console.

CanWrite returns true if the stream can be written or false if the stream is closed or is read-only.

Handle gets the operating system file handle for the file associated with the FileStream. If the file has been closed, this property will return the value –1.

IsAsync returns true if the FileStream was opened asynchronously or false if it was opened synchronously.

Length retrieves the length of the stream in bytes. This will be equal to the current length of the associated file.

Name returns the name of the file associated with the FileStream.

Position is used to get or set the current position in the stream.

Public instance methods

```
public override IAsyncResult BeginRead(byte[] array, int offset, int numBytes,
        AsyncCallback userCallBack, object stateObject)
public override IAsyncResult BeginWrite(byte[] array, int offset, int numBytes,
        AsyncCallback userCallBack, object stateObject)
```

BeginRead() begins an asynchronous read operation. The method attempts to read the specified number of bytes into a byte array beginning at the designated offset. The userCallBack parameter refers to a method that is called when the asynchronous read operation is complete. The stateObject parameter is an object that is used to identify this read operation from other requests. The return value is a reference to the asynchronous read. An exception is thrown if array is a null reference, if either of the integer inputs is invalid, or if the read was attempted past the end of file.

BeginWrite() is similar to BeginRead() except it performs an asynchronous write operation.

```
public override void Close()
```

Close() is used to close the invoking FileStream and releases any resources associated with it. Any data written to the buffer is sent to the underlying repository or data source before the stream is closed. This method calls the protected Dispose() method passing it a true value. This means that both managed and unmanaged resources associated with the FileStream are released. An IOException is thrown if an I/O error occurs while the stream is being closed.

```
public override int EndRead(IAsyncResult result)
public override void EndWrite(IAsyncResult result)
```

EndRead() waits for a pending asynchronous read operation to complete. The return value is the number of bytes read from the stream. The result parameter is a reference to the asynchronous read. An exception is thrown if result is a null reference, if result did not originate from a BeginRead() method on the current stream, or if the method is called multiple times.

EndWrite() waits for an asynchronous write operation to complete and blocks until it does. The result parameter is a reference to the asynchronous write. An exception is thrown if result is a null reference, if result did not originate from a BeginWrite() method on the current stream, or if the method is called multiple times.

```
public override void Flush()
public virtual void Lock(long position, long length)
```

Flush() empties all buffers used by the FileStream. Any buffered data is written to the underlying device. An exception is thrown if an I/O error occurs during the flush or if the stream was closed when this method was invoked.

Lock() prevents access by other processes to the file associated with the FileStream. The position and length parameters are the beginning and extent of the range (in bytes) to be locked. To remove the lock, have the FileStream invoke the UnLock() method. An ArgumentOutOfRangeException is thrown if either of the input arguments is negative.

```
public override int Read(out byte[] array, int offset, int count)
public override int ReadByte()
```

Read() reads a sequence of bytes from the invoking stream and places the data into the specified byte array. The offset parameter is the point in the array at which to start copying. The count parameter is the number of bytes to be read. The return value is the total number of bytes that were actually read into the array. An exception is thrown if array is a null reference, if offset or count are out of range, if the stream does not support reading, if this method was called after the stream was closed, or if some other I/O error occurred

ReadByte() reads a byte from the underlying stream and returns the byte cast into a 32-bit integer value. The method will return −1 if the end of the stream has been reached. An exception is thrown if the stream does not support both writing and seeking or if this method was called after the stream was closed.

```
public override long Seek(int offset, SeekOrigin origin)
public override void SetLength(long value)
public virtual void Unlock(long position, long length)
```

Seek() sets the current position within the stream according to the specified byte offset relative to the specified origin. The return value is the new position of the stream. An exception is thrown if the stream does not support seeking, if the input arguments are out of bounds, or if this method was called after the stream was closed.

SetLength() sets the length of the stream in bytes to the specified value. If value is less than the current length of the stream, the stream will be truncated. An exception is thrown if the stream does not support both writing and seeking or if value is less than zero.

Unlock() restores access to other processes to a file that was previously locked. The position and length parameters are the beginning and extent of the range (in bytes) to be unlocked. An ArgumentOutOfRangeException is thrown if position or length is negative.

```
public override void Write(byte[] array, int offset, int count)
public override void WriteByte(byte value)
```

Write() writes data from the specified byte array to the FileStream. The offset parameter is the point in the buffer at which to begin extracting data. The count parameter is the number of bytes to be written to the current stream. If the write is successful, the position of the stream is advanced by the number of bytes written. An exception is thrown if array is a null reference, if the offset or count parameters are out of range, or if the stream does not support writing.

WriteByte() writes the specified byte to the current position in the stream. An exception is thrown if the stream does not support writing or if the method was called after the stream was closed.

Protected instance methods

```
protected override void Dispose(bool disposing)
```

Dispose() immediately releases the resources allocated to the FileStream. If disposing is true, both the managed and the unmanaged resources are released. If it is false, only the unmanaged resources are released.

FileStream objects are used in many of the examples in this chapter. See the examples in the *BinaryReader class, BinaryWriter class, BufferedStream class, FileMode enumeration,* and *StreamReader class* sections for demonstrations of how a FileStream can be used.

MemoryStream class

The MemoryStream class creates streams that use memory as their backing store rather than a disk or network connection. A MemoryStream encapsulates data that is stored as an unsigned byte array. This data is directly accessible in memory providing an alternative to having to write data to disk. The MemoryStream class provides a method that transfers the contents of a MemoryStream to another byte I/O stream.

Syntax

```
public class MemoryStream : Stream
```

Hierarchy

```
Object   ---   MarshalByRefObject   ---   Stream   ---   MemoryStream
```

Constructors

```
public MemoryStream()
public MemoryStream(int capacity)
public MemoryStream(byte[] buffer)
public MemoryStream(byte[] buffer, bool writable)
public MemoryStream(byte[] buffer, int index, int count)
public MemoryStream(byte[] buffer, int index, int count, bool writable)
public MemoryStream(byte[] buffer, int index, int count, bool writable,
                                                bool publiclyVisible)
```

MemoryStream() creates a MemoryStream object. The no-argument constructor initializes an empty memory stream with an expandable capacity that is initially zero. You can specify an initial capacity value if you like. The stream can be intialized with the contents of a byte array. In this case, the length of the MemoryStream cannot be set to a value greater than the initial length of the byte array taking into account the starting index. The writable parameter indicates whether the stream can be written to. The default is true. If publiclyVisible is true, the unsigned byte array that the stream is based on can be accessed using the GetBuffer() method.

Properties

```
public override bool CanRead {get;}
public override bool CanSeek {get;}
public override bool CanWrite {get;}
public virtual int Capacity {get; set;}
public override long Length {get;}
public override long Position {get; set;}
```

CanRead returns true if the current stream supports reading or false if the stream is closed or only supports writing.

CanSeek returns true if the stream supports seeking. If this property value is false, attempts to access or change the length or position of the stream will cause an exception to be thrown.

CanWrite returns true if the stream can be written or false if the stream is closed or is read-only.

Capacity gets or sets the number of bytes allocated to the stream.

Length retrieves the current length of the stream in bytes.

Position is used to get or set the current position in the stream.

Public instance methods

```
public override void Close()
public override void Flush()
public virtual byte[] GetBuffer()
```

Close() closes the invoking MemoryStream for reading and writing. This method calls the protected Dispose() method passing it a true value. This means that both managed and unmanaged resources associated with the MemoryStream are released. The buffer of a MemoryStream is still available after the stream has been closed.

Flush() overrides the version of this method defined in the Stream class so that no action is performed.

GetBuffer() returns the array of unsigned bytes that initialized the MemoryStream. If the MemoryStream was not initalized with a byte array, the current contents of the MemoryStream are returned. To use this method, the MemoryStream must have the publiclyVisible parameter set to true. An UnauthorizedAccessException is thrown if a MemoryStream with publiclyVisible set to false calls this method.

```
public override int Read(out byte[] buffer, int offset, int count)
public override int ReadByte()
```

Read() reads a block of bytes from the stream and places the data into the specified byte array. The offset parameter is the point in the buffer at which to start reading. The count parameter is the number of bytes to be read. The return value is the total number of bytes that were actually read into the array. An exception is thrown if buffer is a null reference, if offset or count are out of range, or if this method was called after the stream was closed.

ReadByte() reads a byte from the underlying stream and returns the byte cast into a 32-bit integer value. The method will return –1 if the end of the stream has been reached. An ObjectDisposeException is thrown if the stream that calls this method has been closed.

```
public override long Seek(int offset, SeekOrigin origin)
public override void SetLength(long value)
public virtual byte[] ToArray()
```

Seek() sets the current position within the stream according to the specified byte offset relative to the specified origin. The return value is the new position of the stream. An exception is thrown if origin is an invalid seek origin, if offset is out of bounds, or if the stream that calls this method has been closed

`SetLength()` sets the length of the stream in bytes to the specified value. If `value` is less than the current length of the stream, the stream will be truncated. An exception is thrown if the current stream does not support writing or if `value` is out of bounds.

`ToArray()` returns a byte array containing the entire contents of the stream.

```
public override void Write(byte[] buffer, int offset, int count)
public override void WriteByte(byte value)
public virtual void WriteTo(Stream stream)
```

`Write()` writes data from the specified byte array to the `MemoryStream`. The `offset` parameter is the point in the buffer at which to begin extracting data. The `count` parameter is the number of bytes to be written to the current stream. The return value is the number of bytes successfully written. An exception is thrown if `buffer` is a null reference, if the `offset` or `count` parameters are out of range, if the stream does not support writing, or if the stream that calls this method is closed.

`WriteByte()` writes the specified byte to the current position in the stream. An exception is thrown if the stream does not support writing, if the end of the stream has been reached and the stream capacity cannot be modified, or if the stream that calls this method is closed.

`WriteTo()` writes the contents of the invoking `MemoryStream` to the specified stream. An exception is thrown if `stream` is a null reference or if either the invoking stream or the target stream is closed.

Protected instance methods

```
protected override void Dispose(bool disposing)
```

`Dispose()` immediately releases the resources allocated to the `MemoryStream`. If `disposing` is true, both the managed and the unmanaged resources are released. If it is false, only the unmanaged resources are released.

Example: MemoryStream class

In this example, a `MemoryStream` is used to write and subsequently read some data to memory. The `Write()` method is used to write the contents of a byte buffer to memory. The byte buffer holds the characters that make up a `String`. Once the data is written, the position of the `MemoryStream` is reset to zero, and the contents of the stream are read back into the program using the `ReadByte()` method.

```
using System;
using System.IO;

public class MemoryDemo
{
  public static void Main()
  {
    int i;

    //=================================================
    // A data string is created and its characters are
```

```
    //   placed in a byte buffer.
    //====================================================

    String str = "This is some data";
    byte[] buf = new byte[str.Length];
    for(i=0; i<str.Length; ++i)
    {
      buf[i] = (byte)str[i];
    }


    //====================================================
    //   A MemoryStream is used to write the contents of
    //   the byte array to memory.
    //====================================================

    MemoryStream ms = new MemoryStream();
    ms.Write( buf, 0, buf.Length);


    //====================================================
    //   The MemoryStream reads the contents of the stream
    //   back into the program. First the position of
    //   the stream is reset to zero.
    //====================================================

    ms.Position = 0;

    while ( (i=ms.ReadByte()) != -1)
    {
      Console.Write((char)i);
    }
    Console.WriteLine();

    ms.Close();
  }
}
```

Output:

```
This is some data
```

Binary I/O streams

The System.IO namespace provides two classes for reading and writing binary representations of primitive data types and strings. One of the advantages to using binary I/O is that it is a more compact data format. You can store more data in less disk space. You can also read and write primitive data types directly. You don't have to convert them to and from characters or bytes. Some of the disadvantages of binary I/O is that binary can be system-dependent. A binary file created on one computer may not be readable on another. You also can't see what is in a binary file by pulling it into a text editor as you can with an ASCII data file.

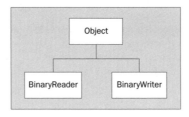

The class hierarchy for the BinaryReader and BinaryWriter classes is shown above. Both classes derive directly from the Object class. They don't derive from the MarshalByRefObject class so instances of them cannot be used as remote objects. They also do not derive from the Stream class so they don't inherit any methods for reading and writing data.

BinaryReader class

The BinaryReader class reads binary data from an input stream. While a BinaryReader can read Strings, it is primarily used for reading primitive data types as binary values according to a specific encoding scheme.

Syntax

```
public class BinaryReader : IDisposable
```

Hierarchy

```
Object  ---  BinaryReader
```

Constructors

```
public BinaryReader(Stream input)
public BinaryReader(Stream input, Encoding encoding)
```

BinaryReader() creates a BinaryReader object. You can specify an encoding scheme if you like. If you don't, UTF-8 Encoding is used. Encoding schemes are discussed in more detail in Chapter 26. A BinaryReader does not exist on its own. It is always associated with, or wrapped around, an underlying byte stream such as a FileStream.

Properties

```
public virtual Stream BaseStream {get;}
```

BaseStream provides access to the underlying stream associated with the BinaryReader. The underlying stream is the Stream instance that was provided to the BinaryReader constructor. This property should be used with caution as using the underlying stream can cause data loss and/or corruption.

Public instance methods

```
public virtual void Close()
public virtual int PeekChar()
```

`Close()` is used to close the invoking `BinaryReader` and its underlying stream. This method calls the protected `Dispose()` method passing it a `true` value. This means that both managed and unmanaged resources associated with the `BinaryReader` are released.

`PeekChar()` returns the next available character from the stream or –1 if the end of the stream has been reached. This method does not advance the byte or character position. An `IOException` is thrown if an I/O error occurs.

```
public virtual int Read()
public virtual int Read(byte[] buffer, int index, int count)
public virtual int Read(char[] buffer, int index, int count)
```

`Read()` is used to read character or byte data from an input stream. The first version reads the next character from the input stream and advances the current position of the stream. The method returns the character that was read or –1 if the end of the stream has been reached. The second and third versions attempt to read `count` elements of a byte or character array starting at position `index`. The return value is the number of bytes or characters actually read. An exception is thrown if `buffer` is a null reference or if the integer arguments are out of range.

```
public virtual bool ReadBoolean()
public virtual byte ReadByte()
public virtual byte[] ReadBytes(int count)
public virtual char ReadChar()
public virtual char[] ReadChars(int count)
public virtual decimal ReadDecimal()
public virtual double ReadDouble()
public virtual short ReadInt16()
public virtual int ReadInt32()
public virtual long ReadInt64()
public virtual sbyte ReadSByte()
public virtual float ReadSingle()
public virtual string ReadString()
public virtual ushort ReadUInt16()
public virtual uint ReadUInt32()
public virtual ulong ReadUInt64()
```

These methods read primitive data from the input stream. The names of the methods indicate the type of data read. Once the data is read, the position of the stream is advanced by the size of the data type that was read. For example, the `ReadDouble()` method will read a `double` from the stream and advance the position of the stream by eight bytes. The `ReadString()` method returns a `String` that is prefixed with its length, encoded as an integer, seven bits at a time. All of these methods will throw an exception if the end of the stream is reached during the read or if another type of I/O error occurs.

Protected instance methods

```
protected virtual void Dispose(bool disposing)
protected virtual void FillBuffer(int numBytes)
protected int Read7BitEncodedInt()
```

`Dispose()` immediately releases the resources allocated to the `BinaryReader`. If `disposing` is true, both the managed and the unmanaged resources are released. If it is false, only the unmanaged resources are released.

`FillBuffer()` fills the internal buffer with the specified number of bytes read from the input stream. An exception is thrown if the end of the stream is reached during the read or if another type of I/O error occurs.

`Read7BitEncodedInt()` reads a 32-bit, compressed format integer. This method is often used to read data that was written by the `BinaryWriter.Write7BitEncodedInt()` method. An exception is thrown if the end of the stream is reached during the read or if another type of I/O error occurs.

The `BinaryReader` class is demonstrated in the `BinaryWriter` class section.

BinaryWriter class

A `BinaryWriter` class writes primitive data types to an output stream in a binary format. The `BinaryWriter` class also supports the writing of `Strings` according to a specific encoding scheme. Binary tends to be more compact than ASCII or other formats and takes less disk space to store the same amount of data.

Syntax

```
public class BinaryWriter : IDisposable
```

Hierarchy

```
Object   ---   BinaryWriter
```

Constructors

```
protected BinaryWriter()
public BinaryWriter(Stream output)
public BinaryWriter(Stream output, Encoding encoding)
```

`BinaryWriter()` is the `BinaryWriter` class constructor. The protected constructor is used with derived classes of `BinaryWriter`. The public constructors create a `BinaryWriter` that is wrapped around the specified byte stream. You can specifiy an encoding scheme if you like. If an encoding scheme is not provided, `UTF8Encoding` will be used.

Fields

```
public static readonly BinaryWriter Null
protected Stream OutStream;
```

`Null` is a read-only, system-provided `BinaryWriter` with no backing store.

`OutStream` is a `Stream` object representing the underlying stream of the `BinaryWriter`. This is equivalent to the `BaseStream` property

Properties

```
public virtual Stream BaseStream {get;}
```

`BaseStream` provides access to the underlying output stream associated with the `BinaryWriter`.

Public instance methods

```
public virtual void Close()
public virtual void Flush()
public virtual long Seek(int offset, SeekOrigin origin)
```

Close() is used to close the invoking BinaryWriter and its underlying stream. This method calls the protected Dispose() method passing it a true value. This means that both managed and unmanaged resources associated with the BinaryWriter are released.

Flush() empties all buffers used by the BinaryWriter. Any buffered data is written to the underlying device. It is a good idea to call this method at the end of the output process to ensure that all buffered data has been written to the output stream.

Seek() is somewhat misnamed because it actually sets the position within the current output stream. It attempts to set the position according to the specified byte offset relative to the specified origin. The return value is a long and represents the new position of the stream.

```
public virtual void Write(bool value)
public virtual void Write(byte value)
public virtual void Write(byte[] buffer)
public virtual void Write(char c)
public virtual void Write(char[] buffer)
public virtual void Write(decimal value)
public virtual void Write(double value)
public virtual void Write(short value)
public virtual void Write(int value)
public virtual void Write(long value)
public virtual void Write(sbyte value)
public virtual void Write(float value)
public virtual void Write(string value)
public virtual void Write(ushort value)
public virtual void Write(uint value)
public virtual void Write(ulong value)
public virtual void Write(byte[] buffer, int index, int count)
public virtual void Write(char[] buffer, int index, int count)
```

Write() writes the specified value or values to the underlying output stream. The method is overloaded to accept all primitive variable types and Strings as input parameters. Once the value is written to the stream, the stream position is advanced by the appropriate amount. String and character data is written according to the encoding associated with the BinaryWriter. The default encoding is UTF8Encoding. Strings are prefixed with a single byte or word containing the length of the String. Byte or character arrays can be written out in their entirety or a subset defined by a starting index and a count can be written. All of these methods will throw an IOException if an I/O error occurs during the write.

Protected instance methods

```
protected virtual void Dispose(bool disposing)
protected void Write7BitEncodedInt(int value)
```

Dispose() immediately releases the resources allocated to the BinaryWriter. If disposing is true, both the managed and the unmanaged resources are released. If it is false, only the unmanaged resources are released.

`Write7BitEncodedInt()` writes the specified integer as a 32-bit, compressed format integer.

Example: BinaryWriter class

This example shows a `BinaryWriter` and `BinaryReader` in action as they are used to read and write a number of primitive data type values. An array of `double` values is created as well as a `BinaryWriter` that is wrapped around a `FileStream` associated with the file `data.out`. The `BinaryWriter` writes the number of elements and the array elements themselves to the file. The `BinaryWriter` is closed.

A `BinaryReader` is then created associated with the same file. The contents of the file are read back into the program, and just to make sure everything worked properly the values are displayed.

```
using System;
using System.IO;

public class BinaryWriterDemo
{
  public static void Main()
  {
    //===================================================
    //  An array containing double values is created.
    //===================================================

    double[] data = {1.23, 45.6, 19.87, 3.89, 34.5};

    //========================================================
    //  A BinaryWriter is wrapped around a FileStream that
    //  connects to a file named "data.out".
    //========================================================

    BinaryWriter writer = new BinaryWriter(
                      new FileStream("data.out", FileMode.Create));

    //========================================================
    //  The number of values and the values themselves are
    //  written to the output stream as binary data.
    //========================================================

    writer.Write(data.Length);

    foreach(Double d in data)
    {
      writer.Write( d);
    }

    writer.Close();

    //========================================================
    //  Now let's read the data file using a BinaryReader.
    //========================================================
```

```
BinaryReader reader = new BinaryReader(
                        new FileStream("data.out", FileMode.Open));

//=============================================================
//  Values are read from the binary data file. First, the
//  number of values contained in the file is read and then
//  the values themselves.
//=============================================================

int count = reader.ReadInt32();

double[] newData = new double[count];
for(int i=0; i<newData.Length; ++i)
{
  newData[i] = reader.ReadDouble();
}


//=============================================================
//  Just to show that everything worked properly, the values
//  are written to standard output.
//=============================================================

for(int i=0; i<newData.Length; ++i)
{
  Console.WriteLine("element {0} value is {1}",i,newData[i] );
}

reader.Close();
  }
}
```

Output:

```
element 0 value is 1.23
element 1 value is 45.6
element 2 value is 19.87
element 3 value is 3.89
element 4 value is 34.5
```

Just for fun, pull the data.out file into a text editor. One of the drawbacks of binary I/O is you can't look at your data as you could with an ASCII data file.

Character I/O streams

Character I/O streams, as their name would suggest, are used to read and write character data. Character streams don't exist on their own. They are always associated with an underlying byte stream, file, string, or StringBuilder. Once nice aspect of character I/O is that you can write out ASCII files that can be viewed in a text editor or on your console screen. There is also no need to convert strings or other character data to and from bytes.

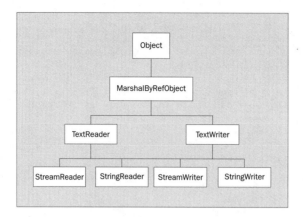

The character stream class hierarchy is shown above. All character stream classes inherit from the `Object` and `MarshalByRefObject`. The inheritance from `MarshalByRefObject` indicates that a character stream instance can be used as a remote object. `TextReader` and `TextWriter` are abstract classes that provide common character I/O functionality used by their derived classes. A `StreamReader` or `StreamWriter` is associated with an underlying byte stream or file. They define methods to read or write characters or strings. `StringReaders` and `StringWriters` are associated with an underlying string or `StringBuilder`.

TextReader class

The `TextReader` class is the base class for classes designed to read character data. The `StreamReader` and `StringReader` classes are derived from `TextReader`. By default, the `TextReader` class is not thread-safe, but the `Synchronized()` method can be used to place a thread-safe wrapper around a `TextReader`.

Syntax

```
public abstract class TextReader : MarshalByRefObject, IDisposable
```

Hierarchy

```
Object   ---   MarshalByRefObject   ---   TextReader
```

Constructors

protected TextReader()

`TextReader()` is a protected constructor used by derived classes of `TextReader`.

Fields

public static readonly TextReader Null

`Null` represents a `TextReader` with no data to read from. Reading from `TextReader.Null` is equivalent to reading from the end of the stream.

Public static methods

```
public static TextReader Synchronized(TextReader reader)
```

Synchronized() places a thread-safe wrapper around the specified TextReader and returns the wrapped version. An ArgumentNullException is thrown if reader is a null reference.

Public instance methods

```
public virtual void Close()
public virtual int Peek()
```

Close() closes the invoking TextReader and releases any resources associated with it. This method calls the protected Dispose() method passing it a true value. This means that both managed and unmanaged resources associated with the TextReader are released.

Peek() returns the next character in the stream but does not remove it from the stream. The method returns –1 if there are no more characters to be read or if the stream does not support seeking. An IOException is thrown if an I/O error occurs during the peek.

```
public virtual int Read()
public virtual int Read(out char[] buffer, int index, int count)
public virtual int ReadBlock(out char[] buffer, int index, int count)
public virtual string ReadLine()
public virtual string ReadToEnd()
```

Read() is used to read character data from the underlying stream. The no-argument version reads the next character from the stream and advances the character position by one character. The return type is an integer, and the return value will be –1 if no more characters are available. The second version attempts to read count characters from the input stream. The characters are placed into the specified buffer starting at the specified index. The return value is the number of characters actually read or zero if the end of the stream has been reached. An exception is thrown if buffer is a null reference, if index or count is out of bounds, or if some other I/O error occurs.

ReadBlock() is similar in function to the second version of Read() except it blocks until the read operation is finished.

ReadLine() reads a line of characters from the input stream and returns the data as a String or returns null if the end of the string has been reached. A line is defined as a sequence of characters followed either by a line feed or by a carriage return immediately followed by a line feed. An exception is thrown if an I/O error occurs during the read.

ReadToEnd() reads the remaining characters in the stream and returns them as a single String. An exception is thrown if an I/O error occurs during the read.

Protected instance methods

```
protected virtual void Dispose(bool disposing)
```

Dispose() immediately releases the resources allocated to the TextReader. If disposing is true, both the managed and the unmanaged resources are released. If it is false, only the unmanaged resources are released.

TextWriter class

The `TextWriter` class is the base class for classes designed to write character data to a stream. The `StreamWriter` and `StringWriter` are two of the classes that derive from `TextWriter`. The `TextWriter` class is by default not thread-safe. The `Synchronized()` method can be used to put a thread-safe wrapper around a `TextWriter`.

Syntax

```
public abstract class TextWriter : MarshalByRefObject, IDisposable
```

Hierarchy

```
Object  ---  MarshalByRefObject  ---  TextWriter
```

Constructors

```
protected TextWriter()
protected TextWriter(IFormatProvider provider)
```

`TextWriter()` creates a `TextWriter` object. These protected constructors are provided for use by derived classes of `TextWriter`.

Fields

```
protected char[] CoreNewLine
public static readonly TextWriter Null
```

`CoreNewLine` stores the newline characters that the `TextWriter` can use.

`Null` represents a `TextWriter` with no backing store. Any write methods called by this object will simply return without any data being written.

Properties

```
public abstract Encoding Encoding {get;}
public virtual IFormatProvider FormatProvider {get;}
public virtual string NewLine {get; set;}
```

`Encoding` retrieves the character encoding scheme used by the stream.

`FormatProvider` returns an `IFormatProvider` containing any culture-specific formatting information used by the `TextWriter`.

`NewLine` returns or sets the line terminator used by the `TextWriter`. The default line terminator is a carriage return followed by a line feed.

Public static methods

```
public static TextWriter Synchronized(TextWriter writer)
```

`Synchronized()` places a thread-safe wrapper around the specified `TextWriter` and returns the wrapped version. An `ArgumentNullException` is thrown if `writer` is a null reference.

Public instance methods

```
public virtual void Close()
public virtual void Flush()
```

Close() closes the invoking TextWriter and releases any resources allocated to it. This method is implemented such that it calls the Dispose() method passing it a true value.

Flush() empties all buffers used by the TextWriter. Any buffered data is written to the underlying device.

```
public virtual void Write(bool value)
public virtual void Write(char value)
public virtual void Write(char[] buffer)
public virtual void Write(char[] buffer, int index, int  count)
public virtual void Write(decimal value)
public virtual void Write(double value)
public virtual void Write(int value)
public virtual void Write(long value)
public virtual void Write(float value)
public virtual void Write(string value)
public virtual void Write(uint value)
public virtual void Write(ulong value)
public virtual void Write(object value)
public virtual void Write(string format, object obj)
public virtual void Write(string format, object objA, object objB)
public virtual void Write(string format, object objA, object objB,
                                                    object objC)
public virtual void Write(string format, params object[] objs)
```

Write() writes a text representation of the input argument to the text stream. In many cases, the text representation is acquired by calling the ToString() method. There are versions that allow you to specify a format string. An exception is thrown if the format string is invalid, if an object argument is a null reference, or if another I/O error occurs.

```
public virtual void WriteLine()
public virtual void WriteLine(bool value)
public virtual void WriteLine(char value)
public virtual void WriteLine(char[] buffer)
public virtual void WriteLine(char[] buffer, int index, int  count)
public virtual void WriteLine(decimal value)
public virtual void WriteLine(double value)
public virtual void WriteLine(int value)
public virtual void WriteLine(long value)
public virtual void WriteLine(float value)
public virtual void WriteLine(string value)
public virtual void WriteLine(uint value)
public virtual void WriteLine(ulong value)
public virtual void WriteLine(object value)
public virtual void WriteLine(string format, object obj)
public virtual void WriteLine(string format, object objA, object objB)
public virtual void WriteLine(string format, object objA, object objB,
                                                    object objC)
public virtual void WriteLine(string format, params object[] objs)
```

WriteLine() does the same thing as Write() except a line terminator is placed at the end of the line. The no-argument version simply writes a line terminator to the text stream.

Protected instance methods

```
protected virtual void Dispose(bool disposing)
```

Dispose() immediately releases the resources allocated to the TextWriter. If disposing is true, both the managed and the unmanaged resources are released. If it is false, only the unmanaged resources are released.

StreamReader class

The StreamReader class represents a TextReader that can read character data from a file or an underlying byte stream. The data is read according to an encoding scheme. The default encoding scheme is UTF-8. Typically, a StreamReader is used for reading lines of information from a standard text file. By default, this class is not thread-safe.

Syntax

```
public class StreamReader : TextReader
```

Hierarchy

```
Object  ---  MarshalByRefObject  ---  TextReader  ---  StreamReader
```

Constructors

```
public StreamReader(Stream stream)
public StreamReader(Stream stream, bool detectEncodingFromByteOrderMarks)
public StreamReader(Stream stream, Encoding encoding)
public StreamReader(Stream stream, Encoding encoding, bool detectEncodingFromData)
public StreamReader(Stream stream, Encoding encoding, bool detectEncodingFromData,
                    int bufferSize)
public StreamReader(string path)
public StreamReader(string path, bool detectEncodingFromData)
public StreamReader(string path, Encoding encoding)
public StreamReader(string path, Encoding encoding, bool detectEncodingFromData)
public StreamReader(string path, Encoding encoding, bool detectEncodingFromData,
                    int bufferSize)
```

StreamReader() creates a StreamReader object. The StreamReader can be associated with an underlying byte stream or with a file designated by path. If the detectEncodingFromData parameter is true, the system will attempt to discern the encoding scheme by looking at the first three bytes of the stream. You can explicitly specify an encoding scheme or use the default, which is UTF-8. If both an encoding scheme and the detectEncodingFromData parameter are provided the system will first try to detect the encoding scheme from the data and if unsuccessful will use the user-specified encoding scheme. A buffer size can also be specified. The default buffer size is 4096 bytes.

Fields

```
public static readonly StreamReader Null
```

Null represents a StreamReader that is wrapped around an empty stream.

Properties

```
public virtual Stream BaseStream {get;}
public virtual Encoding CurrentEncoding {get;}
```

BaseStream returns the underlying stream associated with the StreamReader.

CurrentEncoding retrieves the character encoding scheme used by the StreamReader.

Public instance methods

```
public override void Close()
public void DiscardBufferedData()
public override int Peek()
public override int Read()
public override int Read(out char[] buffer, int index, int count)
public override string ReadLine()
public override string ReadToEnd()
```

Close() closes the invoking StreamReader and releases any resources associated with it. This method calls the Dispose() method passing it a true value.

DiscardBufferedData() causes the invoking StreamReader to discard any data it is holding in its buffer.

Peek() returns the next character in the stream but does not remove it from the stream. The method returns –1 if there are no more characters to be read or if the stream does not support peeking. An IOException is thrown if an I/O error occurs during the peek.

Read() is used to read character data from an input stream. The no-argument version reads the next character from the strream, returns the character as an int, and advances the character position by one character. The return value will be –1 if the end of the stream is reached. The second version attempts to read count characters from the input stream and place the characters into the specified buffer starting at the specified index. The return value is the number of characters actually read. An exception is thrown if buffer is a null reference, if the index or count arguments are out of bounds, or if some other I/O error occurs during the read.

ReadLine() reads a line of characters from the current stream and returns the line as a String or returns null if the end of the stream has been reached. A line is defined as a sequence of characters followed either by a line feed or by a carriage return immediately followed by a line feed. An exception is thrown if an I/O error occurs during the read.

ReadToEnd() reads the remaining characters in the stream and returns them as a single String. An exception is thrown if an I/O error occurs during the read.

Protected instance methods

```
protected override void Dispose(bool disposing)
```

Dispose() immediately releases the resources allocated to the StreamReader. If disposing is true, both the managed and the unmanaged resources are released. If it is false, only the unmanaged resources are released.

Example: StreamReader class

This example shows how a `StreamReader` can be used to perform a very common operation, namely reading data from an input file. The `Area.txt` input file contains one line of data, "radius 2.0", consisting of a variable name and its value. A `StreamReader` uses the `ReadLine()` method to read this line of data into the program as a `String`. The `Split()` method from the `String` class then splits the input `String` into the substrings "radius" and "2.0". The "2.0" `String` is converted to a `double`.

A `StreamWriter` is then created and used to write the radius and area of the circle to an output file named `Area.out`.

```csharp
using System;
using System.IO;

public class StreamRW
{
  public static void Main()
  {
    double radius;

    //=========================================================
    //  A StreamReader is used to read a line of input from
    //  a file. The input line is split into substrings and
    //  the desired value is converted to a double.
    //=========================================================

    StreamReader sr = new StreamReader(
                        new FileStream("Area.txt", FileMode.Open));
    String[] strings = sr.ReadLine().Split(null);
    radius = Convert.ToDouble( strings[strings.GetUpperBound(0)] );

    //=========================================================
    //  A StreamWriter is used to write the output to a file.
    //=========================================================

    StreamWriter sw = new StreamWriter(
                        new FileStream("Area.out", FileMode.OpenOrCreate));

    sw.WriteLine("radius is {0}",radius);
    sw.WriteLine("area is {0}",radius*radius*Math.PI);

    sw.Flush();
    sw.Close();
    sr.Close();
  }
}
```

Output: contents of the `Area.out` file:

```
radius is 2
area is  12.566370614
```

StreamWriter class

A StreamWriter is a TextWriter that is used to write character data to either a file or an underlying byte stream. The data is written according to an encoding scheme associated with the StreamWriter. The default encoding scheme is UTF-8. Any text file created with a StreamWriter will have three byte order marks at the beginning of the file to identify the encoding scheme.

Syntax

```
public class StreamWriter : TextWriter
```

Hierarchy

```
Object  ---  MarshalByRefObject  ---  TextWriter  ---  StreamWriter
```

Constructors

```
public StreamWriter(Stream stream)
public StreamWriter(Stream stream, Encoding encoding)
public StreamWriter(Stream stream, Encoding encoding, int bufferSize)
public StreamWriter(string path)
public StreamWriter(string path, bool append)
public StreamWriter(string path, bool append, Encoding encoding)
public StreamWriter(string path, bool append, Encoding encoding,
                                                    int bufferSize)
```

StreamWriter() creates a StreamWriter object. The StreamWriter can be associated with an underlying byte stream or with a file designated by a path. A buffer size can be specified. The default buffer size is 4096 bytes. If the append parameter is true, data is appended to the file. If it is false, the file is overwritten.

Fields

```
public static readonly StreamWriter Null
```

Null represents a StreamWriter with no backing store. Any write methods called by this object will simply return without any data being written. You might use this during the development and testing of an application to simulate a write operation without actually writing anything to disk.

Properties

```
public virtual bool AutoFlush {get; set;}
public virtual Stream BaseStream {get;}
public override Encoding Encoding {get;}
```

AutoFlush indicates or specifies whether the StreamWriter will flush its buffer after every write operation. If the property value is true, it flushes. If it is false, it doesn't.

BaseStream returns the underlying stream associated with the StreamWriter.

Encoding retrieves the character encoding scheme used by the StreamWriter.

Public instance methods

```
public override void Close()
public override void Flush()
public override void Write(char value)
public override void Write(char[] buffer)
public override void Write(char[] buffer, int index, int count)
public override void Write(string value)
```

`Close()` closes the invoking `StreamWriter` and its underlying stream. This method calls the `Dispose()` method passing it a true value.

`Flush()` empties all buffers of the invoking `StreamWriter`. Any buffered data is written to the underlying stream. An exception is thrown if the `StreamWriter` has been closed or if an I/O error occurs during the flush.

`Write()` writes one or more characters or a string to the output stream. The `index` parameter is the starting position in the character buffer at which to start extracting data and `count` is the number of characters to write to the stream. An exception is thrown if `buffer` is a null reference, if the `index` or `count` arguments are out of bounds, or if another I/O error occurs during the write.

Protected instance methods

```
protected override void Dispose(bool disposing)
```

`Dispose()` immediately releases the resources allocated to the `StreamWriter`. If `disposing` is true, both the managed and the unmanaged resoureces are released. If it is false, only the unmanaged resources are released.

For an example of the `StreamWriter` class, see the `StreamReader` class section where a `StreamWriter` is used to write output to a file.

StringReader class

The `StringReader` class represents a `TextReader` that is associated with a `String` rather than with a file or underlying byte stream.

Syntax

```
public class StringReader : TextReader
```

Hierarchy

```
Object --- MarshalByRefObject --- TextReader --- StringReader
```

Constructors

```
public StringReader(string str)
```

`StringReader()` creates a `StringReader` object that reads from the specified `string`.

Public instance methods

```
public override void Close()
public override int Peek()
```

Close() closes the invoking StringReader and releases any resources associated with it. This method calls the Dispose() method passing it a true value.

Peek() returns the next character in the stream but does not remove it from the stream. The method returns –1 if there are no more characters to be read or if the stream does not support peeking. An ObjectDisposedException is thrown if the invoking StringReader has been closed.

```
public override int Read()
public override int Read(out char[] buffer, int index, int count)
public override string ReadLine()
public override string ReadToEnd()
```

Read() is used to read character data from the underlying string. The no-argument version reads the next character from the string, returns the character as an int, and advances the character position by one character. The return value will be –1 if no more characters are available. The second version attempts to read count characters from the input string. The characters are placed into the specified buffer starting at the specified index. The return value is the number of characters actually read or zero if the end of the string has been reached. An exception is thrown if buffer is a null reference, if the index or count arguments are out of bounds, or if the current StringReader is closed.

ReadLine() reads a line of characters from the underlying string and returns the line as a String or returns null if the end of the underlying string has been reached. A line is defined as a sequence of characters followed either by a line feed or by a carriage return immediately followed by a line feed. An exception is thrown if an I/O error occurs during the read

ReadToEnd() reads the remaining characters in the stream and returns them as a single String. An exception is thrown if an I/O error occurs during the read.

Protected instance methods

```
protected override void Dispose(bool disposing)
```

Dispose() immediately releases the resources allocated to the StringReader. If disposing is true, both the managed and the unmanaged resoureces are released. If it is false, only the unmanaged resources are released.

StringWriter class

A StringWriter is a TextWriter derived class that writes information to an underlying StringBuilder.

Syntax

```
public class StringWriter : TextWriter
```

Hierarchy

```
Object  ---  MarshalByRefObject  ---  TextWriter  ---  StringWriter
```

377

Constructors

```
public StringWriter()
public StringWriter(StringBuilder sb)
public StringWriter(IFormatProvider provider)
public StringWriter(StringBuilder sb, IFormatProvider provider)
```

StringWriter() creates a StringWriter object. The no-argument version creates a new StringBuilder object and associates it with the StringWriter. If a StringBuilder object is provided, any subsequent writing will be done to that object. An IFormatProvider can also be specified to provide some culture-specific formatting information for the string.

Properties

```
public override Encoding Encoding {get;}
```

Encoding retrieves the character encoding scheme used by the StringWriter.

Public instance methods

```
public override void Close()
public virtual StringBuilder GetStringBuilder()
public override string ToString()
public override void Write(char value)
public override void Write(string value)
public override void Write(char[] buffer, int index, int count)
```

Close() closes the invoking StringWriter. This method calls the Dispose() method passing it a true value.

GetStringBuilder() returns the underlying StringBuilder associated with the invoking StringWriter object.

ToString() returns the characters that have been written to the StringWriter as a String.

Write() writes one or more characters from a character buffer to the underlying StringBuilder. The index parameter is the starting position in the character buffer at which to start extracting data and count is the number of characters to write to the stream. If index and count are not provided, the character or string is appended onto the end of the StringBuilder. An exception is thrown if buffer is a null reference, if the index or count arguments are out of bounds, or if the StringWriter has been closed.

Protected instance methods

```
protected override void Dispose(bool disposing)
```

Dispose() immediately releases the resources allocated to the StringWriter. If disposing is true, both the managed and the unmanaged resources are released. If it is false, only the unmanaged resources are released.

Example: StringWriter class

In this example, a `StringWriter` is created with a default underlying `StringBuilder`. The `StringWriter` writes two strings to the `StringBuilder` and the contents of the `StringBuilder` are printed.

```
using System;
using System.IO;
using System.Text;

public class StringWriterDemo
{
  public static void Main()
  {
    StringWriter writer = new StringWriter();
    writer.Write("This is some data. ");
    writer.Write("I forgot to add this");

    Console.WriteLine(writer.GetStringBuilder());
    writer.Close();
  }
}
```

Output:

```
This is some data. I forgot to add this
```

I/O enumerations

The `System.IO` namespace defines a number of enumerations that are used to provide input parameters for many I/O function members. The enumeration values define access to a file, file attributes, how a file will be opened, and how a file can be shared between processes.

FileAccess enumeration

The `FileAccess` enumeration contains constants that define access to a file. Some of the places the `FileAccess` enumeration elements are used are in the `File`, `FileInfo`, and `FileStream` constructors.

Syntax

```
public enum FileAccess
```

Members

`Read` provides read access to a file.

`ReadWrite` indicates both read and write access to the file.

`Write` signifies that there is write access to the file.

For an example of the `FileAccess` enumeration, see the example in the *FileMode enumeration* section where a `FileAccess` constant is used to open a log file.

FileAttributes enumeration

The `FileAttributes` enumeration contains members that provide attributes for files and directories. The member values can be combined in a bitwise manner. For example, to indicate that a file is both read-only and a system file you would write:

```
FileAttributes.ReadOnly | FileAttributes.System
```

Syntax

```
public enum FileAttributes
```

Members

`Archive` marks the file for backup or removal.

`Compressed` indicates that the file is compressed.

`Device` is reserved for future use.

`Directory` signifies that the file is a directory.

`Encrypted` indicates that the file or directory is encrypted.

`Hidden` says that the file is hidden and will not show up in a normal directory listing.

`Normal` indicates that the file is normal and has no other attributes.

`NotContentIndexed` means that the file will not be indexed by the operating system's content indexing service.

`Offline` specifies that the file is offline and its data is not readily available.

`ReadOnly` means that the file is read-only.

`ReparsePoint` indicates that the file contains a block of user-defined data associated with a directory or file.

`SparseFile` marks the file as being a sparse file. Sparse files are typically large data files that contain mostly zeros.

`System` indicates that the file is a system file, one that is part of the operating system or used exclusively by the operating system.

`Temporary` specifies that the file is temporary and should be deleted by the application when it is no longer needed.

FileMode enumeration

The `FileMode` enumeration contains constants that define how the operating system should open a file. A `FileMode` parameter is used with many of the constructors and methods that return a `FileStream` object.

Syntax

```
public enum FileMode
```

Members

`Append` opens a file and seeks the end of the file. If the file does not exist, it is created. The file can only be written to when it is opened with this parameter.

`Create` creates a new file or overwrites a file if it already exists.

`CreateNew` creates a new file. If the file already exists, an exception is thrown.

`Open` tells the operating system to open an existing file.

`OpenOrCreate` will open a file if it exists or create it if it does not.

`Truncate` indicates that a file will be opened and then truncated so its size is zero bytes.

Example: FileMode enumeration

The `FileModeDemo` class updates an access log file whenever the program is run. The intent is for the log to be a continuing history. To ensure that the file is not overwritten, the file mode is set to "`Append`". The file access must also be set to "`Write`".

Run this program a few times and check the contents of the `access.log` file each time.

```
using System;
using System.IO;

public class FileModeDemo
{
  public static void Main()
  {

    //=========================================================
    //   A StreamWriter is connected to an access log file.
    //   The file mode is set to "Append" so the file won't
    //   be overwritten.
    //=========================================================

    StreamWriter sw = new StreamWriter(
        new FileStream("access.log", FileMode.Append, FileAccess.Write));
```

```
//=========================================================
//  The current time and date are written to the log file.
//=========================================================

sw.WriteLine("File accessed "+
        DateTime.Now.ToLongTimeString()+"   "+
        DateTime.Now.ToLongDateString());

sw.Flush();
sw.Close();
    }
}
```

Output: This is a sample of the contents of the access.log file (this will vary):

```
File accessed 9:00:20 AM Wednesday, November 21, 2001
File accessed 9:02:20 AM Wednesday, November 21, 2001
File accessed 9:03:47 AM Wednesday, November 21, 2001
```

FileShare enumeration

The FileShare enumeration contains constants that define whether two or more processes can simultaneously access, or share, the same file. It is possible to split the definition into different parts. For instance, a file can be designated so it allows multiple processes to read from it but not write to it.

Syntax

```
public enum FileShare
```

Members

None indicates that the file does not allow sharing of any kind.

Read allows multiple processes to simultaneously read from the file.

ReadWrite permits full sharing of the file. It can be both read from and written to simultaneously by two or more processes.

Write signifies that the file can be opened for writing by more than one process but can only be read by one process at a time.

File system manipulation classes

In addition to classes that encapsulate data streams and enumerations that define file attributes and other things, the System.IO namespace defines a number of classes that can access, investigate, and even modify the file system of a computer system. You should be somewhat careful when using these classes because they give you a lot of power to change (or even overwrite) your files and directories.

FileSystemInfo class

The FileSystemInfo class is the base class of the DirectoryInfo and FileInfo classes. FileSystemInfo provides fields, properties, and methods that are common to its derived classes.

Syntax

```
public abstract class FileSystemInfo : MarshalByRefObject
```

Hierarchy

```
Object  ---  MarshalByRefObject  ---  FileSystemInfo
```

Constructors

```
protected FileSystemInfo()
```

FileSystemInfo() is a protected constructor used by derived classes of FileSystemInfo.

Fields

```
protected string FullPath
protected string OriginalPath
```

FullPath is the fully qualified path of the directory or file.

OriginalPath is the relative or absolute path originally specified by the user when defining the object.

Properties

```
public FileAttributes Attributes {get; set;}
public DateTime CreationTime {get; set;}
public abstract bool Exists {get;}
public string Extension {get;}
public virtual string FullName {get;}
public DateTime LastAccessTime {get; set;}
public DateTime LastWriteTime {get; set;}
public string Name {get;}
```

Attributes returns or changes the attributes associated with the file or directory.

CreationTime gets or sets a DateTime object containing the creation time of the file or directory.

Exists returns true if the file or directory exists.

Extension retrieves the file name extension.

FullName returns the full path of the directory or file.

LastAccessTime returns or sets a DateTime object containing the time at which the file or directory was last accessed. This property will return null if the file system does not support this information.

LastWriteTime returns or sets a DateTime object containing the time at which the file or directory was last written to. This property will return null if the file system does not support this information.

Name retrieves the name of the file or directory. For directories, the return value will be only the last directory in the hierarchy, Blah rather than C:\Program Files\Blah

Public instance methods

```
public abstract void Delete()
public void Refresh()
```

Delete() deletes a file or directory.

Refresh() refreshes the state of the FileSystemInfo object. This method can be called before attempting to access attribute information to ensure that the attributes are up to date.

Directory class

The Directory class defines a number of static methods for creating, moving, and iterating through directories and subdirectories. For the methods that take a path argument, this can be either a relative or an absolute path and may point to a file or directory. Because the Directory class methods are static and can be called from anywhere, they perform a security check before proceeding.

Syntax

```
public sealed class Directory
```

Hierarchy

```
Object   ---   Directory
```

Public static methods

```
public static DirectoryInfo CreateDirectory(string path)
public static void Delete(string path)
public static void Delete(string path, bool recursive)
public static bool Exists(string path)
```

CreateDirectory() creates all directories and subdirectories according to the specified path. By default the new directories will allow full read/write access to all users. An exception is thrown if the path argument is invalid.

Delete() attempts to delete the directory indicated by the specified path. The first version will only delete the directory if it is empty. If the directory is not empty, it will not be deleted and an IOException will be thrown. If the recursive parameter is set to be true, subdirectories and files within a specified directory will also be deleted. An exception is thrown if the path argument is invalid.

Exists() returns true if the specified path points to an existing directory or false if it does not.

```
public static DateTime GetCreationTime(string path)
public static string GetCurrentDirectory()
public static string[] GetDirectories(string path)
```

```
public static string[] GetDirectories(string path, string searchPattern)
public static string GetDirectoryRoot(string path)
public static string[] GetFiles(string path)
public static string[] GetFiles(string path, string searchPattern)
public static string[] GetFileSystemEntries(string path)
public static string[] GetFileSystemEntries(string path, string
                                                        searchPattern)
public static DateTime GetLastAccessTime(string path)
public static DateTime GetLastWriteTime(string path)
public static string[] GetLogicalDrives()
public static DirectoryInfo GetParent(string path)
```

GetCreationTime() returns a DateTime object containing the date and time at which a directory at the specified path was created. An exception is thrown if the path argument is invalid.

GetCurrentDirectory() retrieves a String representation of the current directory location. A SecurityException is thrown if the caller doesn't have the proper permission.

GetDirectories() returns the subdirectories of the directory at the specified path. The searchPattern might be part of a directory name such as "CSHARP*". An exception is thrown if the path argument is invalid.

GetDirectoryRoot() returns a String containing the fully qualified name of path. An exception is thrown if the path argument is invalid or if the caller doesn't have the proper permission.

GetFiles() returns a String array containing the names of the files in the directory at the specified path. A searchPattern can be specified to limit the search. An example of a search pattern string might be "*.txt". An exception is thrown if the path argument is invalid.

GetFilesSystemEntries() returns a String array containing the files and directories in the specified path. A searchPattern can be specified to limit the search. An example of a search pattern string might be "C*", which would search for directories whose names begin with "C". An exception is thrown if the path argument is invalid or if the caller doesn't have the proper permission.

GetLastAccessTime() retrieves a DateTime object containing the date and time at which the directory at the specified path was last accessed. An exception is thrown if the path argument is invalid or if the caller doesn't have the proper permission.

GetLastWriteTime() retrieves a DateTime object containing the date and time that the directory at the specified path was last written to. An exception is thrown if the path argument is invalid or if the caller doesn't have the proper permission.

GetLogicalDrives() returns a String array containing the names of the logical drives on your computer. The Strings will take the form "<drive letter>:\". An exception is thrown if the caller does not have the proper permission or if an I/O error occurs.

GetParent() returns a DirectoryInfo object containing information about the parent directory of the directory at the specified path. An exception is thrown if the path argument is invalid or if the caller doesn't have the proper permission.

```
public static void Move(string sourceDirectoryPath, string destDirectoryPath)
```

`Move()` moves a directory and all of its contents from a source directory path to a destination directory path. This method will throw an exception if an illegal move is attempted, for instance, if you try to move a directory to a name and location that already exists, if the paths are invalid, or if the caller does not have the proper permission.

```
public static void SetCreationTime(string path, DateTime creationTime)
public static void SetCurrentDirectory(string path)
public static void SetLastAccessTime(string path, DateTime creationTime)
public static void SetLastWriteTime(string path, DateTime creationTime)
```

`SetCreationTime()` changes the creation time of the directory at the specified path to the date and time contained by the specified `DateTime` object. An exception is thrown if the `path` or `creationTime` argument is invalid.

`SetCurrentDirectory()` sets the current directory to the one at the specified path. An exception is thrown if the `path` argument is invalid.

`SetLastAccessTime()` changes the date and time that a directory was last accessed to the date and time contained by the specified `DateTime` object. An exception is thrown if the `path` argument is invalid or if the caller doesn't have the proper permission.

`SetLastWriteTime()` changes the date and time that a directory was last written to to the date and time contained by the specified `DateTime` object. An exception is thrown if the `path` argument is invalid or if the caller doesn't have the proper permission.

Example: Directory class

This example uses the methods defined in the `Directory` class to determine if a file exists in a directory. The `GetFiles()` and `GetCurrentDirectory()` methods are used to fill a `String` array with the names of the files in the current directory. The `Directory` class methods used in this example can throw various exceptions so they are placed in a `try-catch` block. To simplify the code listing only one `catch` block corresponding to a generic `Exception` is included. The file names are then compared against a user-specified file name.

```
using System;
using System.IO;

public class DirectoryDemo
{
  public static void Main()
  {
    bool exists = false;

    //==========================================================
    //  The user is queried for the name of an input file.
    //==========================================================

    Console.Write("enter input file name: ");
    String input = Console.ReadLine();
```

```
//=========================================================
//   The GetCurrentDirectory() and GetFiles() methods are
//   used to get a listing of the files in the current
//   directory.
//=========================================================

try
{
 String[] files = Directory.GetFiles(Directory.GetCurrentDirectory());

   //=============================================================
   //   The return value from the GetFiles() method includes the
   //   full file path. This path is removed from the file
   //   names and the input file name is compared against the files
   //   that exist in the current directory.
   //=============================================================

   int length = Directory.GetCurrentDirectory().Length;

   for(int i=0; i<files.GetLength(0); ++i)
   {
     if ( input == files[i].Substring(length+1))
     {
       exists = true;
       break;
     }
   }
 }
 catch (Exception e)
 {
   Console.WriteLine("exception occurred: "+e);
 }

   //=============================================================
   //   This reports whether the user-specified file exists in the
   //   current directory.
   //=============================================================

   if (exists)
   {
     Console.WriteLine("file exists");
   }
   else
   {
     Console.WriteLine("file does not exist");
   }
 }
}
```

When you run this program, try it with a file that exists in the current directory, making sure you use the correct capitalization (this program is case-sensitive). Then try it with a filename that doesn't exist.

DirectoryInfo class

The `DirectoryInfo` class is similar to the `Directory` class in that it defines methods for creating, moving, and obtaining information about directories and files. The `DirectoryInfo` class methods are different in that they are instance methods and are called using a `DirectoryInfo` object without the security check that is done with the `Directory` class methods.

Syntax

```
public sealed class DirectoryInfo : FileSystemInfo
```

Hierarchy

```
Object  ---  MarshalByRefObject  ---  FileSystemInfo  ---  DirectoryInfo
```

Constructors

```
public DirectoryInfo(string path)
```

`DirectoryInfo()` creates a `DirectoryInfo` object that is associated with the specified path. The path can point to a directory or a file.

Properties

```
public override bool Exists {get;}
public override string Name {get;}
public DirectoryInfo Parent {get;}
public DirectoryInfo Root {get;}
```

`Exists` returns true if the directory associated with the `DirectoryInfo` object exists and false if it does not.

`Name` retrieves the name of the directory associated with the `DirectoryInfo` object.

`Parent` returns a `DirectoryInfo` object corresponding to the parent directory of the current `DirectoryInfo` object. This property will return null if there is no parent.

`Root` returns a `DirectoryInfo` object that represents the root of the path associated with the current `DirectoryInfo` object.

Public instance methods

```
public void Create()
public DirectoryInfo CreateSubdirectory(string path)
public override void Delete()
public void Delete(bool recursive)
```

`Create()` creates a new directory based on the path associated with the invoking `DirectoryInfo` object.

`CreateSubdirectory()` creates a directory or subdirectories according to the specified path. The path can be relative to the invoking `DirectoryInfo` object. The new directories will allow full read/write access to all users. An exception is thrown if the `path` argument is invalid or if the caller doesn't have the proper permission.

`Delete()` attempts to delete the directory represented by the invoking `DirectoryInfo` object. The first version will only delete the directory if it is empty. If the directory is not empty, it will not be deleted and an `IOException` will be thrown. If the recursive parameter is set to be true, subdirectories and files within a specified directory will also be deleted. An exception will also be thrown if the caller doesn't have the proper permission.

```
public DirectoryInfo[] GetDirectories()
public DirectoryInfo [] GetDirectories(string searchPattern)
public FileInfo[] GetFiles()
public FileInfo[] GetFiles(string searchPattern)
public FileSystemInfo[] GetFileSystemInfos()
public FileSystemInfo[] GetFileSystemInfos(string searchPattern)
```

`GetDirectories()` returns an array of `DirectoryInfo` objects representing the subdirectories of the directory associated with the invoking `DirectoryInfo`. A `searchPattern` parameter can be specified to limit the extent of the search. For instance if "S*" was the search pattern, only directories that began with the letter "S" would be sought. An exception is thrown if `searchPattern` is a null reference or if the caller doesn't have the proper permission.

`GetFiles()` returns a `FileInfo` array containing information about the files in the current directory. A `searchPattern` can be specified to limit the search. An example of a search pattern string might be "*.txt". An exception is thrown if `searchPattern` is a null reference or if the caller doesn't have the proper permission

`GetFileSystemInfos()` returns a strongly-typed `FileSystemInfo` array containing information about all of the files and directories in the current directory. A `searchPattern` can be specified to limit the search. An example of a search pattern string might be "C*", which would search for fields and directories whose names begin with "C". An exception is thrown if `searchPattern` is a null reference or if the caller doesn't have the proper permission

```
public void MoveTo(string destDirectoryPath)
```

`MoveTo()` moves a `DirectoryInfo` object and its contents to a new path. This method will throw an exception if an illegal move is attempted, for instance, if you try to move a directory to a location that already exists. An exception is thrown if the destination path is invalid or if the caller doesn't have the proper permission.

```
public override string ToString()
```

`ToString()` returns a `String` representing the full path associated with the invoking `DirectoryInfo` object.

Example: DirectoryInfo class

In this example, a `DirectoryInfo` object is used to create and manipulate subdirectories of the current directory. The `CreateSubdirectory()` and `MoveTo()` methods are demonstrated.

```
using System;
using System.IO;
```

```
public class DirectoryDemo
{
  public static void Main()
  {

    //========================================================
    //  A DirectoryInfo object is obtained for the current
    //  working directory.
    //========================================================

    try
    {
      DirectoryInfo di = new DirectoryInfo(Directory.GetCurrentDirectory());

      //========================================================
      //  The CreateSubdirectory() method is used to create
      //  two subdirectories.
      //========================================================

      di.CreateSubdirectory("blah");
      DirectoryInfo chowDI = di.CreateSubdirectory("chow");

      //========================================================
      //  The MoveTo() method is used to change the name of
      //  the "chow" directory to "dinner". The rest of the
      //  path stays the same.
      //========================================================

      chowDI.MoveTo("dinner");
    }
    catch (Exception e )
    {
      Console.WriteLine("exception occurred: "+e);
    }
  }
}
```

When you run this example you will notice two new directories, "blah" and "dinner", have been created.

File class

The File class provides a series of static methods for creating, deleting, moving, and opening files. There are also methods that create various types of FileStream and StreamReader objects. Because the File class methods are static and can be called at any time, the methods perform a security check before proceeding.

Syntax

```
public sealed class File
```

Hierarchy

```
Object  ---  File
```

Public static methods

```
public static StreamWriter AppendText(string path)
public static void Copy(string sourceFileName, string destFileName)
public static void Copy(string sourceFileName, string destFileName,
                                                    bool overwrite)
public static FileStream Create(string path)
public static FileStream Create(string path, int bufferSize)
public static StreamWriter CreateText(string path)
public static void Delete(string path)
public static bool Exists(string path)
```

AppendText() returns a StreamWriter that can be used to append text to the file at the specified path. If the file does not exist, it will be created. An exception is thrown if the path is invalid or if the caller doesn't have the proper permission.

Copy() copies an existing file to a new file. The two file names cannot be the same unless overwrite is set to be true. An exception is thrown if either path is invalid or if the caller doesn't have the proper permission.

Create() creates a file according to the specified fully qualified path and returns a FileStream object that can access the newly created file. If the file already exists, it is replaced. You can specify the size of the FileStream buffer if you like. An exception is thrown if the path is invalid or if the caller doesn't have the proper permission.

CreateText() returns a StreamWriter than can be used to write text to a newly created file at the specified path. An exception is thrown if the path is invalid or if the caller doesn't have the proper permission.

Delete() deletes the file located at the specified path. An exception is thrown if the path is invalid or if the caller doesn't have the proper permission.

Exists() returns true if a file exists at the specified path. If the path is the location of a directory, the method returns false. An exception is thrown if the path is invalid.

```
public static FileAttributes GetAttributes(string path)
public static DateTime GetCreationTime(string path)
public static DateTime GetLastAccessTime(string path)
public static DateTime GetLastWriteTime(string path)
```

GetAttributes() returns a FileAttributes object containing attribute information for the file located at the specified path. An exception is thrown if the path is invalid.

GetCreationTime() returns a DateTime object containing the date and time at which the file was created. An exception is thrown if the path is invalid or if the caller doesn't have the proper permission.

GetLastAccessTime() returns a DateTime object containing the date and time that the specified file was last accessed. An exception is thrown if the path is invalid or if the caller doesn't have the proper permission.

`GetLastWriteTime()` returns a `DateTime` object containing the date and time that the specified file was last written to. An exception is thrown if the path is invalid or if the caller doesn't have the proper permission.

```
public static void Move(string sourceFileName, string destFileName)
```

`Move()` moves a file to a new location and allows for the file name to be changed. An exception is thrown if either path is invalid or if the caller doesn't have the proper permission.

```
public static FileStream Open(string path, FileMode mode)
public static FileStream Open(string path, FileMode mode, FileAccess access)
public static FileStream Open(string path, FileMode mode, FileAccess access,
                             FileShare share)
public static FileStream OpenRead(string path)
public static StreamReader OpenText(string path)
public static FileStream OpenWrite(string path)
```

`Open()` returns a `FileStream` object that can be used to access the specified file according to the specified mode. File access and file sharing conventions can also be provided. The defaults are for read/write access and for the file to be unshared. The file at the specified path must already exist. An exception is thrown if the path is invalid or if the caller doesn't have the proper permission.

`OpenRead()` returns a `FileStream` object that can access the specified file in a read-only manner. An exception is thrown if the path is invalid or if the caller doesn't have the proper permission.

`OpenText()` returns a `StreamReader` object that can be used to read text from an existing file at the specified path. An exception is thrown if the path is invalid or if the caller doesn't have the proper permission.

`OpenWrite()` returns a `FileStream` object that can be used to read or write to the file at the specified path. An exception is thrown if the path is invalid or if the caller doesn't have the proper permission.

```
public static void SetAttributes(string path, FileAttributes attributes)
public static void SetCreationTime(string path, DateTime time)
public static void SetLastAccessTime(string path, DateTime time)
public static void SetLastWriteTime(string path, DateTime time)
```

`SetAttributes()` assigns the specified `FileAttributes` object to the file located at the specified path. An exception is thrown if the path is invalid.

`SetCreationTime()` sets a new creation date for the file at the specified path. The new creation time is contained in a `DateTime` object. An exception is thrown if the path is invalid or if the caller doesn't have the proper permission.

`SetLastAccessTime()` specifies the last time the file at the specified path was accessed. The access time is contained in the specified `DateTime` object. An exception is thrown if the path is invalid or if the caller doesn't have the proper permission.

`SetLastWriteTime()` sets the last time the specified file was written to. This time is contained in the specified `DateTime` object. An exception is thrown if the path is invalid or if the caller doesn't have the proper permission.

Example: File class

In this example, a File object is used to ensure that a copy of an output file is made before it is overwritten. The Exists() method is used to determine if the file "FileDemo.out" exists. If it does, the Copy() method is invoked to make a copy of the file. The file is then created or overwritten with an output string.

Run this example twice. The first time you run it, the file "FileDemo.out" will be created. Now run it again. You will see that a file "FileDemo.out.save" has been created with the contents of the previous output file.

```
using System;
using System.IO;

public class FileDemo
{
  public static void Main()
  {

    //================================================
    //  A file name and output string are defined.
    //================================================

    String str = "This is the output from FileDemo";
    String fileName = "FileDemo.out";

    //=======================================================
    //  The Exists() method is used to determine if the
    //  file already exists. If it does, the Copy() method
    //  is used to make a copy of the file.
    //=======================================================

    if ( File.Exists(fileName) )
    {
      File.Copy(fileName, fileName+".save", true);
    }

    //==========================================================
    //  The Create() method returns a FileStream that is connected
    //  with the file. A StreamWriter is wrapped around the
    //  FileStream and writes the output string to the file.
    //==========================================================

    StreamWriter sw = new StreamWriter(File.Create(fileName));

    sw.WriteLine(str);

    sw.Flush();
    sw.Close();
  }
}
```

FileInfo class

The `FileInfo` class defines methods to create, copy, delete, move, and open files. There are also methods that return `FileStream` objects. The `FileInfo` class is similar in function to the `File` class except the `FileInfo` class methods are instance rather than static methods. The `FileInfo` methods offer slightly better performance because they do not perform a security check before proceeding.

Syntax

```
public sealed class FileInfo : FileSystemInfo
```

Hierarchy

```
Object  ---  MarshalByRefObject  ---  FileSystemInfo  ---  FileInfo
```

Constructors

```
public FileInfo(string filePath)
```

`FileInfo()` creates a `FileInfo` object that is associated with the file at the specified file path.

Properties

```
public DirectoryInfo Directory {get;}
public string DirectoryName {get;}
public override bool Exists {get;}
public long Length {get;}
public override string Name {get;}
```

`Directory` returns a `DirectoryInfo` object containing information about the parent directory of the file associated with the `FileInfo` object.

`DirectoryName` returns a `String` object containing the name of the parent directory of the file associated with the `FileInfo` object.

`Exists` returns true if the file represented by the `FileInfo` object exists.

`Length` returns the size of the current file in bytes.

`Name` returns a `String` containing the name of the file.

Public instance methods

```
public StreamWriter AppendText()
public void CopyTo(string destFileName)
public void CopyTo(string destFileName, bool overwrite)
public FileStream Create()
public StreamWriter CreateText()
public override void Delete()
public void MoveTo(string destFileName)
```

`AppendText()` returns a `StreamWriter` that can be used to append text to the file associated with the invoking `FileInfo` object.

CopyTo() copies the file represented by the FileInfo object to a new file. A file cannot be overwritten unless overwrite is set to be true. An exception is thrown if the destination path is invalid or if the caller doesn't have the proper permission.

Create() returns a FileStream object that can access a newly created file. The new file will have read/write access to all users.

CreateText() returns a StreamWriter than can be used to write text to a newly created file. The new file will have read/write access to all users. An exception is thrown if the destination file is a directory, if the disk is read-only, or if the caller doesn't have the proper permission.

Delete() deletes the file associated with the invoking FileInfo object. An exception is thrown if the file is a directory or if the caller doesn't have the proper permission.

MoveTo() moves the file associated with the FileInfo object to a new location and allows for the file name to be changed. An exception is thrown if the destination path is invalid or if the caller doesn't have the proper permission.

```
public FileStream Open(FileMode mode)
public FileStream Open(FileMode mode, FileAccess access)
public FileStream Open(FileMode mode, FileAccess access, FileShare share)
public FileStream OpenRead()
public StreamReader OpenText()
public FileStream OpenWrite()
```

Open() returns a FileStream object that can be used to access the file represented by the FileInfo object according to the specified mode. File access and file sharing conventions can also be provided. The defaults are for read/write access and for the file to be unshared. An exception is thrown if the file is not found, if the file is already open, or if the caller doesn't have the proper permission.

OpenRead() returns a FileStream object that provides read-only access to the file associated with the invoking FileInfo object. An exception is thrown if the file is a directory or already opened.

OpenText() returns a StreamReader object with UTF-8 encoding that be used to read text from an existing file. An exception is thrown if the file is a directory, is already opened, of if the caller doesn't have the proper permission.

OpenWrite() returns a FileStream object that can be used to read or write to the file represented by the invoking FileInfo object. An exception is thrown if the file is read-only or a directory.

```
public override string ToString()
```

ToString() returns the fully qualified path of the file associated with the invoking FileInfo object.

Example: FileInfo class

In this short example, a FileInfo object is associated with a file that doesn't exist. The Create() method is used to create the file and connect it to a StreamWriter. The StreamWriter writes a line of text to the file.

```
using System;
using System.IO;

public class FileInfoDemo
{
  public static void Main()
  {

    //========================================================
    //  A FileInfo object is used to create a text file
    //  and connect a StreamWriter to it.
    //========================================================

    FileInfo fi = new FileInfo("blah.txt");
    StreamWriter sw = fi.CreateText();

    sw.WriteLine("Hello there");

    sw.Flush();
    sw.Close();
  }
}
```

Output (contents of blah.txt):

```
Hello there
```

Summary

In this chapter we've looked at the I/O facilities available in the .NET Framework, predominantly from the System.IO namespace. We've looked at byte streams, binary I/O streams, character I/O streams, I/O enumerations, and file system manipulation classes.

C# Programmers reference C# Programmers reference C# Programmers refere
Programmers reference C# Programmers reference C# Programmers refere
Programmers reference C# Programmers reference C# Programmers refere
Programmers reference C# Programmers reference C# Programmers refere
Programmers reference C# Programmers reference C# Programmers refere
Programmers reference C# Programmers reference C# Programmers refere
Programmers reference C# Programmers reference C# Programmers refere
Programmers reference C# Programmers reference C# Programmers refen
mmers reference C# Programmers reference C# Programmers refere
rs reference C# Programmers reference C# Programmers refere
ference C# Programmers reference C# Programmers refere
nce C# Programmers reference C# Programmers refere
C# Programmers reference C# Programmers refere
Programmers reference C# Programmers refere
ogram reference C# Programmers refere
reference Programmers refere
ce Programmers refere
Programmers refere
mers refere
rs refere
Programmers refere
Programmers refere
Programmers refere
Programmers refere
Programmers refere
Programmers refere
Programmers refere
Programmers refere
Programmers refere
C# Programmers refere
ce C# Programmers refere
ence C# Programmers refere
erence C# Programmers refere
eference C# Programmers refere
reference C# Programmers refere
Programmers reference C# Programmers reference C# Programmers refere
Programmers reference C# Programmers reference C# Programmers refere
Programmers reference C# Programmers reference C# Programmers refere
Programmers reference C# Programmers reference C# Programmers refere
Programmers reference C# Programmers reference C# Programmers refen

C#

25

Reflection

Reflection is a generic term for the ability the .NET Framework provides to peer inside an application and see what makes it tick. Reflection allows you to access information about and manipulate the metadata, assemblies, modules, types, and members that make up an application without looking at the actual code listings. The access is performed via library or executable files.

The classes, enumerations, and structures that facilitate reflection are contained in the System.Reflection namespace. In this chapter we will explore the key elements of the namespace. We will cover the application hierarchy classes, member information classes, and other important members of the namespace. We will learn how to dynamically create objects at runtime in a process called late binding. We will also explore how reflection, under the right circumstances, allows you to access and modify otherwise inaccessible property and field data.

Application hierarchy classes

A .NET Framework application can be characterized as a hierarchy of code elements. At the top of the hierarchy is the application domain. An application domain is an isolated environment in which applications execute. An application domain can be thought of as a container for assemblies and types when they are loaded by the runtime.

The next level down in the type hierarchy is the assembly. An assembly is a collection of one or more modules or other resources and a manifest containing metadata about the assembly and its contents. A module is a library file, an executable file, or another type of resource such as an image. Assemblies can consist of one or more physical files. Below the module level in the hierarchy are types and type members. In this section we will discuss the Assembly and Module classes that encapsulate an assembly and a module.

CLR — Common Language Runtime

Assembly class

The Assembly class encapsulates a reusable, self-describing entity known as an assembly. Assemblies are the building blocks of Common Language Runtime applications and are similar to the DLLs and EXEs of a Win32 application. Assemblies assist in the deployment of run-time applications by providing the framework for the runtime to understand the contents of an application and to resolve issues such as versioning, security, and scope resolution.

Versioning
Security
scope resolution

An assembly will contain a manifest, one or more modules, and an optional set of resources. The manifest contains metadata that describes the assembly including the assembly name, version number, security permissions, and contents of the assembly. A module can be an executable file, as library, or another resource such as an image file.

The `Assembly` class does not define any constructors but does define a number of static methods that return an `Assembly` object.

Syntax

```
public class Assembly : IEvidenceFactory, ICustomAttributeProvider, ISerializable
```

Hierarchy

```
Object   ---   Assembly
```

Properties

```
public virtual string CodeBase {get;}
public virtual MethodInfo EntryPoint {get;}
public virtual Evidence Evidence {get;}
public virtual string FullName {get;}
public bool GlobalAssemblyCache {get;}
public virtual string Location {get;}
```

`CodeBase` returns the physical location of the `Assembly` as it was originally specified.

`EntryPoint` returns a `MethodInfo` object representing the entry point of the `Assembly`. A null reference is returned if the `Assembly` has no entry point.

`Evidence` retrieves an `Evidence` object containing information that includes signatures and code origin locations.

`FullName` returns a `String` containing the display name of the `Assembly` including the assembly name, version number, and culture designation.

`GlobalAssemblyCache` returns true if the assembly was loaded from the global assembly cache and false if it was not. (The global assembly cache is used to store assemblies intended to be shared by multiple applications: an assembly library, in other words.)

`Location` returns a `String` containing the location of the loaded file that contains the manifest for the assembly. This will often be the same as the name of the assembly.

Public static methods

```
public static string CreateQualifiedName(string assemblyName, string typeName)
```

`CreateQualifiedName()` returns a `String` containing the name of a specified type qualified by the display name of its assembly. For example, if the `Tree` class is defined in the `MyForest` assembly, its qualified name would be "`Tree.MyForest`".

```
public static Assembly GetAssembly(Type type)
public static Assembly GetCallingAssembly()
public static Assembly GetEntryAssembly()
```

```
public static Assembly GetExecutingAssembly()
```

GetAssembly() returns an Assembly object in which a specified type is defined. The input argument should represent the desired class that will be defined in the Assembly. An ArgumentNullException is thrown if type is a null reference.

GetCallingAssembly() retrieves the Assembly of the instance in which this method is called.

GetEntryAssembly() returns an Assembly representing the type that defines the entry point of an application, the Main() method that is initially executed.

GetExecutingAssembly() retrieves the Assembly that the current code is running from.

```
public static Assembly Load(AssemblyName name)
public static Assembly Load(AssemblyName name, Evidence assemblySecurity)
public static Assembly Load(byte[] rawAssembly)
public static Assembly Load(byte[] rawAssembly, byte[] rawSymbolStore)
public static Assembly Load(byte[] rawAssembly, byte[] rawSymbolStore, Evidence
                           assemblySecurity)
public static Assembly Load(string displayName)
public static Assembly Load(string displayName, Evidence assemblySecurity)
```

 Load() loads an Assembly object according to an AssemblyName, a byte array representing a Common Object File Format (COFF)-based image containing an emitted assembly, or an assembly display name. (Additional information about COFF files can be found at http://www.microsoft.com/hwdev/hardware/PECOFF.asp.) An Evidence object containing security policy information can be provided. An exception is thrown if rawAssembly is a null reference, or if name or displayName do not correspond to a valid assembly or display name.

```
public static Assembly LoadFrom(string assemblyFile)
public static Assembly LoadFrom(string assemblyFile, Evidence securityEvidence)
```

LoadFrom() loads an Assembly based on the name or path of the file that contains the manifest of the assembly. The assembly is loaded into the domain of the caller. The securityEvidence parameter provides security information for loading the assembly. An exception is thrown if assemblyFile is a null reference or otherwise invalid or if this method was called without the required permissions.

Public instance methods

```
public object CreateInstance(string typeName)
public object CreateInstance(string typeName, bool ignoreCase)
public object CreateInstance(string typeName, bool ignoreCase, BindingFlags
                           bindingAttr, Binder binder, object[] constructorArgs,
                           CultureInfo info, object[] activationAttributes)
```

CreateInstance() locates the specified type from the invoking assembly and returns an instance of this type using the system activator. This method can be used to perform something called late binding that is described later in this chapter. The ignoreCase parameter indicates whether the search for the specified type will be case-sensitive. The third version allows the specification of search attributes, a binding object, constructor arguments, cultural information, and activation attributes. An exception is thrown if typeName is an empty string, if typeName is a null reference, or if the specified constructor cannot be found.

```
public virtual object[] GetCustomAttributes(bool inherit)
public virtual object[] GetCustomAttributes(Type attributeType, bool inherit)
```

GetCustomAttributes() retrieves the custom attributes associated with the invoking Assembly. You can gain access to all of the custom attributes or only those of a specified type. The inherit parameter, though included in the argument list, is ignored. An exception is thrown if attributeType is a null reference or is not a valid type.

```
public virtual Type[] GetExportedTypes()
```

GetExportedTypes() returns an array containing the exported types defined in this Assembly.

```
public virtual FileStream GetFile(string name)
public virtual FileStream[] GetFiles()
public virtual FileStream[] GetFiles(bool getResourceModules)
```

GetFile() returns a FileStream object connected with the specified file in the file table of the manifest of the invoking Assembly object. The name parameter should not include the file path, just the file name. This method allows you to read the contents of the included file. For example, if the file "Sport.dll" was contained in an assembly of the same name you could write

```
Assembly assembly = Assembly.Load("Sport");
FileStream stream = assembly.GetFile("Sport.dll");
byte[] buf = new byte[stream.Length];
stream.Read(buf, 0, (int)stream.Length);
```

The byte buffer would contain the contents of the Sport.dll file. This method will throw an exception if name is a null reference, if the file could not be loaded, or if the caller does not have the proper permission.

GetFiles() fills an array of FileStream objects connected to all of the files in the file table of the assembly manifest. If getResourceModules is true, resource modules will be included in the list.

```
public Module[] GetLoadedModules()
public Module[] GetLoadedModules(bool getResourceModules)
```

GetLoadedModules() returns an array of Module objects representing all of the loaded modules that are part of the invoking Assembly. If getResourceModules is true, resource modules will be included in the list.

```
public virtual ManifestResourceInfo GetManifestResourceInfo(string resourceName)
public virtual string[] GetManifestResourceNames()
public virtual Stream GetManifestResourceStream(string resourceName)
public virtual Stream GetManifestResourceStream(Type type, string resourceName)
```

GetManifestResourceInfo() returns an object that contains information about the specified resource's topology. An ArgumentNullException is thrown if resourceName is a null reference.

GetManifestResourceNames() fills a String array with the names of all the resources in the invoking Assembly.

GetManifestResourceStream() opens an I/O stream to the specified manifest resource. The type parameter refers to a type whose namespace will be used to scope (or identify) the resource.

```
public Module GetModule(string name)
public Module[] GetModules()
public Module[] GetModules(bool getResourceModules)
```

GetModule() retrieves a Module object corresponding to the specified module in the invoking Assembly.

GetModules() fills an array containing all of the modules that are part of the current Assembly. If getResourceModules is true, resource modules will be included in the list.

```
public virtual AssemblyName GetName()
public virtual AssemblyName GetName(bool copiedName)
```

GetName() returns an AssemblyName object for the invoking Assembly. An AssemblyName object contains information such as the name, version number, and code base of the assembly. If copiedName is true and if the Assembly was shadow copied, the code base will be set to the assembly location after it was copied.

```
public virtual void GetObjectData(SerializationInfo info, StreamingContext
                                  context)
```

GetObjectData() initializes a SerializationInfo object with the information needed to reinstantiate the invoking Assembly from a serialized (persistently stored) state. The context parameter contains the destination context of the serialization.

```
public virtual AssemblyName[] GetReferencedAssemblies()
public virtual Assembly GetSatelliteAssembly(CultureInfo info)
public virtual Assembly GetSatelliteAssembly(CultureInfo info, Version version)
```

GetReferencedAssemblies() fills an array with AssemblyName objects for all the assemblies referenced by the invoking Assembly.

GetSatelliteAssembly() returns a satellite Assembly of the invoking Assembly for the specified culture. A satellite assembly is a localized version of a default, or culture-neutral, assembly. A Version object that defines the version of the satellite assembly can be provided as well. An exception is thrown if info is a null reference or if the satellite assembly cannot be found. This method doesn't generate a satellite assembly. It merely retrieves an existing one.

```
public virtual Type GetType(string name)
public virtual Type GetType(string name, bool throwOnError)
public virtual Type GetType(string name, bool throwOnError, bool ignoreCase)
public virtual Type[] GetTypes()
```

GetType() returns a Type object from the invoking Assembly corresponding to the specified name. If throwOnError is set to be true and the type is not found, an exception is thrown. If it is false and the type is not found, a null reference is returned. If ignoreCase is true, the system will ignore case while searching for the type corresponding to the input parameter name. An ArgumentNullException is thrown if name is a null reference.

GetTypes() returns an array filled with a Type object for every type defined in the Assembly.

```
public virtual bool IsDefined(Type attributeType, bool inherit)
```

IsDefined() returns true if a custom attribute identified by the specified Type is defined in the Assembly. For this implementation of IsDefined() the inherit parameter is ignored. An ArgumentNullException is thrown if attributeType is a null reference.

```
public Module LoadModule(string moduleName, byte[] rawModule)
public Module LoadModule(string moduleName, byte[] rawModule, byte[]
                         rawSymbolStore)
```

LoadModule() loads a Module object with a resource file or a byte array containing a COFF-based image containing an emitted module. The moduleName parameter must correspond to a file name in the invoking Assembly's manifest. A byte array containing the symbols for the module can also be loaded. An exception is thrown if moduleName or rawModule is a null reference, if they don't represent a valid file entry or module, or if the caller doesn't have the proper permission.

```
public override string ToString()
```

ToString() returns the full, or display, name of the assembly.

Events

```
public event ModuleResolveEventHandler ModuleResolve
```

ModuleResolve occurs when the common language class loader is unable to resolve a reference to an internal module. The event handler receives an argument of type ResolveEventArgs.

Example: Assembly class

This example demonstrates the process of dynamically loading, creating, and using a type at runtime. This process is known as late binding. We start off by defining an abstract class named Sport. This class defines a protected field and two abstract methods that are intended to return the name of a sport and the duration of the games or matches.

Compile the Sport.cs file using the command:

```
csc /t:library Sport.cs
```

```csharp
using System;

public abstract class Sport
{
   protected string name;
   public abstract string GetDuration();
   public abstract string GetName();
}
```

We next define a file named `SomeSports.cs` that contains three derived classes of `Sport`. Each class implements the `GetName()` and `GetDuration()` method.

Compile the `SomeSports.cs` file using the command:

`csc /t:library /r:Sport.dll SomeSports.cs`

```csharp
using System;

public class Football : Sport
{
  public Football()
  {
    name = "Football";
  }

  public override string GetDuration()
  {
    return "four 15 minute quarters";
  }

  public override string GetName()
  {
    return name;
  }
}

public class Hockey : Sport
{
  public Hockey()
  {
    name = "Hockey";
  }

  public override string GetDuration()
  {
    return "three 20 minute periods";
  }

  public override string GetName()
  {
    return name;
  }
}

public class Soccer : Sport
{
  public Soccer()
  {
    name = "Soccer";
  }
```

```
    public override string GetDuration()
    {
      return "two 45 minute halves";
    }

    public override string GetName()
    {
      return name;
    }
}
```

The `AssemblyDemo` class uses reflection to dynamically create a `Sport` derived class instance at runtime. The user specifies the assembly to be examined on the command line. An `Assembly` object is created corresponding to the command line entry. The `GetTypes()` and `GetName()` methods are used to extract all of the types contained in the assembly and list their names.

From this list the user makes a type selection. The `IsSubclassOf()` method checks to see if the selected type is a derived class of `Sport`. If it is, a `ConstructorInfo` object is created and used to create an instance of the selected type. The instance is then used to call the `GetName()` and `GetDuration()` methods.

`AssemblyDemo.cs` is compiled with the command:

csc /r:Sport.dll AssemblyDemo.cs

Note that nowhere in the compilation command or in the `AssemblyDemo` class is there any reference to the `SomeSports.dll` assembly or to the `Football`, `Hockey`, or `Soccer` classes.

```
using System;
using System.Reflection;

public class AssemblyDemo
{
  public static void Main(string[] args)
  {
    int i,j;
    //===================================================================
    //  First the command line arguments are evaluated. If there isn't
    //  at least one, a usage message is printed.
    //===================================================================

    if ( args.GetLength(0) < 1 )
    {
      Console.WriteLine("usage is AssemblyDemo <library_name>");
    }
    else
    {

      //===================================================================
```

```
    //  An Assembly object is obtained from the command line argument.
    //==============================================================

    Assembly assembly = Assembly.LoadFrom(args[0]);

    //=======================================================
    //  The GetTypes() method is used to obtain the types
    //  contained in the Assembly. The types are displayed
    //  and the user is prompted to select one of them.
    //=======================================================

    Type[] types = assembly.GetTypes();
    Console.WriteLine(assembly.GetName().Name+" contains the following types");

    for (i=0; i<types.GetLength(0); ++i)
    {
      Console.WriteLine("\t ("+i+")  "+types[i].Name);
    }

    i = types.Length - 1;
    Console.Write("make selection (0-"+ i +"): ");

    j = Convert.ToInt32(Console.ReadLine());
    Console.WriteLine();

    //=================================================================
    //  If the Type object corresponding to the user's selection
    //  represents a derived class of Sport, a ConstructorInfo
    //  object corresponding to the no-argument constructor is
    //  obtained. The ConstructorInfo uses the Invoke() method to
    //  create an instance of whatever type was specified by the user.
    //  This object then calls its GetName() and GetDuration() methods.
    //=================================================================

      if ( types[j].IsSubclassOf(typeof(Sport)) )
      {
        ConstructorInfo ci = types[j].GetConstructor(new Type[0]);
        Sport sport = (Sport)ci.Invoke(new Object[0]);

        Console.WriteLine(sport.GetName()+" has "+
                 sport.GetDuration());
      }
      else
      {
        Console.WriteLine(types[j].Name+
                 " is not a sub-class of Sport");
      }
    }
  }
}
```

The command to run this program is "`AssemblyDemo SomeSports.dll`". Here is the output if you select the `Hockey` option.

```
SomeSports contains the following types
      (0)    Football
      (1)    Hockey
      (2)    Soccer
make selection (0-2):   1

Hockey has three 20 minute periods
```

One of the benefits of using late binding is that you can add additional classes to the `SomeSports.cs` file without needing to change or even recompile the `AssemblyDemo.cs` program.

Module class

The `Module` class allows you to access information about a module. A module is a `.dll` or `.exe` file containing one or more classes and/or interfaces. A module can represent more than one namespace. One or more modules deployed as a unit with a manifest file make up an assembly. The `Module` class defines no constructors. To acquire a `Module` object, use the `GetLoadedModules()`, `GetModule()`, or `GetModules()` methods defined in the `Assembly` class.

Syntax

```
public class Module : ISerializable, ICustomAttributeProvider
```

Hierarchy

```
Object   ---   Module
```

Fields

```
public static readonly TypeFilter FilterTypeName
public static readonly TypeFilter FilterTypeNameIgnoreCase
```

`FilterTypeName` returns an instance of a `TypeFilter` delegate that can be used to filter the list of types defined in a module. The filtering is performed in a case-sensitive manner. A `TypeFilter` delegate calls a method that takes two arguments: a `Type` and an object representing a filter criterion. This field can be used as an input parameter to the `FindTypes()` method.

`FilterTypeNameIgnoreCase` is similar in function to `FilterTypeName` except the search is case-insensitive.

Properties

```
public Assembly Assembly {get;}
public virtual string FullyQualifiedName {get;}
public string Name {get;}
public string ScopeName {get;}
```

Assembly retrieves the Assembly associated with the invoking Module.

FullyQualifiedName returns the fully qualified name and path of the module represented by the Module object.

Name returns the module name without the path.

ScopeName returns the module name without the path.

Public instance methods

```
public virtual Type[] FindTypes(TypeFilter filter, object filterCriteria)
public virtual object[] GetCustomAttributes(bool inherit)
public virtual object[] GetCustomAttributes(Type attributeType, bool inherit)
```

FindTypes() returns an array containing the types of classes accepted by the specified filter according to the specified criterion. The search criterion is commonly a string. The static fields defined in the Module class can be used for the TypeFilter argument. A ReflectionTypeLoadException is thrown if one or more classes in the module could not be loaded.

GetCustomAttributes() returns an array containing the custom attributes associated with the module represented by the invoking Module object. If a Type is specified, the search will only include custom attributes of that type. If no Type is specified, all custom attributes are returned. If the inherit parameter is true, the array will include attributes inherited from base classes. An ArgumentNullException is thrown if attributeType is a null reference.

```
public FieldInfo GetField(string fieldName)
public FieldInfo GetField(string fieldName, BindingFlags bindingAttr)
public FieldInfo[] GetFields()
```

GetField() returns a FieldInfo object containing information about the specified field. Binding attributes can be provided to control the search for the specified field. An ArgumentNullException is thrown if fieldName is a null reference.

GetFields() retrieves an array of FieldInfo objects corresponding to all of the fields implemented by a class.

```
public MethodInfo GetMethod(string methodName)
public MethodInfo GetMethod(string methodName, Type[] parameterTypes)
public MethodInfo GetMethod(string methodName, BindingFlags bindingAttr,
                    Binder binder, CallingConventions callConvention,
                    Type[] parameterTypes, ParameterModifier[] modifiers)
public MethodInfo[] GetMethods()
```

GetMethod() returns a MethodInfo object containing information about the specified method. You can narrow the search by providing the parameter types, binding flags, calling convention, and parameter modifiers. An ArgumentNullException is thrown if either methodName or parameterTypes is a null reference

GetMethods() returns an array of MethodInfo objects containing information about all the global methods defined in the module.

409

```
public virtual void GetObjectData(SerializationInfo info, StreamingContext
                                                          context)
public X509Certificate GetSignerCertificate()
```

GetObjectData() loads the information needed to serialize and deserialize the invoking Module object into the specified SerializationInfo object. The context parameter provides the serialization context. An ArgumentNullException is thrown if info is a null reference.

GetSignerCertificate() returns an X509Certificate representing the signer certificate for the module. If the module is not signed, this method returns null.

```
public virtual Type GetType(string className)
public virtual Type GetType(string className, bool ignoreCase)
public virtual Type GetType(string className, bool throwOnError, bool
                                                               ignoreCase)
public virtual Type[] GetTypes()
```

GetType() returns a Type object for the specified class. The return value is null if the class does not exist within the module. The search for the class is case-sensitive unless ignoreCase is set to true. If the throwOnError parameter is true, a TypeLoadException will be thrown if there is an error while loading the Type. An exception will also be thrown if the className argument is invalid or if the caller doesn't have the required permission.

GetTypes() returns an array of Type objects representing all of the classes contained in the module. An exception is thrown if any of the classes could not be loaded or if the caller doesn't have the required permission.

```
public virtual bool IsDefined(Type attributeType, bool inherit)
public bool IsResource()
```

IsDefined() returns true if an attribute of the specified type is defined on the module. The inherit parameter is ignored in this method. An ArgumentNullException is thrown if attributeType is a null reference

IsResource() returns true if the invoking Module represents a resource.

```
public override string ToString()
```

ToString() returns the name of the module represented by the Module object.

Protected instance methods

```
protected virtual MethodInfo GetMethodImpl(string methodName, BindingFlags
         bindingAttr, Binder binder, CallingConventions callConvention, Type[]
         parameterTypes, ParameterModifier[] modifiers)
```

GetMethodImpl() returns a MethodInfo object containing information about the implementation of the specified method. The method is identified according to the parameter types, binding flags, calling convention, and parameter modifiers.

Example: Module class

The SomeSports.dll assembly used in the *Assembly class* section example consists of a module named SomeSports.dll and a manifest. In this example, a Module file associated with the SomeSports.dll module is used to search for a particular type that may be defined in the module.

The GetModule() method is used to return a reference to a Module object associated with SomeSports.dll. The Module calls the FindTypes() method to search the contents of the module for a type named "Football". The static FilterTypeName field is used as the TypeFilter argument for FindTypes().

In this case, the Football type will be found. At this point, the example proceeds exactly as the example in the *Assembly class* section. The Type object accesses a Football class constructor to create an instance of the class. The Football instance then invokes the GetName() and GetDuration() methods.

The ModuleDemo.cs file should be compiled using the following command:

```
csc /r:Sport.dll ModuleDemo.cs
```

```
using System;
using System.Reflection;

public class ModuleDemo
{
  public static void Main(string[] args)
  {
    //=======================================================
    //  An Module object is obtained representing the
    //  SomeSports.dll library file.
    //=======================================================

    Assembly assembly = Assembly.Load("SomeSports");
    Module module = assembly.GetModule("SomeSports.dll");

    //=======================================================
    //  Search the module for the type named "Football".
    //  If it is found, use  MethodInfo objects to invoke the
    //  methods on an instance of Football.
    //=======================================================

    Type[] types = module.FindTypes(Module.FilterTypeName, "Football");

    if ( types.Length != 0 )
    {
      ConstructorInfo ci = types[0].GetConstructor(new Type[0]);
      Sport sport = (Sport)ci.Invoke(new Object[0]);

      Console.WriteLine(sport.GetName()+" has "+sport.GetDuration());
    }
```

```
    else
    {
        Console.WriteLine("type not found");
    }
  }
}
```

Output:

```
Football has four 15 minute quarters
```

You can also use the "*" wildcard in the search criteria. For instance, specifying the search criterion as "F*" would return all types whose name begins with 'F'.

Member information classes

One of the primary uses of reflection is to expose information about types and type members contained in assemblies and modules. The System.Reflection namespace defines a variety of classes to do this. The member information class hierarchy is shown below.

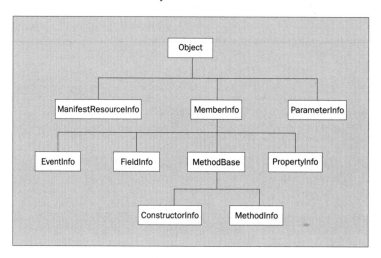

The member information class hierarchy defines two abstract base classes: MemberInfo and MethodBase. These classes define function and data members common to the specific member information classes that are derived from them. The other member information classes contain information about constructors, events, fields, manifest resource files, methods, parameters, and properties.

The member information classes can do more than expose information. They can also be used as part of a process known as late binding where an object is dynamically created at runtime. In addition to this, member information classes can be used to invoke constructors or methods and can even be used to access private data members and properties.

MemberInfo class

The `MemberInfo` class defines methods that are used to reveal the attributes of a member and to access member metadata. The `MemberInfo` class is the base class of the `EventInfo`, `FieldInfo`, `MethodBase`, `PropertyInfo`, and `Type` classes.

Syntax

```
public abstract class MemberInfo : ICustomAttributeProvider
```

Hierarchy

```
Object   ---   MemberInfo
```

Constructors

```
protected MemberInfo()
```

`MemberInfo()` is a protected constructor that can be used by derived classes of `MemberInfo`.

Properties

```
public abstract Type DeclaringType {get;}
public abstract MemberTypes MemberType {get;}
public abstract string Name {get;}
public abstract Type ReflectedType {get;}
```

`DeclaringType` returns the `Type` object for the class that declares the member represented by the current `MemberInfo` object.

`MemberType` retrieves a `MemberTypes` object containing information about the type of this member.

`Name` gets a `String` containing the name of this member.

`ReflectedType` returns the `Type` of the class object that was used to create this instance of `MemberInfo`.

Public instance methods

```
public abstract object[] GetCustomAttributes(bool inherit)
public abstract object[] GetCustomAttributes(Type attributeType, bool
                                                          inherit)
public abstract bool IsDefined(Type attributeType, bool inherit)
```

`GetCustomAttributes()` returns an array containing the custom attributes associated with the member represented by the invoking `MemberInfo` object. If a `Type` is specified, the search will only include custom attributes of that type. If no `Type` is specified, all custom attributes are returned. If the `inherit` parameter is true, the array will include attributes inherited from base classes.

`IsDefined()` returns true if an attribute of the specified attribute type exists in the member represented by the invoking `MemberInfo` object. If the `inherit` parameter is true, the search will include those attributes defined in base classes.

413

MethodBase class

The MethodBase class is the base class for Reflection classes that deal with methods, specifically the ConstructorInfo and MethodInfo classes. The MethodBase class defines properties and methods common to its derived classes, including the Invoke() method, which can be used to invoke the method or constructor associated with the MethodBase object

Syntax

```
public abstract class MethodBase : MemberInfo
```

Hierarchy

```
Object   ---   MemberInfo   ---   MethodBase
```

Constructors

```
protected MethodBase()
```

MethodBase() is a protected constructor that can be used by derived classes of MethodBase.

Properties

```
public abstract MethodAttributes Attributes {get;}
public virtual CallingConventions CallingConvention {get;}
public bool IsAbstract {get;}
public bool IsAssembly {get;}
public bool IsConstructor {get;}
public bool IsFamily {get;}
public bool IsFamilyAndAssembly {get;}
public bool IsFamilyOrAssembly {get;}
public bool IsFinal {get;}
public bool IsHideBySig {get;}
public bool IsPrivate {get;}
public bool IsPublic {get;}
public bool IsSpecialName {get;}
public bool IsStatic {get;}
public bool IsVirtual {get;}
public abstract RuntimeMethodHandle MethodHandle {get;}
```

Attributes returns an instance of the MethodAttributes enumeration containing values that describe the attributes of the MethodBase object.

CallingConvention retrieves an object representing the calling conventions for this method. The CallingConvention enumeration contains values that define how arguments are passed to and from methods.

IsAbstract returns true if the method represented by the MethodBase is abstract.

IsAssembly returns true if this method can be called by other classes in the same assembly.

IsConstructor returns true if the method represented by the MethodBase is a constructor.

`IsFamily` returns true if access to the method is restricted to members of its class and derived classes.

`IsFamilyAndAssembly` indicates if the method can be called by derived classes that reside in the same assembly.

`IsFamilyOrAssembly` returns true if the method represented by the `MethodBase` can be called by derived classes and by all classes in the same assembly.

`IsFinal` returns true if the method represented by the `MethodBase` is final.

`IsHideBySig` indicates if the method is hidden by a member of the same kind with the same signature in a derived class.

`IsPrivate` returns true if the method represented by the `MethodBase` is private.

`IsPublic` returns true if the method represented by the `MethodBase` is public.

`IsSpecialName` indicates if the method has a special name that might tell a compiler to give it special treatment.

`IsStatic` returns true if the method represented by the `MethodBase` is static.

`IsVirtual` returns true if the method represented by the `MethodBase` is virtual.

`MethodHandle` retrieves a handle to the internal metadata representation of a method.

Public static methods

```
public static MethodBase GetCurrentMethod()
public static MethodBase GetMethodFromHandle()
```

`GetCurrentMethod()` returns a `MethodBase` object representing the method that is currently executing.

`GetMethodFromHandle()` retrieves a `MethodBase` object based on the method's internal metadata representation or handle.

Public instance methods

```
public abstract MethodImplAttributes GetMethodImplementationFlags()
public abstract ParameterInfo[] GetParameters()
```

`GetMethodImplementationFlags()` returns the `MethodImplAttributes` enumeration flags that are associated with the `MethodBase`.

`GetParameters()` returns an array of `ParameterInfo` objects representing the parameters associated with the method or constructor.

```
public object Invoke(object obj, object[] parameters)
public abstract object Invoke(object obj, BindingFlags invokeAttr, Binding
                             binding, object[] parameters, CultureInfo info)
```

Invoke() calls the underlying method or constructor associated with the MethodBase object. The obj parameter is the instance on which the method will be invoked. The parameters input is the argument list that is passed to the invoked method. The return value of Invoke() is the return value of the invoked method cast as an object. The second version lets you specify binding flags, a Binder, and culture-specific information. An exception is thrown if the method represented by the MethodBase is static and obj is a null reference, if the invoked method or constructor throws an exception, if the method is not declared or inherited by the type of obj, if the parameters passed to the method are invalid, or if the caller does not have the required permission.

ConstructorInfo class

The ConstructorInfo class allows you to determine the attributes of a class constructor. It also provides access to constructor metadata and can be used to invoke a constructor. The ConstructorInfo class does not define any public constructors. A ConstructorInfo object can be obtained using the GetConstructors() or GetConstructor() methods defined in the Type class.

The ConstructorInfo class is a derived class of the Object, MemberInfo, and MethodBase classes and has access to the properties and methods defined in those classes.

Syntax

```
public abstract class ConstructorInfo : MethodBase
```

Hierarchy

```
Object   ---   MemberInfo   ---   MethodBase   ---   ConstructorInfo
```

Constructors

```
protected ConstructorInfo()
```

ConstructorInfo() is a protected constructor used by derived classes of ConstructorInfo.

Fields

```
public static readonly string ConstructorName
public static readonly string TypeConstructorName
```

ConstructorName is the string ".ctor" which is the name of the class constructor method as it is stored in metadata.

TypeConstructorName is the string ".cctor" which is the name of the type constructor method as it is stored in metadata.

Properties

```
public override MemberTypes MemberType {get;}
```

`MemberType` returns a `MemberTypes` object representing the type of member that the invoking `ConstructorInfo` object reflects.

Public instance methods

```
public object Invoke(object[] parameters)
public object Invoke(BindingFlags invokeAttributes, Binder binder, object[]
                     parameters, CultureInfo info)
```

`Invoke()` invokes the constructor that the invoking `ConstructorInfo` object reflects. The input parameters for the constructor are provided as arguments to the method. The second version performs the constructor invocation under the constraints of the specified `Binder`, invocation attributes, and cultural information. An exception is thrown if the attempt to access the constructor fails, if the parameters are invalid or an incorrect number of parameters is provided, or if the invoked constructor throws an exception. For an example of using the `Invoke()` method, see the example in the *Assembly class* section.

Example: ConstructorInfo Class

In this example, a `ConstructorInfo` object is used to obtain information about the constructors of a specified class. The `GetConstructors()` method of the `Type` class is used to return a `ConstructorInfo` object for every constructor of the `System.Queue` class. Various `ConstructorInfo` class properties and methods are used to display information about the constructors.

For another example of how to use a `ConstructorInfo` object, see the *Assembly class* section, where a `ConstructorInfo` object is used to create an instance of a user-specified class.

```csharp
using System;
using System.Reflection;

public class CIDemo
{
  public static void Main()
  {
    ParameterInfo[] pi;

    //===============================================================
    //   The GetType() method returns a Type object corresponding
    //   to the System.Collections.Queue class.
    //===============================================================

    Type type = Type.GetType("System.Collections.Queue");
    Console.WriteLine("Constructors for type {0}\n",type.ToString());

    //===============================================================
    //   The GetConstructors() method returns a ConstructorInfo object
    //   for each constructor defined by the Queue class.
    //===============================================================

    ConstructorInfo[] consts = type.GetConstructors();
```

```
        Console.WriteLine("\nNumber of constructors = {0}",
                                            consts.GetLength(0));

    //================================================================
    //  Each ConstructorInfo object calls the GetParameters() method
    //   to obtain a ParameterInfo object for each parameter used by
    //   the constructor. Various ParameterInfo properties are listed.
    //================================================================

    for(int i=0; i<consts.GetLength(0); ++i)
    {
        pi = consts[i].GetParameters();
        Console.WriteLine("\nconstructor {0} takes {1} input parameters",
                                            i,pi.GetLength(0));
        for(int j=0; j<pi.GetLength(0); ++j)
        {
          Console.WriteLine("\tparameter {0}: name={1} type={2}",
                            pi[j].Position,pi[j].Name,pi[j].ParameterType);
        }
      }
    }
  }
```

Output:

```
Constructors for type System.Collections.Queue

Number of constructors = 4

constructor 0 takes 0 input parameters

constructor 1 takes 1 input parameters
        parameter 0: name=capacity type=System.Int32

constructor 2 takes 2 input parameters
        parameter 0: name=capacity type=System.Int32
        parameter 1: name=growFactor type=System.Single

constructor 3 takes 1 input parameters
        parameter 0: name=col type=System.Collections.ICollection
```

EventInfo class

The EventInfo class can expose the attributes of an event. It also provides access to event metadata. The EventInfo class does not define any public constructors. An EventInfo object can be obtained using the GetEvent() or GetEvents() methods from the Type class.

The EventInfo class is a derived class of the Object and MemberInfo classes and has access to the properties and methods defined in those classes.

Syntax

```
public abstract class EventInfo : MemberInfo
```

Hierarchy

```
Object  ---  MemberInfo  ---  EventInfo
```

Constructors

```
protected EventInfo()
```

EventInfo() is a protected constructor used by derived classes of EventInfo.

Properties

```
public abstract EventAttributes Attributes {get;}
public Type EventHandlerType {get;}
public bool IsMulticast {get;}
public bool IsSpecialName {get;}
public override MemberTypes MemberType {get;}
```

Attributes returns the read-only attributes for the event reflected by the EventInfo object.

EventHandlerType retrieves the Type of the underlying event handler delegate associated with the event.

IsMulticast returns true if the event delegate associated with the event is a multi-cast delegate.

IsSpecialName returns true if the EventInfo object has a name with a special meaning. A special name might indicate that some special treatment must be performed on the event.

MemberType gets the member type for the event reflected by the EventInfo object.

Public instance methods

```
public void AddEventHandler(object eventSource, Delegate handler)
public MethodInfo GetAddMethod()
public abstract MethodInfo GetAddMethod(bool nonPublic)
public MethodInfo GetRaiseMethod()
public abstract MethodInfo GetRaiseMethod(bool nonPublic)
public MethodInfo GetRemoveMethod()
public abstract MethodInfo GetRemoveMethod(bool nonPublic)
public void RemoveEventHandler(object eventSource, Delegate handler)
```

AddEventHandler() adds the specified delegate to the multi-cast event delegate maintained by the specified event source. Each time the event source generates the event type reflected by the EventInfo, the method or methods represented by handler will be called. An exception is thrown if eventSource is a null reference or if handler cannot be added to the event delegate.

GetAddMethod() returns a MethodInfo object representing the method used to add an event handler delegate to an event source. The second version of this method can be overridden in a derived class to return a MethodInfo object specifying whether the method should be public or non-public. A SecurityException is thrown if the caller does not have the required permission to call this method.

GetRaiseMethod() returns a MethodInfo object representing the method that is called when an event is generated. The second version of this method can be overridden in a derived class to return a MethodInfo object specifying whether the method should be public or non-public. A SecurityException is thrown if the caller does not have the required permission.

GetRemoveMethod() returns a MethodInfo object representing the method used to remove an event handler delegate from an event source. The second version of this method can be overridden in a derived class to return a MethodInfo object specifying whether the method should be public or non-public. A SecurityException is thrown if the caller does not have the required permission to call this method.

RemoveEventHandler() removes the specified event handler delegate from the specified event source. The method or methods represented by the event handler will no longer be called when the event source generates an event. An exception is thrown if eventSource is a null reference or if handler cannot be removed from the event delegate.

Example: EventInfo Class

In this simple example, an EventInfo object is returned for every event defined in the Assembly class. The EventInfo object is then used to access the event handler type and the methods to add or remove the event handler from an event source.

```
using System;
using System.Reflection;

public class EventInfoDemo
{
  public static void Main()
  {
    Type type = Type.GetType("System.Reflection.Assembly");
    Console.WriteLine("Events for type {0}\n",type.ToString());

    //==============================================================
    //   The GetEvents() method returns an EventInfo object for
    //   each event defined in the class. Various EventInfo
    //   methods are used to display information about the event.
    //==============================================================

    EventInfo[] events = type.GetEvents();
    Console.WriteLine("number of events = {0}\n",events.GetLength(0));

    for(int i=0; i<events.GetLength(0); ++i)
    {
      Console.WriteLine("Event name = {0}",events[i].Name);
      Console.WriteLine("handler type = {0}",events[i].EventHandlerType);
      Console.WriteLine("add method = {0} ",events[i].GetAddMethod().Name);
      Console.WriteLine("remove method = {0} ",
                                events[i].GetRemoveMethod().Name);
    }
  }
}
```

Output:

```
Events for type System.Reflection.Assembly

number of events = 1

Event name = ModuleResolve
handler type = System.Reflect.ModuleResolveEventHandler
add method = add_ModuleResolve
remove method = remove_ModuleResolve
```

FieldInfo class

The FieldInfo class can expose the attributes of a field and can access information contained in field metadata. FieldInfo also facilitates dynamic get and set functionality for the value of the field. The FieldInfo class does not define a public constructor. The GetFields() or GetField() methods from the Type or Module classes can be used to return a reference to a FieldInfo object.

The FieldInfo class is a derived class of the Object and MemberInfo classes and has access to the properties and methods defined in those classes.

Syntax

```
public abstract class FieldInfo : MemberInfo
```

Hierarchy

```
Object  ---  MemberInfo  ---  FieldInfo
```

Constructors

```
protected FieldInfo()
```

FieldInfo() is a protected constructor used by derived classes of FieldInfo.

Properties

```
public abstract FieldAttributes Attributes {get;}
public abstract RuntimeFieldHandle FieldHandle {get;}
public abstract Type FieldType {get;}
public bool IsAssembly {get;}
public bool IsFamily {get;}
public bool IsFamlyAndAssembly {get;}
public bool IsFamlyOrAssembly {get;}
public bool IsInitOnly {get;}
public bool IsLiteral {get;}
public bool IsNotSerialized {get;}
public bool IsPinvokeImpl {get;}
public bool IsPrivate {get;}
public bool IsPublic {get;}
public bool IsSpecialName {get;}
public bool IsStatic {get;}
```

```
public override MemberTypes MemberType {get;}
```

`Attributes` returns the attributes associated with the field reflected by the `FieldInfo` object.

`FieldHandle` retrieves a handle to the internal metadata representation of the field. The handle is only valid in the app domain in which it was obtained.

`FieldType` returns the type of the field.

`IsAssembly` returns true if the field has the `Assembly` attribute set or false if it does not. A field with `Assembly` level visibility can be called by any member within the same assembly.

`IsFamily` returns true if the field has the `Family` attribute set or false if it does not. A field with `Family` level visibility can be accessed by any member in a derived class.

`IsFamilyAndAssembly` returns true if the field has the `FamANDAssem` attribute set or false if it does not. A field with `FamilyAndAssembly` visibility can be accessed from any member in a derived class that is in the same assembly.

`IsFamilyOrAssembly` returns true if the field has the `FamORAssem` attribute set or false if it does not. A field with `FamilyOrAssembly` visibility can be accessed from any member in a derived class or from any member in the same assembly.

`IsInitOnly` returns true if the field has the `InitOnly` attribute set or false if it does not. If this is true, the field can only be initialized and is read-only after that.

`IsLiteral` returns true if the field has the `Literal` attribute set or false if it does not. If it is true, the value of the field is written at compile time and cannot be changed.

`IsNotSerialized` returns true if the field has the `NotSerialized` attribute set or false if it does not.

`IsPinvokeImpl` returns true if the field has the `PinvokeImpl` attribute set or false if it does not. This is relevant when working with unmanaged code.

`IsPrivate` returns true if the field has private access.

`IsPublic` returns true if the field has public access.

`IsSpecialName` returns true if the field has the `SpecialName` attribute set or false if it does not. A special name might indicate to the compiler that the field requires special treatment.

`IsStatic` returns true if the field is static.

`MemberType` returns information about the type of the field reflected by the `FieldInfo` object.

Public static methods

```
public static FieldInfo GetFieldFromHandle(RuntimeFieldHandle handle)
```

`GetFieldFromHandle()` returns a `FieldInfo` object based on the specified handle to an internal metadata representation of a field.

Public instance methods

```
public abstract object GetValue(object obj)
public virtual object GetValueDirect(TypedReference obj)
public void SetValue(object obj, object value)
public abstract void SetValue(object obj, object value, BindingFlags attr, Binder
                             binder, CultureInfo info)
public virtual void SetValueDirect(TypedReference obj, object value)
```

GetValue() returns the value of the field reflected by the invoking FieldInfo object. The input argument obj is an instance of a class that inherits or declares the field and the return value will be the value of the field as defined by obj. If the field is static, the input parameter obj is ignored. An exception is thrown if the field is non-static and obj is a null reference, if obj does not define or inherit the GetValue() method, or if the caller doesn't have the proper permission.

GetValueDirect() is similar to GetValue() except it is not CLS-compliant and the input argument is a managed pointer to a location and a run-time representation of the type that might be stored at that location.

SetValue() changes the value of a field as defined by object obj. The input parameter value is the new value to assign to the field. The second version allows you to specify binding attributes and cultural information. If the field is static, the input parameter obj is ignored. An exception is thrown if the field is an instance field and obj is a null reference, if the type of value cannot be assigned to the field, if the field does not exist on the object, or if the caller doesn't have the required permission.

SetValueDirect() is similar to SetValue() except it is not CLS-compliant. The input argument obj is a managed pointer to a location.

Example: FieldInfo Class

If you look at the Sport.cs code listing in the *Assembly class* section, you will notice that there seems to be no way to change the value of the name field. The field is non-public and there is no Set() method defined in the Sport class. However, it is possible to change the value of the name field using a FieldInfo object.

A Hockey object is created. Hockey is a derived class of Sport. The Hockey object calls the GetType() method to get a Type object corresponding to the Hockey class. The Type object acquires a FieldInfo object corresponding to the name field of that class. The FieldInfo object then calls the SetValue() method and changes the value of the name field for the Hockey object to "Cricket". If the Hockey object calls the GetName() method, the return value is now "Cricket".

We need to reference the assemblies we created earlier at compile time:

```
csc /r:Sport.dll /r:SomeSports.dll FieldInfo.cs
```

```
using System;
using System.Reflection;

public class FieldInfoDemo
```

```
{
    public static void Main()
    {
        //=================================================================
        //   A Hockey object is created. (See the Assembly Class example
        //   for a listing of the Hockey class.) The value of its name
        //   field is printed.
        //=================================================================

        Hockey hk = new Hockey();
        Console.WriteLine("Name is {0}",hk.GetName());

        //=================================================================
        //   A Type object is obtained representing the Hockey class.
        //   The Type object is used to acquire a FieldInfo object
        //   corresponding to the "name" field.
        //=================================================================

        Type type = hk.GetType();
        FieldInfo field = type.GetField("name",BindingFlags.NonPublic|
                                               BindingFlags.Instance);

        //=================================================================
        //   The FieldInfo object calls the SetValue() method to change
        //   the value of the "name" field of the Hockey object. Now when
        //   the Hockey object calls the GetName() method, the modified
        //   name is returned.
        //=================================================================

        field.SetValue(hk,"Cricket");
        Console.WriteLine("name is now {0}",hk.GetName());
    }
}
```

Output:

```
Name is Hockey
name is now Cricket
```

ManifestResourceInfo class

The ManifestResourceInfo class contains information about the manifest resource file. The three properties defined in the class represent the name of the manifest resource file, its containing assembly, and one or more enumeration values that define where the resource file is located.

Syntax

```
public class ManifestResourceInfo
```

Hierarchy

```
Object  ---  ManifestResourceInfo
```

Properties

```
public virtual string FileName {get;}
public virtual Assembly ReferencedAssembly {get;}
public virtual ResourceLocation ResourceLocation {get;}
```

FileName retrieves the name of the manifest resource file.

ReferencedAssembly returns an Assembly object representing the manifest resource's containing assembly.

ResourceLocation gets an instance of a ResourceLocation enumeration containing one or more values defining the location of the manifest resource.

MethodInfo class

The MethodInfo class exposes the attributes of a method and provides access to the metadata associated with the method. The MethodInfo class does not define any public constructors. A MethodInfo object can be obtained using the GetMethod() or GetMethods() methods defined in the Type or Module classes.

Syntax

```
public abstract class MethodInfo : MethodBase
```

Hierarchy

```
Object  ---  MemberInfo  ---  MethodBase  ---  MethodInfo
```

Constructors

```
protected MethodInfo()
```

MethodInfo() is a protected constructor used by derived classes of MethodInfo.

Properties

```
public override MemberTypes MemberType {get;}
public abstract Type ReturnType {get;}
public abstract ICustomAttributeProvider ReturnTypeCustomAttributes {get;}
```

MemberType returns a MemberTypes object identifying this member as a method.

ReturnType retrieves a Type object corresponding to the return value of the method represented by the MethodInfo object.

ReturnTypeCustomAttributes returns an ICustomAttributeProvider object representing the custom attributes for the return type of the method.

Public instance methods

```
public abstract MethodInfo GetBaseDefinition()
```

`GetBaseDefinition()` returns a `MethodInfo` object corresponding to the first definition of the method in the class hierarchy.

Example: MethodInfo Class

This is a modified version of the example presented in the *Assembly class* section. In this version, `MethodInfo` objects are used to invoke methods of a dynamically loaded class. As before, the user inputs an assembly name at the command line. The `GetTypes()` method extracts the types defined in the assembly. The user then selects one of the available types.

The `Type` object corresponding to the user's selection then creates `MethodInfo` objects corresponding to the `GetName()` and `GetDuration()` methods. The `MethodInfo` objects use the `Invoke()` method to call their corresponding methods on an object of the user-specified type created by the `CreateInstance()` method.

The `MethodInfoDemo.cs` file should be compiled using the following command:

```
csc /r:Sport.dll MethodInfoDemo.cs
```

```
using System;
using System.Reflection;

public class MethodInfoDemo
{
  public static void Main(string[] args)
  {
    int i,j;
    //=====================================================================
    // First the command line arguments are evaluated. If there isn't
    // at least one, a usage message is printed.
    //=====================================================================

    if ( args.GetLength(0) < 1 )
    {
      Console.WriteLine("usage is MethodInfoDemo <library_name>");
    }
    else
    {

      //=======================================================
      // An Assembly object is obtained from the command
      // line argument.
      //=======================================================

      Assembly assembly = Assembly.LoadFrom(args[0]);

      //=======================================================
      // The GetTypes() method is used to obtain the types
      // contained in the Assembly. The types are displayed
      // and the user is prompted to select one of them.
      //=======================================================
```

```
          Type[] types = assembly.GetTypes();
          Console.WriteLine(assembly.GetName().Name+
                                      " contains the following types");
          for (i=0; i<types.GetLength(0); ++i)
          {
            Console.WriteLine("\t ("+i+")  "+types[i].Name);
          }

          i = types.Length - 1;
          Console.Write("make selection (0-"+ i +"): ");

          j = Convert.ToInt32(Console.ReadLine());
          Console.WriteLine();

          //===================================================================
          //  If the Type object corresponding to the user's selection
          //  represents a derived class of Sport, then two MethodInfo
          //  objects corresponding to the GetName() and GetDuration()
          //  methods are created. An object of the user-specified type
          //  is created and the MethodInfo objects invoke their associated
          //  methods on that object.
          //===================================================================

          if ( types[j].IsSubclassOf(typeof(Sport)) )
          {
            MethodInfo mi1 = types[j].GetMethod("GetName");
            MethodInfo mi2 = types[j].GetMethod("GetDuration");

            object obj = Activator.CreateInstance(types[j]);

            Console.WriteLine(mi1.Invoke(obj,null)+" has "+
                                            mi2.Invoke(obj,null));
          }
          else
          {
            Console.WriteLine(types[j].Name+ " is not a sub-class of Sport");
          }
        }
      }
    }
```

Output (using the command "MethodInfoDemo SomeSports.dll" and choosing "Football"):

```
SomeSports contains the following types
      (0)     Football
      (1)     Hockey
      (2)     Soccer
make selection(0-2): 0

Football has four 15 minute quarters
```

ParameterInfo class

The `ParameterInfo` class permits access to the attributes and metadata of a parameter. The `ParameterInfo` class does not provide any public constructors. To obtain a `ParameterInfo` object, use the `GetParameters()` method from the `MethodBase` class.

Syntax

```
public class ParameterInfo : ICustomAttributeProvider
```

Hierarchy

```
Object   ---   ParameterInfo
```

Constructors

```
protected ParameterInfo()
```

`ParameterInfo()` is a protected constructor for use by derived classes of `ParameterInfo`.

Fields

```
protected ParameterAttributes AttrsImpl
protected Type ClassImpl
protected object DefaultValueImpl
protected MemberInfo MemberImpl
protected string NameImpl
protected int PositionImpl
```

These protected fields are intended for use by derived classes of `ParameterInfo`. Normal access to the information described by these fields is obtained through the `ParameterInfo` class properties.

`AttrsImpl` retrieves the attributes associated with a parameter.

`ClassImpl` represents the `Type` of the parameter.

`DefaultValueImpl` is the default value of the parameter.

`Membermpl` corresponds to the member in which the parameter is implemented.

`NameImpl` is the name of the parameter.

`PositionImpl` is the zero-based position of the parameter in the parameter list.

Properties

```
public virtual ParameterAttributes Attributes {get;}
public virtual object DefaultValue {get;}
public bool IsIn {get;}
public bool IsLcid {get;}
public bool IsOptional {get;}
public bool IsOut {get;}
public bool IsRetval {get;}
```

```
public virtual MemberInfo Member {get;}
public virtual string Name {get;}
public virtual Type ParameterType {get;}
public virtual int Position {get;}
```

Attributes returns an instance of the ParameterAttributes enumeration containing values that describe the attributes of the parameter.

DefaultValue gets the default value of the parameter or its current value if there is no default.

IsIn returns true if the parameter represented by the ParameterInfo object is an input parameter.

IsLcid returns true if the parameter is a locale identifier.

IsOptional returns true if the parameter is optional.

IsOut returns true if the parameter is an output parameter.

IsRetval returns true if the parameter is a Retval (return value) parameter.

Member retrieves a MemberInfo object representing the member in which the parameter is implemented.

Name returns the name of the parameter.

ParameterType gets the Type of the parameter.

Position returns the position of the parameter in the parameter list.

Public instance methods

```
public virtual object[] GetCustomAttributes(bool inherit)
public virtual object[] GetCustomAttributes(Type attributeType, bool inherit)
```

GetCustomAttributes() returns an array containing the custom attributes associated with the parameter represented by the invoking ParameterInfo object. If a Type is specified, the search will only include custom attributes of that type. If no Type is specified, all custom attributes are returned. The inherit parameter is ignored with this method.

```
public virtual bool IsDefined(Type attributeType, bool inherit)
```

IsDefined() returns true if an attribute of the specified attribute is defined on the parameter. The inherit parameter is ignored in this method.

For an example of ParameterInfo objects in action, see the example in the *ConstructorInfo class* section of this chapter where ParameterInfo objects are used to access information about the input parameters of the Assembly class constructors.

PropertyInfo class

The `PropertyInfo` class allows you to access the attributes and other information associated with a property. The `PropertyInfo` class does not define any public constructors. A `PropertyInfo` object can be obtained using the `GetProperty()` or `GetProperties()` methods defined in the `Type` class.

The `PropertyInfo` class is a derived class of the `Object` and `MemberInfo` classes and has access to the properties and methods defined in those classes.

Syntax

```
public abstract class PropertyInfo : MemberInfo
```

Hierarchy

```
Object   ---   MemberInfo   ---   PropertyInfo
```

Constructors

```
protected PropertyInfo()
```

`PropertyInfo()` is a protected constructor used by derived classes of `PropertyInfo`.

Properties

```
public abstract PropertyAttributes Attributes {get;}
public abstract bool CanRead {get;}
public abstract bool CanWrite {get;}
public bool IsSpecialName {get;}
public override MemberTypes MemberType {get;}
public abstract Type PropertyType {get;}
```

`Attributes` returns an instance of the `PropertyAttributes` enumeration containing values that describe the attributes of the property.

`CanRead` returns true if the property can be read.

`CanWrite` returns true if the property can be set.

`IsSpecialName` returns true if the property has a special name.

`MemberType` returns a `MemberTypes` object representing the type of the property.

`PropertyType` returns the type of the property.

Public instance methods

```
public MethodInfo[] GetAccessors()
public MethodInfo[] GetAccessors(bool nonPublic)
```

`GetAccessors()` returns a `MethodInfo` array representing the `get` and `set` accessors on this property. If `nonPublic` is true, both public and non-public accessors will be returned. If it is false, only public accessors are returned.

```
public MethodInfo GetGetMethod()
public MethodInfo GetGetMethod(bool nonPublic)
```

GetGetMethod() retrieves a MethodInfo object corresponding to the get accessor for this property. If nonPublic is true, a non-public get accessor will be returned. If it is false, only a public get accessor is returned. The return value is null if an appropriate accessor is not found.

```
public abstract ParameterInfo[] GetIndexParameters()
```

GetIndexParameters() returns an array of ParameterInfo objects representing the index parameters for the property.

```
public MethodInfo GetSetMethod()
public MethodInfo GetSetMethod(bool nonPublic)
```

GetSetMethod() retrieves a MethodInfo object corresponding to the set accessor for this property. If nonPublic is true, a non-public set accessor will be returned. If it is false, only a public set accessor is returned. The return value is null if an appropriate accessor is not found.

```
public virtual object GetValue(object obj, object[] index)
public virtual object GetValue(object obj, BindingFlags invokeAttr, Binder binder,
                        object[] index, CultureInfo info)
```

GetValue() returns the value of the property associated with the PropertyInfo object. The obj parameter is the object whose property value will be returned. The index parameter is optional and contains index values for indexed properties. You can also specify binding flags, a Binder, and cultural information. An exception is thrown if the property's get accessor is not found, if the index parameters are invalid, or if the type of obj is different from that of the instance associated with the PropertyInfo object.

```
public virtual void SetValue(object obj, object value, object[] index)
public virtual void SetValue(object obj, BindingFlags invokeAttr,
                    Binder binder, object[] index, CultureInfo info)
```

SetValue() changes the value of the property associated with the PropertyInfo object as it is applied to the object obj. The index parameter is optional and contains index values for indexed properties. You can also specify binding flags, a Binder, and cultural information. An exception is thrown if the property's set accessor is not found, if the index parameters are invalid, or if the type of obj is different from that of the instance associated with the PropertyInfo object.

Example: PropertyInfo Class

In the example from the *FieldInfo class* section, we saw how a FieldInfo object can be used to change the value of a field. A PropertyInfo object can similarly be used to change the value of a property. There is one catch, however. You can only change the value of a property that has a set accessor associated with it. You cannot change the value of a read-only property, one that only has a get accessor.

This example shows how it can be done. A StreamWriter is created and used to write some text to a file. A PropertyInfo object associated with the Position property of the Stream class is then created. The PropertyInfo object calls the SetValue() method to change the value of the Position property associated with the StreamWriter. This resets the position to 0. When text is next written to the stream, it overwrites the previously written text.

```
using System;
using System.Reflection;
using System.IO;

public class PIDemo
{
  public static void Main()
  {
    //==============================================================
    //  A StreamWriter is wrapped around a FileStream that is
    //  connected to the file "output.txt". A line of text
    //  is written to the file.
    //==============================================================

    StreamWriter sw = new StreamWriter(File.Create("output.txt"));
    sw.WriteLine("This is written to output.txt");
    sw.Flush();

    //==============================================================
    //  A Type object corresponding to the Stream class is
    //  used to get a PropertyInfo object representing the
    //  Position property. The PropertyInfo object invokes
    //  the SetValue() method to change the position of the
    //  underlying stream of the StreamWriter.
    //==============================================================

    Type type = Type.GetType("System.IO.Stream");

    PropertyInfo prop = type.GetProperty("Position");
    prop.SetValue(sw.BaseStream,0,new object[0]);

    //==========================================================
    //  The previous text is overwritten by this text.
    //==========================================================

    sw.WriteLine("Where is this output going?");
    sw.Flush();
    sw.Close();
  }
}
```

Output (contents of output.txt):

```
Where is this output going?
```

Other System.Reflection members

This chapter concludes with a brief discussion of four other useful members of the System.Reflection namespace. The Binder class can be used to help identify a function or data member from a list of candidate members. Binder objects are commonly used inputs in reflection and I/O methods. The BindingFlags enumeration contains values that define access control or type operations. The IReflect interface declares methods that are implemented by types that support reflection. Types that implement this interface include the Type and AccessibleObject classes. The Pointer class is used to wrap a managed-memory object around an unmanaged memory pointer.

Binder class

A Binder can be used to assist in the search for a method, constructor, parameter, or field. It can also perform a type conversion on a specified object.

Syntax

```
public abstract class Binder
```

Hierarchy

```
Object  --- Binder
```

Constructors

```
protected Binder()
```

Binder() is a protected constructor used by derived classes of Binder.

Public instance methods

```
public abstract FieldInfo BindToField(BindingFlags bindingAttr, FieldInfo[]
                              match, object fieldValue, CultureInfo info)
public abstract MethodBase BindToMethod(BindingFlags bindingAttr,
      MethodBase[] match, ref object[] args, ParameterModifier[] modifiers,
                      CultureInfo info, string[] names, out object state)
public abstract object ChangeType(object value, Type type, CultureInfo info)
public abstract void ReorderArgumentArray(ref object[] args, object state)
public abstract MethodBase SelectMethod(BindingFlags bindingAttr,
           MethodBase[] match, Type[] types, ParameterModifier[] modifiers)
public abstract PropertyInfo SelectProperty(BindingFlags bindingAttr,
                   PropertyInfo[] match, Type returnType, Type[] indexes,
                                          ParameterModifier[] modifiers)
```

BindToField() returns a FieldInfo object from an array of FieldInfo objects based on the specified binding attributes, field value, and cultural information.

BindToMethod() selects a method to invoke from an assortment of methods. The methods are represented by MethodBase objects. The selection is based on the specified binding attributes, the arguments that will be passed to the method, an array of parameter modifiers, cultural information, and the method name or names. The state parameter is a binder-provided object that keeps track of argument reordering.

`ChangeType()` changes the specified object to the specified type and returns the type-modified object. This method should only be used to perform widening conversions, from a float to a double, for instance, because a narrowing conversion may lose data.

`ReorderArgumentArray()` is called by the Common Language Runtime after a return from the `BindToMethod()` method. `ReorderArgumentArray()` restores the `args` argument to what it was when it came from `BindToMethod()`.

`SelectMethod()` selects a method from a collection of methods based on the specified argument types. Binding attributes and parameter modifiers can also be specified.

`SelectProperty()` returns a property from a selection of properties based on the specified binding attributes, property return type, index types (for indexer-type properties), and parameter modifiers.

BindingFlags enumeration

The `BindingFlags` enumeration contains members that are used to define access control and type operations. They are commonly used as input parameters in reflection and I/O methods to limit or otherwise define the scope of an activity.

Syntax

```
public enum BindingFlags
```

Members

`CreateInstance` specifies that an operation will create an instance of the specified type.

`DeclaredOnly` indicates that inherited members are not considered.

`Default` refers to an empty (meaningless) binding flag.

`ExactBinding` indicates that no type conversions will be permitted on input arguments. The input argument types must match the parameter list type specification.

`FlattenHierarchy` means only static members in the hierarchy are returned. Nested members are not returned.

`GetField` indicates that this operation should return the value of a field.

`GetProperty` indicates that this operation should return the value of a field.

`IgnoreCase` specifies that case should be ignored.

`IgnoreReturn` means that the return value of a member will be ignored.

`Instance` indicates that instance members will be included in a search.

`InvokeMethod` specifies that this operation will invoke a member.

`NonPublic` means that non-public members will be included in the search.

`OptionalParamBinding` is used for operations with members that can have a variable number of parameters.

`Public` indicates that public members will be included in the search.

`SetField` specifies that this operation should set the value of a field.

`SetProperty` indicates that an operation should set the value of a property.

`Static` means that static members will be included in the search.

IReflect interface

The `IReflect` interface declares methods that return `MemberInfo` objects and instances of derived classes of `MemberInfo`. These objects contain information about fields, members, methods, and properties. The interface also declares the `InvokeMember()` method that can be used to invoke a member on a target object. The `Type` and `AccessibleObject` classes implement this interface.

Syntax

```
public interface IReflect
```

Properties

```
Type UnderlyingSystemType {get;}
```

`UnderlyingSystemType` represents the underlying type that represents the `IReflect` object. For example, if a `Type` object was associated with the `String` class the underlying type would be `String`.

Methods

```
FieldInfo GetField(string fieldName, BindingFlags bindingAttr)
FieldInfo[] GetFields(BindingFlags bindingAttr)
```

`GetField()` returns a `FieldInfo` object containing information about the specified field. The binding attributes are used to control the search for the specified field.

`GetFields()` retrieves an array of `FieldInfo` objects corresponding to all of the fields of the current class.

```
MemberInfo[] GetMember(string memberName, BindingFlags bindingAttr)
MemberInfo[] GetMembers(BindingFlags bindingAttr)
```

`GetMember()` returns an array of `MemberInfo` objects for all members that match the specified name. The binding attributes are used to control the search for the members.

`GetMembers()` returns an array of `MemberInfo` objects for all members of the current class. The binding attributes are used to control the search for the members.

```
MethodInfo GetMethod(string methodName, BindingFlags bindingAttr)
MethodInfo GetMethod(string methodName, BindingFlags bindingAttr, Binder
                     binder, Type[] types, ParameterModifiers[] modifiers)
```

435

```
MethodInfo[] GetMethods(BindingFlags bindingAttr)
```

GetMethod() returns a MethodInfo object containing information about the specified method. The binding attributes are used to control the search for the specified method. In addition to a method name, you can also provide a Binder, an array of Types representing the argument types to the method, and an array of parameter modifiers.

GetMethods() returns an array of MethodInfo objects containing information about every method of the current class. The binding attributes are used to control the search for the methods. For instance, they can specify that only information about public methods is returned.

```
PropertyInfo[] GetProperties(BindingFlags bindingAttr)
PropertyInfo GetProperty (string propertyName, BindingFlags bindingAttr)
PropertyInfo GetProperty (string propertyName, BindingFlags bindingAttr,
                 Binder binder,  Type returnType, Type[] types,
                                 ParameterModifiers[] modifiers)
```

GetProperties() returns an array of PropertyInfo objects containing information about every property of the current class. The binding attributes are used to control the search for the properties. For instance, they can specify that only information about public properties is returned.

GetProperty() returns a PropertyInfo object containing information about the specified property. The binding attributes are used to control the search for the specified property. In addition to a property name, you can also specify a Binder, a return type, an array of Types representing the argument types to the method, and an array of parameter modifiers.

```
object InvokeMember(string memberName, BindingFlags invokeAttr, Binder binder,
                 object target, object[] args, ParameterModifiers[] modifiers,
                 CultureInfo info, string[] namedParamters)
```

InvokeMember() is used to invoke the specified member. The invokeAttr and binder arguments represent invocation attributes and binding information. The target is the object on which to invoke the member. The args array contains the number, order, and type of the parameters required by the member. This will be an empty array if there are no parameters. You can also specify parameter modifier and culture-specific information.

Pointer class

The Pointer class provides two static methods for placing or removing an object wrapper of a specified type around a pointer. This is important when dealing with non-CLR code because pointers allow direct access to memory and are not allowed "as-is" in C#. The boxing and unboxing features defined in the Pointer class allow us to deal with unmanaged memory pointers in a managed-memory fashion.

Syntax

```
public sealed class Pointer : ISerializable
```

Hierarchy

```
Object  ---  Pointer
```

Public static methods

```
public static object Box(void* ptr, Type type)
public static void* Unbox(object ptr)
```

Box() provides an object wrapper of the specified type around the specified unmanaged memory pointer. The wrapped object is returned.

Unbox() unwraps a pointer that has previously had an object wrapped around it. The unwrapped pointer is returned.

Summary

In this chapter we've looked at the classes available to us when we want to use reflection in our C# programs. We've looked at the structure of an assembly, and how this can be inspected programmatically.

Programmers reference C# Programmers reference C# Programmers reference

26

Text manipulation

Text is the primary way an application interacts with a user. Text is used to display output, query for input, and present other valuable information to the user. The `System.Text` namespace contains classes that represent ASCII, Unicode, UTF-7, and UTF-8 character encoding schemes. These classes are used to convert character data to an array of bytes and vice versa. You will commonly use these classes when working with byte I/O streams.

The various encoding types are not necessarily compatible. This is an important point when trying to decode byte data read from a file. For example, data written using the Unicode encoding scheme can't be decoded properly with the ASCII, UTF-7, or UTF-8 encoding schemes. This is because the Unicode encoding scheme uses two bytes to represent every character and the other schemes do not. The ASCII, UTF-7, and UTF-8 schemes are compatible when reading and writing ASCII data. For non-ASCII data (characters with integer values greater than 127), none of the schemes are compatible. If your data file is incompatible with the encoding scheme you're using to decode the data, it won't generate an exception – the decoded characters just won't be properly translated.

`System.Text` also contains the `StringBuilder` class. A `String` object is immutable. Once initialized, a string's contents cannot be changed; if you want a different set of characters, a new `String` object must be created. A `StringBuilder` represents a sequence of characters that can be modified without creating a new instance of the `StringBuilder`. A `StringBuilder` can improve performance in a situation where a lot of changes will be made to a string of character data.

Encoding class

The `Encoding` class is the base class for classes that represent encoding schemes. The `Encoding` class defines methods that are used to encode character data into bytes and decode byte arrays into characters. Derived classes of `Encoding` include the `ASCIIEncoding`, `UnicodeEncoding`, `UTF7Encoding`, and `UTF8Encoding` classes. One of the interesting things about the `Encoding` class is that it defines instances of derived classes as static fields.

Syntax

```
public abstract class Encoding
```

Hierarchy

```
Object   ---   Encoding
```

Constructors

```
protected Encoding()
protected Encoding(int codePage)
```

Encoding() is a protected constructor used by derived classes of Encoding. The codePage parameter is an identifier for the encoding scheme. The code page values for the various schemes discussed in this chapter are ASCII = 20127, little-endian Unicode = 1200, big-endian Unicode = 1201, UTF-7 = 65000, and UTF-8 = 65001.

Public static properties

```
public static Encoding ASCII {get;}
public static Encoding BigEndianUnicode {get;}
public static Encoding Default {get;}
public static Encoding Unicode {get;}
public static Encoding UTF7 {get;}
public static Encoding UTF8 {get;}
```

ASCII returns an Encoding object that uses the ASCII encoding scheme.

BigEndianUnicode retrieves an Encoding object for the Unicode format in the big-endian byte order.

Default returns an Encoding object based on the system's current ANSI code page.

Unicode retrieves an Encoding object for the Unicode format using the little-endian byte order.

UTF7 returns an Encoding object based on the UTF-7 format.

UTF8 retrieves an Encoding object representing the UTF-8 format.

Public instance properties

```
public virtual string BodyName {get;}
public virtual int CodePage {get;}
public virtual string EncodingName {get;}
public virtual string HeaderName {get;}
public virtual bool IsBrowserDisplay {get;}
public virtual bool IsBrowserSave {get;}
public virtual bool IsMailNewsDisplay {get;}
public virtual bool IsMailNewsSave {get;}
public virtual string WebName {get;}
public virtual int WindowsCodePage {get;}
```

BodyName returns a name for the encoding scheme that can be used with mail agent body tags. For example, the body name for the US version of the ASCII encoding scheme would be "us-ascii".

CodePage retrieves the code page identifier for the encoding scheme. The code page values for the ASCII, Unicode, UTF 7, and UTF 8 schemes are listed in the *Constructors* section above.

EncodingName returns the name of the encoding scheme.

HeaderName returns a name for the encoding scheme that can be used with mail agent header tags. For example, the header name for the US version of the ASCII encoding scheme would be "us-ascii".

IsBrowserDisplay returns true if the characters decoded using the encoding scheme can be displayed in a browser.

IsBrowserSave returns true if the encoding scheme can be used to save characters displayed in a browser.

IsMailNewsDisplay returns true if the decoded characters can be displayed by news and mail clients, Outlook/Express for example.

IsMailNewsSave returns true if the encoding scheme can be used to save characters displayed in a news or mail client.

WebName retrieves the array of International Assigned Numbers Authority (IANA)-registered names for the encoding. If there is a preferred name, it will be the first name in the String.

WindowsCodePage returns the Windows code page that is closest to the encoding scheme.

Public static methods

```
public static byte[] Convert(Encoding beginEncoding, Encoding endEncoding,
                                                      byte[] bytes)
public static byte[] Convert(Encoding beginEncoding, Encoding endEncoding,
                                    byte[] bytes, int startIndex, int count)
```

Convert() converts the contents of a byte array from one encoding scheme to another. You can convert an entire byte array or a subset of one defined by startIndex and count. The return value is an array containing the converted bytes. An exception is thrown if bytes or either of the Encoding arguments is a null reference or if the integer arguments are out of bounds.

```
public static Encoding GetEncoding(int codePage)
public static Encoding GetEncoding(string encodingName)
```

GetEncoding() returns an Encoding object corresponding to either the specified code page identifier or the name of the encoding scheme. A NotSupportedException is thrown if the input argument is invalid, or if it represents an encoding scheme that is not supported by the local system.

Public instance methods

```
public override bool Equals(object value)
```

Equals() is an overridden version of the method defined in the Object class. It returns true if value is an Encoding object that is equal to the invoking Encoding object.

```
public virtual int GetByteCount(string str)
public virtual int GetByteCount(char[] chars)
public abstract int GetByteCount(char[] chars, int startIndex, int count)
```

GetByteCount() returns the number of bytes required to encode a sequence of characters. The input value can be a String, a character array, or a subset of a character array defined by startIndex and count. An exception is thrown if either the character array or str is a null reference or if the integer arguments are out of bounds.

```
public virtual byte[] GetBytes(string str)
public virtual int GetBytes(string str, int charStartIndex, int charCount,
                                          byte[] bytes, int byteStartIndex)
public virtual byte[] GetBytes(char[] chars)
public virtual byte[] GetBytes(char[] chars, int startIndex, int count)
public abstract int GetBytes(char[] chars, int charStartIndex,
                        int charCount, byte[] bytes, int byteStartIndex)
```

GetBytes() converts a sequence of characters into a sequence of bytes and stores the bytes in a byte array. The characters can either be contained in a String or in a character array. The starting indices of the character and byte arrays as well as the number of characters to convert are specified. The return value is the resulting byte array or the number of bytes that were stored in the byte array. An exception is thrown if either the character array or str is a null reference or if the integer arguments are out of bounds.

```
public virtual int GetCharCount(byte[] bytes)
public abstract int GetCharCount(byte[] bytes, int startIndex, int count)
```

GetCharCount() returns the number of characters that would result if the bytes in the specified byte array were decoded by the invoking Encoding object. You can evaluate this for an entire byte array or a subset of one defined by startIndex and count. An exception is thrown if bytes is a null reference or if the integer arguments are out of bounds.

```
public virtual char[] GetChars(byte[] bytes)
public virtual char[] GetChars(byte[] bytes, int startIndex, int count)
public abstract int GetChars(byte[] bytes, int startByteIndex,
                        int byteCount, char[] chars, int startCharIndex)
```

GetChars() decodes a sequence of bytes into a sequence of characters and stores the characters in a character array. You can convert an entire byte array or a subset of one defined by startByteIndex and byteCount. The return value is either the resulting character array or the number of characters that were stored in the character array. An exception is thrown either if the array is a null reference or if the integer arguments are out of bounds.

```
public virtual Decoder GetDecoder()
public virtual Encoder GetEncoder()
```

GetDecoder() returns the decoder associated with the invoking Encoding object.

GetEncoder() retrieves an encoder associated with the invoking Encoding object. The default implementation simply forwards method calls to the invoking Encoding object. This method can be overridden to provide, for instance, an Encoding object that will maintain a state between successive conversions.

```
public override int GetHashCode()
public abstract int GetMaxByteCount(int charCount)
public abstract int GetMaxCharCount(int byteCount)
public virtual byte[] GetPreamble()
```

`GetHashCode()` returns the 32-bit signed integer hash code for the invoking `Encoding` object.

`GetMaxByteCount()` returns the maximum number of bytes that would be required to encode the specified number of characters.

`GetMaxCharCount()` returns the maximum number of characters that could be decoded from the specified number of bytes.

`GetPreamble()` returns the bytes placed at the beginning of a stream that identify the type of encoding that was used, and can include the Unicode byte order mark.

```
public virtual string GetString(byte[] bytes)
public virtual string GetString(byte[] bytes, int startIndex, int count)
```

`GetString()` returns a `String` containing the decoded bytes of the specified byte array. An entire byte buffer or a subset of one can be decoded. An exception is thrown if `bytes` is a null reference or if the integer arguments are out of bounds.

Example: Encoding class

This simple example demonstrates the use of the `GetString()` method that converts the contents of a byte buffer into a `String`. To see other examples of `Encoding` class methods in action, look to the `ASCIIEncoding`, `Decoder`, `UTF7Encoding`, and `UTF8Encoding` class sections in this chapter.

```csharp
using System;
using System.Text;

public class EncodingDemo
{
  public static void Main()
  {

    //========================================================
    //   A byte array is created with byte representations
    //   of character data.
    //========================================================

    byte[] buf = {0x0061, 0x003d, 0x00c6, 0x00a9,
                  0x0028, 0x0062, 0x002b, 0x0063,
                  0x0029};

    //========================================================
    //   The UTF8 property returns a Encoding object that
    //   uses UTF-8 encoding. This object calls the
    //   GetString() method to convert the byte array to
    //   a String.
    //========================================================

    String str = Encoding.UTF8.GetString(buf);
```

```
            Console.WriteLine(str);
        }
    }
```

Output:

```
    a=Σ(b+c)
```

Note that the command line can be very inaccurate when displaying unicode characters. If the console doesn't produce the desired output (and substitutes a different character instead of a Σ), add the following lines:

```
Using System.IO;
    ...
        FileStream fs = File.Create("EncodingDemo.out");
        fs.Write(buf, 0, buf.Length);
        fs.Close();
    ...
        String str = Encoding.UTF8.GetString(buf);
        Console.WriteLine(str);
    }
```

When you run the code this time, you should have a new file called `EncodingDemo.out` on your system. You can then view the contents of this file in an editor that supports Unicode, for example, Microsoft Word XP. Opening it in Microsoft Word XP brings up the following dialog box:

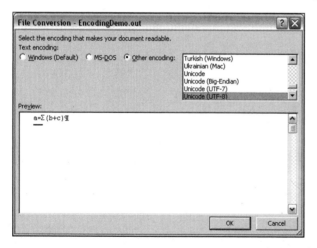

This method applies if you get display errors from the console in the rest of the Unicode examples in this chapter.

ASCIIEncoding class

The ASCIIEncoding class provides the ability to use the ASCII character encoding scheme. The ASCIIEncoding class defines methods that convert strings or character arrays into bytes and to decode byte arrays into a sequence of characters.

In the ASCII encoding scheme, Unicode characters are encoded as single 7-bit ASCII characters. The ASCII character values can range from u\0000 to u\007F (0 to 127). This range is not sufficient to represent the characters used in some languages. Such programs should use Unicode, UTF-7, or UTF-8 encoding.

Syntax

```
public class ASCIIEncoding : Encoding
```

Hierarchy

```
Object   ---   Encoding   ---   ASCIIEncoding
```

Constructors

```
public ASCIIEncoding()
```

ASCIIEncoding() is a no-argument constructor that initializes all fields to their default values.

Public instance methods

```
public override int GetByteCount(string str)
public override int GetByteCount(char[] chars, int startIndex, int count)
public override int GetBytes(string str, int charStartIndex, int charCount,
                                        byte[] bytes, int byteStartIndex)
public override int GetBytes(char[] chars, int charStartIndex,
                        int charCount, byte[] bytes, int byteStartIndex)
```

GetByteCount() returns the number of bytes required to encode a sequence of characters. The input value can be a String or a subset of a character array. An exception is thrown if either the character array or str is a null reference or if the integer arguments are out of bounds.

GetBytes() converts a sequence of characters into a sequence of bytes and stores the bytes in a byte array. The characters can be contained either in a String or in a character array. The starting indices of the character and byte arrays as well as the number of characters to convert are specified. The return value is the number of bytes that were stored in the byte array. An exception is thrown if either the character array or str is a null reference, or if the integer arguments are out of bounds.

```
public override int GetCharCount(byte[] bytes, int startIndex, int count)
public override int GetChars(byte[] bytes, int startByteIndex,
                        int byteCount, char[] chars, int startCharIndex)
```

GetCharCount() returns the number of characters that would result if the bytes in the specified byte array were decoded according to the ASCII encoding scheme. The starting index and number of bytes to decode are specified. An exception is thrown if bytes is a null reference, or if the integer arguments are out of bounds.

`GetChars()` decodes a sequence of bytes into a sequence of characters and stores the characters in a character array. The starting indices of the character and byte arrays as well as the number of bytes to decode are specified. The return value is the number of characters that were stored in the character array. An exception is thrown if either of the arrays is a null reference, or if the integer arguments are out of bounds.

```
public override int GetMaxByteCount(int charCount)
public override int GetMaxCharCount(int byteCount)
```

`GetMaxByteCount()` returns the maximum number of bytes that would be required to encode the specified number of characters. This method can be used to determine a safe byte buffer size for the `GetBytes()` method. An `ArgumentOutOfRangeException` is thrown if `charCount` is less than zero.

`GetMaxCharCount()` returns the maximum number of characters that could be decoded from the specified number of bytes. This method can be used to determine the appropriate character buffer size for the `GetChars()` method. An `ArgumentOutOfRangeException` is thrown if `byteCount` is less than zero.

```
public override string GetString(byte[] bytes)
public override string GetString(byte[] bytes, int startIndex, int count)
```

`GetString()` returns the `String` that results if the specified byte buffer is decoded according to the ASCII scheme. You can decode an entire byte buffer or a subset of one defined by `startIndex` and `count`. An exception is thrown if `bytes` is a null reference or if the integer arguments are out of bounds.

Example: ASCIIEncoding class

In this example, an `ASCIIEncoding` object is used to encode and decode data according to the ASCII encoding scheme. The `ASCIIEncoding` object first converts the elements of a `String` to a byte array and then lists the value of the bytes. The bytes are then written to a file. The `ASCIIEncoding` object then converts the byte data back to characters.

Note that the `String` that is encoded contains only ASCII characters. If the `String` contained higher-value Unicode characters, such as Greek letters or Chinese glyphs, one of the other encoding schemes would have to be used. The non-ASCII character wouldn't cause an exception to be thrown but it would be displayed as another character, possibly a question mark.

```csharp
using System;
using System.IO;
using System.Text;

public class AsciiDemo
{
  public static void Main()
  {
```

```
//=================================================
//  An ASCIIEncoding object and string are created.
//=================================================

ASCIIEncoding encoder = new ASCIIEncoding();

String str = "I like pie";

//=============================================================
//  The ASCIIEncoding object converts the string to a series
//  of bytes according to the ASCII encoding scheme and
//  stores the bytes in a byte buffer. The byte values are
//  written out.
//=============================================================

byte[] buf = new byte[encoder.GetByteCount(str)];
int j = encoder.GetBytes(str, 0, str.Length, buf, 0);

for(int i=0; i<buf.Length; ++i)
{
  Console.WriteLine("byte {0} is {1,2:X}",i,buf[i]);
}
Console.WriteLine();

//=============================================================
//  A FileStream is created and used to write the contents
//  of the byte buffer to a file named "AsciiDemo.out"
//=============================================================

FileStream fs = File.Create("AsciiDemo.out");
fs.Write(buf, 0, buf.Length);
fs.Close();

//=============================================================
//  We now use the ASCIIEncoding object to convert the contents
//  of the byte array back into character data.
//=============================================================

int length = encoder.GetCharCount(buf, 0, buf.Length);
char[] charArray = new char[length];

encoder.GetChars(buf, 0, buf.Length, charArray, 0);
Console.WriteLine(charArray);

  }
}
```

Output:

```
byte 0 is 49
byte 1 is 20
byte 2 is 6C
```

```
byte 3 is 69
byte 4 is 6B
byte 5 is 65
byte 6 is 20
byte 7 is 70
byte 8 is 69
byte 9 is 65

I like pie
```

There are 10 characters in the string (including two whitespace characters) and there are 10 bytes in the byte array.

UnicodeEncoding class

The UnicodeEncoding class is used to convert character data to bytes and vice versa using the Unicode encoding scheme. This scheme encodes each character in UTF-16 format as two consecutive bytes. The byte order can be little-endian (code page = 1200) or big-endian (code page = 1201). In little-endian format, the least significant byte is written and read first. In big-endian format, the most significant byte is written and read first. Unicode files may also contain a byte order mark at the beginning of the file that identifies the type of byte ordering.

Syntax

```
public class UnicodeEncoding : Encoding
```

Hierarchy

```
Object  ---  Encoding  ---  UnicodeEncoding
```

Constructors

```
public UnicodeEncoding()
public UnicodeEncoding(bool bigEndian, bool byteOrderMark)
```

UnicodeEncoding() creates a UnicodeEncoding object. If bigEndian is true, the encoding will use big-endian format. The default is to use little-endian format. If byteOrderMark is true, a byte order mark will be included in the encoding. The default is true.

Fields

```
public const int CharSize
```

CharSize is the Unicode version 2.0 character size in bytes.

Public instance methods

```
public override bool Equals(object value)
```

Equals() is an overridden version of the method defined in the Object class. It returns true if value is an UnicodeEncoding object that is equal to the invoking UnicodeEncoding object.

```
public override int GetByteCount(string str)
public override int GetByteCount(char[] chars, int startIndex, int count)
```

GetByteCount() returns the number of bytes required to encode a sequence of characters. The input value can be a String or a subset of a character array defined by startIndex and count. An exception is thrown if the character array or str is a null reference or if the integer arguments are out of bounds.

```
public override byte[] GetBytes(string str)
public override int GetBytes(string str, int charStartIndex, int charCount,
                                        byte[] bytes, int byteStartIndex)
public override int GetBytes(char[] chars, int charStartIndex,
                        int charCount, byte[] bytes, int byteStartIndex)
```

GetBytes() converts a sequence of characters into a sequence of bytes and stores the bytes in a byte array. The characters can be contained either in a String or in a character array. The starting indices of the character and byte arrays as well as the number of characters to convert are specified. The return value is the resulting byte array or the number of bytes that were stored in the byte array. An exception is thrown if the character array or str is a null reference or if the integer arguments are out of bounds.

```
public override int GetCharCount(byte[] bytes, int startIndex, int count)
public override int GetChars(byte[] bytes, int startByteIndex,
                        int byteCount, char[] chars, int startCharIndex)
```

GetCharCount() returns the number of characters that would result if the bytes in the specified byte array were decoded by the invoking UnicodeEncoding object. The starting index of the byte array and number of bytes to decode are specified. An exception is thrown if bytes is a null reference or if startIndex and count do not specify a valid range.

GetChars() decodes a sequence of bytes into a sequence of characters and stores the characters in a character array. The starting indices of the byte and character arrays are specified along with the number of bytes to decode. The return value is the number of characters that were stored in the character array. An exception is thrown if either array is a null reference or if the integer arguments are out of bounds.

```
public override Decoder GetDecoder()
public override int GetHashCode()
public override int GetMaxByteCount(int charCount)
public override int GetMaxCharCount(int byteCount)
public virtual byte[] GetPreamble()
```

GetDecoder() returns a Decoder associated with the invoking UnicodeEncoding object.

GetHashCode() returns the 32-bit signed integer hash code for the invoking UnicodeEncoding object.

GetMaxByteCount() returns the maximum number of bytes that would be required to encode the specified number of characters.

`GetMaxCharCount()` returns the maximum number of characters that could be decoded from the specified number of bytes.

`GetPreamble()` returns the bytes placed at the beginning of a stream that identify the type of encoding that was used. If the `UnicodeEncoding` object does not use a byte order mark, an empty array is returned.

Example: UnicodeEncoding class

This example is similar to the example from the *ASCIIEncoding class* section. A `UnicodeEncoding` object is used to convert a string into a series of bytes according to the Unicode encoding scheme. In this case, the string includes the Greek letter π. The ASCII encoding scheme would not be able to properly convert this character.

The bytes are placed into a byte array and the byte values are printed out. The `UnicodeEncoding` object is then used to convert the bytes back into a `String` using the `GetString()` method. The `String` is printed out.

```
using System;
using System.Text;

public class UnicodeDemo
{
  public static void Main()
  {

    UnicodeEncoding encoder = new UnicodeEncoding();
    String str = "I like "+'\u03a0';

    //=============================================================
    //   The UnicodeEncoding object converts the string to a series
    //   of bytes according to the Unicode encoding scheme and
    //   stores the bytes in a byte buffer. The byte values are
    //   printed out.
    //=============================================================

    byte[] buf = new byte[encoder.GetByteCount(str)];
    int j = encoder.GetBytes(str, 0, str.Length, buf, 0);

    for(int i=0; i<buf.Length; ++i)
    {
       Console.WriteLine("byte {0} is {1,2:X}",i,buf[i]);
    }
    Console.WriteLine();

    //=============================================================
    //   We now use the UnicodeEncoding object to convert the
    //   contents of the byte array back into a string.
    //=============================================================

    String str2 = encoder.GetString(buf);
```

```
        Console.WriteLine(str2);
    }
}
```

Output:

```
byte 0 is 49
byte 1 is  0
byte 2 is 20
byte 3 is  0
byte 4 is 6C
byte 5 is  0
byte 6 is 69
byte 7 is  0
byte 8 is 6B
byte 9 is  0
byte 10 is 65
byte 11 is  0
byte 12 is 20
byte 13 is  0
byte 14 is A0
byte 15 is  3

I like π
```

Notice that there are now 16 bytes in the byte buffer. This is because there were eight characters in the string and Unicode encoding uses two bytes to represent each character. Also note that for the ASCII characters, the first byte in the Unicode encoding scheme is the same as the byte used in the ASCII encoding scheme.

UTF7Encoding class

The UTF7Encoding class is used to convert character and byte data using the UCS Transformation Format, 7-bit (UTF-7) formatting scheme. This coding supports all Unicode characters. Characters with integer values of 127 and less are represented by a single byte. Characters with integer values greater than 127 are represented with multiple bytes. The code page value assigned to the UTF-7 encoding scheme is 65000.

Syntax

```
public class UTF7Encoding :  Encoding
```

Hierarchy

```
Object  ---  Encoding  ---  UTF7Encoding
```

Constructors

```
public UTF7Encoding()
public UTF7Encoding(bool allowOptionals)
```

UTF7Encoding() creates a UTF7Encoding object. The allowOptionals parameter determines how the UTF7Encoding object handles characters whose integer value is larger than 127. If allowOptionals is true, these characters are represented by an optional character (!, #, $, %, etc.) instead of with a modified base-64 character. By default allowOptionals is false.

Public instance methods

```
public override int GetByteCount(char[] chars, int startIndex, int count)
public override int GetBytes(char[] chars, int charStartIndex, int charCount,
                            byte[] bytes, int byteStartIndex)
```

GetByteCount() returns the number of bytes required to encode count characters in the specified character array starting at index startIndex. An exception is thrown if chars is a null reference, or if the integer arguments are out of bounds.

GetBytes() converts a sequence of characters into a series of bytes that are placed into a byte array. The starting indices of the character and byte arrays as well as the number of characters to convert are specified. The return value is the number of bytes that were stored in the byte array. An exception is thrown if chars or bytes is a null reference, or if the integer arguments are out of bounds.

```
public override int GetCharCount(byte[] bytes, int startIndex, int count)
public override int GetChars(byte[] bytes, int startByteIndex, int byteCount,
                            char[] chars, int startCharIndex)
```

GetCharCount() returns the number of characters that would result if the bytes in the specified byte array were decoded by the invoking UTF7Encoding object. The starting index of the byte array and number of bytes to decode are specified. An exception is thrown if bytes is a null reference or if startIndex and count do not specify a valid range.

GetChars() decodes a sequence of bytes into a sequence of characters and stores the characters in a character array. The starting indices of the byte and character arrays are specified along with the number of bytes to decode. The return value is the number of characters that were stored in the character array. An exception is thrown if chars or bytes is a null reference, if bytes contains an invalid sequence of bytes, or if the integer arguments are out of bounds.

```
public override Decoder GetDecoder()
public override Encoder GetEncoder()
public override int GetMaxByteCount(int charCount)
public override int GetMaxCharCount(int byteCount)
```

GetDecoder() returns a Decoder associated with the invoking UTF7Encoding object.

GetEncoder() returns an Encoder associated with the invoking UTF7Encoding object. The default implementation simply forwards method calls by the Encoder back to the invoking UTF7Encoding object.

GetMaxByteCount() returns the maximum number of bytes that would be required to encode the specified number of characters.

GetMaxCharCount() returns the maximum number of characters that could be decoded from the specified number of bytes.

452

Example: UTF7Encoding class

In this example a UTF7Encoding object is used to encode the string "I like π". The GetBytes() method converts the string to a series of bytes that are stored in a byte array. The contents of the array are written out. The encoder then converts the bytes back into a String.

There are a total of 12 bytes in the byte array. The seven ASCII characters at the beginning of the string are represented by one byte each. The byte values are the same as were seen in the *ASCIIEncoding class* example. The Greek character at the end of the string requires five bytes. This is a UTF-7 modified base-64 character representation of the character π.

```
using System;
using System.Text;

public class UTF7Demo
{
  public static void Main()
  {

    UTF7Encoding encoder = new UTF7Encoding(true);
    String str = "I like "+'\u03a0';

    //=============================================================
    //   The UTF7Encoding object converts the string to a series
    //   of bytes according to the UTF 7 encoding scheme and
    //   stores the bytes in a byte buffer. The byte values are
    //   printed out.
    //=============================================================

    byte[] buf = new byte[encoder.GetByteCount(str)];
    int j = encoder.GetBytes(str, 0, str.Length, buf, 0);

    for(int i=0; i<buf.Length; ++i)
    {
      Console.WriteLine("byte {0} is {1,2:X}",i,buf[i]);
    }
    Console.WriteLine();

    //=============================================================
    //   We now use the UTF7Encoding object to convert the
    //   contents of the byte array back into a string.
    //=============================================================

    Console.WriteLine(encoder.GetString(buf));
  }
}
```

Output:

```
byte 0 is 49
byte 1 is 20
```

```
byte 2 is 6C
byte 3 is 69
byte 4 is 6B
byte 5 is 65
byte 6 is 20
byte 7 is 2B
byte 8 is 41
byte 9 is 36
byte 10 is 41
byte 11 is 2D

I like π
```

UTF8Encoding class

The UTF8Encoding class permits character to byte conversions using the UCS Transformation Format, 8-bit (UTF-8) encoding scheme. The UTF-8 scheme supports all Unicode characters. Characters with integer values of 127 and less are represented by a single byte. Characters with integer values greater than 127 are represented with two bytes. The code page value assigned to UTF-8 encoding is 65001.

Syntax

```
public class UTF8Encoding : Encoding
```

Hierarchy

```
Object  ---  Encoding  ---  UTF8Encoding
```

Constructors

```
public UTF8Encoding()
public UTF8Encoding(bool emitIdentifier)
public UTF8Encoding(bool emitIdentifier, bool throwError)
```

UTF8Encoding() creates a UTF8Encoding object. If the emitIdentifier parameter is true, a Unicode byte order mark in UTF-8 must be emitted when encoding. If the throwError parameter is true, an exception will be thrown if invalid bytes are detected.

Public instance methods

```
public override bool Equals(object value)
```

Equals() returns true if value is a UTF8Encoding object that is equal to the invoking UTF8Encoding object.

```
public override int GetByteCount(string str)
public override int GetByteCount(char[] chars, int startIndex, int count)
```

GetByteCount() returns the number of bytes required to encode a sequence of characters. The input value can be a String or a subset of a character array defined by startIndex and count. An exception is thrown if the character array or str is a null reference or if the integer arguments are out of bounds.

```
public override byte[] GetBytes(string str)
public override int GetBytes(string str, int charStartIndex,
                    int charCount, byte[] bytes, int byteStartIndex)
public override int GetBytes(char[] chars, int charStartIndex,
                    int charCount, byte[] bytes, int byteStartIndex)
```

GetBytes() converts a sequence of characters into a series of bytes that are stored in a byte array. The characters can be contained either in a String or in a character array. The starting indices of the character and byte arrays as well as the number of characters to convert are specified. The return value is the resulting byte array or the number of bytes that were stored in the byte array. An exception is thrown if the array or str is a null reference or if the integer arguments are out of bounds.

```
public override int GetCharCount(byte[] bytes, int startIndex, int count)
public override int GetChars(byte[] bytes, int startByteIndex,
                    int byteCount, char[] chars, int startCharIndex)
```

GetCharCount() returns the number of characters that would result if the bytes in the specified byte array were decoded by the invoking UTF8Encoding object. The starting index of the byte array and number of bytes to decode are specified. An exception is thrown if bytes is a null reference, or if the integer arguments are out of bounds.

GetChars() decodes a sequence of bytes into a sequence of characters and stores the characters in a character array. The starting indices of the byte and character arrays are specified along with the number of bytes to decode. The return value is the number of characters that were stored in the character array. An exception is thrown if chars or bytes is a null reference, if bytes contains an invalid sequence of bytes, or if the integer arguments are out of bounds.

```
public override Decoder GetDecoder()
public override Encoder GetEncoder()
```

GetDecoder() returns a Decoder associated with the invoking UTF8Encoding object.

GetEncoder() returns an Encoder associated with the invoking UTF8Encoding object. The default implementation simply forwards method calls by the Encoder back to the invoking UTF8Encoding object.

```
public override int GetHashCode()
public override int GetMaxByteCount(int charCount)
public override int GetMaxCharCount(int byteCount)
public virtual byte[] GetPreamble()
```

GetHashCode() returns the 32-bit signed integer hash code for the invoking UTF8Encoding object.

GetMaxByteCount() returns the maximum number of bytes that would be required to encode the specified number of characters.

GetMaxCharCount() returns the maximum number of characters that could be decoded from the specified number of bytes.

GetPreamble() returns the bytes placed at the beginning of a stream that identify the type of encoding that was used. If the UTF8Encoding object does not use a byte order mark, an empty array is returned.

Example: UTF8Encoding class

This example is similar to the example in the *UTF7Encoding class* section except in this example a UTF8Encoding object is used to encode the string "I like π". The GetBytes() method converts the String to a series of bytes that are stored in a byte array. The contents of the array are written out. The encoder then converts the bytes back into a String.

The UTF-8 encoding scheme is a little more efficient than the UTF-7 scheme in that higher value characters only require two bytes to represent them. Compare the output of this example with the output from the UTF7Encoding class example. The first seven bytes, those representing the ASCII characters, are the same, but the bytes that represent the Greek character are different.

```
using System;
using System.Text;

public class UTF8Demo
{
  public static void Main()
  {

    UTF8Encoding encoder = new UTF8Encoding(true);
    String str = "I like "+'\u03a0';

    //=============================================================
    //   The UTF8Encoding object converts the string to a series
    //   of bytes according to the UTF 8 encoding scheme and
    //   stores the bytes in a byte buffer. The byte values are
    //   printed out.
    //=============================================================

    byte[] buf = new byte[encoder.GetByteCount(str)];
    int j = encoder.GetBytes(str, 0, str.Length, buf, 0);

    for(int i=0; i<buf.Length; ++i)
    {
      Console.WriteLine("byte {0} is {1,2:X}",i,buf[i]);
    }
    Console.WriteLine();

    //=============================================================
    //   We now use the UTF8Encoding object to convert the
    //   contents of the byte array back into a string.
    //=============================================================
```

```
        Console.WriteLine(encoder.GetString(buf));
    }
}
```

Output:

```
byte 0 is 49
byte 1 is 20
byte 2 is 6C
byte 3 is 69
byte 4 is 6B
byte 5 is 65
byte 6 is 20
byte 7 is CE
byte 8 is A0

I like π
```

Decoder class

The abstract `Decoder` class defines a class used to convert a sequence of bytes into characters. A `Decoder` will maintain state between successive conversions allowing it to properly decode a character whose bytes may span multiple blocks of data. The `Decoder` class defines no public constructors (and is abstract anyway). The usual way to obtain a `Decoder` object is to have an `Encoding` object invoke the `GetDecoder()` method.

Syntax

```
public abstract class Decoder
```

Hierarchy

```
Object   ---   Decoder
```

Constructors

```
protected Decoder()
```

`Decoder()` is a protected constructor provided for use by derived classes of `Decoder`.

Public instance methods

```
public abstract int GetCharCount(byte[] bytes, int startIndex, int count)
public abstract int GetChars(byte[] bytes, int startByteIndex,
                        int byteCount, char[] chars, int startCharIndex)
```

`GetCharCount()` returns the number of characters that would result if the bytes in the specified byte array were decoded. The starting index of the byte array and number of bytes to decode are specified. An exception is thrown if `bytes` is a null reference, or if the integer arguments are out of bounds.

GetChars() decodes a sequence of bytes into a sequence of characters and stores the characters in a character array. The starting indices of the byte and character arrays are specified as well as the number of bytes to decode. The return value is the number of characters that were stored in the character array. An exception is thrown if either chars or bytes is a null reference, or if the integer arguments are out of bounds.

Example: Decoder class

Decoder objects are particularly useful when the bytes that make up a Unicode character might span multiple reads. For instance, say a Unicode character is represented by two bytes and the buffer size for a read operation is 4096 bytes. It is possible that the first byte of the character might be read in as the 4096th byte of one read operation and the second byte might be read in as the first read of the next read operation. Because a Decoder maintains state between successive read operations, the character can be properly reconstructed.

This example demonstrates how this is done. A Decoder object corresponding to the UTF-8 encoding scheme is obtained using the GetDecoder() method. The Decoder will decode bytes that represent the String "a+d=Σ(b+c)". The bytes are stored in two byte buffers. The 'Σ' character is represented by two bytes. The first byte is at the end of the first byte buffer. The second byte of the 'Σ' character is at the beginning of the second byte buffer.

This presents no problem to the Decoder. It reconstructs the String with successive calls to the GetChars() method keeping track of how many characters were decoded in the first call to the method. The reconstructed String is then printed out.

```
using System;
using System.Text;

public class DecoderDemo
{
  public static void Main()
  {

    //=================================================
    //   The GetDecoder() method returns a reference
    //   to a Decoder object.
    //=================================================

    Decoder decoder = Encoding.UTF8.GetDecoder();

    //===================================================
    //   Two byte arrays are created. The bytes correspond
    //   to Unicode character data. One of the characters
    //   is represented by two bytes. The first byte is at
    //   the end of buf1. The second byte is at the
    //   beginning of buf2.
    //===================================================

    byte[] buf1 = {0x0061, 0x002b, 0x0064, 0x003d, 0x00c6};
```

```
        byte[] buf2 = {0x00a9, 0x0028, 0x0062, 0x002b, 0x0063, 0x0029};

        char[] charArray = new char[10];

        //============================================================
        //  The Decoder calls the GetChars() method to decode the
        //  bytes from the two byte arrays. Because the Decoder
        //  maintains state between successive conversions, it is
        //  able to reconstruct the two-byte character even though
        //  the bytes are stored in different buffers.
        //============================================================

        int i = decoder.GetChars(buf1, 0, buf1.Length, charArray, 0);
        decoder.GetChars(buf2, 0, buf2.Length, charArray, i);

        Console.WriteLine(charArray);
    }
}
```

Output:

```
a+d=Σ(b+c)
```

Encoder class

The Encoder class represents an object that is used to convert a sequence of characters into bytes. An Encoder will maintain state between successive conversions allowing it to properly encode a character sequence that may span multiple blocks of data. The Encoder class defines no public constructors. The usual way to obtain an Encoder object is to have an Encoding object invoke the GetEncoder() method.

Syntax

```
public abstract class Encoder
```

Hierarchy

```
Object  ---  Encoder
```

Constructors

```
protected Encoder()
```

Encoder() is a protected constructor provided for use by derived classes of Encoder.

Public instance methods

```
public abstract int GetByteCount(char[] chars, int startIndex,
                                            int count, bool flush)
public abstract int GetBytes(char[] chars, int charStartIndex,
                        int charCount, byte[] bytes, int byteStartIndex)
```

GetByteCount() returns the number of bytes required to encode a sequence of characters contained in a character array. The index of the character array at which to start the evaluation and the number of characters to evaluate are specified. If the flush parameter is true, the Encoder will flush its internal state following the conversion. An exception is thrown if chars is a null reference, or if the integer arguments are out of bounds.

GetBytes() converts a sequence of characters from a character array into a sequence of bytes and stores the bytes in a byte array. The starting indices of the character and byte arrays, as well as the number of characters to convert, are specified. If flush is true, the Encoder will flush its internal state following the conversion. The return value is the number of bytes that were stored in the byte array. An exception is thrown if either chars or bytes is a null reference, or if the integer arguments are out of bounds.

StringBuilder class

A StringBuilder represents a sequence of characters that can be modified without creating a new instance of the class. This is in contrast to the String class that encapsulates an immutable sequence of characters. In a situation where a lot of changes will be made to a character string, using a StringBuilder instead of a String will improve performance. When you are finished modifying a StringBuilder, its contents can easily be placed into a String.

Syntax

```
public sealed class StringBuilder
```

Hierarchy

```
Object  ---  StringBuilder
```

Constructors

```
public StringBuilder()
public StringBuilder(int capacity)
public StringBuilder(string value)
public StringBuilder(int capacity, int maxCapacity)
public StringBuilder(string value, int capacity)
public StringBuilder(string value, int startIndex, int length, int capacity)
```

StringBuilder() creates a StringBuilder object. The no-argument constructor returns an empty StringBuilder with a capacity of 16 characters. The capacity of the StringBuilder will automatically be increased if the StringBuilder length reaches its capacity. An initial string, an initial capacity, and a maximum capacity can be specified. If startIndex and length parameters are provided, the StringBuilder will be initialized with a substring of the specified String.

Properties

```
public int Capacity {get; set;}
public chars this[int index] {get; set;}
public int Length {get; set;}
public int MaxCapacity {get;}
```

Capacity returns or changes the capacity of the StringBuilder.

`this` is the indexer for the `StringBuilder` class. It is used to get or set the character at the specified position.

`Length` retrieves or sets the length of the `StringBuilder`. If this value is set to be less than its current length, the `StringBuilder` is truncated. Attempting to set `Length` less than zero or greater than `MaxCapacity` causes an `ArgumentOutOfRangeException`.

`MaxCapacity` returns the maximum capacity of the `StringBuilder`.

Public instance methods

```
public StringBuilder Append(bool value)
public StringBuilder Append(byte value)
public StringBuilder Append(char value)
public StringBuilder Append(char value, int repeatCount)
public StringBuilder Append(char[] value)
public StringBuilder Append(char[] value, int startIndex, int count)
public StringBuilder Append(decimal value)
public StringBuilder Append(double value)
public StringBuilder Append(short value)
public StringBuilder Append(int value)
public StringBuilder Append(long value)
public StringBuilder Append(object value)
public StringBuilder Append(sbyte value)
public StringBuilder Append(float value)
public StringBuilder Append(string value)
public StringBuilder Append(string value, int startIndex, int count)
public StringBuilder Append(ushort value)
public StringBuilder Append(uint value)
public StringBuilder Append(ulong value)
```

`Append()` appends a value to the end of the invoking `StringBuilder`. In many cases the `ToString()` method is used to implicitly convert the input argument to a `String` first. The return value is a reference to the modified `StringBuilder`. The `repeatCount` parameter adds that number of characters. Specifying a `startIndex` and a `count` means a substring of the character array or `String` will be appended.

```
public StringBuilder AppendFormat(string format, object obj)
public StringBuilder AppendFormat(string format, object objA, object objB)
public StringBuilder AppendFormat(string format, object objA, object objB,
                                                          object objC)
public StringBuilder AppendFormat(string format, param object[] objs)
public StringBuilder AppendFormat(IFormatProvider provider, string format,
                                                    param object[] objs)
```

`AppendFormat()` appends a formatted string to the end of the invoking `StringBuilder` and returns a reference to the modified `StringBuilder`. An `IFormatProvider` can be specified to provide some culture-specific formatting information. The format string will contain zero or more format specifiers of the form `{N,W:F}` where `N` is a zero-based integer indicating the argument to be formatted, `W` is optional and defines the width of the formatted value, and `F` is a formatting code. The objects provide the arguments to the formatted string. For example:

```
double d = 0.18;
StringBuilder sb = new StringBuilder();
sb.AppendFormat("percentage is {0:P}",d);
```

The above is an example of using AppendFormat() to express a double as a percentage.

```
public int EnsureCapacity(int capacity)
public new bool Equals(StringBuilder sb)
```

EnsureCapacity() checks the current capacity of the invoking StringBuilder against the specified value. If the current capacity is less than capacity, it is increased to that value.

Equals() returns true if the invoking StringBuilder and sb contain the same sequence of characters.

```
public StringBuilder Insert(int index, bool value)
public StringBuilder Insert(int index, byte value)
public StringBuilder Insert(int index, char value)
public StringBuilder Insert(int index, char[] value)
public StringBuilder Insert(int index, char[] value, int startIndex,
                                                      int count)
public StringBuilder Insert(int index, decimal value)
public StringBuilder Insert(int index, double value)
public StringBuilder Insert(int index, short value)
public StringBuilder Insert(int index, int value)
public StringBuilder Insert(int index, long value)
public StringBuilder Insert(int index, object value)
public StringBuilder Insert(int index, sbyte value)
public StringBuilder Insert(int index, float value)
public StringBuilder Insert(int index, string value)
public StringBuilder Insert(int index, string value, int repeatCount)
public StringBuilder Insert(int index, ushort value)
public StringBuilder Insert(int index, uint value)
public StringBuilder Insert(int index, ulong value)
```

Insert() places the specified value into the invoking StringBuilder at the specified position. In many cases the ToString() method is used to implicitly convert the input argument to a String first. The return value is a reference to the modified StringBuilder. Specifying a startIndex and a count means a substring of the character array will be inserted. The repeatCount parameter indicates the number of times the specified String will be inserted.

```
public StringBuilder Remove(int startIndex, int count)
```

Remove() removes the specified number of characters starting at the specified index from the invoking StringBuilder. A reference to the modified StringBuilder is returned. An ArgumentOutOfRangeException is thrown if the integer arguments are out of bounds.

```
public StringBuilder Replace(char oldChar, char newChar)
public StringBuilder Replace(string oldString, string newString)
public StringBuilder Replace(char oldChar, char newChar, int startIndex, int
                                                      count)
```

```
public StringBuilder Replace(string oldString, string newString, int startIndex,
                                                                  int count)
```

Replace() replaces all of the instances of a character or String in the invoking StringBuilder. A reference to the modified StringBuilder is returned. The replacement can be performed throughout the entire StringBuilder or over a subset of it defined by startIndex and count. An ArgumentOutOfRangeException is thrown if the integer arguments are out of bounds.

```
public override string ToString()
public string ToString(int startIndex, int length)
```

ToString() converts the invoking StringBuilder to a String. You can convert the entire contents of the StringBuilder or a subset of it defined by startIndex and count. An ArgumentOutOfRangeException is thrown if the integer arguments are out of bounds.

Example: StringBuilder class

The big advantage of using the StringBuilder class over the String class is that you can make changes to a StringBuilder without creating a new instance of it. If there is a situation where an application will be making a lot of changes to a character string, using a StringBuilder will improve the performance of the code.

This example compares the performance difference between a String and a StringBuilder when they are used to execute a character replacement. An instance of each class is created and initialized with the same string of characters. Both instances then perform a character replacement by calling the Replace() method. To highlight the differences, the replace operation is performed many times.

The time it takes each loop to execute is computed as well as the additional memory that needs to be allocated to perform the loop. The StringBuilder doesn't need any additional memory allocation because the same instance is modified each time. Not only does the String take longer to execute the loop but there is memory overhead as well because a new String instance is created every time the Replace() method is called.

```
using System;
using System.Text;
using System.Threading;

public class SBDemo
{
  public static void Main()
  {
    int maxIteration = 500000;
    long startTime, startMemory, stringMemory, sbMemory;
    double stringTime, sbTime;

    StringBuilder sb = new StringBuilder("On your marks");
    String str = "On your marks";

    //=====================================================
```

```
    //  Evaluate the performance of a StringBuilder as it
    //  performs a character replacement over and over.
    //=======================================================

    startMemory = GC.GetTotalMemory(false);
    startTime = DateTime.Now.Ticks;

    for(int i=0; i<maxIteration; ++i)
    {
      sb.Replace('m','g');
    }

    sbTime = (DateTime.Now.Ticks - startTime)/1.0e+7;
    sbMemory = GC.GetTotalMemory(false) - startMemory;

    //=======================================================
    // Now see how a string performs doing the same thing.
    //=======================================================

    startMemory = GC.GetTotalMemory(false);
    startTime = DateTime.Now.Ticks;

    for(int i=0; i<maxIteration; ++i)
    {
      str = str.Replace('m','g');
    }

    stringTime = (DateTime.Now.Ticks - startTime)/1.0e+7;
    stringMemory = GC.GetTotalMemory(false) - startMemory;

    Console.WriteLine("StringBuilder Loop Results: \n");
    Console.WriteLine("   elapsed time     = {0} seconds",sbTime);
    Console.WriteLine("   memory allocated = {0} bytes",sbMemory);
    Console.WriteLine("\nString Loop Results: \n");
    Console.WriteLine("   elapsed time     = {0} seconds",stringTime);
    Console.WriteLine("   memory allocated = {0} bytes",stringMemory);
  }
}
```

Output:

```
StringBuilder Loop Results:

    elapsed time     =  0.046875 seconds
    memory allocated =  0

String Loop Results:

    elapsed time     =  0.125 seconds
    memory allocated =  57240
```

Summary

In this chapter we've looked at the different classes available in the `System.Text` namespace, which represent various character encoding schemes, including ASCII, Unicode, UTF-7, and UTF-8. We've also looked at the `StringBuilder` class, which gives us a performance boost and flexibility when working with a string of character data.

Programmers reference C# Programmers reference C# Programmers reference

27

Regular expressions

A regular expression is a sequence of characters that defines a pattern that can be used to match a set of strings. The sequence of characters may include escape characters, other special characters, and character sequences that refine the search. A regular expression is used in the implementation of the "search" and "replace" functionality of a document editor or any application that manipulates character data. This chapter provides details of the regular expression classes that are provided in the `System.Text.RegularExpressions` namespace that exists in the .NET Framework.

The hierarchy of the classes discussed in this chapter is shown below. The `Regex` class encapsulates a regular expression. In addition to finding matches in text, a `Regex` object can be used to split a string or replace characters in a string. The `Match`, `Capture`, and `Group` classes represent three search components. A match occurs when an instance of the regular expression is found in the text being searched. A match will contain one or more capturing groups represented by the `Group` class. The number of groups depends on how the regular expression was defined. The `Capture` class encapsulates a capture string. A `Group` will contain one or more `Captures`.

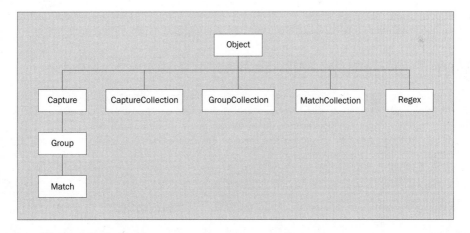

Also found in the namespace are classes that represent collections of `Groups`, `Matches`, and `Captures`. These collection classes all define a method to obtain an `IEnumerator` that can be used to iterate through the collection as well as an indexer to return a reference to an individual element of the collection.

Capture class

The Capture class represents a substring of a successful capture. A capture occurs when a match is found between a regular expression and part of a String. The Capture class is the base class of the Group and Match classes. The Capture class does not define any constructors. To obtain a Capture object, use the Captures property of the Group class.

Syntax

```
public class Capture
```

Hierarchy

```
Object   ---   Capture
```

Properties

```
public int Index {get;}
public int Length {get;}
public string Value {get;}
```

Index retrieves the position in the original String of the first character of the captured substring.

Length returns the length of the captured substring.

Value returns the captured substring.

Public instance methods

```
public override string ToString()
```

ToString() returns the captured substring.

For an example of the Capture class, see the example in the *Match class* section where the Value property is used to display the captures that result from a regular expression search.

CaptureCollection class

The CaptureCollection class represents a collection of capture substrings. The collection is read-only. The CaptureCollection class defines no constructors. A CaptureCollection can be obtained through the Captures property of the Group class. The elements of a CaptureCollection can be accessed using the GetEnumerator() method or by using the CaptureCollection class indexer.

Syntax

```
public class CaptureCollection : ICollection, IEnumerable
```

Hierarchy

```
Object   ---   CaptureCollection
```

Properties

```
public int Count {get;}
public bool IsReadOnly {get;}
public bool IsSynchronized {get;}
public Capture this[int i] {get;}
public object SyncRoot {get;}
```

Count returns the number of items in the CaptureCollection.

IsReadOnly returns true if the collection is read-only. The default is true. If you created a read-write derived class of CaptureCollection you would define this property to return false.

IsSynchronized returns true if access to the collection is synchronized.

this[] is the indexer for the CaptureCollection. It returns the Capture object at the specified index.

SyncRoot gets an object that can be used to synchronize access to the collection. Synchronized operations are performed on the SyncRoot rather than on the CaptureCollection itself.

Public instance methods

```
public void CopyTo(Array array, int arrayIndex)
public IEnumerator GetEnumerator()
```

CopyTo() copies all of the elements of the invoking CaptureCollection into the specified Array starting at the specified index. The length of the destination Array must be at least as large as the length of the CaptureCollection added to arrayIndex. An exception is thrown if array is a null reference, or if arrayIndex is out of bounds.

GetEnumerator() returns an IEnumerator that can be used to iterate through the elements of the CaptureCollection.

For an example of the CaptureCollection class, see the example in the *Match class* section where a CaptureCollection is obtained for each group resulting from a regular expression search.

Group class

The Group class encapsulates a single capturing group. A group may contain zero or more capture substrings. A Group can be used to supply a collection of Capture objects. The Group class defines no constructors. A collection of Group objects can be obtained through the Groups property of the Match class. Instances of the Group class are not guaranteed to be thread-safe.

Syntax

```
public class Group : Capture
```

The Group class is a derived class of the Object and Capture classes and has access to the properties and methods defined in those classes.

Hierarchy

```
Object  ---  Capture  ---  Group
```

Properties

```
public CaptureCollection Captures {get;}
public bool Success {get;}
```

Captures retrieves a collection of all of the captures matched by the capturing group. The collection may have zero elements if there were no captures.

Success returns true if there was at least one substring captured by the group.

Public static methods

```
public static Group Synchronized(Group inner)
```

Synchronized() places a thread-safe wrapper around the specified Group and returns a reference to the wrapped Group.

For an example of the Group class, see the example in the *Match class* section where a series of Group objects are used to display the results from a regular expression search.

GroupCollection class

The GroupCollection class represents a collection of captured groups. The collection is read-only. The GroupCollection class defines no constructors. A GroupCollection can be obtained through the Groups property of the Group class. The elements of a GroupCollection can be accessed using the GetEnumerator() method or by using the GroupCollection class indexer.

Syntax

```
public class GroupCollection : ICollection, IEnumerable
```

Hierarchy

```
Object  ---  GroupCollection
```

Properties

```
public int Count {get;}
public bool IsReadOnly {get;}
public bool IsSynchronized {get;}
public object SyncRoot {get;}
public Group this[int groupNumber] {get;}
public Group this[string groupName] {get;}
```

Count returns the number of items in the GroupCollection.

IsReadOnly returns true if the collection is read-only, which is the default. If you defined a read-write derived class of GroupCollection, it would have this property return false.

IsSynchronized returns true if access to the collection is thread-safe.

SyncRoot gets an object that can be used to synchronize access to the collection. Synchronized operations are performed on the SyncRoot rather than on the GroupCollection itself.

this[] is the indexer for the GroupCollection. It returns the Group object corresponding to the specified group number or name.

Public instance methods

```
public void CopyTo(Array array, int arrayIndex)
public IEnumerator GetEnumerator()
```

CopyTo() copies all of the elements of the invoking GroupCollection into the specified Array starting at the specified index. The length of the destination Array must be at least as large as the length of the GroupCollection added to arrayIndex.

GetEnumerator() returns an IEnumerator that can be used to iterate through the elements of the GroupCollection.

For an example of using the GroupCollection class, see the example in the *Match class* section where a GroupCollection is used to obtain information about the Groups that result from a regular expression search.

Match class

The Match class encapsulates a single regular expression match. A single match can involve multiple capturing groups. The Match class defines no constructors. You can obtain a reference to a single Match object using the Match() method from the Regex class. A series of Match objects can be contained in a MatchCollection. An instance of the Match class is not guaranteed to be thread-safe.

Syntax

```
public class Match : Group
```

Hierarchy

```
Object  ---  Capture  ---  Group  ---  Match
```

The Match class is a derived class of the Object, Capture, and Group classes, and has access to the properties and methods defined in those classes.

Properties

```
public static Match Empty {get;}
public virtual GroupCollection Groups {get;}
```

Empty represents a failed match.

Groups returns a collection of all capture groups matched by the regular expression. The first element of the GroupCollection is a reference to the Match object itself.

Public static methods

```
public static Match Synchronized(Match inner)
```

Synchronized() places a thread-safe wrapper around the specified Match and returns a reference to the wrapped Match.

Public instance methods

```
public Match NextMatch()
public virtual string Result(string replacement)
```

NextMatch() returns the next match to the regular expression in the search string. When there are no more matches, the Match.Empty field is returned.

Result() returns an expanded version of what the specified replacement pattern would be. For example:

```
String str = match.Result("$1$2");
```

The above syntax would return the concatenated capture substrings contained in the second and third capturing groups associated with the Match instance match.

Example: Match class

This example demonstrates how to conduct a regular expression search using the static version of the Matches() method from the Regex class. The various components of the search results are investigated by going down the Match-Group-Capture hierarchy. When going through this example it's useful to keep in mind the relationships between the various regular expression elements.

❑ A regular expression can generate one or more matches (a Match instance)

❑ A match will consist of one or more capture groups (a Group instance)

❑ A group will contain one or more capture substrings (a Capture instance)

A string of text is defined that contains two URLs. We want to conduct a regular expression search that will pick out the URLs, with groups that will contain the entire URL and the protocol and address components by themselves. Our regular expression search pattern is defined as "\b(\S+)://(\S+)?\b". The "\b" characters at the beginning and end mean that the search will be restricted to word boundaries. The "\S+" syntax means it will search for one or more non-whitespace characters before the text "://" and it will search for one or more non-whitespace characters after the text "://". The braces indicate that the results from this part of the search will be placed into a separate group. A listing of some of the more commonly used regular expressions can be found at the end of this chapter.

The Matches() method searches the input string for the text defined by the regular expression search pattern. The resulting Match objects are returned as the contents of a MatchCollection. Each Match object in the MatchCollection accesses its Groups property to obtain a GroupCollection containing the Group objects associated with the Match. Each Group object accesses its Captures property to return a CaptureCollection containing the capture substrings associated with each Group. All of these elements are printed out.

Each `Match` object in this example will have three `Group` objects associated with it. In this case, there will be one group for the entire match string, one for the protocol part of the URL, and one for the address part.

```csharp
using System;
using System.Collections;
using System.Text.RegularExpressions;

public class MatchDemo
{
  public static void Main()
  {

    //================================================
    //  This is the String that will be searched.
    //================================================

    String str = "Information about other wonderful "+
      "Wrox books can be found at http://www.wrox.com. "+
      "Or for you spotted toad aficionados, look to "+
      "https://www.spottedtoad.net for wonderful "+
      "photos of these magnificent creatures";

    //========================================================
    //  The '@' character preceding the search pattern tells
    //  the C# compiler to ignore anything it may interpret
    //  as an escape sequence.
    //========================================================

    String pattern = @"\b(\S+)://(\S+)?\b";

    //========================================================
    //  The Matches() method searches the String for matches
    //  with the search pattern. The Matches are returned
    //  in a MatchCollection. The GetEnumerator() method
    //  returns an IEnumerator that is used to print out
    //  the matches.
    //========================================================

    MatchCollection matches = Regex.Matches(str,pattern);

    Console.WriteLine("number of matches is {0}",matches.Count);

    IEnumerator matchEnum = matches.GetEnumerator();

    while ( matchEnum.MoveNext() )
    {
      Console.WriteLine(matchEnum.Current);
    }
    Console.WriteLine();

    //============================================================
```

```
        //  Each Match object accesses its Groups property to return
        //  a collection of the Group objects associated with the
        //  Match. The values of the Groups are printed out.
        //=============================================================

        for (int i=0; i<matches.Count; ++i)
        {

            GroupCollection groups = matches[i].Groups;

            Console.WriteLine("In match {0}, "+
                    "there are {1} groups",i,groups.Count);

            IEnumerator groupEnum = groups.GetEnumerator();

            while ( groupEnum.MoveNext() )
            {
                Console.WriteLine(groupEnum.Current);
            }
            Console.WriteLine();

            //=============================================================
            //  Each Group object accesses its Captures property to return
            //  a collection of the Capture objects associated with the
            //  Group. The values of the capture substrings are printed out.
            //=============================================================

            for (int j=0; j<groups.Count; ++j)
            {

                CaptureCollection captures = groups[j].Captures;

                Console.WriteLine("Group {0}, "+
                        "has {1} capture",j,captures.Count);

                for (int k=0; k<captures.Count; ++k)
                {
                    Console.WriteLine(captures[k].Value);
                }
                Console.WriteLine();
            }
        }
    }
}
```

Output:

```
number of matches is 2
http://www.wrox.com
https://www.spottedtoad.net

In match 0 there are 3 groups
```

```
http://www.wrox.com
http
www.wrox.com

Group 0 has 1 capture
http://www.wrox.com

Group 1 has 1 capture
http

Group 2 has 1 capture
www.wrox.com

In match 1 there are 3 groups
https://www.spottedtoad.net
https
www.spottedtoad.net

Group 0 has 1 capture
https://www.spottedtoad.net

Group 1 has 1 capture
https

Group 2 has 1 capture
www.spottedtoad.net
```

MatchCollection class

The MatchCollection class represents a collection of matches found by iteratively searching for a regular expression in an input String. The collection is read-only. The MatchCollection class defines no constructors. A MatchCollection can be obtained using the Matches() method of the Regex class.

Syntax

```
public class MatchCollection : ICollection, IEnumerable
```

Hierarchy

```
Object  ---  MatchCollection
```

Properties

```
public int Count {get;}
public bool IsReadOnly {get;}
public bool IsSynchronized {get;}
public Match this[int i] {get;}
public object SyncRoot {get;}
```

Count returns the number of items in the MatchCollection.

`IsReadOnly` returns `true` if the collection is read-only. The `MatchCollection` class implementation returns `true`. If you defined a read-write derived class of `MatchCollection`, it would set this property to be `false`.

`IsSynchronized` returns `true` if access to the collection is synchronized.

`this[]` is the indexer for the `MatchCollection`. It returns the `Match` object at the specified index.

`SyncRoot` gets an object that can be used to synchronize access to the collection. Synchronized operations are performed on the `SyncRoot` rather than on the `MatchCollection` itself.

Public instance methods

```
public void CopyTo(Array array, int arrayIndex)
public IEnumerator GetEnumerator()
```

`CopyTo()` copies all of the elements of the invoking `MatchCollection` into the specified `Array` starting at the specified index. The length of the destination `Array` minus `arrayIndex` must be at least as large as the length of the `MatchCollection`.

`GetEnumerator()` returns an `IEnumerator` that can be used to iterate through the elements of the `MatchCollection`.

For an example of using the `MatchCollection` class, see the example in the *Match class* section where a `MatchCollection` is used to obtain information about the `Match` objects that result from a regular expression search.

Regex class

The `Regex` class encapsulates a regular expression. A `Regex` object is immutable, meaning that once it is initialized with its match parameters they cannot be changed. This class also defines a number of static methods that allow you to perform regular expression searches and other operations without having to create a `Regex` object. These static methods in effect create a temporary `Regex` object, similar to a local variable, which is discarded after the operation is complete.

Syntax

```
public class Regex : Serializable
```

Hierarchy

```
Object  ---  Regex
```

Constructors

```
protected Regex()
public Regex(string pattern)
public Regex(string pattern, RegexOptions options)
```

`Regex()` creates a `Regex` object. The `pattern` parameter is the regular expression pattern to match. The `options` parameter consists of one or more elements from the `RegexOptions` enumeration and is used to modify the search. The protected constructor is for use by `Regex` derived classes.

Properties

```
public RegexOptions Options {get;}
public bool RightToLeft {get;}
```

Options retrieves whatever options were passed to the Regex constructor.

RightToLeft returns true if the regular expression search will be conducted right-to-left.

Public static methods

```
public static void CompileToAssembly(RegexCompilationInfo[] regexes,
                                                    AssemblyName name)
public static void CompileToAssembly(RegexCompilationInfo[] regexes,
                    AssemblyName name, CustomAttributeBuilder[] attrs)
public static void CompileToAssembly(RegexCompilationInfo[] regexes,
    AssemblyName name, CustomAttributeBuilder[] attrs, string resourceFile)
```

CompileToAssembly() compiles one or more Regex objects into an Assembly. This can be used to create a permanent library of commonly used Regex objects. The regexes parameter is an array of objects describing the regular expressions to compile. The attrs parameter is an array of objects detailing the attributes of the assembly. A resource file name can also be provided. An ArgumentNullException is thrown if name or regexes is a null reference.

```
public static string Escape(string str)
```

Escape() converts whitespace and metacharacters (\, *, +, ?, |, {, }, (,), ^, $, ., #, and whitespace) contained in the specified string into their equivalent escape codes and returns a String containing the converted values.

```
public static bool IsMatch(string input, string pattern)
public static bool IsMatch(string input, string pattern,
                                            RegexOptions options)
```

IsMatch() returns true if the regular expression contained in the pattern parameter finds a match in the input String. One or more elements from the RegexOptions enumeration can be used to modify the search.

```
public static Match Match(string input, string pattern)
public static Match Match(string input, string pattern, int startIndex,
                                                    int length)
public static Match Match(string input, string pattern,
                                            RegexOptions options)
```

Match() searches the specified input String for the regular expression defined in the pattern parameter. The entire String can be searched or a subset of it. The return value is a Match object representing the first match or the Match.Empty field if no match is found. One or more elements from the RegexOptions enumeration can be used to modify the search.

```
public static MatchCollection Matches(string input, string pattern)
public static MatchCollection Matches(string input, string pattern,
                                            RegexOptions options)
```

Matches() searches the specified input String for all occurrences of the regular expression defined in the pattern parameter. The entire string can be searched or a subset of it. The return value is a collection of Match objects found by the search. If no matches are found, an empty collection is returned. One or more elements from the RegexOptions enumeration can be used to modify the search.

```
public static string Replace(string input, string pattern,
                                           MatchEvaluator evaluator)
public static string Replace(string input, string pattern,
                          MatchEvaluator evaluator, RegexOptions options)
public static string Replace(string input, string pattern,
                                              string replacment)
public static string Replace(string input, string pattern,
                             string replacment, RegexOptions options)
```

Replace() replaces every occurrence of a character pattern with a replacement String. A MatchEvaluator delegate can be specified to provide custom verifications or other operations when the replace is performed. One or more elements from the RegexOptions enumeration can be used to modify the search. The modified String is returned.

```
public static string[] Split(string input, string pattern)
public static string[] Split(string input, string pattern,
                                          RegexOptions options)
```

Split() splits the specified input String into substrings using the specified regular expression character pattern as the delimiter. One or more elements from the RegexOptions enumeration can be used to modify the search.

```
public static string Unescape(string str)
```

Unescape() reverses the effects of the Escape() method in that it converts any escape code characters in the input String into their metacharacter equivalents.

Public instance methods

```
~Regex()
```

~Regex() is equivalent to the Finalize() method. It forces a Regex object to free resources allocated to it before the object is garbage collected.

```
public string[] GetGroupNames()
public int[] GetGroupNumbers()
public string GroupNameFromNumber(int i)
public int GroupNumberFromName(string name)
```

GetGroupNames() returns an array containing the capturing group names for the regular expression. If the capturing groups are not explicitly named, they will be assigned numbers.

GetGroupNumbers() retrieves the numbers assigned to the capturing groups associated with a regular expression.

`GroupNameFromNumber()` gets the name of the specified group number. If no name has been assigned to the group, the number is returned.

`GroupNumberFromName()` returns the group number corresponding to the specified group name. If the named group does not exist, -1 is returned.

```
public bool IsMatch(string input)
public bool IsMatch(string input, int startIndex)
```

`IsMatch()` returns `true` if the regular expression associated with the invoking `Regex` object finds a match in the specified `String`. You can search the entire `String` or a subset of it starting at character position `startIndex`.

```
public Match Match(string input)
public Match Match(string input, int startIndex)
```

`Match()` determines if the regular expression associated with the invoking `Regex` object finds a match in the specified `String`. The entire `String` can be searched or a subset of it. The return value is a `Match` object representing the match or the `Match.Empty` field if no match is found.

```
public MatchCollection Matches(string input)
public MatchCollection Matches(string input, int startIndex)
```

`Matches()` searches the specified input `String` for all occurrences of the regular expression associated with the invoking `Regex` object. You can search the entire `String` or a subset of it starting at character position `startIndex`. The method returns a collection of `Match` objects found by the search. If no matches are found, an empty collection is returned.

```
public string Replace(string input, MatchEvaluator evaluator)
public string Replace(string input, MatchEvaluator evaluator, int count)
public string Replace(string input, MatchEvaluator evaluator, int count,
                                                      int startIndex)
public string Replace(string input, string replacment)
public string Replace(string input, string replacment, int count)
public string Replace(string input, string replacment, int count,
                                                      int startIndex)
```

`Replace()` replaces one or more occurrences of the character pattern defined by the regular expression associated with the invoking `Regex` object with a replacement `String`. A `MatchEvaluator` delegate can be specified to provide custom verifications or other operations when the replace is performed. If a `count` is specified, this is the maximum number of occurrences that will be replaced. If the `count` parameter is not provided, every occurrence will be replaced. The entire `String` can be searched or the search can begin at character position `startIndex`. The modified `String` is returned.

```
public string[] Split(string input)
public string[] Split(string input, int count)
public string[] Split(string input, int count, int startIndex)
```

`Split()` splits the specified input `String` into substrings using the regular expression associated with the invoking `Regex` object as the delimiter. The `count` parameter is the maximum number of times the `String` will be split even if more matches exist. The `startIndex` parameter is the character position within the `String` at which to start the splitting.

```
public override string ToString()
```

ToString() returns the regular expression associated with the invoking Regex object as a String.

Example: Regex class

One of the useful things about the regular expressions is that they allow you to perform intelligent search and replace operations. In this example, an input String is defined as "ted wanted the other ted to do it". We want to capitalize the 't' in each instance of "ted" without changing "wanted" to "wanTed".

Your first impulse may be to use the Replace() method defined in the String class, but what search pattern do you use? If you replace "ted" with "Ted" it will replace all three. If you use " ted " and " Ted " (with a space before and after the word), it will only capitalize the 't' in the second "ted".

The answer is to use a regular expression that constrains the search to word boundaries. This is done by using the "\b" character before and after the search string in the regular expression. The Replace() method from the Regex class can then be used to perform the proper substitution.

```
using System;
using System.Collections;
using System.Text.RegularExpressions;

public class RegexDemo
{
  public static void Main()
  {

    //=====================================================
    //   Define a regular expression search pattern and
    //   define an input and replacment String.
    //   The '@' character preceding the search pattern
    //   tells the C# compiler to ignore anything it may
    //   interpret as an escape sequence.
    //=====================================================

    String input = "ted wanted the other ted to do it";
    String pattern = @"\b(ted)\b";
    String replace = "Ted";

    //=====================================================
    //   Create a Regex object based on the search pattern.
    //   The Replace() method searches the input String
    //   and replaces any regular expression matches with
    //   the replacement String.
    //=====================================================

    Regex regex = new Regex(pattern);
    String newString = regex.Replace(input, replace);

    Console.WriteLine(newString);
```

```
        }
    }
```

Ouput:

```
    Ted wanted the other Ted to do it
```

RegexOptions enumeration

The `RegexOptions` enumeration defines constants that are used to specify regular expression options.

Syntax

```
    public enum RegexOptions
```

Members

`Compiled` indicates that the regular expression has been compiled to an assembly using the `Regex.CompileToAssembly()` method. The assembly represents a library of regular expressions.

`ECMAScript` enables ECMAScript-compliant behavior for the regular expression. ECMAScript is a standard scripting language based on JavaScript. This flag can only be used in conjunction with the `Compiled`, `IgnoreCase`, and `Multiline` flags.

`ExplicitCapture` specifies that only captures explicitly tied to a named or numbered group will be saved. Text surrounded only by braces is treated as a non-capturing group. This constant removes the need for the "?:" syntax.

`IgnoreCase` permits case-insensitive matching.

`IgnorePatternWhitespace` eliminates unescaped whitespace from the search pattern.

`Multiline` changes the meaning of the '^' and '$' characters to mean the beginning and end of a line rather than of the entire `String`.

`None` means that no options are set.

`RightToLeft` specifies that the search will be conducted from right-to-left instead of the default left-to-right.

`SingleLine` indicates single-line mode. The '.' character now matches every character including the newline character.

Regular expression modifiers

The following is a list and description of some of the commonly used modifiers used in regular expressions. For a complete list, you may want to visit http://msdn.microsoft.com/. To see examples of regular expressions in action, see the examples in the *Match class* and *Regex class* sections.

481

In addition to the modifiers described here, you can use the standard escape sequences "\n", "\t", "\r", and so on in regular expressions.

Match quantifier modifiers

These modifiers define the number of required matches and are placed after the character or group to be searched for.

Syntax	Description
*	Match 0 or more times
+	Match 1 or more times
?	Match 0 or 1 times
{n}	Match exactly n times
{n,}	Match at least n times
{n,m}	Match at least n times but not more than m times

Character match modifiers

These modifiers are used to represent a character of a given type. With the exception of the "\s" modifier, the character itself is undefined.

Syntax	Description
.	Match any character except newline
\w	Match any alphanumeric character plus "_"
\W	Match a non-alphanumeric character
\s	Match a whitespace character
\S	Match a non-whitespace character
\d	Match a digit character
\D	Match a non-digit character

Position modifiers

These modifiers define where in the string to look for a match.

Syntax	Description
\b	Match only at a word boundary
\B	Match a non-word boundary
\A	Match only at the beginning of the string
\Z	Match only at the end of the string or line
\z	Match only at the end of a string
^	Match at the beginning of a line

Case modifiers

These modifiers define the case of the characters being searched for.

Syntax	Description
\l	Lowercase next character
\L	Lowercase until \E modifier
\u	Uppercase next character
\U	Uppercase until \E modifier
\E	Terminate case specification

Grouping modifiers

These modifiers are used to define capturing groups and to define a group of characters from which to match.

Syntax	Description
[character_list]	Matches any character in the list
[^character_list]	Matches any character not in the list
[c1-c2]	Matches any character between c1 and c2
()	Defines a capturing group
(?<name>)	Defines a named capturing group
(?<number>)	Defines a numbered capturing group
(?:)	Specifies a non-capturing group

Summary

In this chapter we've taken a look at the System.Text.RegularExpressions namespace, and the classes it provides us for working with regular expressions. While we've not concentrated too heavily on the syntax of regular expressions, we've had a look through some commonly-used expression modifiers that can be put together to form a complex expression.

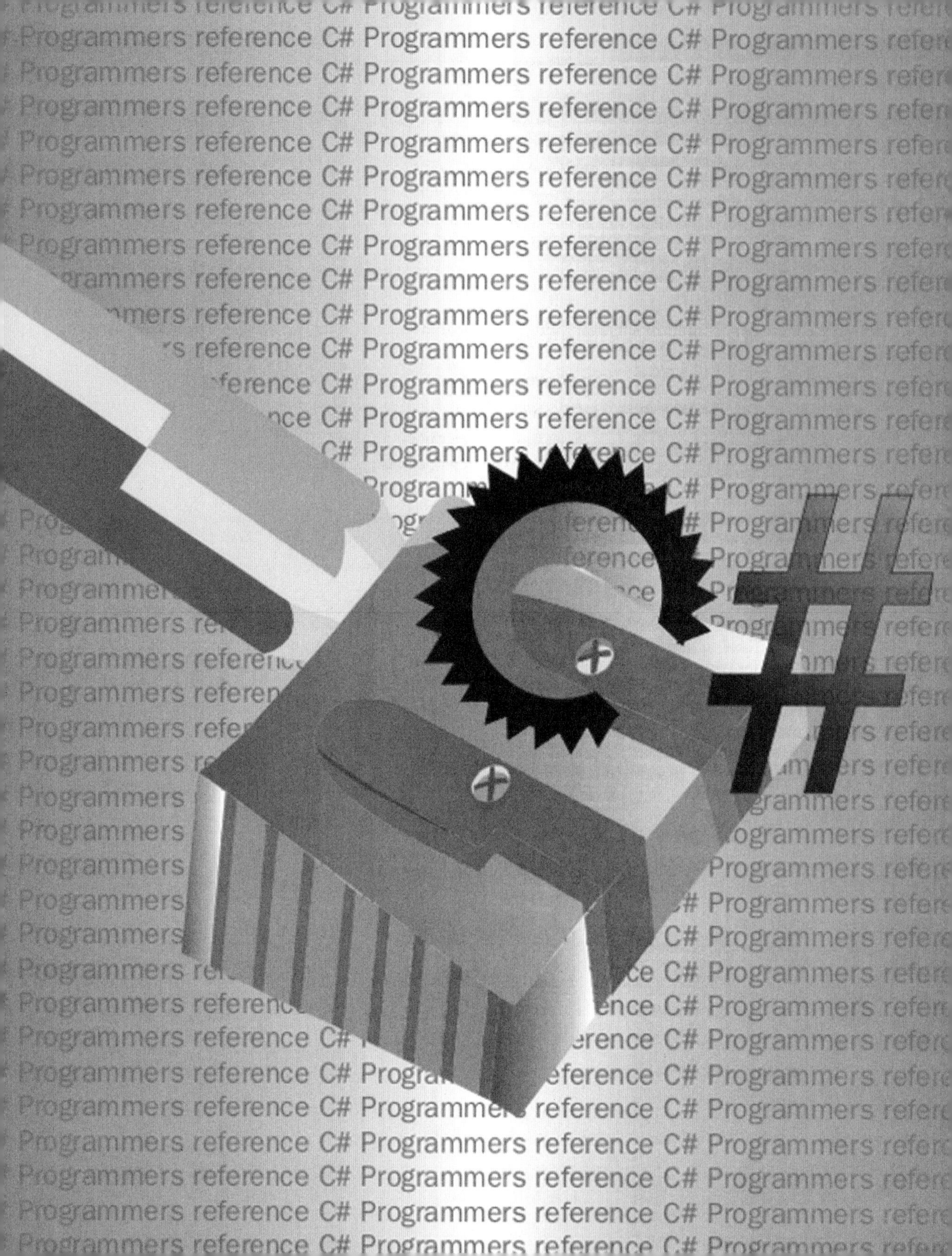
Programmers reference C#

28

Threading

The System.Threading namespace contains the interfaces, enumerations, delegates, and classes that enable multi-threaded programming and synchronized access to various programming elements. A simple program will likely only have one thread of execution, but more complicated programs may have many threads running at the same time. One may be reading data from a file, while another performs a computation, while a third runs animation on the screen. The Thread class encapsulates an execution thread and provides methods to create, start, suspend, and abort threads. The ThreadPool class represents a collection of system-managed worker threads that can be used to perform various tasks.

The Monitor class encapsulates a monitor lock that's used to give synchronized access to an object. The Interlocked class provides methods to increment, decrement, compare, or exchange values **atomically** – that is, in a single operation making the process thread-safe. The Mutex class defines a mutually exclusive lock, also known as a **mutex**, that facilitates exclusive access to a shared resource. The ReaderWriterLock class provides I/O locks for threads that read and write data. The System.Threading namespace also defines the Timer class – a useful tool that can be employed to call a delegate after a specified period of time.

Synchronization basics

A synchronized element is one that only one thread at a time may access – it could be a local variable, a field, a thread, or some other shared resource. Access to an object in a multi-threaded environment is governed by the thread that holds the lock on that object at a particular moment in time. The lock may be a monitor lock, a mutex lock, or a read-write lock. Respectively, the Monitor, Mutex, and ReaderWriterLock classes encapsulate these locks.

Threads can try to acquire a lock, release a lock they own, or wait until notified by another thread that a lock they want is available. A **ready queue** contains threads that wish to acquire the lock on the object, while a **waiting queue** contains threads that are waiting for notification of a change in an object's state. A block of code will generally be placed between the syntax for acquiring a lock and the syntax for releasing the lock. The block of code defines processes for which synchronized access is required.

You can also synchronize access to a code element using the lock keyword, which was first introduced in Chapter 11. A lock statement is really just a syntactical shortcut for the Monitor.Enter() and Monitor.Exit() methods. For instance, the syntax:

```
Monitor.Enter(obj);

// Code to execute

Monitor.Exit(obj);
```

is entirely equivalent to:

```
lock(obj)
{
   // Code to execute
}
```

Application domains

An important innovation in the way .NET handles processes and threads is the concept of the **application domain** (or **AppDomain**), which provides a way of isolating threads within the same process. Previously, developers have faced a stark choice: isolate components in separate processes, which has a significant performance cost; or place components in the same process, with the danger that a problem in one will cause the whole application to crash.

Application domains allow us to separate blocks of code that are running in the same process. Each application domain is allocated a share of the virtual memory block for the process, and the CLR's type-safety checking ensures that one domain cannot access the data of another. However, note that there isn't a one-to-one correlation between threads and application domains – several threads can execute within a single domain, and threads may cross domain boundaries.

Thread class

The Thread class is the basic class that represents a thread of execution. It provides methods for creating, controlling, and changing the attributes of a thread, including its status and priority. The Join() method can be used to block subsequent code activity until the invoking Thread exits. The Suspend() and Abort() methods can be used to stop the execution of the invoking Thread. The Interrupt() method can interrupt a Thread that is blocking in a join, sleep, or wait state.

Syntax

```
public sealed class Thread
```

Hierarchy

```
Object --- Thread
```

Constructors

```
public Thread(ThreadStart start)
```

Thread() creates a Thread object. The start parameter is the delegate that will be called when the Start() method is invoked.

Public static properties

```
public static Context CurrentContext {get; }
public static IPrincipal CurrentPrincipal {get; set;}
public static Thread CurrentThread {get;}
```

CurrentContext returns the current context of the executing thread.

CurrentPrincipal gets or sets the thread's current principal. It returns an implementation of the IPrincipal interface, which contains information about the thread's identity and the user group to which it belongs.

CurrentThread retrieves a reference to the currently executing thread.

Public instance properties

```
public ApartmentState ApartmentState {get; set;}
public CultureInfo CurrentCulture {get; set;}
public CultureInfo CurrentUICulture {get; set;}
public bool IsAlive {get;}
public bool IsBackground {get; set;}
public string Name {get; set;}
public ThreadPriority Priority {get; set;}
public ThreadState ThreadState {get;}
```

ApartmentState retrieves or sets the apartment state of the thread. The apartment state determines whether the thread will run in a single-threaded or multi-threaded mode. The default value of this property is Unknown.

CurrentCulture returns or specifies the cultural information of the thread. This information will include the name, language, and calendar of the culture assigned to the thread.

CurrentUICulture gets or sets the UI cultural information of the thread. The resource manager will use this information at runtime to determine how things should look on the screen.

IsAlive returns true if the thread has been started and is still alive.

IsBackground returns true if the thread is running (or will run) in the background. The set accessor can specify whether the thread is a background thread. A background thread differs from a foreground thread in that it does not have to complete execution or be terminated before a process that invoked it can terminate.

Name retrieves or specifies the name of the thread. If a thread is not given a name, its name is the empty string.

Priority gets or sets the thread priority. The default value is Normal.

ThreadState returns the state of the thread. The default value is Unstarted.

Public static methods

The CLR provides a local data store in which threads can store their data. This data store is specific to a thread, and even child threads cannot access the data. The Thread class has six methods for dealing with this store:

```
public static LocalDataStoreSlot AllocateDataSlot()
public static LocalDataStoreSlot AllocateNamedDataSlot(string name)
public static void FreeNamedDataSlot(string name)
public static object GetData(LocalDataStoreSlot slot)
public static LocalDataStoreSlot GetNamedDataSlot(string name)
public static void SetData(LocalDataStoreSlot slot, object data)
```

AllocateDataSlot() allocates an unnamed data slot on all existing threads. A data slot is a local memory entity used to store thread-specific data. A slot allocated with this method will be freed when the thread expires.

AllocateNamedDataSlot() allocates a named data slot on all existing threads. Named data slots must be freed explicitly.

FreeNamedDataSlot() frees a previously allocated named data slot on all threads.

GetData() retrieves the object stored in the specified slot of the current thread for that thread's current domain.

GetNamedDataSlot() retrieves the specified named data slot.

SetData() places the specified object into the specified data slot on the currently running thread, for that thread's current domain.

```
public static AppDomain GetDomain()
public static int GetDomainID()
```

GetDomain() returns information about the application domain in which the current thread is running.

GetDomainID() returns the identification number for the domain in which the current thread is running.

```
public static void ResetAbort()
```

ResetAbort() cancels an abort operation. To call this method, an application must have ControlThread permission. When a Thread is terminated, either by completing its execution or by calling the Abort() method, a ThreadAbortException is thrown. This method prevents the ThreadAbortException from terminating the thread. An exception is thrown if this method was not invoked on the current thread, or if the caller did not have the required permission.

```
public static void Sleep(int millisecondsTimeout)
public static void Sleep(TimeSpan timeout)
```

Sleep() suspends the current thread (puts it to sleep) for a specified period of time. An ArgumentOutOfRangeException is thrown if the value of the timeout is less than zero or greater than MaxValue.

Public instance methods

```
public void Abort()
public void Abort(object stateInfo)
```

Abort() raises a ThreadAbortException that will initiate the process of killing the thread. The finally blocks of all try statements are executed before the thread dies, and thread and process-based locks are released. Because of this, the thread may not stop immediately. The Join() method can be used to ensure that the thread has stopped. If Abort() is called on a thread that hasn't been started, the thread will abort when it is started. A SecurityException is thrown if the caller does not have the proper permission to call this method.

```
public void Interrupt()
public void Join()
public bool Join(int millisecondsTimeout)
public bool Join(TimeSpan timeout)
```

Interrupt() interrupts a thread that is blocking in a join, sleep, or wait state. If it is not in one of these states, it will be interrupted when it next begins to block. A SecurityException is thrown if the caller does not have the proper permission to call this method.

Join() waits for the invoking Thread to die, and returns when it does. The method can wait forever, or until the timeout period specified by the integer or TimeSpan arguments expires. The versions that return a Boolean return true if the Thread died, and false if the timeout period expired. An exception is thrown if the value of the timeout is less than zero or greater than MaxValue, or if the caller does not have the proper permission to call this method.

```
public void Resume()
public void Start()
public void Suspend()
```

Resume() resumes a suspended Thread. An exception is thrown if the Thread is not in a suspended state, or if the caller does not have the proper permission to call this method.

Start() starts the Thread by invoking the ThreadStart delegate that was provided to the Thread constructor. Exceptions are thrown if the thread has already been started, if there is not enough memory to start the thread, if the thread that calls this method is a null reference, or if the caller does not have the proper permission to call this method.

Suspend() suspends the invoking Thread. If the Thread is already suspended, the method does nothing. An exception is thrown if the Thread has not been started, if the Thread is dead, or if the caller does not have the proper permission to call this method.

Protected instance methods

```
~Thread()
```

~Thread() is the destructor for the Thread class. This method is normally called by the system when the thread is garbage collected.

Example: Thread class

Every example in this chapter makes use of the Thread class. To complement those, here's a simple example that demonstrates the use of some of the Thread class methods. In it, three Threads are created, named, and started. After a 0.5 second delay, the first Thread is suspended.

An attempt is made to abort the third Thread by invoking the Abort() method, which throws a ThreadAbortException. The Count() method defines a catch block that catches any ThreadAbortExceptions. The catch block identifies the Thread that caused the exception and resets the abort. The execution of the reset Thread then continues to the next statement after the catch block.

Back in the Main() method, the second Thread calls the Join() method. This prevents any subsequent lines of code from executing until the second Thread is finished. When the second Thread finishes, the execution of the first Thread is resumed.

```
using System;
using System.Threading;

public class ThreadDemo
{
  public static void Main()
  {
    ThreadDemo demo = new ThreadDemo();

    // Three Threads are created and named. When the threads
    // are started, they call the Count() method.
    Thread one = new Thread(new ThreadStart(demo.Count));
    Thread two = new Thread(new ThreadStart(demo.Count));
    Thread three = new Thread(new ThreadStart(demo.Count));

    one.Name = "Thread one";
    two.Name = "Thread two";
    three.Name = "Thread three";

    one.Start();
    two.Start();
    three.Start();

    // After a delay of 0.5 seconds, the first Thread is
    // suspended and an attempt is made to abort the third.
    Thread.Sleep(500);
    one.Suspend();
    three.Abort();

    // The second Thread calls the Join() method. This prevents
    // any subsequent lines of code from executing until the
    // second Thread is finished. When the second Thread is
    // finished, the execution of the first Thread is resumed.
    two.Join();
    one.Resume();
```

```
    }

    // The Count() method has each Thread go through a
    // for loop. Any aborts that are called are reset.

    public void Count()
    {
      try
      {
        for(int i = 0; i < 5; ++i)
        {
          Console.WriteLine("{0}: {1}", Thread.CurrentThread.Name, i);
          Thread.Sleep(200);
        }
      }
      catch(ThreadAbortException e)
      {
        Console.WriteLine("\nAttempt to abort " + Thread.CurrentThread.Name);
        Console.WriteLine(e.Message);
        Console.WriteLine("Abort reset\n");
        Thread.ResetAbort();
      }
      Console.WriteLine(Thread.CurrentThread.Name + ": out of for loop");
    }
  }
```

Output:

```
Thread one: 0
Thread two: 0
Thread three: 0
Thread one: 1
Thread two: 1
Thread three: 1
Thread one: 2
Thread two: 2
Thread three: 2

Attempt to abort Thread three
Exception of type System.Threading.ThreadAbortException was thrown.
Abort reset

Thread three: out of for loop
Thread two: 3
Thread two: 4
Thread two: out of for loop
Thread one: 3
Thread one: 4
Thread one: out of for loop
```

ThreadStart delegate

The ThreadStart delegate is passed to the Thread class constructor. It references the method that is initially called when a Thread is started. The delegate refers to a method that takes no arguments and has a return type of void.

Syntax

```
public delegate void ThreadStart()
```

Every example in this chapter passes a ThreadStart delegate to the Thread constructor.

ThreadPriority enumeration

The ThreadPriority enumeration contains constants that define a thread's priority. A thread with a higher priority is more likely to run than one with a lower priority.

Syntax

```
public enum ThreadPriority
```

Constants

The ThreadPriority constants are listed here in order of highest to lowest priority value. The default priority is Normal.

Highest
AboveNormal
Normal
BelowNormal
Lowest

ThreadState enumeration

The ThreadState enumeration contains constants that indicate the current execution state of a Thread. A Thread will always be in at least one of the states defined in this enumeration. The constants can be combined in a bitwise manner to describe a Thread that is in more than one state at the same time. There are some restrictions; for example, you cannot designate the state of a Thread to be both Aborted and Unstarted.

Syntax

```
public enum ThreadState
```

Constants

Constant	Description
Aborted	The Thread has been aborted.
AbortRequested	The Abort() method has been called, but the Thread has not yet aborted.
Background	The Thread is running as a background thread.
Running	The Start() method has been called and the Thread is executing.
Stopped	The Thread has stopped.
StopRequested	The Thread has been requested to stop.
Suspended	The Thread has been suspended.
SuspendRequested	The Thread is being requested to suspend its activities.
Unstarted	The Thread has not yet called the Start() method.
WaitSleepJoin	The Thread is blocking because it called either the Wait(), Sleep(), or Join() method.

Interlocked class

The Interlocked class provides static methods that are used to synchronize access to a variable that's shared by multiple threads. There are methods to increment, decrement, compare, and replace a value atomically.

A method does something atomically when it performs its function in a single operation. A standard increment operation, for example, takes place in two parts: the value is incremented, and the updated value is stored. It's possible to have a situation where one thread could increment the value, and a second thread could increment the value again before the first thread has a chance to store it. Because the Interlocked methods work atomically, they remove the possibility of this type of thread conflict.

Syntax

```
public sealed class Interlocked
```

Hierarchy

```
Object --- Interlocked
```

Public static methods

```
public static long Increment(ref long value)
public static int Increment(ref int value)
```

Increment() increments the specified value and returns the incremented value.

```
public static int Decrement(ref int value)
public static long Decrement(ref long value)
```

Decrement() decrements the specified value and returns the decremented value.

```
public static int Exchange(ref int location, int newValue)
public static float Exchange(ref float location, float newValue)
public static object Exchange(ref object location, object newValue)
```

Exchange() sets the value of location to newValue. Integer values, single-precision floating point values, and objects can be exchanged. The original value of location is returned.

```
public static int CompareExchange(ref int destValue,
                                  int replaceValue, int compareValue)
public static float CompareExchange(ref float destValue,
                                    float replaceValue, float compareValue)
public static object CompareExchange(ref object destValue,
                                     object replaceValue, object compareValue)
```

CompareExchange() compares destValue and compareValue. If they are equal, destValue is replaced with replaceValue. Integer values, single-precision floating point values, and object references can be compared. The original destination value (destValue) is returned.

Monitor class

The Monitor class provides synchronized access to objects (or to a synchronized block within an object) using the concept of a **lock**. Monitor locks are similar to critical sections in Win32 programming – a thread that has the monitor lock on an object is the only thread that may access that object. The Monitor class defines a number of static methods for acquiring and transferring a lock. There are also methods to perform operations on the threads in the ready and waiting queues.

A Monitor is associated with a given object on demand. The Monitor class provides no constructor: a Monitor object cannot be instantiated.

Syntax

```
public sealed class Monitor
```

Hierarchy

```
Object --- Monitor
```

Public static methods

```
public static void Enter(object obj)
public static void Exit(object obj)
```

Enter() attempts to obtain the monitor lock for the specified object. This method will block if another thread holds the lock. An ArgumentNullException is thrown if obj is a null reference.

Exit() releases the monitor lock for the specified object. Another thread is now able to acquire the lock. An exception is thrown if obj is a null reference, or if the current thread does not own the lock for obj.

```
public static void Pulse(object obj)
public static void PulseAll(object obj)
```

`Pulse()` is invoked by the thread that holds the lock on the specified object to inform the next thread in the waiting queue of a change in the object's state; this thread is then moved to the ready queue. The thread that invoked `Pulse()` releases the lock, allowing the next thread in the ready queue to acquire it. This method must be invoked from within a synchronized block of code. An exception is thrown if `obj` is a `null` reference, or if the current thread does not own the lock for `obj`.

`PulseAll()` is invoked by the thread that holds the lock on the specified object to inform all the threads in the waiting queue of a change in the object's state. All of the threads in the waiting queue are moved to the ready queue. The thread that invoked `PulseAll()` releases the lock, allowing the next thread in the ready queue to acquire it. This method must be invoked from within a synchronized block of code. An exception is thrown if `obj` is a `null` reference, or if the current thread does not own the lock for `obj`.

```
public static bool TryEnter(object obj)
public static bool TryEnter(object obj, int millisecondsTimeout)
public static bool TryEnter(object obj, TimeSpan timeout)
```

`TryEnter()` attempts to acquire the monitor lock of the specified object under certain conditions. The first version tries to get the lock without blocking. The second and third versions will block, but only for the specified time interval. The method returns `true` if the method was successful, or `false` if it was not. An exception is thrown if `obj` is a `null` reference, if `obj` is a value type, or if the time interval argument is invalid.

```
public static bool Wait(object obj)
public static bool Wait(object obj, int millisecondsTimeout)
public static bool Wait(object obj, TimeSpan timeout)
public static bool Wait(object obj, int millisecondsTimeout,
                        bool exitContext)
public static bool Wait(object obj, TimeSpan timeout)
```

`Wait()` releases the monitor lock and places the invoking thread into the waiting queue. The thread can then be moved to the ready queue if another thread invokes the `Pulse()` or `PulseAll()` methods. If a time interval is specified, this is the maximum time to wait before the method returns. If `exitContext` is true, the synchronization domain for the context (if any) is exited before the wait and the lock is reacquired after it. The method returns `true` if the wait succeeds and `false` if the wait was unsuccessful or the time interval expired. This method must be invoked from within a synchronized block of code.

Example: Monitor locks

This example is a variation on the classic producer-consumer example. The `MonitorDemo` class defines an initially empty `Queue` as a data member, and then starts two threads. The first of these calls the `AddItem()` method that adds elements to the queue, while the second calls the `RemoveItem()` method that removes elements from it.

The problem here is that the `RemoveItem()` thread has intentionally been given a higher thread priority than the `AddItem()` method. This means `RemoveItem()` will execute preferentially: it will remove items from the `Queue` faster than the `AddItem()` method can add them. Attempting to remove an item from an empty `Queue` will cause an `InvalidOperationException` to be thrown.

We can avoid this situation by using `Monitor` class methods. The `RemoveItem()` method calls `Enter()` to acquire the lock for the `Queue`. If there aren't any elements in the `Queue`, the `Wait()` method is called to release the lock and place the thread in a waiting state. When it reacquires the lock, it removes an element from the `Queue`. `AddItem()` similarly acquires the lock for the `Queue` using a `lock` statement. It adds an element to the `Queue`, and calls the `Pulse()` method to inform any waiting threads that they can reacquire the lock.

```
using System;
using System.Threading;
using System.Collections;

public class MonitorDemo
{
  Queue queue;

  public MonitorDemo()
  {
    queue = new Queue();
  }

  public static void Main()
  {
    MonitorDemo demo = new MonitorDemo();

    // Two Thread objects are created. One is used to add items to a
    // Queue. The other removes items from the Queue. The addThread is
    // slowed down to set up a potential InvalidOperationException.
    Thread addThread = new Thread(new ThreadStart(demo.AddItem));
    addThread.Priority = ThreadPriority.BelowNormal;
    Thread removeThread = new Thread(new ThreadStart(demo.RemoveItem));

    addThread.Start();
    removeThread.Start();
  }

  // The RemoveItem() method acquires the lock for the Queue. If there
  // aren't any elements in the Queue, the Wait() method is called to
  // give up the lock. The method then blocks further activity until the
  // lock is reacquired. When it is, an element is removed from the Queue.
  public void RemoveItem()
  {
    for(int i = 0; i < 4; ++i)
    {
      Monitor.Enter(queue);
      if(queue.Count < 1)
        Monitor.Wait(queue);

      queue.Dequeue();
      Console.WriteLine("Queue has {0} items", queue.Count);
      Monitor.Exit(queue);
    }
  }
```

```
    // The AddItem() method acquires the lock for the Queue. An element
    // is added to the Queue. The Pulse() method is called to notify
    // any waiting threads that they can reacquire the lock.
    public void AddItem()
    {
      for(int i = 0; i < 4; ++i)
      {
        lock(queue)
        {
          queue.Enqueue("queue item");
          Console.WriteLine("Queue has {0} items", queue.Count);
          Monitor.Pulse(queue);
        }
      }
    }
  }
```

Output:

```
Queue has 1 items
Queue has 0 items
Queue has 1 items
Queue has 0 items
Queue has 1 items
Queue has 0 items
Queue has 1 items
Queue has 0 items
```

If you remove the monitor lock syntax in the AddItem() and RemoveItem() methods, this program will throw an InvalidOperationException when run, because RemoveThread() is called before AddThread().

WaitHandle class

The WaitHandle class is the base class for Win32 synchronization handles. It is used to manage access to shared resources – it provides methods for waiting until objects have been **signaled**. (A signaled object is one that will not block a thread waiting on it.) Derived classes include the Mutex, AutoResetEvent, and ManualResetEvent classes.

Syntax

```
public abstract class WaitHandle : MarshalByRefObject, IDisposable
```

Hierarchy

```
Object --- MarshalByRefObject --- WaitHandle
```

Constructors

```
public WaitHandle()
```

497

`WaitHandle()` is used by derived classes of `WaitHandle`.

Fields

```
protected static readonly IntPtr InvalidHandle
public const int WaitTimeout
```

`InvalidHandle` represents an invalid synchronization handle.

The `WaitTimeout` constant is an integer value that indicates that a call to the `WaitAny()` method has timed out and no object has been signaled.

Properties

```
public virtual IntPtr Handle {get; set;}
```

`Handle()` accesses or sets the native operating system handle.

Public static methods

```
public static bool WaitAll(WaitHandle[] waitHandles)
public static bool WaitAll(WaitHandle[] waitHandles,
                            int millisecondsTimeout, bool exitContext)
public static bool WaitAll(WaitHandle[] waitHandles, TimeSpan timeout,
                                            bool exitContext)
```

`WaitAll()` returns when all of the `WaitHandle` objects in the specified array are signaled, or if a specified timeout period expires. If `exitContext` is `true` and the method was executed in a synchronized context, this context is exited before the wait and reacquired after it. The return value is `true` if all of the `WaitHandle` objects were signaled, or `false` if the method timed out. An exception is thrown if `waitHandles` is a `null` reference, or if it contains duplicate elements.

```
public static int WaitAny(WaitHandle[] waitHandles)
public static int WaitAny(WaitHandle[] waitHandles, int millisecondsTimeout,
                                            bool exitContext)
public static int WaitAny(WaitHandle[] waitHandles, TimeSpan timeout,
                                            bool exitContext)
```

`WaitAny()` returns when any of the `WaitHandle` objects in the specified array are signaled, or if a specified timeout period expires. If `exitContext` is `true` and the method was executed in a synchronized context, this context is exited before the wait and reacquired after it. The return value is the array index of the signaled object, or the `WaitTimeout` constant if no object was signaled before the timeout period expired. An exception is thrown if `waitHandles` is a `null` reference, or if it contains duplicate elements.

Public instance methods

```
public virtual void Close()
```

`Close()` closes the invoking handle. This method calls the `Dispose()` method, passing it a `true` value.

```
public virtual bool WaitOne()
public virtual bool WaitOne(int millisecondsTimeout, bool exitContext)
public virtual bool WaitOne(TimeSpan timeout, bool exitContext)
```

WaitOne() returns when the invoking WaitHandle object is signaled, or when a specified timeout period expires. The no-argument version will block indefinitely until the current WaitHandle receives a signal. An exception is thrown if waitHandles is a null reference, or if it contains duplicate elements. The return value is true if the method was successful.

Protected instance methods

```
protected virtual void Dispose(bool explicitDisposing)
~WaitHandle()
```

Dispose() releases the resources allocated to the handle. If explicitDisposing is true, both the managed and unmanaged resources are released. If it is false, only the unmanaged resources are released.

~WaitHandle() is the destructor for the class. This method is normally called by the system when the WaitHandle is garbage collected.

The WaitHandle class is shown in action in the example in the *Mutex class* section, where the WaitOne() method is used to request the mutex lock.

Mutex class

The Mutex class represents a mutually exclusive lock that permits exclusive access to a shared resource. Once a thread acquires the mutex lock, any additional threads wishing to access the shared resource are suspended until the lock is released. The WaitOne() method of the WaitHandle class can be used to request the mutex lock. The ReleaseMutex() method can be called to release the lock.

Syntax

```
public sealed class Mutex : WaitHandle
```

Hierarchy

```
Object --- MarshalByRefObject --- WaitHandle --- Mutex
```

Constructors

```
public Mutex()
public Mutex(bool initiallyOwned)
public Mutex(bool initiallyOwned, string mutexName)
public Mutex(bool initiallyOwned, string mutexName, out bool gotOwnership)
```

Mutex() creates a Mutex object. Setting initallyOwned to true indicates that the thread already has access to the resource. Furthermore, a name can be given to the Mutex instance, while the gotOwnership parameter will be set to true if initiallyOwned is true. Otherwise, it will be false.

Public instance methods

```
public void ReleaseMutex()
```

ReleaseMutex() releases the mutex *once*. A thread can place multiple claims to a mutex by calling the Wait() method multiple times; to release ownership of the mutex lock, ReleaseMutex() must be called the same number of times.

Example: Mutex locks

This example shows how a Mutex object can be used to give exclusive access to a block of code inside a subroutine. Two Threads are created, both of which call the Increment() method when started. This method simply cycles through a for loop, printing out the current value. We want each thread to finish its for loop before the next thread begins.

The initial listing of the code is shown below. Both Threads have equal, unsynchronized access to the code inside the Increment() method, and will run through their version of the for loop at the same time:

```
using System;
using System.Threading;

public class MutexDemo
{
  private Mutex mutex;

  public MutexDemo()
  {
    mutex = new Mutex();
  }

  public static void Main()
  {
    MutexDemo demo = new MutexDemo();

    // Two Threads are created. When started, they
    // both try to access the Increment() method.
    Thread inc = new Thread(new ThreadStart(demo.Increment));
    inc.Name = "Increment one";
    Thread inc2 = new Thread(new ThreadStart(demo.Increment));
    inc2.Name = "Increment two";

    inc.Start();
    inc2.Start();
  }

  // The Increment() method increments a value.
  public void Increment()
  {
    for(int i = 0; i < 4; ++i)
    {
```

```
        Console.WriteLine(Thread.CurrentThread.Name + ": value is {0}", i);
        Thread.Sleep(5);
      }
    }
  }
}
```

Output:

```
Increment one:   value is 0
Increment two:   value is 0
Increment one:   value is 1
Increment two:   value is 1
Increment one:   value is 2
Increment two:   value is 2
Increment one:   value is 3
Increment two:   value is 3
```

This was not what we wanted – we wanted the first thread to print out all of its values before the next thread began to print its values. To get the code to do this, a Mutex object is used to give a thread a mutually exclusive lock on the code inside the Increment() method. This is done by having a Mutex object invoke the WaitOne() method that it inherits from the WaitHandle class. The mutex lock is released by calling the ReleaseMutex() method.

The modified Increment() method is shown below. When the modified code is run, the first thread completes its for loop before the second thread begins.

```
// The WaitOne() method is called to give the current Thread the
// mutex lock on the for loop. The Thread has exclusive access to
// the for loop until the ReleaseMutex() method is called.
public void Increment()
{
  mutex.WaitOne();

  for(int i = 0; i < 4; ++i)
  {
    Console.WriteLine(Thread.CurrentThread.Name + ": value is {0}", i);
    Thread.Sleep(5);
  }

  mutex.ReleaseMutex();
}
```

Output:

```
Increment one:   value is 0
Increment one:   value is 1
Increment one:   value is 2
Increment one:   value is 3
Increment two:   value is 0
Increment two:   value is 1
Increment two:   value is 2
Increment two:   value is 3
```

ReaderWriterLock class

The `ReaderWriterLock` class provides locks for threads that are used to read and write data. It supports nested reader and writer locks, and allows you to change the type of lock associated with a thread, or to restore a lock status to a previous state. A `ReaderWriterLock` object can acquire either a reader lock or a writer lock, but it cannot have both at the same time. A `ReaderWriterLock` object can support at most one writer, but it can deal with multiple readers.

Syntax

```
public sealed class ReaderWriterLock
```

Hierarchy

```
Object --- ReaderWriterLock
```

Constructors

```
public ReaderWriterLock()
```

`ReaderWriterLock()` creates a `ReaderWriterLock` object with default properties.

Properties

```
public bool IsReaderLockHeld {get;}
public bool IsWriterLockHeld {get;}
public int WriterSeqNum {get;}
```

`IsReaderLockHeld` returns `true` if the current thread holds the reader lock.

`IsWriterLockHeld` returns `true` if the current thread holds the writer lock.

`WriterSeqNum` retrieves the sequence number associated with the `ReaderWriterLock`. The sequence number will be 1 if the `ReaderWriterLock` has not acquired a writer lock, and 2 if it has.

Public instance methods

```
public void AcquireReaderLock(int millisecondsTimeout)
public void AcquireReaderLock(TimeSpan timeout)
public void AcquireWriterLock(int millisecondsTimeout)
public void AcquireWriterLock(TimeSpan timeout)
```

`AcquireReaderLock()` attempts to acquire the reader lock for the current thread. It will keep attempting to do this for the specified time period. A `millisecondsTimeout` value of -1 indicates an infinite timeout period. This method supports nested reader locks, and the calling thread will block if another thread has the writer lock.

`AcquireWriterLock()` tries to acquire the writer lock for the current thread. It will keep attempting to do this for the specified time period. A `millisecondsTimeout` value of -1 indicates an infinite timeout period. This method supports nested writer locks, and the calling thread will block if another thread has the reader lock, and deadlock if it holds the reader lock itself. The `UpgradeToWriterLock()` method can be used to prevent such a deadlock.

```
public bool AnyWritersSince(int seqNum)
```

AnyWritersSince() returns true if there have been any intermediate write operations since the sequence number for this instance was obtained.

```
public LockCookie ReleaseLock()
public void ReleaseReaderLock()
public void ReleaseWriterLock()
public void RestoreLock(ref LockCookie cookie)
```

ReleaseLock() releases any locks associated with the invoking ReaderWriterLock object, including any nested locks. The LockCookie struct identifies the lock; currently this defines no data or function members.

ReleaseReaderLock() releases the reader lock if it is held by the invoking thread. If the thread also holds the writer lock, it too will be released.

ReleaseWriterLock() releases the writer lock (as long as this was not a nested call to release the lock). This method will throw an ApplicationException if the invoking thread is holding the reader lock.

RestoreLock() undoes any changes to the lock status of the invoking thread that were caused by calling the ReleaseLock() method.

```
public void DowngradeFromWriterLock(ref LockCookie cookie)
public LockCookie UpgradeToWriterLock(int millisecondsTimeout)
public LockCookie UpgradeToWriterLock(TimeSpan timeout)
```

DowngradeFromWriterLock() undoes any change in the lock status that resulted from a previous call to the UpgradeToWriteLock() method.

UpgradeToWriterLock() changes a reader thread to a writer thread. It will keep attempting to do this for the specified time period. A millisecondsTimeout value of –1 indicates an infinite timeout period. This method is used to avoid possible exceptions or deadlocks that can occur when a thread holds both the reader and writer locks.

Example: ReaderWriterLock class

In this example, a ReaderWriterLock object is used to control access to an integer stored in memory. Three Threads are created: the first calls the WriteSome() method and writes a value to memory; the other two read the stored value. There is a potential problem in that we don't want the reader threads to do anything until the writer thread has finished writing the value.

The way to ensure this is with a ReaderWriterLock object that acquires the writer lock for the writer thread. The reader threads try to acquire the reader lock, but they can't do so until the writer thread releases the writer lock, which it does after it writes the value to memory. The reader threads then acquire the reader lock and read the value.

```
using System;
using System.IO;
using System.Threading;

public class RWDemo
{
  ReaderWriterLock rwlock;
  int value;
  byte[] buf = new byte[1];
  MemoryStream stream;

  public RWDemo()
  {
    rwlock = new ReaderWriterLock();
    value = 4;
    stream = new MemoryStream();
  }

  public static void Main()
  {
    RWDemo demo = new RWDemo();

    Thread one = new Thread(new ThreadStart(demo.ReadSome));
    Thread two = new Thread(new ThreadStart(demo.ReadSome));
    Thread three = new Thread(new ThreadStart(demo.WriteSome));

    one.Start();
    two.Start();
    three.Start();
  }

  // The WriteSome() method writes an integer to memory.
  // The AcquireWriterLock() method grabs the writer lock for
  // the current Thread. When the writing is complete, the
  // ReleaseWriterLock() method releases the lock.
  public void WriteSome()
  {
    rwlock.AcquireWriterLock(-1);
    Thread.Sleep(1000);
    buf[0] = (byte)value;
    stream.Position = 0;
    stream.Write(buf, 0, buf.Length);
    Console.WriteLine("Value written was {0}", value);
    rwlock.ReleaseWriterLock();
  }

  // The ReadSome() method reads an integer from memory.
  // The AcquireReaderLock() method grabs the reader lock for
  // the current Thread. When the reading is complete, the
  // ReleaseReaderLock() method releases the lock.
  public void ReadSome()
  {
    Thread.Sleep(1000);
```

```
        rwlock.AcquireReaderLock(-1);
        stream.Position = 0;
        Console.WriteLine("Value read was {0}", stream.ReadByte());
        rwlock.ReleaseReaderLock();
    }
}
```

Output:

```
    Value written was 4
    Value read was 4
    Value read was 4
```

If you comment out the `Acquire...Lock()` and `Release...Lock()` method calls in the `WriteSome()` and `ReadSome()` methods, the output you get is this:

```
    Value read was -1
    Value read was -1
    Value written was 4
```

The -1 value means there was no data to read.

ThreadPool class

While multi-threaded programming can be much more efficient than single-threaded programming, there is an overhead involved in creating threads. However, Windows allows us to make more effective use of multiple threads by maintaining a pool of threads for each process. Instead of creating a new thread for each operation, Windows will assign an existing worker thread from the pool to incoming operations (or generate a new thread if the pool is empty).

The `ThreadPool` class encapsulates this pool of worker threads that are managed by the system and monitor the status of wait operations queued to the thread pool. The thread pool is also used by timers, and can be used to process work items unrelated to wait operations. The thread pool is created by calling the `QueueUserWorkItem()` method, or when a timer-queue timer or registered wait operation queues a callback function.

Syntax

```
    public sealed class ThreadPool
```

Hierarchy

```
    Object --- ThreadPool
```

Public static methods

```
    public static bool BindHandle(IntPtr osHandle)
```

`BindHandle()` binds the specified operating system handle to the thread pool. A `SecurityException` is thrown if the caller does not have the proper permission to call this method.

```
public static bool QueueUserWorkItem(WaitCallback callback)
public static bool QueueUserWorkItem(WaitCallback callback, object state)
```

`QueueUserWorkItem()` sends a user work item to the thread pool queue. The `callback` parameter is executed when a thread in the thread pool picks up a work item. The `state` parameter is an object passed to the delegate when serviced from the thread pool. The return value is `true` if the method was successful.

```
public static RegisteredWaitHandle RegisterWaitForSingleObject(
                WaitHandle waitObject, WaitOrTimerCallback callback,
                object state, int millisecondsTimeout, bool executeOnce)
public static RegisteredWaitHandle RegisterWaitForSingleObject(
                WaitHandle waitObject, WaitOrTimerCallback callback,
                object state, long millisecondsTimeout, bool executeOnce)
public static RegisteredWaitHandle RegisterWaitForSingleObject(
                WaitHandle waitObject, WaitOrTimerCallback callback,
                object state, TimeSpan timeout, bool executeOnce)
public static RegisteredWaitHandle RegisterWaitForSingleObject(
                WaitHandle waitObject, WaitOrTimerCallback callback,
                object state, uint millisecondsTimeout, bool executeOnce)
```

`RegisterWaitForSingleObject()` registers the specified `WaitHandle` object with the thread pool. The `callback` parameter is a delegate to call when the handle is signaled. The `state` parameter is an object passed to the delegate. The operation is given a timeout value, with -1 indicating an infinite timeout period. If `executeOnce` is `true`, the delegate is only called once. If this is `false`, a worker thread will invoke the delegate when `waitObject` is in a signaled state, or when the specified timeout period expires. The return value is an object representing the native handle. An `ArgumentOutOfRangeException` is thrown if the value of the timeout argument is less than -1.

Example: ThreadPool class

In this quick example of using the `ThreadPool` class, we define a simple thread function that has an `Object` parameter – this is a requirement for any function that's intended to be executed on a thread from the thread pool. `SimpleThreadFunc()` reports on today's date, outputs its thread ID, and discovers how many threads are left in the pool, before sleeping for a second and handing control back to the `Main()` method.

The `Main()` method itself just queues ten calls to this function for execution by threads in the pool, and then waits for them all to finish.

```
using System;
using System.Threading;

public class PoolingDemo
{
    void SimpleThreadFunc(Object obj)
```

```
   {
      // Display the passed parameter
      Console.Write("Today is {0}: ", obj);
      Console.WriteLine("Thread ID {0} in SimpleThreadFunc()",
                        AppDomain.GetCurrentThreadId().ToString());
      int nWorkerThreads;
      int nIOThreads;

      // Get the available thread count
      ThreadPool.GetAvailableThreads(out nWorkerThreads, out nIOThreads);
      Console.WriteLine("Available worker threads: {0}",
                        nWorkerThreads.ToString());
      Thread.Sleep(1000);
   }

   public static void Main()
   {
      PoolingDemo demo = new PoolingDemo();

      // Declare the string
      String strToday = DateTime.Today.ToShortDateString();

      // Use process-wide ThreadPool thread(s) to call SimpleThreadFunc()
      for(int i = 0; i < 10; i++)
      {
         ThreadPool.QueueUserWorkItem(
                        new WaitCallback(demo.SimpleThreadFunc), strToday);
      }

      // Give enough time for the work items to finish
      Thread.Sleep(10000);
   }
}
```

Output:

```
Today is 27/02/2002: Thread ID 1604 in SimpleThreadFunc()
Available worker threads: 24
Today is 27/02/2002: Thread ID 1624 in SimpleThreadFunc()
Available worker threads: 23
Today is 27/02/2002: Thread ID 988 in SimpleThreadFunc()
Available worker threads: 22
Today is 27/02/2002: Thread ID 1604 in SimpleThreadFunc()
Available worker threads: 22
Today is 27/02/2002: Thread ID 1624 in SimpleThreadFunc()
Available worker threads: 22
Today is 27/02/2002: Thread ID 1640 in SimpleThreadFunc()
Available worker threads: 21
Today is 27/02/2002: Thread ID 988 in SimpleThreadFunc()
Available worker threads: 21
Today is 27/02/2002: Thread ID 1616 in SimpleThreadFunc()
```

```
Available worker threads: 20
Today is 27/02/2002: Thread ID 1604 in SimpleThreadFunc()
Available worker threads: 20
Today is 27/02/2002: Thread ID 1624 in SimpleThreadFunc()
Available worker threads: 20
```

The important thing to notice from this output is that despite making ten requests for work, only five different threads are actually used. Threads in the pool are recycled when they finish their work, minimizing the use of resources without compromising the performance of your code. As an aside, we can see that the thread pool initially makes 25 threads available.

Timeout class

The Timeout class defines a field representing a time interval. This field is used by methods that suspend a thread for a period of time.

Syntax

```
public sealed class Timeout
```

Hierarchy

```
Object --- Timeout
```

Fields

```
public const int Infinite
```

Infinite defines an infinite timeout. The field has a numerical value of -1.

Timer class

The Timer class is used to call a delegate after a specified period of time. A worker thread from the thread pool calls the delegate when the timer expires. Timers can be updated after they are created, and a pending Timer can be canceled. Threads often use timers to wake themselves up after a certain amount of time has passed. The thread will use one of the Wait() functions to be notified when the timer expires.

The Timer class won't work on operating systems that predate Windows 2000. An exception will be thrown if you try to run Timers on older Windows versions.

Syntax

```
public sealed class Timer : IDisposable
```

Hierarchy

```
Object --- Timer
```

Constructors

```
public Timer(TimerCallback callback, object state, int dueTime,
                                                   int period)
public Timer(TimerCallback callback, object state, long dueTime,
                                                   long period)
public Timer(TimerCallback callback, object state, TimeSpan dueTime,
                                                   TimeSpan period)
public Timer(TimerCallback callback, object state, uint dueTime,
                                                   uint period)
```

Timer() creates a Timer object. The callback parameter is the delegate that's called when the timer expires; it is passed the state object when this happens. The dueTime parameter is the time (in milliseconds, or represented by a TimeSpan object) after which the timer should expire. If the period parameter is zero, the timer will execute once. If period is greater than zero, the timer is periodic and will reset itself each time the period elapses.

Protected instance methods

```
~Timer()
```

~Timer() is the destructor for this class. This method is normally called by the system after garbage collection of the Timer.

Public instance methods

```
public bool Change(int dueTime, int period)
public bool Change(long dueTime, long period)
public bool Change(TimeSpan dueTime, TimeSpan period)
public bool Change(uint dueTime, uint period)
```

Change() modifies the expiration time and period of the invoking Timer. The method returns true if the values were successfully reset.

```
public void Dispose()
public bool Dispose(WaitHandle notifyObject)
```

Dispose() stops and/or removes a Timer. The first version releases all resources allocated to the invoking Timer. The second version deletes the Timer from the timer queue. The notifyObject parameter is a WaitHandle that is signaled when the method is successful. The return value is true if the method was successful. A NullReferenceException is thrown if notifyObject is a null reference.

Example: Timer class

In this example, a Timer object is used to suspend and resume the operation of a Thread. First of all, a Thread is created. When started, the Thread invokes the Count2() method, which increments a value. The Count2() method also defines a Timer object that calls the Blah() method when it expires, passing it a reference to the current Thread. The Blah() method suspends the Thread if it is not suspended, and resumes the Thread if it is suspended.

The main execution thread then calls the `Count()` method that does the same thing as `Count2()`, but without the `Timer`.

```csharp
using System;
using System.Threading;

public class TimerDemo
{
  public static void Main()
  {
    TimerDemo demo = new TimerDemo();

    // A Thread is created and when started calls the Count2()
    // method. The main execution thread calls the Count() method.
    Thread thread2 = new Thread(new ThreadStart(demo.Count2));
    thread2.Name = "Thread two";
    thread2.Start();
    demo.Count();
  }

  // The Count() method increments a value.
  public void Count()
  {
    for(int i = 0; i < 8; ++i)
    {
      Console.WriteLine("Main thread count is {0}", i);
      Thread.Sleep(100);
    }
  }

  // The Count2() method starts a Timer and then increments a value.
  // The Timer calls the Blah() method passing it a reference to the
  // current Thread.
  public void Count2()
  {
    Timer timer = new Timer(new TimerCallback(Blah),
                            Thread.CurrentThread, 400, 800);
    for(int i = 0; i < 8; ++i)
    {
      Console.WriteLine("{0}: count is {1}", Thread.CurrentThread.Name, i);
      Thread.Sleep(100);
    }
  }

  // The Blah() method is called when a Timer expires. If the Thread
  // passed as an argument is suspended, it is resumed. Otherwise,
  // the Thread is suspended.
  public static void Blah(object obj)
  {
    Thread t = (Thread)obj;
    if(t.ThreadState == (ThreadState.WaitSleepJoin|ThreadState.Suspended))
```

```
            t.Resume();
        else
            t.Suspend();
    }
}
```

Output:

```
Main thread: count is 0
Thread two: count is 0
Main thread: count is 1
Thread two: count is 1
Main thread: count is 2
Thread two: count is 2
Main thread: count is 3
Thread two: count is 3
Main thread: count is 4
Thread two: count is 4 -> Thread two suspended here
Main thread: count is 5
Main thread: count is 6
Main thread: count is 7
Thread two: count is 5 -> Thread two resumes here
Thread two: count is 6
Thread two: count is 7
```

Summary

.NET is intrinsically a multi-threaded environment. Although many of the .NET objects are type-safe by design, some are not – or they're only type-safe as static fields. Multi-threaded programming requires special care when there is the potential for multiple threads to access shared resources simultaneously.

In this chapter, we have looked at the classes provided by the .NET Framework for manipulating threads. We have seen how to create, suspend, and abort threads, and how to place interlocked, monitor, or mutex locks on shared resources that may be accessed by multiple threads.

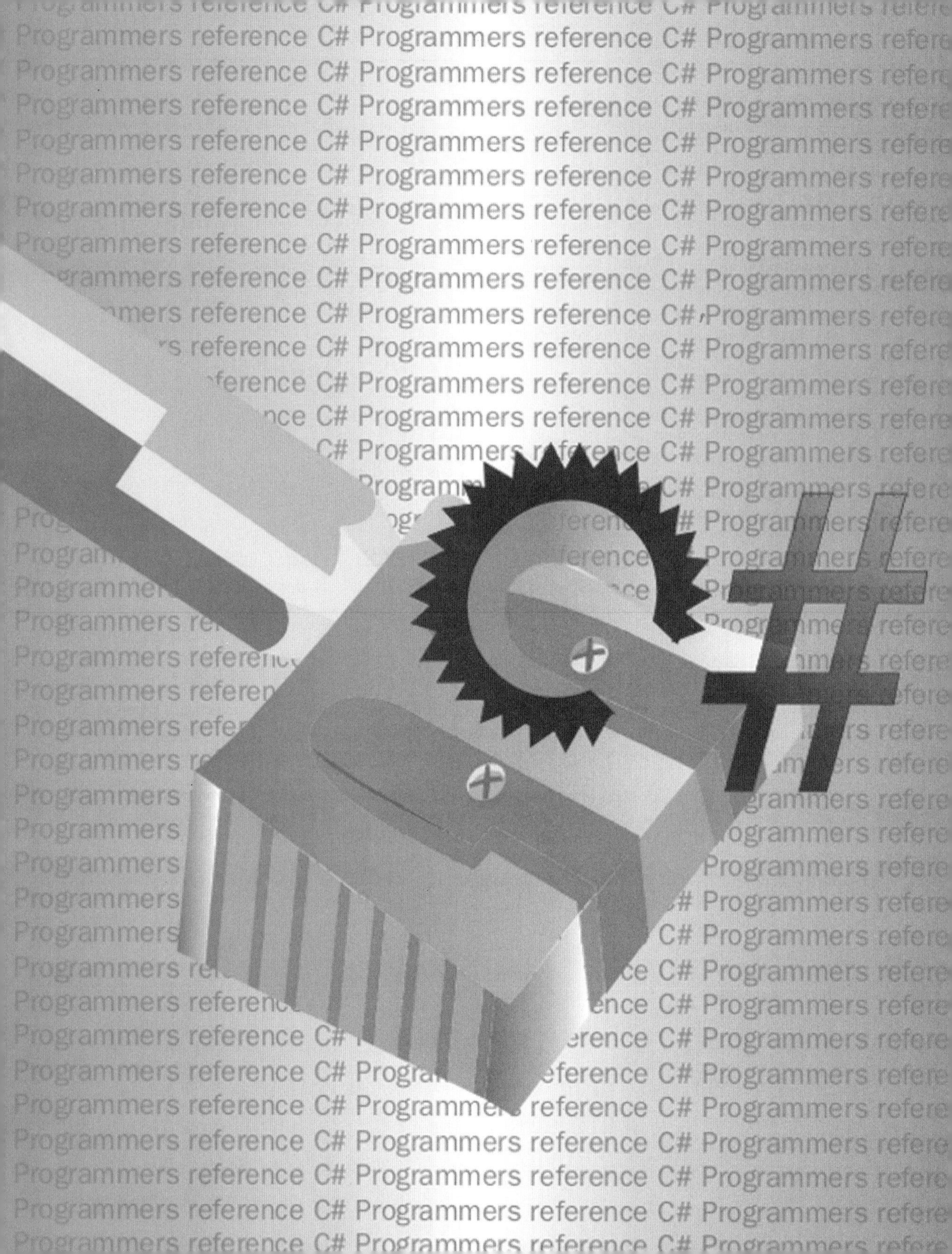
Programmers reference C#

C# keywords

These are keywords that have special meaning in the C# language. We've discussed most of these earlier in the book. You will use these keywords all the time when developing your C# codes. Because these words are reserved, you can't use them as names of types or of type members. For instance, you might want to name an IEnumerator instance enum, but you can't because enum is a C# keyword.

Here is a list of the C# keywords and a brief description of what they do.

Keyword	Description
abstract	Indicates a class or method that is meant to be overridden. An abstract member has no implementation code.
as	A casting operator that returns null if the cast fails.
base	Passes a call to a base class implementation.
bool	A predefined type equivalent to the System.Boolean type. It represents a boolean value.
break	A jump statement used to exit from a loop or switch statement.
byte	A predefined type equivalent to the System.Byte type. It represents an 8-bit unsigned integer.
case	Defines a value that is compared against the values in a previous switch statement. If the values match, the code following the case statement is executed.
catch	Defines a block of code that is executed if a specified type of exception is thrown. Also see try and finally.
char	A predefined type equivalent to the System.Char type. It represents a single 16-bit Unicode character.
checked	Forces the Common Language Runtime to throw an exception if an arithmetic overflow occurs.
class	Designates a type as a class. A class is a reference type that can contain both data and function members.
const	Indicates that the value of a local variable or field cannot be changed.
continue	A jump statement used to return to the top of the loop.
decimal	A predefined type equivalent to the System.Decimal type. It represents a 128-bit high precision decimal value.

Table continued on following page

Keyword	Description
default	Designates a block of code in a `switch` statement that is executed if none of the `case` statement values match the `switch` statement value.
delegate	Specifies that a type is a delegate. Delegates are generic references to methods of a given argument list and return type. Delegates are used extensively in the C# event model.
do	Part of a `do-while` conditional statement. The block of code following the `do` keyword will execute at least once whether or not the condition is satisfied.
double	A predefined type equivalent to the `System.Double` type. It represents a 64-bit double-precision floating-point value.
else	Part of an `if-else` or `if-else if-else` conditional statement. The `else` block is executed if the preceding conditional statements are not satisfied.
enum	A value type representing a collection of named constants.
event	Indicates that a delegate will be used as an event-handling delegate.
explicit	An operator that defines a user-defined explicit cast conversion operator. Generally this will convert a built-in type to a user-defined type or vice versa. Explicit conversion operators must be invoked with a cast.
extern	Indicates that a method will be implemented externally, in another programming language.
false	A Boolean literal.
finally	Defines a block of code that is executed when the program control leaves a `try` block. See also the `try` and `catch` keywords.
fixed	Fixes a reference type at a given memory location while a block of code executes.
float	A predefined type equivalent to the `System.Float` type. It represents a 32-bit single precision floating-point value.
for	Defines a loop statement that executes as long as a specified condition holds.
foreach	Used to iterate through the elements of a collection.
goto	A jump statement that redirects the execution to another point in the code.
if	Defines a conditional statement. If the condition following an `if` statement is satisfied, the subsequent block of code is executed.
implicit	An operator that defines a user-defined implicit cast conversion operator. Generally this will convert a built-in type to a user-defined type or vice versa. Implicit conversion operators must be invoked with a cast.
in	Part of the iteration syntax in a `foreach` statement. The `in` keyword is placed between the variable name and the collection to be iterated over.
int	A predefined type equivalent to the `System.Int32` type. It represents a 32-bit signed integer value.
interface	An interface declares the signatures of properties, indexers, events, and methods without provided their implementation. The implementation is left to classes and structs that implement the interface.
internal	An access modifier. A code element with `internal` access is available to other types in the same assembly.

Keyword	Description
is	A comparison operator that compares the types of two objects.
lock	Used in multi-threaded programming to place a mutual exclusion lock (mutex) around a variable.
long	A predefined type equivalent to the System.Int64 type. It represents a 64-bit signed integer value.
namespace	Defines a collection of types.
new	Used to call a reference-type constructor or create an instance of a struct. Also used to hide an inherited method with the same signature.
null	A literal that represents an undefined reference type.
object	A predefined type equivalent to the System.Object type.
operator	Used to define an operator.
out	Allows a variable to be initialized by a function member. An out variable can be passed to a function before it is initialized.
override	A modifier that indicates that a method or operator will override a virtual or abstract method or an operator of the same name defined in a base class.
params	Applied to an input parameter of a method to indicate that one or more instances of the specified type may be passed to the method.
private	An access modifier. A code element with private access is only available inside the type in which the code element is defined.
protected	An access modifier. A code element with protected access is available to the type in which the code element is defined and to derived types of the type in which it is defined.
public	An access modifier. A code element with public access is freely available inside or outside of the type in which the code element is defined.
readonly	Indicates that the value of a field is read-only except when it is declared inside a constructor.
ref	Causes a value type or primitive input parameter to be passed to a method as a reference type.
return	A jump statement used to exit a method. The execution returns to the point after the method call statement.
sbyte	A predefined type equivalent to the System.SByte type. It represents an 8-bit signed integer.
sealed	A method or class that is sealed cannot be overridden or derived from.
short	A predefined type equivalent to the System.Int16 type. It represents a 16-bit signed integer value.
sizeof	An operator that returns the size of a value type in bytes.
stackalloc	Returns a pointer to a block of memory allocated on the stack.
static	A static code element is associated with the type in which it is defined rather than with an instance of the type.
string	A predefined type equivalent to the System.String type. It represents a Unicode character string.

Table continued on following page

Keyword	Description
struct	A struct is a value-type encapsulation construct that can contain data and function members.
switch	Defines a value that is compared against the values in subsequent case statements.
this	References the current instance of a type.
throw	Causes an exception to be thrown.
true	A Boolean literal.
try	Part of an exception-handling block of code. The try block contains code that might throw an exception. See also the catch and finally keywords.
typeof	An operator that returns the Type of the argument passed to it.
uint	A predefined type equivalent to the System.UInt32 type. It represents a 32-bit unsigned integer value.
ulong	A predefined type equivalent to the System.UInt64 type. It represents a 64-bit unsigned integer value.
unchecked	Suppresses overflow checking.
unsafe	Marks a block of code, method, or class that contains pointer operations.
ushort	A predefined type equivalent to the System.UInt16 type. It represents a 16-bit unsigned integer value.
using	When applied to a namespace, the using keyword lets you access the types in the namespace without having to specify the fully qualified type name. Also used for defining finalization scope.
virtual	A method modifier indicating that the method can be overridden.
void	The return type for methods that don't return anything.
volatile	Indicates that a field can be modified by the operating system, some type of hardware device, or a concurrently executing thread.
while	Part of the while and do-while conditional statements. The while keyword defines a condition. While the condition is true, an associated block of code will execute.

C#
Programmers reference C# Programmers reference C# Programmers reference

Naming conventions

Other than a few restrictions (not using a keyword, not starting a class name with a number, etc.), you have a lot of flexibility when naming your code elements. You could, for instance, capitalize every other letter in a method name. However, a chaotic approach to naming conventions and styles would be very frustrating to anyone else who had to work with your code.

It is important to remember that C# is an object-oriented programming language. Your data and function members will all be encapsulated in a class or struct. The names of the type, data members, and function members should be consistent with each other and each name should describe the functionality or nature of the item to which it is attributed.

To this end, the .NET framework has defined a series of naming guidelines to promote a uniform style amongst C# programs. It's a good idea for you to follow these guidelines. The following sections are a summary of the complete naming convention document that can be found at:

http://msdn.microsoft.com/library/default.asp?url=/library/en-
us/cpgenref/html/cpconnamingguidelines.asp

Capitalization style

There are three basic capitalization styles used in C#. With the Pascal style, the first letter of a name is capitalized and the first letter of every subsequent concatenated word is capitalized. For example you might have a method named `GetAirDensity()`. With the Camel style, the first letter of each name is lower case. The first letter of subsequent concatenated words is upper case. For instance, you might define a protected instance field named `unitCost`. The third capitalization style is for all letters to be capitalized. This is reserved for names and identifiers that are only one or two letters long.

The following lists indicate which style to use when naming a given code element.

Pascal

- ❏ class
- ❏ enumeration
- ❏ enumeration value
- ❏ event
- ❏ read-only static field

- interface
- method
- namespace
- property
- public instance field

Camel

- parameter
- protected instance field

You will notice that most of the time the Pascal style is used. As a rule of thumb, things external to a type use Pascal style. Internal elements use Camel style. Most code elements that use the Pascal style will begin with one capital letter. The exception to this is interface names that begin with a capital "I" followed by the interface name. The first two letters of the interface name are capitalized.

General naming guidelines

You cannot name a code element the same as one of the reserved C# keywords. Do not use names that are the same as namespace names defined in the .NET Framework. When choosing method names, be careful not to select one that is the same as a method from a base class unless you intend to override or hide that method. For instance, you should avoid defining an Equals() method in your user-defined class since this will conflict with the Equals() method defined in the Object class.

Case sensitivity

A general .NET Framework naming guideline is to not create namespaces or other code elements whose names differ only by case. This is to avoid conflicts for languages that are case-insensitive. For example, you shouldn't define a Bailey namespace and a bailey namespace. If you follow the capitalization guidelines given above, you will probably avoid case conflicts.

Abbreviations

The following guidelines are suggested by the .NET Framework to standardize the look and use of abbreviations in naming code elements. You should not use abbreviations as part of identifier names. Calling a method GetDensity() is preferable to naming it GetDens(). You can, however, use well known acronyms to replace lengthy phrase names. Instead of calling a method GetUserInterface(), name it GetUI(). Do not use acronyms that are not commonly known.

Code element-specific naming guidelines

The following are Microsoft's recommended naming guidelines for various code elements. These should give you a general idea of how to select names and apply the proper style to the various components that will make up your program.

Attributes

Attribute class names should follow the class name guidelines. In addition to this, attribute class names should end with "Attribute".

Classes

A class name should be a noun or noun phrase. Class names use the Pascal capitalization style. You should avoid using abbreviations in class names, and class names should not contain the underscore character, "_". A derived class name should, if possible, include a reference to its base class. An example of this is the `AssemblyLoadEventArgs` class, which is a derived class of the `EventArgs` class.

Enumerations

Enumerations use the Pascal capitalization style for their type and value names. The "Enum" suffix should not be used for `enum` type names, and abbreviations should be avoided. A plural name should be applied to enumeration types that represent bit fields.

Events and event handlers

Event handler method names should end in the suffix "EventHandler". The arguments to the event handler method should be named `sender` and `e`. The `sender` parameter is of type object and is the event source. The e parameter is an instance of a derived class of `EventArgs`. Event names are often verbs.

Fields

Instance field names should use the Camel style, except public instance fields, which use the Pascal style. Abbreviations should be used sparingly and should be commonly understood by developers. Static field names use the Pascal capitalization style and should be a noun or noun phrase. Abbreviations of nouns can also be used.

Interfaces

Interfaces in C# use the so-called Hungarian notation in that their names should begin with a capital "I". Beyond this, the naming conventions for interfaces are similar to those of classes. Interface names should follow the Pascal capitalization style. Abbreviations should be used sparingly. The underscore character should not be used.

Methods

Method names should be verbs or verb phrases. They employ the Pascal capitalization style. The method name should clearly describe what the method does. Abbreviations can be used if it is clear what the abbreviated word is.

Namespaces

Namespace names should use the Pascal capitalization style. The first part of a namespace name is generally a company or organization name. This helps ensure that the namespace will be unique if it is incorporated into a library of namespaces. The second part of a namespace name is the name of the associated technology followed by optional feature and design names. The various parts of a namespace name are separated by periods.

```
Eloret.GasModels.Thermodynamic
```

Do not define a namespace and a class with the same name. In the above example, you should not define a `Thermodynamic` class.

Parameters

Parameter names use the Camel capitalization style. The names should be descriptive such that their usage can be ascertained from the name.

Properties

Property names use the Pascal capitalization style and should be a noun or noun phrase. Oftentimes a property name is the same as the field it exposes (apart from the case of the first letter) or has the same name as its underlying type.

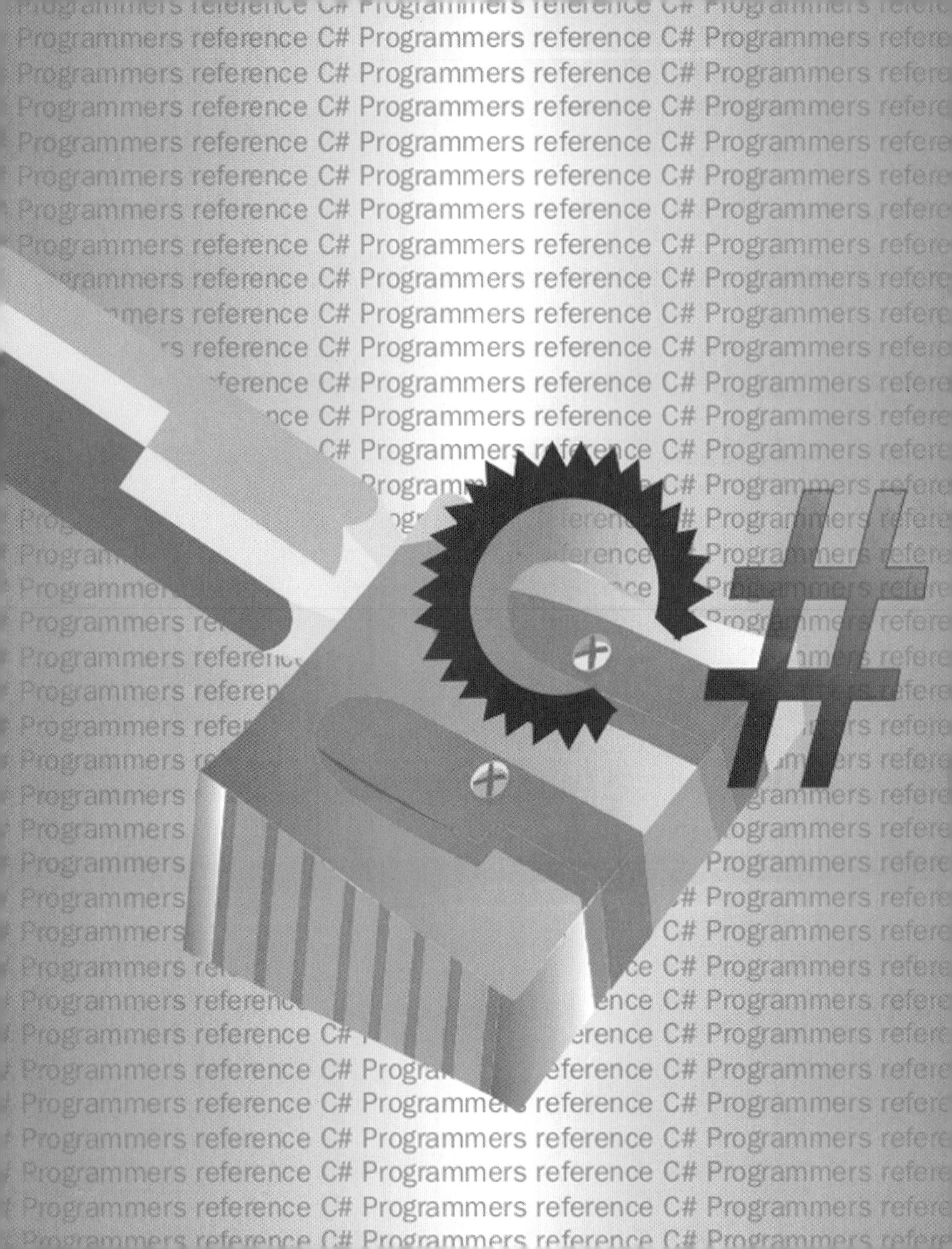
Programmers reference C#

Index

Sybols

Q

R

T